THE

CONTRIBUTORS

FRANK VICTOR DAWES was born in London and worked as a journalist on Fleet Street and for the BBC. The author of *Not in Front of the Servants,* he was a member of the British Guild of Travel Writers and the editorial consultant for this guidebook.

ANTHONY BURTON has written several books on the industrial history of England—and one on the history of beer and pubs. He wrote and presented several television series about England's industrial heritage for the BBC.

BRYN FRANK is the author of *Everyman's England* and *Short Walks in English Towns.* He is a regular contributor to *British Heritage* and *In Britain* magazines, and he writes occasionally about travel in the U.K. for the London *Evening Standard.*

SUSAN GROSSMAN was born in London, where she lives. Editor of both *The Best of Britain Guide* (American Express) and *Upbeat* magazine, she frequently writes about hotels and restaurants.

ALEX HAMILTON is the author of seven works of fiction and a travel book on the Trans-Siberian railway. He is a winner of the Fitzgerald Award for travel writing and is travel editor of the British national daily *The Guardian.*

KATIE LUCAS, the author of a best-selling book on walking tours of London, runs a London-based specialized British tours company.

ANGELA MURPHY, a longtime London resident, is a freelance journalist who has contributed to a number of guidebooks, including the *Shell Weekend Guide Book* to England and the *Hachette Guide to Great Britain.*

PAUL MURPHY's first book, *The Guiness Guide to Superlative London,* won the 1989 Guidebook of the Year award from the London Tourist Board. Since then he has stopped guiding tourists around the capital and has become a regular contributor to many travel guides.

DAVID WICKERS contributes regularly to several major British publications, and is travel editor of *Marie Claire* magazine and travel correspondent of the London *Sunday Times*. In 1992 he was named U.K. Travel Writer of the Year.

THE BERLITZ
TRAVELLERS GUIDES

THE BERLITZ TRAVELLERS GUIDE TO LONDON

Fourth Edition

ALAN TUCKER
General Editor

BERLITZ PUBLISHING COMPANY, INC.
New York, New York

BERLITZ PUBLISHING COMPANY LTD.
Oxford, England

THE BERLITZ TRAVELLERS GUIDE
TO LONDON
Fourth Edition

Berlitz Trademark Reg U.S. Patent and Trademark Office
and other countries—Marca Registrada

Published by Berlitz Publishing Company, Inc.
257 Park Avenue South, New York, New York 10010, U.S.A.

Distributed in the United States by
the Macmillan Publishing Group

Distributed elsewhere by Berlitz Publishing Company Ltd.
Berlitz House, Peterley Road, Horspath, Oxford OX4 2TX, England

ISBN 2-8315-1710-9
ISSN 1057-4751

Designed by Beth Tondreau Design
Cover design by Dan Miller Design
Cover photograph © Marty Loken/Allstock
Maps by Mark Stein Studios
Illustrations by Bill Russell
Fact-checked by Doram Tamari
Fact-checked in London by Paul Murphy
Edited by Patricia Fogarty

Printed in the United States of America
1 3 5 7 9 10 8 6 4 2

THIS GUIDEBOOK

The Berlitz Travellers Guides are designed for experienced travellers in search of exceptional information that will enhance the enjoyment of the trips they take.

Where, for example, are the interesting, out-of-the-way, fun, charming, or romantic places to stay? The hotels described by our expert writers are some of the special places, in all price ranges except for the very lowest—not just the run-of-the-mill, heavily marketed places in advertised airline and travel-wholesaler packages.

We are *highly* selective in our choices of accommodations, concentrating on what our insider contributors think are the most interesting or rewarding places, and why. Readers who want to review exhaustive lists of hotel and resort choices as well, and who feel they need detailed descriptions of each property, can supplement the *Berlitz Travellers Guide* with tourism industry publications or one of the many directory-type guidebooks on the market.

We indicate the approximate price level of each accommodation in our description of it (no indication means it is moderate in local, relative terms), and at the end of every chapter we supply more detailed hotel rates as well as contact information so that you can get precise, up-to-the-minute rates and make reservations.

The Berlitz Travellers Guide to London highlights the more rewarding parts of the city and the surrounding countryside so that you can quickly and efficiently home in on a good itinerary.

Of course, this guidebook does far more than just help you choose a hotel and plan your trip. *The Berlitz Travellers Guide to London* is designed for use *in* London. Our writers, each of whom is an experienced travel journalist who lives in the city or in the part of the environs he or she covers, tell you what you really need to know, what you can't find out so easily on your own. They identify and describe the truly out-of-the-ordinary restaurants, shops, activities, and sights, and tell you the best way to "do" the destination.

Our writers are highly selective. They bring out the significance of the places they *do* cover, capturing the personality and the underlying cultural and historical resonances of a city or region—making clear its special appeal.

The Berlitz Travellers Guide to London is full of reliable information. We would like to know if you think we've left out some very special place. Although we make every effort to provide the most current information available about every destination described in this book, it is possible too that changes have occurred before you arrive. If you do have an experience that is contrary to what you were led to expect by our description, we would like to hear from you about it.

A guidebook is no substitute for common sense when you are travelling. Always pack the clothing, footwear, and other items appropriate for the destination, and make the necessary accommodation for such variables as altitude, weather, and local rules and customs. Of course, once on the scene you should avoid situations that are in your own judgment potentially hazardous, even if they have to do with something mentioned in a guidebook. Half the fun of travelling is exploring, but explore with care.

ALAN TUCKER
General Editor
Berlitz Travellers Guides

Root Publishing Company
350 West Hubbard Street
Suite 440
Chicago, Illinois 60610

CONTENTS

MAPS

THE
BERLITZ
TRAVELLERS
GUIDE
TO
LONDON

Greater London

miles 0 — 2

kilometers 0 — 3

HARROW

HARROW-ON-THE-HILL

WEMBLEY

A40

EALING

ACTON

A406

WOOD GREEN

HIGHGATE

A1

Hampstead Heath

A41

HAMPSTEAD

KILBURN

MAIDA VALE

Regent's Park

PADDINGTON

A40(M)

A40

CENTRAL LONDON

Hyde Park

Westminster Bridge

KENSINGTON

WESTMINSTER

HAMMERSMITH

A4

CHELSEA

Albert Bridge

Battersea Bridge

M4

A4

A4

To Heathrow Airport

CHISWICK

Hammersmith Bridge

FULHAM

Putney Bridge

Battersea Park

BATTERSEA

KEW

BARNES

Royal Botanic Gardens

MORTLAKE

A205

CLAPHAM

RICHMOND

Richmond Bridge

PUTNEY

River Thames

A3

BALHAM

River Thames

TWICKENHAM

Richmond Park

A3

WANDSWORTH

HAM

Wimbledon Common

Hampton Court Palace

HAMPTON

WIMBLEDON

OVERVIEW

By Frank Victor Dawes

Frank Dawes was born in London and worked as a journalist on Fleet Street and for the BBC. The author of Not in Front of the Servants, *he was a member of the British Guild of Travel Writers and the editorial consultant for this guidebook.*

From an orbiting satellite 450 miles up, the River Thames is the most outstanding feature of London, a sinuous dark ribbon winding across the purple blotch of mostly built-up land within the circle of the M 25 motorway. And indeed London's river is *the* connecting thread through the kaleidoscopic pattern of widely varying localities stretching 35 miles from Heathrow Airport in the west to Dartford Tunnel in the east.

Since the once mighty Port of London moved downriver toward the estuary to accommodate container ships, the river has assumed greater significance for tourism. Pleasure-boat traffic is on the increase and oceangoing cruise ships have returned, the smaller ones mooring in the shadow of Tower Bridge. London City Airport, operating STOL (short takeoff and landing) flights to other cities in the U.K. and to Continental Europe, occupies the site of the old Royal Docks, and an eight-square-mile area of East London waterfront is undergoing the greatest rebuilding operation since the Great Fire of 1666. This is nothing less than a new city grafted onto the old.

London's history may go back to Roman times, when as the walled city of Londinium it was the trading center from which all roads radiated, but it is now a capital gearing itself for the 21st century. The Beefeaters at the Tower of London, the Guards at Buckingham Palace, and the Household Cavalry still provide a flash of scarlet and gleaming steel, the popular image of London along with double-decker buses and black cabs, but other familiar images have gone the way of pea-soup November fogs. Since deregulation the buses no longer have to be red and may well be green, gray, or even yellow. The sight of a City businessman wearing a bowler hat is rare enough to turn heads in busy streets where hardly anything is weird enough to merit a second glance. No longer does Fleet Street reverberate through the night to the roar of the presses spewing out millions of newspapers; their offices are now dispersed throughout the capital, survived on the street by the journalists' church of St. Bride, the well-known pub Ye Olde Cheshire Cheese (where, after centuries, the spreading of sawdust on the floor ceased only in 1991 because of stricter fire regulations), and the preserved façades of the Daily Express and Daily Telegraph buildings.

North, South, and Just Beyond

The importance of what jazz musician George Melly calls "the transpontine divide" cannot be over-emphasized. The Thames is a cultural as well as a geographical frontier, whereas the traditional divide between East End and West End is becoming less and less relevant. It is no exaggeration to say that in modern London true Cockneys "born within the sound of Bow Bells" (the bells of St. Mary-le-Bow, on Cheapside) are hard to find. To a surprising extent, citizens who hail from other parts of the country or the world regard themselves instead as North of the River or South of the River people. While it may be true that the north has long enjoyed a monopoly on affluence (and visitors), the myth that South London is inferior and alien territory occupied largely by gangsters and used-car dealers is put about by folk who live north of the river.

They perversely ignore the existence of the South Bank Arts Centre and the reconstruction of Shakespeare's Globe Theatre on its original site in what in Tudor times was the capital's theaterland around Bear Gardens on Bankside. The 1,500-seat theater is not due for completion until the mid-1990s, but a permanent exhibition on Shakespearean life, a shopping precinct, and a piazza overlooking the Thames are open to the public. And what about the Oval for cricket and Wimbledon for tennis, the charming Georgian and Victorian villages of Dulwich and Blackheath, the parklands of Richmond and Kew, or Greenwich, the maritime heart of England? And while a few years ago it might have been difficult to find good places to dine in a South London dominated by fish-and-chip takeouts and ethnic Indian and Chinese restaurants, that has now changed, most noticeably in places such as Clapham, Balham, and Wandsworth. Here, too, are some of the least-spoiled pubs, many serving Youngs bitter, a full-bodied South London beer. Captain Cook took a glass or two of something even stronger at the Angel in Rotherhithe between global explorations, and earlier the Pilgrims had gathered at the nearby Mayflower (then The Shippe) before embarking on their voyage to the New World.

For the inquiring visitor, not all the jewels of London are to be found in the Tower. Many of the historic buildings and country villages in the surrounding shires that have been swallowed up by the expanding metropolis survive and are worth seeking out. Eltham Palace and Downe House (where Charles Darwin lived and wrote *On the Origin of Species by Means of Natural Selection*) are on the southeastern outskirts. The Baroque Moor Park north toward Watford, the village clustered around the famous school that Churchill attended at Harrow-on-the-Hill, and the 500-year-old tithe barn in the village of Harmondsworth half a mile from Heathrow's runways— these are just a few of many such examples. Watch for the blue plaque—a sign on buildings where famous people have lived. There are nearly 600 dotted around the capital, and *The Blue Plaque Guide,* available from bookshops, details them all.

Seeing London from the Water and the Rails

Like all great capital cities, London can be overwhelming at first sight. Where to begin? Much depends of course on the time available, but if possible let the river make the introductions before you explore *both* banks in depth. To the west, royal Windsor Castle and Cardinal Wolsey's Hampton Court are reminders that the water by which they stand was once the main metropolitan highway, at its apogee in Tudor times. Embraced by the Thames as it rolls along toward London is Richmond Park, 2,500 green acres first enclosed as a hunting ground by Charles I in 1637 and still roamed by red and fallow deer. Not far away, and also overlooking the river, the Royal Botanic Gardens at Kew were established in 1759 and now cover 300 acres, with a magnificently restored Victorian Palm House and the new multi-environment Princess of Wales Conservatory.

Most of the previously mentioned popular "sights" and a good many others can be seen from a boat on the river as it winds its way through the heart of the capital from Chelsea Embankment under no fewer than ten bridges, including the London Bridge that replaced the one now to be found at Lake Havasu in Arizona. Riverbus catamarans ply the waters from ten piers between Chelsea Harbour and Greenwich (Tel: 512-0555) with departures every 20 minutes Monday through Friday and half-hourly on weekends. The catamarans now stop at St. Katharine Pier (convenient for the Tower of London and Tobacco Dock shopping mall) and the new Canary Wharf. A moderately priced Explorer Ticket can be used throughout the day starting at 9:30 A.M. from the West End and City to Docklands and Greenwich. The Thames flows past the palaces of Lambeth (spiritual) and Westminster (temporal), where Parliament sits, and past the ancient City of London, within whose square mile lies the Bank of England and the Stock Exchange, and which has been governed since the 12th century by a corporation of aldermen and liverymen. Its boundaries are guarded by iron dragons bearing shields embossed with heraldic devices, and the policemen's helmets are distinctively different from those worn by the rest of London's "bobbies."

The best view of Tower Bridge and the Norman Tower of London is from the water, especially if the vessel you are on is large enough to require the opening of the bridge's twin bascules (which occurs only a few times a week these days). One of the most enjoyable excursions—and a rewarding introduction to London—is down the river from Charing Cross Pier to Greenwich on the south bank. There you can see something of Britain's seafaring tradition in the Maritime Museum, tread the deck of the *Cutty Sark* (the last remaining tea clipper), learn about the history of Greenwich mean time at the Old Royal Observatory, and, in the courtyard, straddle a brass strip denoting the Prime Meridian (Longitude 0°), with a foot in each hemisphere. The Queen's House in the former royal hunting park at Greenwich is one of the few surviving masterpieces of 17th-century architect Inigo Jones, and the first Palladian-style house in England to be restored to its original pristine elegance and opened to visitors. On Croom's Hill is a unique Fan Museum with more than 2,000 exhibits.

An alternative and intriguing way of getting to Greenwich is to board one of the computer-driven trains of the Docklands Light Railway at Tower Gateway; in contrast, adjacent at Tower Hill remnants of Roman Londinium are on display in the gardens. The train proceeds swiftly through the vast building site of the new London, with its glass-and-concrete tower blocks and converted warehouses, to Island Gardens on the Isle of Dogs. On the opposite side of the river is an array of classical buildings, an inspiring prospect unchanged since Canaletto painted it two centuries ago, except that the sailing ships have gone. The view from the other side is now dominated by Canary Wharf, the tallest office tower (803 feet/245 meters) in London and, for the time being, in Europe. A foot tunnel, with access by a vast creaking elevator, runs under the river here.

The constant juxtaposition of ancient and modern is one of the fascinations of London. The Docklands Light Railway is an innovation, just as the tube was the world's first deep-level electric railway when it was opened a century ago. In its heyday in the 1930s, it set the pace for graphic design as well as efficient operations, but today it is increasingly compared, not always favorably, to the underground systems of other major cities. For graffiti it took over where the New York City subway system left off in 1989, although efforts are being made to end the defacing as New York has tried to do.

Still, more than 90 percent of the nine million overseas visitors who come to London each year use the Underground to get about, and two-thirds use the buses. If you seek the old-fashioned civilities, with a little sightseeing along the way, go by bus. A Visitor Travelcard, available for purchase outside Britain from British Rail offices and travel agents, offers virtually unlimited travel for one to seven days on the tube, buses, Docklands Light Railway, and British Rail within London and suburban zones. The card comes with a set of discount vouchers for Madame Tussaud's, the London Zoo, and other tourist attractions. London Transport has a travel shop at 55 Broadway next to St. James's Park Underground station, or telephone (222-1234) for 24-hour information.

Neighborhoods

For the visitor who wants more than the usual whistle-stop tour of the Tower of London, St. Paul's Cathedral, Westminster Abbey, and Big Ben, this guide covers a variety of up-and-coming neighborhoods in addition to those that are familiar to readers who know a bit about London already.

We range from the capital-letter City (that is to say, the area within the original Roman walls) to the West End and beyond, on to Hampstead, Camden Town, Islington, and some of the other less well known "villages" that make up the urban patchwork, then to the new city of Docklands. Markets such as Smithfield for meat and Covent Garden for fruit and vegetables may have lost their original purpose but are as vibrantly alive as ever with new ideas and styles. Literary Bloomsbury, in contrast, has changed hardly at all, although parts of the library at the British Museum are being relocated to a new site near St. Pancras Station.

Ethnic quarters such as Soho, with its Chinatown, its strip shows, sleazy clubs, and good restaurants of many nationalities, and Notting Hill, with its famous open-air antiques market, are where the pulse of London life is at its strongest. Even though violence and crime are on the increase, and the visitor should be aware of this, these are far from being "no go" areas.

The East End holds interest for anyone who wants to know about succeeding waves of immigrants, from the 16th-century Huguenots to the Jews and Irish Catholics of the 19th century and the Bengalis and Bangladeshis who make up a sizable minority of the population today. The Cockney dialect, or one version of it, can still be heard amid a variety of other accents and tongues.

The West End, Mayfair, and Knightsbridge are, as ever, the magnet for those who come to London for dining and dancing, theater and entertainment, and, above all, shopping (see the relevant sections below). Chelsea, whose associations with royalty and the literati go back centuries, experienced its heyday as the birthplace of "Swinging London" in the 1960s and is now somewhat faded. However, Chelsea still has a "villagey" air, enhanced by the river flowing past its southern doorsteps, as do those parts of Hammersmith and Chiswick fortunate enough to have a frontage on the north bank of the Thames.

Seasonal London

The list of attractions never stops growing, and ranges from a tour of Lord's Cricket Ground to Rock Circus, a permanent waxworks exhibition of such stars as the Beatles and the Rolling Stones backed by music (in the restored London Pavilion on Piccadilly Circus). Whatever the season, London's calendar is always full, from the New Year's Eve celebrations in Trafalgar Square, where thousands gather to hear Big Ben, to the setting up of the annual Christmas tree from Norway and the switching on of the illuminations in Oxford Street, Bond Street, and Regent Street.

Spring comes to the river with the annual boat race between Oxford and Cambridge universities, run over a course from Putney to Mortlake. In high summer straw boaters, Champagne, and hospitality marquees line the banks at Henley—and the rowing seems almost incidental. In July the Worshipful Companies of Vintners and Dyers, accompanied by representatives of the Queen, conduct an annual Swan Upping, from Sunbury to Pangbourne, during which the birds are counted and marked.

The Easter Parade in Battersea Park, and the London Marathon from Greenwich to Westminster Bridge and the Chelsea Flower Show, both in May, are signs that what used to be called "the Season" can't be far behind. The Flower Show arrives with a fanfare and all the imperial pomp of two grand military parades: Beating the Retreat and Trooping the Colour (the latter celebrating the Queen's *official* birthday). Her Majesty lends that invaluable "royal touch" to the English summer when she rides in an open coach over the turf at Royal Ascot, greets the guests at a garden party in the grounds of Buckingham Palace, or appears unexpectedly in the Royal Box at Wimbledon.

Visitors with an artistic bent might be more attracted to the Royal Academy of Arts' Summer Exhibition, the "Proms" at the Albert Hall (the series of annual Promenade Concerts conducted by Sir Henry Wood from 1895 to 1944 and still keeping his memory green), or open-air concerts on the grounds of Kenwood House on Hampstead Heath or Marble Hill at Richmond (take a picnic hamper and blanket). On August Bank Holiday, Caribbean carnival comes to Notting Hill and the streets are filled with spectacular floats and costumes and the beat of steel bands—a festive indication of London's multicultural mix.

The approach of winter is signaled by Fireworks Nights, held all over on November 5 to commemorate the foiling of Guy Fawkes's plot to blow up Parliament in 1605. Less than a week later the City of London lets its hair down for the annual Lord Mayor's Show, when the worthy elected to that office rides in a gilded coach to the Law Courts followed by a variety of floats and bands.

London Oases

London is full of quiet corners such as the Chelsea Physic Garden, which dates from 1673 and is the second-oldest botanic garden in Britain (after Oxford's), and, five minutes from Marble Arch, Tyburn Convent, which offers peaceful sanctuary beside a replica of the Tyburn Tree, the gallows that stood nearby. The nuns still pray for the highwaymen and martyrs hanged there. As well as these quaint oases, the capital has wide acres of parkland, commons, gardens, green spaces, and stretches of open water offering escape from the rush and the traffic's roar.

Hampstead Heath, with its panoramic views of St. Paul's Cathedral and the city from the northern heights, attracted such notable intellectuals and artists as Karl Marx, John Constable, and Robert Louis Stevenson, who described it as "the most delightful place for air and scenery in London." The commons of Wimbledon, Wandsworth, Clapham, and Blackheath are strung across south London like a necklace of emeralds, ever open to walkers, riders, and kite-flyers. But London's crowning glories are the royal parks that lie at its heart and were once the grounds of palaces. Hyde Park, originally a hunting ground for Henry VIII, has boating and swimming on a lake called the Serpentine, and horseback riding in Rotten Row. Its open tree-dotted grassland merges imperceptibly at the west with the more formal Kensington Gardens and the Round Pond adjoining Kensington Palace, where Princess Margaret and other members of the royal family have their apartments. Security is tight, but it's not unusual to catch a glimpse of them driving past, apparently unnoticed by the crowds at large.

Regent's Park, laid out by John Nash, who also designed many of the elegant Regency terraces encircling it, is the home of the London Zoo, whose role is evolving into that of an environmental center rather than a place where animals are kept behind bars. The park also contains a boating lake, a notable rose garden, and an open-air theater. The canal that skirts it is used for pleasure cruises from Little Venice to the west and Camden Town. Green Park and St. James's Park, flanking Buckingham Palace—whose private grounds are discreetly hidden away behind a high, spiked brick wall—provide something like countryside between the traffic fumes of Piccadilly, Whitehall, and Grosvenor Place. Just off the Mall, the broad avenue that sweeps arrow-straight from Trafalgar Square to the palace, is Clarence House, where Queen Elizabeth, the Queen Mother (affectionately known as the "Queen Mum"), has her London home. Buckingham Palace and its outdoor military rituals, spiced by the occasional wave of a white-gloved hand as the Queen rides by, are the focus of most visitors' attention.

The royal parks provide the green backdrop to the spontaneous and continuous entertainment that draws visitors to London from across the world. Next to Old Father Thames himself, they are the city's most enduring inheritance, changeless and open to all.

Day Trips

The choice of fascinating places to visit within a day of London covers all points of the compass. Nor is the Channel that separates England from the Continent a serious barrier (see The Coast of France and Belgium section below) with the opening of the new Channel Tunnel between Folkestone, England, and Calais, France, in mid-1994. This shuttle of high-speed trains carrying vehicles and passengers through twin tunnels will provide an alternative to the existing surface ferries. Those who travel on the surface of the Channel rather than under it won't miss out on the views of the White Cliffs, although their journey will take a little longer.

If you prefer to keep your day trips within the shores of England, there are plenty of famous and historic places to see within an hour or two by car, bus, or train. Motorways such as the M 25, which girds London, have made it easier to get around this relatively small and crowded island, but traffic can be heavy at times.

It is worth considering sitting back and enjoying the marvelous scenery from a train or the bus, which is even cheaper and just as convenient. In fact, our Day Trips from London chapter is designed primarily for rail and bus travellers.

We have spread the net as wide as possible to include lesser-visited places such as Warwick and Royal Tunbridge Wells along with the more popular places such as Windsor, Stratford-upon-Avon, Bath, and Canterbury, which are crammed with tourists at peak times. Likewise, Oxford and Cambridge, those two ancient seats of learning that are always paired although miles apart geographically, are nonetheless each well within day-trip radius of London.

In what Paul Theroux called "The Kingdom by the Sea," you are never far from the lap of the waves on sand or shingle, and we have selected three places along the south coast within easy reach of London—Brighton, baronial Arundel, and Portsmouth.

Whichever trips you choose, you will find a vast array of museums, castles, historic houses, and exhibitions to fill a day, and guided tours galore to ease the way if that is more comfortable or convenient for you.

USEFUL FACTS

When to Go

There is never an off-season for London and southern England. Although many people prefer to come in May, when the azaleas and rhododendrons in some of the lovely gardens are in full bloom, others might prefer year-end holiday time, when they can enjoy a typically English Christmas, with all the trimmings of log fires and pantomimes.

London's major tourist season is July and August; as a result hotels, restaurants, and theaters are often heavily or fully booked. The stately homes and gardens in the region also experience their full share of the tourist torrent then. All things considered, spring and autumn are much better times to visit. The weather in Britain is entirely unpredictable, but these two seasons are also often the nicest. Spring can be wonderful, with mild, sunny weather and the trees coming into leaf. Autumn, with its glorious, hazy-sunny days, often lasts until Christmas. But England is, after all, an island, with a maritime climate subject to the winds and weather of the Atlantic.

What to Wear

London is a huge city, but don't let that put you off; most of the best-known sights are close together, enabling you to see a great deal in two or three days. (You could just as well spend the rest of your life trying to learn about it—

and not exhaust its wonders.) It is really a collection of small villages, each with its own heart and ambience. But London is definitely a walking city, so make sure you bring some sensible shoes.

The things you are least likely to need are very dressy evening clothes. The English tend to underdress rather than overdress, unless it is a very grand ball, at which time the family tiara gets an outing. If evening clothes are needed by visitors during their trip, it will probably be easier to rent rather than take up a lot of space in your luggage. There are several evening-dress rental shops listed in the Yellow Pages. Even for the opera and the theater, however, people here really don't dress up much, unless it is a gala or premiere. Many people go out in the evening straight from their place of work, so day dress is the norm in the evening as well.

The climate in southern England is temperate, which means the temperature rarely rises above 80° F (27° C) or falls below 30° F (just under 0° C). Contrary to what most visitors have been led to believe, London does not have a great deal of rain. It does, however, have a lot of weather of every sort—and it is entirely unpredictable, so it is just not possible to tell anyone what to bring to wear. Perhaps the most sensible thing to do is to dress in layers—the classic British compromise. Another solution is to travel light and buy when you get here, as the clothes, especially knitwear, are of very good quality.

Getting In

From North America, there are now direct flights to London's Heathrow or Gatwick airports from Atlanta, Boston, Chicago, Dallas/Fort Worth, Los Angeles, Montreal, New York, San Francisco, Toronto, and other cities. Among the many major airlines flying the North America–Britain route are Air Canada, Air India, American, British Airways, British Caledonian, USAir, Virgin Atlantic, and World. Qantas and British Airways fly the long route between Britain and Australia.

The London airports are well connected to the central city by public transportation. Heathrow is on the Underground (Piccadilly Line; 50 minutes from the airport to Piccadilly Circus, with stops in the hotel area around Harrods as well), which is very convenient. If you are planning on taking the Underground from the city center to Heathrow, however, it is essential that you know from which terminal you are departing. One Underground stop serves Terminals 1, 2, and 3; another serves Terminal 4—and if you get off at the wrong stop, you will end up walking miles with your baggage.

You can also take a Flight Line 777 bus from Gatwick or Heathrow to Victoria Coach Station. London Transport's Express Airbus connects with Heathrow only and makes stops throughout central London. The A1 Airbus goes to Victoria coach (bus) and railway stations; the A2 goes to Euston Station. The trip from Heathrow to central London usually takes less than an hour, and the fare is £5. Taxis take about the same time and charge around £38.

An efficient and much cheaper alternative is offered by London Airways Car Service (Tel: 071-403-2228; Fax: 071-403-5015), which charges a flat rate of £15 for a journey between any address in central London and Heathrow Airport and £25 to Gatwick for up to four passengers.

The fastest way to get from Gatwick to London is by train. This extremely efficient service runs directly from the Gatwick main terminal every 15 minutes, with trains reaching Victoria Station in just 30 minutes. Hourly Flight Line 777 buses also connect Gatwick with Victoria Coach Station and take 70 to 80 minutes.

Ferries link southern England with dozens of ports on the Continent and in Ireland. The two major Continental lines are P & O, which serves Dover–Calais, Dover–Ostend, Felixstowe–Zeebrugge, Portsmouth–Cherbourg, Portsmouth–Le Havre, and Portsmouth–Bilbao (Tel: 0304-20-33-88 in Dover or 081-575-8555 in London); and Sealink Stena Line, which serves Dover–Calais, Dover–Dunkirk, Harwich–Hook of Holland, Southampton–Cherbourg, and Newhaven–Dieppe (Tel: 0233-64-70-47). The trip across the Channel can take anywhere from a few hours to a full day or night, depending on your destination. The fastest crossing is by hovercraft (summer only) with Hoverspeed, which makes the trip from Dover to Calais in just 35 minutes. (Tel: 0304-24-02-41 in Dover or 081-554-7061 in London.)

For those who enjoy a longer sea voyage, the Cunard Line's *Queen Elizabeth II* makes the transatlantic crossing in style, from New York to Southampton, April through December.

Entry Documents

A passport is required of all travellers entering Britain, with the exception of citizens of other EC countries, who need only present an identity card. Citizens of the U.S.,

Commonwealth nations (Canada, Australia, and New Zealand), South Africa, and many other countries do not need a visa. Britain imposes strict anti-rabies measures, and all pets entering the country must be quarantined for a minimum of six months; unless you are moving to Britain, leave the pets at home.

For visits to the coast of France and Belgium, see the "Getting Around" section at the end of the Day Trips from London chapter.

Getting Around on Day Trips

If you are travelling from London on a day trip, be forewarned that there are many different train stations, each serving a different part of the country. Here are the ones you're most likely to use: Charing Cross serves southeastern England; Liverpool Street, East Anglia and Cambridge; Paddington, western England and southern Wales; Victoria, southern England; and Waterloo, southwestern England. (For more information about train service, see the "Getting Around" section at the end of the London chapter.)

Several discount passes for train travel are available. The most popular is the BritRail Pass, available for both first-class and second-class travel, which allows holders unlimited travel through England, Scotland, and Wales for periods of 8, 15, 22, or 30 days. The BritRail Pass is sold only outside of Britain, at British Rail offices or through travel agents.

National Express is Britain's nationwide bus network. Of special interest to overseas visitors is the Tourist Trail Pass, which provides unlimited travel for any consecutive period of 5, 8, 15, 22, or 30 days. Adult prices start at £65. Alternatively you may wish to consider buying a BritExpress card, which entitles you to a discount of 30 percent off all standard fares on every journey you make in any consecutive 30-day period; it costs £12. Tel: 730-0202.

Most major car-rental agencies have offices at London's airports and train stations. You must be 21 years of age (25 with some firms) and present a valid driver's license; an international driver's license is not required. Driving is on the left, and motorists from the United States, Canada, and other countries where driving is on the right may have difficulty adjusting to this orientation. Be extremely careful. The same holds for pedestrians— remember to look both ways before crossing the street.

(For getting around in London itself, see the section following London Museums, in the London chapter.)

Local Time

Britain observes Greenwich mean time (GMT), five hours ahead of the east coast of North America (four ahead of the Canadian Atlantic Provinces) and nine hours behind Sydney, Australia.

Telephoning

The country code for Britain is 44..The London area has been split into two area codes: (071) for inner London and (081) for outer London. In the London chapter that follows, we have given the area code only if it is (081); if it does not appear, you can assume that the area code is (071). When dialing from outside Britain, do not include the initial 0 in city codes.

To make a public-telephone call, put 10p (pence) into the coin slot in the telephone box if it has a *pink* band on the exterior. Dial the number you require and speak; when you hear an insistent beeping tone you will need to feed more money into the box to continue the call. For a box with a *green* band on the exterior you will need a green telephone card, which can be purchased at most newsstands. You insert the card into the slot and make your call. From either type, if you wish to speak to the operator, dial 100. For London directory inquiries dial 142 (when you are in London), and for directory inquiries in other regions, dial 192.

Currency

The unit of currency in Britain is the pound sterling (denoted as £), which is divided into units of 100 pence. There are coins for 1p, 2p, 5p, 10p, 20p, 50p, and £1, and notes in denominations of £5, £10, £20, and £50. Check postings in banks and in daily newspapers for the current rate of exchange.

In the main hall at most airports there is a bank where you can change foreign currency into pounds and pence. Outside airports, banks are always open Monday through Friday between 9:30 A.M. and 3:30 P.M. There are many bureaux de change around London, and most hotels will change money as well. Many branches are now open later, some until 5:00 P.M., and some also open on Saturday mornings.

At press time, the English pound converted to the U.S. dollar at the rate of £1.00 to $2.00.

Room Rates

Hotel room rates listed for London are for double rooms, double occupancy. Rates are projections for 1994 and, unless otherwise stated, do not include breakfast. (This rule is reversed, however, in the sections on places outside London, where the prices given include breakfast.) As prices are subject to change, always double-check before booking. The rates given may or may not include service charges and taxes; be sure to inquire about these charges, as they can add a significant amount to the cost of a room.

You may want to ask about two- or three-day weekend and mid-week deals, or "breaks," which can reduce the cost of staying in some hotels considerably. Prices also may vary seasonally.

Tipping

Always check on the menu in a restaurant to see whether it includes a service charge; if it doesn't, leave 10 to 15 percent. For porters and bellhops, 50p per bag is the norm, with the minimum £1. Tip hairdressers and taxi drivers 10 to 15 percent. For extraordinary services rendered, tip the hotel hall porter a suitable extra amount when you depart (beyond the service charge included in your bill).

Business Hours

Sunday is a day for strolling in the parks and going to church. Tourist areas aside, very few shops are open, many restaurants are closed, and even some museums don't open until 2:00 P.M. During the week most pubs now stay open continuously from 11:00 A.M. to 11:00 P.M. On Sundays they open at noon and close from 3:00 P.M. to 7:00 P.M., then open until 10:30 P.M..

Shops generally open at 9:00 A.M. and close at 5:30 P.M., except for the one evening a week when shops in some districts of London stay open until 8:00 P.M.—Wednesdays in Knightsbridge and Kensington, and Thursdays on Oxford Street. Shops and most banks are closed for bank holidays.

Holidays

Bank holidays are Christmas Day and Boxing Day (December 26), New Year's Day, Good Friday and Easter Monday, May Day (the first Monday in May), Spring Whit Bank Holiday (the last Monday in May), and August Bank Holiday (the last Monday in August).

Medical Problems

If you should need medical help or a doctor, ask the receptionist of your hotel, as most hotels have one they can call on. If they don't, Medical Express, a 24-hour medical partnership, can be reached at 499-1991. For pharmaceuticals, Bliss the Chemist, at Marble Arch (Tel: 723-6116), is open daily from 9:00 A.M. until midnight. If you need an ambulance, dial 999, which is also the number for the police and the fire brigade.

Electric Current

Voltage in Britain is 220/240, 50 HZ, which means that an adapter or converter, plus an adapter plug, is necessary for North American appliances.

Information

Offices of the British Tourist Authority, located in cities and towns across Britain, provide maps, booklets on sights and travel itineraries, accommodations listings, tips on travel passes and tourist discount passes, and a wealth of other information. BTA offices abroad are extremely helpful when you are planning a trip. Major offices are located at: Suite 701, 551 Fifth Avenue, New York, NY 10176 (Tel: 212-986-2200; Fax: 212-986-1188); Suite 1510, 625 North Michigan Avenue, Chicago, IL 60611 (Tel: 312-787-0490; Fax: 312-787-7746); Suite 450, 350 South Figueroa Street, Los Angeles, CA 90071 (Tel: 213-628-3525; Fax: 213-687-6621); Suite 470, 2580 Cumberland Parkway, Atlanta, GA 30339-3909 (Tel: 404-432-9635; Fax: 404-432-9641); Suite 450, 111 Avenue Road, Toronto, Ontario M5R 3J8 Canada (Tel: 416-925-6326; Fax: 416-961-2175); 123 Lower Baggot Street, Dublin 2, Ireland (Tel: 01-614-188; Fax: 01-785-280); Suite 305, 3rd Floor, Dilworth Building, Corner Customs and Queen Streets, Auckland 1, New Zealand (Tel: 09-303-1446; Fax: 09-377-6965); and 201 Clarence Street, Sydney, N.S.W. 2000, Australia (Tel: 02-267-4555; Fax: 02-267-4442).

—Paul Murphy

BIBLIOGRAPHY

PETER ACKROYD, *Dickens' London*. Ackroyd sets the scene and then leaves it to Dickens's writings and to excellent photographs to bring Victorian London alive.

————, *Hawksmoor*. This powerful and atmospheric novel can best be described as a supernatural thriller, combining a vivid account of London life, centered on the work of the great architect Nicholas Hawksmoor, with an investigation into 20th-century murders.

LINDSAY BAREHAM, *A Guide to London's Ethnic Restaurants*. A noted restaurant critic describes where to go to enjoy regional food from around the world.

PAUL BARKSHIRE, *London Villages*. A photographic record of the quiet rural spots, villages, and country houses that have been absorbed into the city.

NICHOLAS BARTON, *The Lost Rivers of London*. The story of London's rivers, other than the Thames, many now running underground—including the famous River Fleet, now covered over by Fleet Street.

ROBERT BAYLIS, *Pilgrim's London*. A guide to London's Christian heritage, this is not just a description of the capital's many churches but also covers monuments, portraits, and buildings associated with famous Christians.

JOHN BETJEMAN, *City of London Churches*. The former poet laureate was famous for his love of ecclesiastical architecture. Here he describes his favorite churches with his usual enthusiasm, at the same time demonstrating his special gift for identifying the odd and unusual detail.

Blue Plaque Guide. A comprehensive gazetteer of London houses that have once been home to famous men and women.

MARY CATHCART BORER, *The Story of Covent Garden*. The whole story of this area in the heart of London, from convent garden to fruit and flower market on to more recent years and the battle for conservation.

ARTHUR BYRON, *London Statues*. A comprehensive guide to the city's outdoor statues and sculpture.

G. COUCH AND W. FORRESTER, *Access in London*. This is a guidebook intended specifically for the physically impaired and others who have trouble getting around.

EDWIN COURSE, *London's Railways*. A full and detailed description of London's rail system and its history.

ALIZINA STONE DAK AND BARBARA SLOAN HENDERSHOTT, *Mystery Readers' Walking Guide to London*. A series of fascinating walks around Central London, each one following the path of a well-known mystery writer.

ANDREW DAVIES, *Literary London*. A street-by-street guide to the authors who have lived in London and written about London, and so also a guide to the London they described.

DANIEL DEFOE, *Journal of the Plague Years* (1724-1726). Defoe, best known as a novelist, was also a great essayist. He combined his talents to good effect in producing this convincing account of London during the Great Plague of 1664–1665.

CHARLES DICKENS, *Barnaby Rudge, Bleak House, David Copperfield, Dombey and Sons, Little Dorrit, Nicholas Nickleby, The Old Curiosity Shop, Oliver Twist, Our Mutual Friend, The Pickwick Papers*. No one did more to create the image we now have of 19th-century London than Dickens. His novels mostly portray a city of narrow alleys, dirt, and discomfort, but also a growing city, a place of excitement and exhilaration.

SIR ARTHUR CONAN DOYLE, *The Complete Sherlock Holmes*. 221B Baker Street, the home of Sherlock Holmes, is probably the most famous fictitious address in London. Doyle's novels and short stories are packed with descriptions of all aspects of London life in the last century.

ANDREW DUNCAN, *London Museums and Galleries Guide*. A straightforward, practical guide.

NELL DUNN, *Poor Cow* and *Up the Junction*. These two novels, evocations of working-class London in the 1960s, present a vivid picture of life in the inner suburbs.

SUSANNE EBEL AND DOREEN IMPNEY, *Guide to London's Riverside*. The Thames has a central place in the story of London's development, and this guidebook tells the story in terms of the riverside of today.

GEORGE AND WEEDON GROSSMITH, *Diary of a Nobody*. A hilarious account of life in suburban London at the turn of the century.

SANDRA F. GUSTAFSON, *Cheap Eats in London*. A guide to more than a hundred cheap but good establishments, ranging from pubs and tearooms to wine bars and restaurants.

JASON HAWKES AND FELIX BARKER, *London from the Air*. Stunning aerial photographs showing the London of the 1990s.

JOHN HILLABY, *John Hillaby's London*. A very personal account of walks off the beaten track: as much a story of the people of London as of places.

HENRY JAMES, *London Life* (1889). The great North American novelist is more usually associated with the country house than the city, but here he turns his refined attention to life among the upper classes at the turn of the century.

MICHAEL JENNER, *London Heritage*. A portrait of London's historical remains from Roman times to the beginning of this century.

MICHAEL LEAPMAN (editor), *The Book of London*. The story of London's development up to the present day, with sections on a variety of topics covering all aspects of life and work in the city.

———, *A History of the Thames*. The Thames has had a central role in London's development. In this book its story is told in words and in pictures from the works of Canaletto to modern photographers.

NORMAN LEBRECHT, *Music in London*. A guide to the past and present of the city's musical life, especially useful for visitors.

KATIE LUCAS, *London Walkabout*. The author, who runs a British tours company, gives details of a number of walks through London, each one fully described and enlivened with historical notes and anecdotes.

IAN NAIRN, *Nairn's London*. The classic guidebook, revised by Peter Gasson in a new edition. The late Ian Nairn was one of the most idiosyncratic of architectural writers, always controversial and always stimulating.

SAMUEL PEPYS, *Diary*. These famous diaries cover the years 1660 to 1669, a momentous period that included the restoration of the monarchy and the disasters of the Great Plague and Great Fire.

NIKOLAUS PEVSNER, *London (1): Cities of London and Westminster; London (2): South; London (3): North West*. These volumes in the Penguin "Buildings of England" series are indispensable guides for all serious students of architecture, with full details of all the buildings of note in the area.

FREDERICK A. POTTLE (editor), *Boswell's London Journal, 1762–1763*. Boswell is best known for his biography of Dr. Samuel Johnson, which also depicts London life, but it is the journal that gives the more intimate picture of city life in the 18th century, life enjoyed to the full by the young Scotsman.

V. S. PRITCHETT, *London Perceived*. A classic description of London by a distinguished author.

ROGER PROTZ, *The Best Pubs in London*. A guide to both the best pubs and the best beer by the former editor of *The Good Beer Guide*.

ANN SAUNDERS, *Art and Architecture of London*. A scholarly, fully illustrated treatment of the subject.

RICHARD TRENCH AND ELLIS HILLMAN, *London Under London: A Subterranean Guide*. A fascinating guide to the world beneath London's pavements. A book full of surprises.

PETER VANSITTART, *London, A Literary Companion*. London in all its moods, and at its quirkiest, from E.M. Forester setting fire to models of suburbia to Dr. Johnson performing a citizen's arrest.

JOHN TALBOT WHITE, *Country London*. A guide to parks and commons, riverside walks and woodlands. A series of walks is described, each one appropriate to a particular time of year.

—*Anthony Burton*

LONDON

By David Wickers with Bryn Frank

David Wickers, a longtime resident of London, is travel correspondent for the Sunday Times *of London, travel editor of* Marie Claire *magazine, and a regular contributor to several other magazines and newspapers in the United Kingdom. In 1992 he was named U.K. Travel Writer of the Year. Bryn Frank is the author of several books about Britain. He has also contributed to* National Geographic, *among many other publications and guidebooks. He is the former editor of the monthly travel and feature magazine* In Britain. *Both he and David Wickers are members of the British Guild of Travel Writers.*

Most people seeing Stonehenge for the first time say "Isn't it small!" Many a traveller who has somehow missed out on London before will exclaim "Isn't it green!" That simple statement will stop commuters in their tracks, but it's true. City office workers—we use the capital letter advisedly, for "the City" denotes the square mile, the original London now devoted mainly to commerce—may *think* they have been shoehorned into their desk space, but the fact remains that this great metropolis contains enough unspoiled parkland to make it seem like a garden city.

It's one thing to soak up the sun in one of the royal parks—it doesn't take a sophisticated tourist to tumble across St. James's Park, Green Park, Kensington Gardens, or Hyde Park and lay out his or her picnic. But there are precious copses and greenery besides: in the Inns of Court (where young lawyers are trained and household names among law firms have their chambers); in the Embankment Gardens by the Thames, close to the Savoy Hotel; and in Berkeley Square.

Zoological Gardens

Regent's Park

To Hampstead

HAMPSTEAD ROAD

MAIDA VALE

WELLINGTON RD.

Regent's Canal

PARK RD.

St

Euston Station

Marylebone Station

MARYLEBONE RD.

TOTTENHAM CT. RD.

PADDINGTON

WESTWAY

EDGWARE RD.

CUMBERLAND PL.

GREAT CUMBERLAND ST.

BAKER ST.

Cosmopolitan

Oxford Circus

NEW

Paddington Station

BRYANSTON ST.

OXFORD ST.

SOHO

NOTTING HILL

QUEENSWAY

BAYSWATER

BAYSWATER RD.

Caribbean Carnival

Marble Arch

WEST END

REGENT ST.

National Galler

Entertainment
5 SHOPS

Kensington Gardens

Hyde Park

PARK LANE

Piccadilly Circus

Trafalgar Sq.

MAYFAIR

American
Express

THE MALL

PICCADILLY

Green Park

KENSINGTON RD.

KNIGHTSBRIDGE

GROSVENOR PL.

BIR CAG

To Heathrow Airport

Queen's Gate

Victoria and Albert Museum

KNIGHTSBRIDGE

Harrods

Buckingham Palace

KENSINGTON

SLOANE ST.

BELGRAVIA

VICTORIA

CROMWELL RD.

BROMPTON RD.

BUCKINGHAM PALACE RD.

Victoria Station

WES

To Hammersmith and Richmond

EARL'S COURT

Sloane Sq.

avant-garde

PIMLICO

CHELSEA
artist + writer's home

FULHAM RD.

BEAUFORT ST.

LIMERSTON ST.

KING'S RD.

Chelsea Bridge

To Hampton Court

Albert Bridge

River Thames

QUEENSTOWN RD.

Palace of King Henry VIII

Battersea Bridge

Battersea Park

Thus it is possible to find quiet in the heart of the city. For some it is the inner courtyard of the Wallace Collection (of fine art) in Manchester Square; for others it is a stroll around the expensive quarter that is Mayfair, or the somber granite banks and financial institutions of the City, or the London University enclave of Bloomsbury, easy on the eye and almost untouched by recent development.

They say London is a collection of villages. Understanding the difference between the City and the West End is a great help in London. Not knowing the difference is like going to Oxford or Cambridge and asking, "Where is the university?"—it is actually all around you, in separate colleges.

Strictly speaking, "the City" means the area within the original Roman walls, and it is interesting to note that the original transmural expansion was made by those who were actually banned from the old city, such as actors and brothel-keepers, as well as certain privileged classes, including monks, aristocrats, lawyers, and foreigners, who could afford to ignore the protection afforded by the city walls. If you should visit the Smithfield market area (the streets around it, especially nearby Clerkenwell, have seen a massive financial investment, and the area is becoming stylish and interesting), remember that it first grew to prominence in the 12th century as a place where produce was sold just outside the city walls. Houndsditch, a street near Liverpool Street Station (gateway to East Anglia), is another name that evokes memories of the City walls, and is so called because of the dead dogs that were often found in a stream that circled the walls.

By the 16th century London was bursting at the seams, as the capital grew on both sides of the Thames. Then came the Great Plague and Great Fire of 1665 and 1666, respectively, which, rather than bringing about the demise of London, paved the way for its rebirth.

But the term "City" remains, and for many people, as we hope to show, it is as full of interest as the West End, where the shops and conventional entertainment are located. Certainly, unless you venture into the famous "square mile" and beyond it toward the East End, you will never really feel the pulse of London.

There are several contenders for our opening pages, but we begin with London's river, "Old Father" Thames, and let the current carry us east to the City, the hub of finance, and its fringing areas. Then we leap back west into the center of town to feel the pulse of Covent Garden, with its historic roots but distinctly contemporary flavor. Nearby are Bloomsbury with its museums and literary associations, cosmopolitan Soho, and the West End's major stores. Mayfair, their neighbor to the west, could be dubbed American London, being home to the U.S. embassy, but Westminster, the seat of the British Parliament and various government offices south of the West End, is undiluted U.K.

Moving still farther west, we take a turn upmarket to Belgravia and Knightsbridge, among the city's most affluent neighborhoods. Nearby Chelsea also has its share of wealthy residents, although the style is a shade more avant-garde. But this is just as well; otherwise the culture shock between Knightsbridge and Notting Hill, northwest across Hyde Park, famous for its annual carnival when London's Caribbean population takes to the streets in a pageant of calypso and reggae, would be hard to take. Farther west still, both Richmond and Hampton Court, the palace of King Henry VIII, are green gems.

Not that the west enjoys a monopoly of urban greenery. In the north, Regent's Park, with its zoo, is one exception; it's also close to both Madame Tussaud's Waxworks Museum and Camden Lock's weekend market, both major tourist draws. Islington and Hampstead, farther north, are great places for exploring interesting small shops (Islington for antiques, Hampstead for clothes, though neither exclusively so). Hampstead also has the bonus of the best of London's open spaces: the rural landscapes of the Heath.

Back toward the east of the City is the epicenter of Cockney London, the East End, with its Jewish and, more recently, Indian and Pakistani populations. And nearby on the river is the newest "village" of London, the Docklands area, a vast landscape of formerly abandoned docklands that has been, and is still being, transformed into residential and commercial properties. From this newest neighborhood in London you can walk through a tunnel under the River Thames that will bring you face to face with Greenwich, one of its most historic.

MAJOR INTEREST

The Thames
A boat tour
Tower of London
South Bank Arts Centre

CENTRAL LONDON

The City
St. Paul's Cathedral
Museum of London
Fleet Street
The Strand
Courtauld Institute Galleries
Inns of Court

Covent Garden
Royal Opera House
Shopping

Bloomsbury
British Museum
Georgian squares

Soho
Ethnic restaurants
Chinatown
Jazz

West End
Oxford Street and Regent Street for shopping
Wallace Collection
Royal Academy of Arts
Piccadilly Circus
Theater

Mayfair
Grosvenor and Berkeley squares

Westminster
Buckingham Palace (Changing of the Guard)
St. James's Park
National Gallery
Cabinet War Rooms (Churchill's bunker)
Houses of Parliament
Westminster Abbey
Tate Gallery

Dulwich Village
Dulwich Picture Gallery

LONDON WEST

Knightsbridge—Belgravia
Harrods and other shops
Hyde Park

Chelsea
Old houses of literary greats
Shopping on the King's Road

South Kensington
Victoria and Albert Museum and other museums

Richmond
Walks along the Thames
Kew Gardens

Hampton Court

Notting Hill
Annual Caribbean Carnival
Portobello Road market and art galleries

LONDON NORTH

Marylebone Road
Madame Tussaud's Waxworks Museum
Planetarium
Baker Street

Hampstead
Hampstead Heath
Highgate hilltop village

Camden Town
Camden Lock weekend market
Music venues and restaurants
London Zoo and Regent's Park
Nash terraces
Regent's Canal boat tours

Islington
Antiques shops and markets
Sadler's Wells Theatre

LONDON EAST

East End
Cockney ambience
Petticoat Lane market
Kosher and Indian food

Docklands
St. Katharine's Dock
New commercial and residential development
Docklands Light Railway
Canary Wharf

Greenwich
Maritime history
Old Royal Observatory

The Thames

Although there is no single London, there is a significant single divide between the north and south: the River Thames. As you move upstream (west) from Tower Bridge, there are more than a dozen bridges linking its northern and southern banks. Despite the ease with which one can cross from one side to the other, however, the emotional divide between north and south London is deeply rooted. While the south has always had its pockets of prosperity in such places as Dulwich Village and Blackheath, joined now by Battersea, Greenwich, Clapham, and a number of other recently gentrified boroughs, the north has long enjoyed a monopoly on affluence. More to the point, as far as the traveller is concerned, south London has its attractions, but they are widely scattered. There is a greater concentration of attractions—from stylish shops to seasoned sights—north of the river.

London happened because of its river. Its commercial significance was the city's raison d'être. Today, although the forest of masts and rigging, bustling warehouses, cranes, and general state of economic frenzy that dominated the area in the past have all but disappeared from the scene, the Thames is still the most essential element in London's chemistry.

Among the world's great rivers the Thames ranks very low. Its entire length runs only a little more than 200 miles, making it a mere stream in contrast to, say, the 4,000 miles of the Amazon or even Europe's 1,000-mile-long Rhine. And it is not always a pretty sight, especially at low tide when its muddy banks are exposed. But while a boat ride along the Seine may be hard to beat when it comes to romance, Paris's river cannot hold a candle to the Thames for the sheer interest sustained by the passing panorama.

The Thames was once the main highway of London, and in Victorian times people used to "take the water" much as we now "catch a bus"; the penny steamers were packed with day-trippers. With the development of the Docklands area, boating on the Thames has once again become popular, and both pleasure craft and Riverbuses are plentiful. The fares on the Riverbuses are reasonable, and the departures punctual. The best seats are at the front, where you can see the landmarks on both riverbanks. (For more information, see "Boat Excursions" in the Getting Around section, below.) In the 1950s the Thames was so filthy that anyone who had the misfortune to fall in was rushed off to have his stomach pumped. Today perch, trout, and even the occasional salmon have been fished from its waters. The Thames has been granted a new lease on life, one in which leisure has taken the place of commerce, and its importance as a focal point of any visit to London is of greater significance now than it has ever been.

A sightseeing boat ride is one of the best ways to enjoy the Thames. Starting from **Westminster Pier**, right beside Westminster Bridge across the road from the Houses of Parliament, regularly scheduled boats depart in either direction. You'll drift past several of the most important sights in the city, and while most cry out for far closer scrutiny than from the rails of a passing launch, at least the ride—backed by a commentary—is an apt introduction to the London cityscape.

Less easy to arrange, but a big bonus if it does come your way, is the sight of Thames-side London from the air. Many a weary transatlantic passenger is enlivened by the sight of Tower Bridge dwarfing the White Tower, which was built by William the Conqueror as the earliest part of the Tower of London and renders the nearby City church of All Hallows by the Tower pathetically small. Naval history buffs will spot H.M.S. *Belfast,* the doughty World War II cruiser, and the child in all of us will probably think the Palace of Westminster looks like a toy fortress painstakingly assembled by a twelve-year-old. The tower of Big Ben is more noticeable for its clockface than its Victorian fripperies, and, as on the ground, a lot of people are surprised at the way the Victoria Tower, at the westerly, House of Lords end of the palace, dominates.

When the light is right, you will also notice from the air how flat the eastern approaches to the city are, and how serpentine the course of the Thames actually is (most maps simplify its progress). That flatness is one reason the spectacular Thames Flood Barrier (see the end of the Docklands section, below) was built. Another thing the observant or regular air traveller will notice is how much greenery there is in the city. On one swath of undeveloped land, Hackney Marshes, there is enough space to fit *one hundred* football fields side by side.

The Tower of London

The most historically important riverside sight is the Tower of London. First built of wood by William the Conqueror in 1067, then converted to stone a decade later, it protected the king's capital both from invaders sailing upstream from the Channel and from conquered Londoners who might challenge his authority. The tower's most famous historical role, however, was as a prison to a score of leading figures, including the Little Princes (both allegedly murdered in the Bloody Tower), Thomas More, Anne Boleyn, Sir Walter Raleigh, Guy Fawkes, and, the last in the line, Rudolf Hess. Many were to pass through Traitors' Gate, the main water entrance, never to see daylight again.

Although the tower is one of those "obvious" sights that the majority of Londoners probably haven't visited since their childhood, its popularity with visitors is enormous. Apart from the impressive antiquity of the place, there are two other aspects of a tower visit that will linger in the memory long after your knowledge of its history has faded. First is the **Crown Jewels**, which include the five-pound crown said to have been worn by all British monarchs, including Queen Elizabeth II, since Charles II (and maybe even earlier), as well as the crown of the Queen Mother, which incorporates the enormous Koh-i-Noor diamond.

The second memory will be of the **Beefeaters**—more officially, the Yeoman Warders—whose history dates from their role as bodyguards to Henry VII in the 15th century. You can see them at their most spectacular—though you need to make a written application to the Resident Governor of the Tower to do so—at the Ceremony of the Keys, the closing of the main gates of the tower every evening at 10:00. Before you leave the tower, be sure to count the ravens. There are always a minimum complement of six, and legend dictates that when they no longer flap about the place, the tower and England will fall. Try to arrive early to avoid the crowds—reentry tickets are available to enable you to go out to eat. The earlier or the later in the day you go, the better.

Tower Bridge

Immediately in front of the tower is Tower Bridge, probably the single most widely recognized landmark in the entire city. Though your visit may not coincide with the impressive opening yawn of its road section—or bascules—as it only occurs roughly three times a week, the bridge nevertheless makes a stunning picture. It took eight years to build and was opened in 1894 with great pomp and ceremony by the Prince of Wales, later King Edward VII. At the time it was hailed as one of the great engineering wonders of the world. In its heyday the bridge opened for river traffic some 50 times a day and required a permanent staff of more than 100, including a few whose only job was to collect the horse droppings (presumably so they wouldn't cascade down the opening bascules onto waiting traffic).

The bridge cost more than £1 million to build, and in the early 1980s £2.5 million was the price of converting it into a tourist attraction. Today you can get acquainted with the bridge from the walkway, the topmost, latticed structure linking the two great Gothic Revival towers. The walkway and several tower rooms constitute a **museum**, with exhibits illustrating the history of the bridge (including, for those who miss it, pictures of the bridge with its jaws wide open for passing ships; one photograph shows a bus that failed to stop and was caught straddling the gap). Best of all, the walkways afford one of the best views of the Thames to be had.

When describing London from the air we mentioned the church of All Hallows by the Tower. This is just one of the many exquisite city churches, overlooked by all too many travellers, that can be havens of tranquillity in an inevitably noisy and crowded metropolis—and they are repositories of London history. Among other favorites are nearby **St. Helen's**, on Bishopsgate, which dates from the 12th century and is rich in monuments, and **St. Giles Without Cripplegate**, which is about 600 years old and is where Shakespeare is said to have attended the baptism of his nephew in 1604. ("Without" in the name denotes that it was built outside the city walls; St. Giles is in the Barbican Arts Centre northwest of the Tower.)

If you can only spare the time to see one such church, though, make it **All Hallows by the Tower**, on Byward Street. For one thing, it combines well with a visit to the Tower itself. The foundation is A.D. 675, but the present building is 13th century. The registers give details of the marriage here of John Quincy Adams, who was to become the sixth president of the United States, and of the baptism of William Penn on October 23, 1644. In the undercroft (underground room) is a Roman pavement *in situ* and a model of Roman London.

Having mentioned some favorite London churches, we

should note that many people consider the handsomest London church of all to be **St. Martin-in-the-Fields**, on Trafalgar Square (see below under Westminster). Apart from its physical charms and its very popular lunchtime concerts, it offers visitors a rare chance every year—during the Harvest Festival service held in October—to see some of London's Pearly Kings and Queens, an East End hierarchy whose "royal family" wear suits decorated with hundreds of buttons, many made of mother-of-pearl (hence the name); they collect vast sums for charity.

South Bank Arts Centre

The place in central London that offers the most intimate relationship with the Thames is the South Bank Arts Centre, by Waterloo Bridge. In front of the Royal Festival Hall, built for the Festival of Britain in 1951, there is a broad promenade along which to stroll, lean, and watch the passing barge traffic or gaze across the river at the Houses of Parliament. The **Royal Festival Hall** was an architectural triumph in its time, but you may not feel the same accolades can be applied to its neighbors. You will no doubt form a strong opinion about the newer buildings in the complex—the stark concrete presences that house the **Queen Elizabeth Hall** (staging a wide range of musical events from blues to classical concerts), the **Purcell Room** (a small theater used for recitals and chamber music), the **Hayward Gallery** (mounting major art exhibitions, contemporary and historic), the **National Theatre**, and the **National Film Theatre**. The Hayward Gallery generates much more pleasure inside than out, and is known for its imaginative but not outlandish contemporary exhibitions, as well as for its "borrowings" from major museums—more than a quarter of a million people visited the recent Toulouse-Lautrec exhibition.

The newest attraction, opened in 1988, is the **Museum of the Moving Image** (affectionately known as MOMI), the largest museum in the world devoted to cinema and television. It traces the history of film from the Chinese shadow plays of 2000 B.C. to the latest in optical-disc technology. The style of presentation here is interactive; the museum is full of evocative images and cinema memorabilia, plus opportunities to get involved in activities such as editing a film and reading a script from an autocue. There are also high-quality temporary exhibitions. Another new development here is Gabriel's Wharf, next to the National Theatre, which features a colorful food market on Fridays, with some stalls open on Sundays.

The new **Riverside Walk** (signposted) now allows pedestrians to walk from County Hall, opposite the Houses of Parliament, to beyond Tower Bridge with just a minor detour. The walk passes the **Clink Museum**, displaying torture instruments and other penal artifacts on the site of a 15th-century prison, and the new **Hay's Galleria** shopping, office, and restaurant complex. From the walk you can also gain access to the cruiser H.M.S. *Belfast*.

Central London

St. Paul's Cathedral

Unmistakably, St. Paul's Cathedral *is* London. Designed by Sir Christopher Wren, the great 17th-century church now sits rather uncomfortably in its surroundings, not unlike an aging, legally protected tenant who occupies a prime parcel of fast-appreciating real estate. Look at a selection of old paintings of London, and St. Paul's, with its curvaceous dome and squat twin towers, reigns magnificently over the skyline. Even in pictures taken during the 1940s the cathedral's environs lie around its ankles.

Today the cathedral is both hidden and dwarfed by clusters of uninspired office buildings, all fed by revenues from the City's commerce. Prince Charles has even gone on record as decrying such works as "carbuncles." Poor old St. Paul's looks pitiably ill at ease in this setting, and, architectural gem though it is, it no longer works the way Wren intended it to.

When you do occasionally catch a glimpse of the cathedral rising above the skyline of modern London—from the southern bank of the Thames near Blackfriars Bridge, for example, or looking east down Fleet Street or from a riverboat—it is superb. The dome, a giant pewter tureen from the outside, ornately painted within, is one of the cathedral's most impressive features. Depending on whether you are gazing at it from within or without, the size varies; the interior of the dome is actually a false ceiling, best appreciated from the neck-saving perspective afforded by the famous Whispering Gallery, named after its unusual acoustics, which allow a *sotto voce* murmur on the far side of the dome to be carried around the circumference and be heard by an ear held next to the opposite wall.

If you have time after seeing St. Paul's, walk eastward along Queen Victoria Street and look for the narrow Edwardian frontage of **Sweetings**, a classic London restaurant (lunchtimes only) little known to outsiders that serves top-quality fish dishes to discriminating merchant bankers. Best of all, because it's quick and informal it's not expensive.

THE CITY

St. Paul's is arguably more a symbol of the City of London than of London the city, a confusing matter for first-time visitors but a distinction that is easy to explain. The City of London is both the oldest section of town and London's financial heart, the place that bore the brunt of 1987's Black October, when share prices plummeted. It is an official city-within-a-city. Its foundation was laid by the Romans in A.D. 43, when they built the first bridge over the Thames and declared the existence of Londinium, defending their new outpost with a wall. Fragments of their protective perimeter can still be seen today (next to the Museum of London, for example), while the names Ludgate, Aldgate, and Bishopsgate remain as testimony to the wall's existence.

The Museum of London

Visitors with more than a slight curiosity about historic London should first stop by the Museum of London, on the street called (evocatively) London Wall, which explains the story of the capital from prehistoric times. It is an unprepossessing modern building, its entrance opening directly onto the pedestrian walkway that connects the Barbican Centre (see below) with the rest of the City. But the building's youth lends itself to exciting, contemporary displays and light, airy galleries.

Pity the unfortunate person whose task it was to whittle down a potentially mammoth collection into a few choice exhibits that would best portray London's history. The galleries are open-plan and chronologically ordered, so it makes sense to start on the upper floor with The Thames in Prehistory, followed by Roman, Saxon and Medieval, Tudor, and Early Stuart London. Downstairs, mock shop fronts, transport exhibits, and video screens are part of the Late Stuart, Georgian, Early 19th-century, Imperial, 20th-century, and Ceremonial London displays (the latter includes the Lord Mayor's State Coach, built in 1757 and still used in the annual Lord Mayor's Show). Other galleries specialize in prints, drawings, and paintings of London, as well as costumes and textiles. Now move on to roam the streets.

Around in the City

In medieval times the City expanded to roughly a square mile (677 acres). Today British and major international banks, insurance companies, commodity exchanges, and other financial firms have their headquarters within the historic Square Mile originally bordered by the medieval wall. More than 300,000 people pour in during the day from suburbia, but walk these streets on weekends or at night and you will hardly meet a soul.

The Great Fire of 1666 (described so vividly in Samuel Pepys's *Diary*), the wartime Blitz, and postwar redevelopment have proved to be in the worst interests of conservation. Evidences of old London are thin on the ground, although 3,000-year-old Celtic crematory urns have been found beneath Fenchurch Street, and the foundations of the Rose Theatre, built in 1587, have recently been uncovered during excavations made prior to the building of yet another office tower. One of the finest collections of Elizabethan and Tudor London artifacts is the "Cheapside Hoard," the contents of an Elizabethan jeweler's shop that was buried, only to be rediscovered in 1912. It is now displayed in the Museum of London.

There's more to see in the little-known **Shakespeare Globe Museum**, Bear Gardens, Bankside, on the south side of the river more or less opposite St. Paul's, including a reconstructed Elizabethan theater and a Rose Theatre reconstruction. Here also is Sam Wanamaker's ambitious project, the rebuilding of the **Globe Theatre**, scheduled for completion in the mid-1990s. Built along traditional Elizabethan lines, the Globe will hold 1,500 people for Shakespearean performances under open skies and natural light.

If you're blessed with a sense of imagination you can get a feeling of the City's past from present-day names. Cheapside—the name comes from the Saxon *ceap,* meaning "to barter"—was the site of a market in the Middle Ages, while nearby Poultry and Milk streets had more specific retail functions. In the Middle Ages, the **Guildhall**, on Wood Street a short walk southeast from the Museum of London, was the nerve center of the City, with a cluster

The City

0   yards   300

0   meters   300

of Livery Halls (for example, the Apothecaries' Hall, the Goldsmiths' Hall, and the Haberdashers' Hall) around it. These were the headquarters of the Guilds of London, which looked after the interests of various merchant and artisan members, and maintained professional standards. Visitor access to the Livery Halls is sometimes possible by prior arrangement; Tel: 260-1460 for further information. Dating from the period 1411–1435, the Hall of the Corporation of the City of London, to give the Guildhall its official name, is still recognizably medieval in parts, although the lower section of the Great Hall, the porch, and the crypt were damaged by the Great Fire of 1666 and bombed in 1940; they were restored in the early 1950s. The Court of the Common Council of the City of London meets here every third Thursday, and the public is admitted. And within the contemporary fabric of City life you will still find numerous references to sheriffs, aldermen, and the early trade guilds. The Guildhall also houses the world's oldest clock museum, in the new library.

Pepys is one of very few 17th-century writers who is read today. His description of the Great Fire is still riveting: "Poor people staying in their houses as long as till the very fire touched them.... The poor pigeons I perceive were loath to leave their houses, but hovered about the windows and balconies till some of them were burned and fell down.... The churches, houses and all on fire and flaming at once, and a horrid noise the flames made, and the cracking of houses and their ruine...."

Signs that the City is a separate entity include the uniforms of local policemen, similar but not quite the same as those worn in the rest of London (they have red-and-white armbands and different helmets), and various unique ceremonies, culminating in the Lord Mayor's Show to mark the annual election of the new top official. Even the Queen is traditionally escorted into the City by the lord mayor. And each December the Worshipful Company of Butchers presents a boar's head to the lord mayor in thanks for the City's giving the butchers access to the Fleet, once a tributary of the Thames, where they could clean the "entrails of beasts."

The **Barbican Arts Centre**, the City's newest grand-scale development, on Silk Street, grew out of an enormous hole in the ground, a 60-acre bomb site just to the east of the Museum of London. In addition to its trade exhibitions, concerts (it's home to the London Symphony Orchestra), stage plays (many by the resident Royal Shakespeare Company), conferences, and art exhibitions, the Barbican is a place where some 5,000 people live. It is also a place that visitors love to hate, not only for its out-of-the-way location and overpoweringly harsh design but also for the confusion that any simple movement within its labyrinthine confines seems to involve. The name "Barbican" originally came from an Arabic word meaning "house on the wall"; it denotes a structure from which watch was kept on the northern routes of the city. There is little of the old Roman Wall left in the City, but you can view the remains of a Roman fort at Cripplegate. The latter can be viewed from the Barbican Centre as well as from a window in the Museum of London.

Just outside the City's official boundary is **Wesley's Chapel** (see the map of Islington, later in the chapter). At 47 City Road, the chapel is very much a place of pilgrimage for Methodists. The first stone in this, "the mother church of Methodism," was laid by John Wesley in 1777, and the great man preached here during the last years of his life, living in the house next door until his death in 1791. (He is buried in the graveyard behind the chapel.) Bun Hill Fields, just opposite, is an ancient Saxon burial ground ("Bone" Hill Fields) that was used between 1623 and 1852 as a nonconformist cemetery. Its famous dead include John Bunyan (1688), Daniel Defoe (1731), and William Blake (1827).

Other City sights to see include the Stock Exchange, the Bank of England (with its new museum tracing the Bank's history), the Mansion House (official residence of the lord mayor), and the futuristic Lloyd's insurance building, built like the Centre Georges Pompidou in Paris with its insides on the outside. Just north of London Bridge on Fish Street Hill is the **Monument**, which commemorates the Great Fire (it started in a bakery that, at 202 feet, was situated as far from the base of the monument as the monument is tall). It was designed by Wren, who, were he to climb to the top today, might well be tempted to leap to the bottom after seeing the clutter around his more famous edifice. It used to be one of the City's best-known viewpoints, but it has been dwarfed by recent development. A Latin inscription at the base (with a translation) tells that Charles II— prompted by Wren—petitioned Parliament to rebuild while the ruins of the fire were still smoking. A nearby notice says "No lift. Just 311 steps."

Never does the City come so entertainingly alive for the ordinary visitor as on the day of the Lord Mayor's Proces-

sion, held on the second Saturday in November. You'll
have every chance, if you stand along the well-publicized
route, to see the newly sworn-in lord mayor, who in 1994
will be upholding an 805-year-old tradition. During his (or
her) term the lord mayor will make about 1,000 official
appearances, eat 600 formal meals, and make about 800
speeches. You can see the lord mayor's 236-year-old coach
at other times of the year in the Museum of London.

At this point you might like to take a walk south over
London Bridge—not the 19th-century version, which
now stands in Arizona—and have a drink at the 17th-
century pub **The George**, just along on the left down in a
courtyard off Borough High Street. The pub, which appeared in Dickens's *Pickwick Papers* and *Little Dorrit,* is
now owned by the National Trust.

FLEET STREET AREA

Before the redevelopment of London's Docklands you
would have found the office of nearly every national newspaper somewhere along **Fleet Street.** Although the printing trade has been linked with it since the beginning of the
16th century, the high-tech machinations of the Docklands
have milked Fleet Street of her successful sons (*The Times,*
the *Sunday Times,* the *Daily Telegraph,* and the *News of the
World* among them). No major newspapers are now located on Fleet Street, but the spirit of the past still resides a
few steps off the street in **El Vino's** wine bar and **Ye Olde
Cheshire Cheese** pub, a remarkable throwback to the 17th
century and watering hole of Dickens, Tennyson, Thackeray, Conan Doyle, and Theodore Roosevelt. Don't ignore
the street—one of its most beautiful landmarks is the Art
Deco former *Daily Express* building at number 121, a
world of glass and polished chrome—or its offshoots
either. Just behind the south side of Fleet Street, on the east
side of Salisbury Court, is the church of **St. Bride**, known as
the "wedding cake" and designed by Wren in 1701, with
the tallest of his steeples.

St. Paul's, towering above Ludgate Circus, forms an
impressive eastern anchor to Fleet Street. Start walking
the length of the street from there and, between the
former homes of media giants, you'll come across traditional tobacconists, topsy-turvy Tudor gabled buildings,
Dr. Johnson's House in Gough Square (open to the
public), where the famous dictionary was written between 1749 and 1759, and several large outdoor-clothing

and sports stores. At its western end the road takes a sharp upturn in class as it becomes the Strand.

At the western, Strand end of Fleet Street look for London's last-surviving example in situ of a timber-framed Jacobean town house (number 17), known as **Prince Henry's Room**. It survived only because the Great Fire of 1666 stopped next door. While it would be nice to report that Prince Henry, son of James I, had lodgings here, the name seems to come from the fact that Henry became Prince of Wales in 1610 while the building was being restored. Located within the Inner Temple Gateway and containing an exhibition devoted to Samuel Pepys, the half-timbered house dates from 1610 and has a Jacobean enriched plaster ceiling.

The Strand (or simply Strand) parallels the river (although its pedestrians cannot see the river), thus adding immense value to the buildings along its southern flank, most of which back onto the water. The world-famous Savoy Hotel is without doubt the grandest of these (try to have breakfast in its delightful **River Room**), though its neighbor, **Somerset House,** is a close competitor. Built in white Portland stone, the latter used to be the headquarters of the Registrar General of Births, Deaths, and Marriages; it now houses the less popular Board of Inland Revenue, the Probate Registry, and the very popular **Courtauld Institute Galleries**, where only a third of the collection could be seen at any one time. Painters represented in this impressive collection include numerous 19th-century masters—Bonnard, Degas, van Gogh, Seurat, Manet, Monet, Cézanne—as well as Rubens, Michelangelo, Brueghel, Dürer, Tintoretto, Rembrandt, Gainsborough, Bellini, and Kokoschka. The **Savoy Hotel** has as its forecourt the only road in Great Britain where you are obliged to drive on the right side. This dates back to a special privilege granted by Parliament to allow Savoy Theatre-goers (the theater stands adjacent to the hotel) to dismount from their carriages directly into the theater. If you are lucky enough to be invited to join a party dining at the Savoy, don't be surprised if you are seated next to Kaspar the cat; he is the Savoy's own model puss brought in to avoid unlucky parties of 13.

Other worthy sights in the area include the Wren-designed **St. Clement Danes** church (the bells ring out the "Oranges and Lemons" nursery rhyme at 9:00 A.M., noon, 3:00 P.M., and 6:00 P.M., Monday through Friday, but the interior is of little interest to most visitors), the Royal Courts of Justice (see below), and the traffic-ridden, semi-circular street known as the Aldwych, with the BBC's Bush House, the **London School of Economics** (officially the London School of Economics and Political Science) nearby on Houghton Street, and, on the opposite side of the Aldwych, on Strand Lane, the **Roman Bath**—an important source of cleanliness in its heyday, now owned by the National Trust (although its authenticity is disputed). Restored in the 17th century, the Roman Bath is open to the public by appointment only; Tel: 798-2063, 24 hours in advance.

Benjamin Franklin had lodgings at 36 Craven Street, off the Strand, during the time he lived in England as a man of substance and agent for Pennsylvania (from 1757 to 1762 and again, after a brief return to America, from 1764 to 1775). He had first come to London in 1724 after a family quarrel, and at that time stayed about 18 months.

THE INNS OF COURT

Apart from its journalistic associations, Fleet Street (along with its offshoot, Chancery Lane) cuts through the heart of legal London. The "Big Four," all a short stroll from one another, are the four Inns of Court: Gray's Inn, Lincoln's Inn, Middle Temple, and Inner Temple (the last two are part of the Temple complex; the other two, separate from each other, are off to the north). Together, they have been the linchpins of Britain's closely knit legal community since the 14th century. A stroll through the cloistered courtyards of the inns reveals a tranquil world of fine stone buildings, manicured gardens, and elegant quadrangles. In a few steps you can leave the traffic hubbub of Chancery Lane and find yourself in an atmosphere more reminiscent of Oxford or Cambridge than the City. Any tour of the area should begin with the **Temple**, reached via Middle Temple Lane, one of the tiny side streets off the south side of Fleet Street.

The college-like buildings of the Temple house the two older inns: the **Middle Temple** and the **Inner Temple**. An area called the Outer Temple has long since disappeared, but next to the Inner Temple is the 12th-century **Temple Church**, one of England's last remaining round churches. Originally home to the Knights Templars, a military order founded in Jerusalem in 1118, the Temple was built in the mid-12th century. In the early 14th century, the order was disbanded, and the Temple was let out to students.

In 1292 King Edward I declared that the country's legal system was a mass of shortcomings. Until then all matters of justice had been dealt with by members of the clergy. They were undoubtedly the most literate members of society, but they were still laymen so far as noncanon law was concerned. Edward's desire to professionalize the legal system led to the recruitment of top candidates from the aristocracy. At first the students were scattered around the country, but by the end of the 14th century all barrister pupils were brought to London and accommodated in hostels, or "inns," including the former lodgings of the Knights Templars.

Today each inn is an autonomous entity with its own chapel, library, and dining hall. The latter, a richly decorated room, has always been the focal point; Queen Elizabeth I and her courtiers, for example, were wined and dined in **Gray's Inn**, the most northerly of the inns, off High Holborn, on so many occasions that today's inmates still toast "Good Queen Bess" in a room adorned with relics of a vessel captured during the rout of the Spanish Armada. A number of Shakespeare's plays also debuted in the inns: Gray's Inn saw the first performance of *The Comedy of Errors* in 1594, while the magnificent Middle Temple Hall claims the same honor for *Twelfth Night* in 1602.

The oldest of the four Inns of Court, **Lincoln's Inn**, just east of Kingsway, near the Holborn Underground station and off Lincoln's Inn Fields, can name eleven prime ministers among its members. Records date from the 15th century in this inn, which was built partly on land owned by Henry Lacy, earl of Lincoln, whose lion figures in the inn's badge. The poet John Donne, chaplain of the inn and later dean of St. Paul's Cathedral, laid the foundation stone of the chapel in 1619.

In Britain, unlike in the United States and most other countries, there are two distinct types of lawyer. Barristers represent the prosecution or defense in the high-ranking courts, whereas solicitors—who are forbidden to stand and be heard in these places—handle the nuts-and-bolts paperwork on a case and deal directly with clients. The barrister may never so much as meet those he represents in court. But the laws governing the law are beginning to change; in the near future solicitors are likely to be permitted to represent clients.

While television's pompous, blustering Rumpole of the Bailey is a caricature of British barristers, there is a great deal of snobbishness attached to the inns, and the members of each one adhere to a strict hierarchy. Their interiors are sacrosanct, as they contain the offices (or "chambers") of practicing barristers, whose names are listed beside each doorway.

Over the years these lists have read like the pages of *Who's Who*. Sir Thomas More and several other lord chancellors were members of Lincoln's Inn, the place where rival Prime Ministers Disraeli and Gladstone also qualified as barristers. Sir Francis Bacon was the most famous member of Gray's Inn, and Charles Dickens was apprenticed to one of its lawyers at age 15. Sir Walter Raleigh and Sir Francis Drake were both members of the Middle Temple (it's even rumored that one of its dining-hall serving tables is made of timber from Drake's ship *The Golden Hind*). John Dickinson, a Middle Templar, was the man who coined the phrase "no taxation without representation"; when the American Declaration of Independence was drawn up, five Middle Templars signed the final document. Many prominent North Americans are still honorary members of the inns.

You will undoubtedly catch sight of barristers rushing to and from court in twos and threes, each clutching a bundle of "briefs." By tradition, they do not carry briefcases; all documents are carried openly and bound by a red ribbon (hence the expression "red tape").

Royal Courts of Justice

Having prepared their cases, barristers have only a short walk to work. The Neo-Gothic Royal Courts of Justice on the Strand, home of the High Court and the Court of Appeal of England and Wales, pass judgment on the most important civil cases. The vaulted, cathedral-like Great Hall, supported by granite pillars and hung with oil paintings of former judges and coats of arms, echoes the hushed activity. Barristers, ticking on White Rabbit schedules, their black gowns bloated like sails in a gale-force wind and frizzes (wigs) askew, emerge from one corridor, zip across the hall, and disappear into another. Don't even attempt to follow them; five and a half miles of corridors lead off the hall, and that's a lot of shoe leather if you get lost.

Members of the public whose cases are scheduled for judgment in one of the 64 courts later in the day stand huddled in earnest conversation with solicitors. All the day's cases are listed in showcases. To witness a trial involving murder, robbery, or other such heinous crimes, you have to make your way to the public gallery of the Old Bailey, the most famous criminal court in the world.

The Old Bailey

"Justice is not blind at the Old Bailey," declared the City of London Corporation 87 years ago when the Old Bailey (or the Central Criminal Court, to give it its proper name; located back east near St. Paul's, at Old Bailey and New-gate streets) was built on the site of Newgate Prison, which was demolished in 1902. To emphasize the point, they made sure that their version of the figure of Justice, the statue that sits on the building's green dome holding the scales of justice and the sword of retribution high above the traffic jams, was one of the only ones in the world without a blindfold.

The open area in front of the court building dates from 1783, when public hangings first took place here in an attempt to reduce the riots that often accompanied the journey of prisoners west from Newgate Prison along Oxford Street to the gallows at Tyburn. A plaque at the junction of Bayswater and Edgware roads, close to Marble Arch, marks the site of Tyburn Gallows, fashioned "in a triangular manner" in order to face each of the three roads leading to the junction, and where up to 24 people at a time could be hanged. (The last public execution in England took place at Newgate in 1868, when Michael Barrett was convicted and hanged for the bombing of Clerkenwell Prison, in which 12 died.) Many prisoners did not survive to stand on the gallows, dying as a result of the unsanitary conditions in Newgate, where gaol fever (a form of typhoid) bred. To hide the stench that pervaded the courts, and supposedly to protect against infection, judges held posies of sweet-smelling flowers. Today judges still carry posies on ceremonial occasions as a reminder of the appalling conditions of years gone by.

Criminal justice in England and Wales focuses on the Old Bailey, and within the walls of its 19 courts you can hear the verdicts of major trials, many of which are referred to the High Court judges as a last resort. The most famous and most important cases are heard in the surprisingly small Court Number One, a wood-paneled courtroom whose dock floorboards have creaked under some of the most notorious criminals in the history of 20th-century Britain. These include the U.S.-born Dr. Crippen, accused of murdering his wife, Belle Elmore, and cutting her up into pieces before eloping with his mistress. More recent trials have included that of the "Yorkshire Ripper," the murderer who terrorized that part of the country in the late 1970s.

Not many town houses begin life as a museum, but the house near Lincoln's Inn that Bank of England architect and antiquarian Sir John Soane built was actually designed to house his collection of architectural fragments, prints, antiquities, and paintings. **Sir John Soane's Museum**, 13 Lincoln's Inn Fields, is a museum with a difference. Soane stipulated that his collections remain unaltered. As a result, a fine house of the period, with an eclectic assortment of fine art, antiquities, and furniture, remains as it was in 1813. Instead of hurrying through marble halls you press the doorbell, are admitted with some ceremony, and sign the visitor's book. You're then free to wander slowly through the many-roomed mansion and be impressed by the profusion of mirrors and play of light at almost every angle. There are some domestic touches on the first floor, but mostly you'll be astonished by the sheer flamboyance and originality of the decor, and by the work of artists such as Turner, Canaletto, and Hogarth.

COVENT GARDEN

Cross busy Kingsway, walk down Great Queen Street past the vast Masonic Hall, and you'll find yourself in London's newest village (at least on the visitor's map), Covent Garden. Within the space of a few years, the city's old fruit-and-vegetable market has been transformed into one of the liveliest and loveliest urban centers in Europe.

In underground cellars once used to store bananas, young sophisticates now pick cherries off the ends of tiny paper parasols resting on the edges of cocktail glasses. From stalls in the central Apple Market, where Granny Smiths and Cox's Orange Pippins were once stacked, shoppers now buy elaborately patterned sweaters and scores of other products handmade by the craftspeople who sell them. And in high-ceilinged warehouses that once stored crates of carrots, parsnips, potatoes, and other roots, Filofax clutchers now dine on nouvelle cuisine served by bowtied waiters whose own social background would not permit them to take on such menial and deferential roles anywhere else in Britain.

In an earlier incarnation Covent Garden was also a very fashionable part of town. Inigo Jones designed **St. Paul's**

Church, popularly known as "the actors' church," as well as the Piazza on which it stands, just west of the market. The story has it that the earl of Bedford (the original land-owner) told Jones that his budget would only stretch to cover a barn, so the architect promised the "most beautiful barn in the country." Completed in 1633 as part of London's first square, modeled after the Italian piazzas Jones had studied in his travels, the church was later destroyed by fire but was rebuilt to its original specifications.

The original Theatre Royal, where Nell Gwyn sold oranges, opened in 1662, and soon afterward the **Royal Opera House** opened its doors on Bow Street, off Long Acre. But the area's early elegance did not last long. The presence of the wealthy drew rogues—the poet Dryden was beaten up in an alleyway outside the Bucket of Blood pub, now the Lamb and Flag. It is no coincidence that London's first police force, the Bow Street Runners, was established just around the corner.

Fostered by the security of the strong arm of the law, a new wave of prosperity followed. This renaissance was marked by the construction of the Central Market build-ings in 1830, when the duke of Bedford decided that something smarter was needed to replace the rows of shanty vegetable stalls that had stood their ground since the 17th century. Coffeehouses also flourished; Dr. John-son first met Boswell in a small establishment, now fit-tingly called Boswell's, on Russell Street.

In 1974, after three centuries of commercial activity, the market vendors moved out to modern premises across the River Thames at Nine Elms. They left behind a mass of grimy buildings—and an enormous debate on just what to do with such a potentially prime site on the fringes of the West End. Restoration work on the old buildings was started, but the transition was not accom-plished without opposition—mainly from neighborhood residents, who would have preferred to see the develop-ment of a simple residential community, not an upscale designer village.

The Shopping

The Covent Garden area offers some of the best of Lon-don's shopping—not for basics (there is only one butcher shop, and even that is mostly a purveyor of game) but for fashionable, boutique-type wares. Lots of old traders re-main, including Anello and Davide, the theatrical shoe-makers; the Drury Tea and Coffee Co.; and Stanfords, the

map and travel book shop. Covent Garden itself and neighboring streets such as Long Acre contain scores of galleries and bookshops, clothing boutiques, epicurean and organic food stores, gift shops, and other establishments whose wares all bear a stamp of design that far exceeds the functional.

Many shop fronts are based on original designs, and in the north hall, site of the old Apple Market, a flavor of the old days remains. Forty original wrought-iron stands, salvaged from the Flower Market, are now rented to traders and craftspeople, who sell their goods beneath the magnificent glass roof. As for the Old Flower Market itself— on the eastern side of the Piazza, completed in 1872 and staffed entirely by women—it now houses the **London Transport Museum**'s collection of early buses, trams, trains, trolleybuses, and motor and horse buses; a collection of 1920s and 1930s advertising posters; videos, including one with recollections from people who worked on the London buses; a simulated driver's journey on the Underground; and many interactive displays. The entrance to Britain's first **Theatre Museum** is around the corner on Russell Street, within walking distance of the Royal Opera House and many other theaters. The best place to start a tour here is in the strangely decorated tearoom, and then on to a dramatic show of the British stage and its development from Shakespeare to the present day.

Every day at lunchtime you will find performances by buskers (street performers), all carefully screened by the Covent Garden management, in front of the portico of St. Paul's Church, the very spot where George Bernard Shaw's Eliza Doolittle first met Professor Higgins, as well as under the 1830s roof of the Apple Market.

At night the activity moves to a different rhythm. When the stores close—most not until 8:00 P.M.—people drift to the pubs and wine-and-cocktail bars, then on to restaurants. You can eat inexpensive but sometimes bland African fare at the **Calabash**, Italian at **Orso**, American at **Joe Allen's**, Chinese at **Poon's**, classic English at the **Opera Terrace**, French at **Mon Plaisir** or **Boulestin**, Japanese at **Ajimura**, and Mexican at **Café Pacifico**.

BLOOMSBURY

Sinatra's rendition of Ira Gershwin's lyric, "a foggy day in London town," captures Bloomsbury, north of Covent Garden, in a surprisingly dramatic mood. The British

Museum, he croons, has lost its charm—a curious attribute for such a hefty, solid chunk of masonry, even on the sunniest of days. And, just to correct those misconceptions, London's traditional pea-soup fog, in which Ira Gershwin was no doubt once engulfed, is now only to be experienced in ancient horror movies. In 1956 the Clean Air Act was passed, outlawing the use of coal and wood fires, and regulating industrial emissions.

British Museum

The British Museum, with its magnificent colonnaded façade and entrance on Great Russell Street, is at the heart of Bloomsbury, a fitting edifice for this, the most cerebral area of town. This great repository of treasures, many blatantly stolen from Egypt and other lands at a time when Britain's imperialist arrogance, not to mention its archaeological light-fingeredness, exercised no ethical restraints, is invariably among the top half-dozen priorities of overseas visitors to London (although most Londoners went there the first and last time as children, led by their teacher).

Construction of the present building, with its ancient Greek influences (rather ironic, considering the recent tussle over the fate of the Elgin Marbles), was completed in the middle of the last century. (It displayed the grime of all those years, too, until its recent cleaning.) The building houses a vast collection, spread among some 94 rooms, galleries, and landings. Museum freaks may feel the need to tackle the lot, devoting their entire vacation to poking around. Others will prefer to limit their visits to the essential exhibits. These must, of course, include the **Elgin Marbles** (a set of sculptures and a frieze that were taken from the Parthenon in Athens by Lord Elgin in 1803), if only to see the cause of the dispute between the authorities in Britain and Greece concerning their permanent home. You'll find them displayed in the Duveen Gallery. The Library Galleries contain the **Magna Carta,** one of the most important documents in the annals of democracy, while the prize in the Egyptian Sculpture Gallery is the **Rosetta Stone**. All these rooms are on the ground floor. In the Egyptian Gallery upstairs are the famous mummies, arguably the museum's most fascinating exhibits. You can also have a brief look at the Reading Room, a stunning library in which rows of desks radiate out from a central area beneath a 40-foot dome. The library is scheduled for relocation to a site near St.

Pancras railway station; the move, to begin in 1995, will take until 1999, perhaps longer. Meanwhile, visitors are allowed in at noon, 2:00, 3:00, and 4:00 P.M.

Other Museums

Other Bloomsbury museums include the **Percival David Foundation of Chinese Art**, on Gordon Square, which includes superb porcelains; and the tiny one-room **Jewish Museum** on Upper Woburn Place, Tavistock Square, which in cramped surroundings displays artifacts from Jewish life and religion, including Torah scrolls, Ark curtains, marriage contracts and mugs, Hanukkah lamps, and a rich and elaborately carved synagogue Ark once used as a servants' wardrobe in Chillingham Castle, Northumberland. (The museum is slated to move to larger quarters in May 1994; Tel: 071-388-4525.)

Also worth seeing is the **Dickens House Museum**, 48 Doughty Street, which contains memorabilia from every period of Dickens's life, not just the two years he lived here, much of it set out as it was in his time—with the Dickens drawing room, the study where he worked on *The Pickwick Papers, Oliver Twist, Nicholas Nickleby,* and the beginning of *Barnaby Rudge,* and the dining room where he held regular dinner parties. It also houses one of the most comprehensive Dickens libraries in the world. **Pollock's Toy Museum**, 1 Scala Street across Tottenham Court Road, displays the original "Penny Plain Tuppence Coloured" Toy Theatres, as well as a variety of 19th- and 20th-century toys, some of which can be bought, though not cheaply. Here is a cornucopia of toys: early jigsaws, puppets, dolls, games, and those toy theaters, with examples from the 16th century to the present day, plus a collection of old teddy bears, including Eric, "the oldest known bear."

University of London

If the British Museum represents Bloomsbury's seat of knowledge, the University of London is its seat of learning. American visitors, in particular, will be surprised at the relatively small acreage that such an important educational institution appears to occupy. This is partly because there are no halls of residence as such, but also because several of the surrounding ordinary-looking buildings have been bought by the university for the use of individual faculties.

Located to the rear of the British Museum, on the southwestern side of Russell Square, the main part of the university is a relative newcomer to Bloomsbury—the tall Senate House was begun only in 1932—but because so many of its parts are found in older buildings, its geographical roots seem much older. Among the most important of the larger buildings are University College and, on the opposite side of Gower Street, University College Hospital.

Elsewhere in Bloomsbury

Sadly, the tallest building in Bloomsbury also happens to be one of the ugliest. West of Tottenham Court Road, the British Telecom Tower, also known by its former name, the Post Office Tower, dominates London's skyline (it's the third-tallest structure in London, after Canary Wharf in Docklands and the NatWest Bank building in the City) and is widely despised, though it has a good reason for being here, as its ungainly stature affords the necessary ground clearance for its communications functions. Close by, on and around **Berners Street**, you'll find London's nearest equivalent to New York's garment district. Early in the morning you'll be jostled by people wheeling trolleys of new clothes destined for wholesale and retail outlets. Streetwise shoppers make individual purchases here, though not all businesses will allow retail sales.

On nearby **Charlotte Street** you'll be at the heart of a district of small ethnic restaurants that tend to be less expensive and less chic than those in Knightsbridge or Mayfair. The area is often associated with Greek restaurants, such as the long-established **White Tower** on Percy Street, but there is also a well-known French restaurant, **L'Etoile**, on Charlotte Street.

There are, as in any section of any city, certain monstrosities. But Bloomsbury is one of the corners of Georgian London that has survived fairly well, its leafy squares little changed since their drawing rooms witnessed the frantic exchanges of artistic, literary, and philosophical banter between members of the early-20th-century Bloomsbury Group. Most members of this circle (Virginia Woolf and her sister Vanessa Bell, Rupert Brooke, D. H. Lawrence, art critic Roger Fry, Lytton Strachey, Clive Bell, Maynard Keynes, and E. M. Forster) didn't have far to travel when visiting—they lived on one or another of Bedford, Woburn, Russell, Gordon (Virginia Woolf lived at number 46 before she married), Tavistock, or Fitzroy squares. Sadly, Bloomsbury Square has lost all its original architecture; only **Bedford Square** and **Fitzroy Square** are still lined with their vintage tall and extremely handsome mid-18th-century terraced houses. However, the core of most squares is still a quiet patch of green, though when in the shape of lush gardens they are usually closed to the public (the residents have keys).

Brunswick Square is the blacksheep of Bloomsbury—its dimensions have narrowed and its beauty has disappeared since the construction of an ugly housing block and a small, modern cinema, the Renoir, which was plunked in its center alongside a Safeway supermarket and other commercial outlets.

With all its literary flowering, it's little wonder that Bloomsbury sprouted a spray of publishing houses, many now departed in the face of skyrocketing rents. To see what they produced, try some of the area's many bookshops—**Dillons** is the largest, built to serve the university, its distinctive navy-blue-and-gold window display hogging the northern end of Malet Street. For second-hand or more specialized tomes, head south of Russell Square to the network of narrow streets around Museum Street.

SOHO

Since the beginning of the century Soho has enjoyed a dubious reputation. The name still conjures up images of sleazy clubs, brothels, gambling parlors, and gang plots (both the Italian and Chinese varieties). It is a world where, by night at least, tourists once feared to tread or did so with their adrenaline pumping.

Not so long ago one-third of all its houses were brothels, and, although a great deal has been done to clean up the area, only recently have the authorities begun to stem the tide of sex shops and peep shows that blossomed in their place. Soho is not a no-go. It may not appeal to your taste, but, compared with most other sin centers of the world, it is relatively tame. In any case, it cannot be ignored. To do so would be to turn your back on the highest density of good dining to be found in the whole of London.

The area is anchored on the southeast by Leicester Square and bordered by **Charing Cross Road** (still famous for its bookstores—Foyle's, Zwemmer's, and others) and the shopping thoroughfares of Oxford and Regent streets. **Leicester Square** is a good place to begin a Soho saunter. It is difficult to imagine, despite the grass underfoot and the towering plane trees, that in Henry VIII's time the area was at the heart of a royal hunting ground surrounded by open country and rural villages, with the City of London still a few miles off to the east. (The very name "Soho" is derived from an old hunting cry, the contemporary equivalent being "tallyho.")

The actual square, known originally as Leicester Fields, was named after the earl of Leicester, who built its first town house on what is now the site of the Angus Steak House, on the northern side of the square. Soon other houses went up, in one of the country's earliest spates of property speculation. Once commoners moved in to occupy them, however, the earl moved out. Today the square is a bright-lights mecca that mainly entices out-of-towners in search of a newly released movie (there's also a ticket booth selling seats for same-day theater performances at half price; but don't expect tickets for smash hits—the system works best for second-rank shows and plays).

Many people regard **Soho Square**, in Soho's northeast corner near the intersection of Charing Cross and Oxford Street, as the heart of the area. It is certainly its greenest core, with a statue of King Charles II standing among the trees holding what looks like a spout in one hand. It *is* a spout; the king used to be a fountain "powered" by a row of windmills along what is now Oxford Street. The square was once a garden for the exclusive use of residents, but they departed and the park became public. Today it's a popular summer retreat for lunchtime sandwich-eaters and more than a scattering of winos. A close inspection of the building that looks like a Tudor hunting lodge in the center of the square will reveal that it is mock Tudor. Built in the 1930s, it was modeled after the type of hunting lodge that used to keep the royal heads dry in the event of rain. It is now a tool shed.

Soho's social history is colorfully cosmopolitan. French Huguenots fleeing the consequences of the revocation of the Edict of Nantes, Greeks escaping the Turks, Swiss, Italians, Germans, Jews, and other refugees have all immigrated to Soho in large numbers, most sharing a background of persecution in their home countries. By 1914, for example, one-third of the houses here were occupied by Jews, a figure that will come as a surprise to people who think of the East End as the traditional Jewish district in London.

Dining in Soho

The cosmopolitan mix today is best seen in the enormous number of ethnic restaurants. Stand, for example, on the corner of Leicester Street (just north of the square) and Lisle Street, and you'll see Poon's Chinese restaurant virtually next door to Manzi's Italian fish restaurant, which, just to add to the confusion, used to be a German hotel whose visitors' book recorded Karl Marx and his wife and children as onetime guests.

Among the many echoes of the French accent in Soho is the **French House** at 49 Dean Street, a regular pub but one as close as you're likely to come to a French bar in London (although its characterful owner, Gaston, has retired). The walls are lined with photos of French boxers, and the atmosphere is heavy with not-too-distant memories of Charles de Gaulle, who, during the war, patronized the bar along with other members of the Free French movement. There's also the delightfully bohemian **Pâtisserie Valerie** on Old Compton Street and **Maison Bertaux** on Greek Street, perfect places to rest weary feet while having a coffee and croissant or *gâteau*.

If Londoners had to pick a single street that summed up the essence of Soho, the honors would go to **Old Compton Street**. No more than 300 yards long, it contains an Algerian coffee store, a French restaurant, a Spanish deli, an Italian pizzeria, a Malaysian restaurant, a Vietnamese restaurant, and, one of the most recent arrivals, an American diner called Ed's. The area's diversity is well represented by the newsagent called A. Moroni & Son, who sells just about every newspaper in the world (except for, surprisingly, the *New York Times*). One of the most cheerful streets in Soho is **Berwick Street**, the site of a market since the 1840s. Although it deals mainly in fruit and vegetables, you'll find some clothes and fabrics here as well.

Chinatown

The most recent ethnic group to move into Soho in significant numbers have been the Chinese from Hong Kong. In fact, it wasn't until 1981 that the area in which they settled, centered on the now pedestrianized **Gerrard Street**, was officially recognized as Chinatown. The Chinese have totally revitalized what used to be a run-down, inner-city slum. Although London's Chinatown is far smaller than its counterparts in, say, New York City or San Francisco, the area's shops, restaurants, and overall atmosphere are almost completely Chinese—and, yes, the telephone boxes are shaped like pagodas. There is a large Chinese supermarket, too, on Gerrard Street, and while you are unlikely to need bags of frozen prawns or packets of bean shoots (unless you are staying in an apartment with a kitchen), you will find useful between-meals snacks and cold drinks here at prices much lower than what you'll pay in kiosk and fast-food outlets around Piccadilly and Leicester Square.

Historic Soho

Soho has numerous blue plaques commemorating the famous as well as red lights announcing the presence of the infamous. No matter where you walk in Soho and no matter what ethnic stamp is currently on the street, evidences of its history abound. William Blake was born here, on Marshall Street; Hazlitt died here, on Frith Street. On Gerrard Street you'll spot a plaque that describes the time that John Dryden spent here. Just a few doors along the road, in the house now occupied by the Loon Fung restaurant, Edmund Burke resided. On the opposite side of the street you'll see an original 18th-century building with a portico (now the Loon Moon supermarket) that is famous for a former occupant, the Turk's Head Tavern. The Turk, mentioned by Dickens and by Boswell in his biography of Johnson, was the great literary hangout of the day (the current media hangout is Groucho's, a private club just around the corner on Dean Street).

The parish of Soho was once far grander in scale than it is now, and boasted the church of St. Martin-in-the-Fields (on Trafalgar Square) as its parish church. As the area grew in popularity as a residential section of town, the scale became unmanageable, and the parish was split in two. St. Anne's was built as the new parish church—but, since World War II, all that remains is a tower with a unique barrel-shaped clock, the only one in London. It is best seen from the corner of Romilly and Dean streets, where a new community center represents the spirit of a newer, cleaner Soho, a phoenix rising from an image-poor past.

But back to the blue plaques. Casanova lived on Frith Street and also on nearby Meard Street, which still contains a row of mid-18th-century brick houses, among the oldest in the area. (Chopin gave a recital in one.) Jean-Paul Marat lived on Romilly Street in a house with a distinctive bay-window overhang, or "jetty." He came to London not as a revolutionary but as a doctor, and labored over a treatise on eye diseases while he lived here.

Another unifying Soho theme, apart from its history, sexual notoriety, and good eating, is music. In the 1950s Soho was famous for its coffeehouses, which spawned the U.K.'s first superstars of pop. Though all of the original venues are gone, Soho is still a place to hear music. **Ronnie Scott's** is the jazz epicenter, located opposite a brick building where Mozart came to entertain at the age of eight. Just a few yards away, on the same side of the road at 47 Frith Street, yet another blue plaque marks the spot where, at an embryonic stage in the development of another branch of entertainment, John Baird demonstrated the first television set.

THE WEST END

Although visitors may find the nomenclature geographically confusing—it's in central, not western, London— Londoners never think twice about the West End's location. To them the West End means central shopping (and the theater). If you want to immerse yourself in the commercial heart of town, just mingle with the lunchtime office workers or weekend pilgrims from the suburbs who come to shop here.

Oxford Street

Two miles of crowded sidewalks line Oxford Street, the West End's main artery, which is trampled daily from Marble Arch at its western end to Centrepoint skyscraper at Tottenham Court Road. Its reputation has been carried to all corners of the globe, yet its days as London's premier shopping street seem numbered. There was a time when no self-respecting chain of stores would fail to open a branch on Oxford Street; without the address, a concern would hold little credibility in the retail hierarchy. Nowadays shoppers tend to give its stores a pass, preferring its more fashionable, polished rivals along Kensington High Street, in Covent Garden, and on Fulham Road in Chelsea.

Commercially, at least, it is still viable for a retail outlet to have at least one branch on Oxford Street—Saturday crowds so large that police use megaphones to move people out of the way of oncoming buses cannot be bad for business. (There's even a regular shuttle-bus service that ferries shoplifters to the police station.) But the traditional Oxford Street names would probably be far happier if the tacky discount stores, furiously trying to unload cheap sweatshirts, plastic watches, tasteless imitations, and gimmicky paraphernalia, weren't their neighbors. Even offshoot Carnaby Street, a West End high spot during the swinging 1960s, is now surviving on reputation alone; in reality, its veneer is more than a trifle faded.

Largely it's the quality department stores (Selfridges, John Lewis, Marks and Spencer, C&A, Debenhams, and British Home Stores) that keep the lunchtime, Saturday, and late-night Thursday shopping crowds flowing down Oxford Street. They are the last great British shopping institutions, giant magnets without which Oxford Street would have died long ago.

Marking the street's Park Lane (western) extremity, **Marble Arch** deserves a brief mention. Built by George IV to celebrate England's victory over Napoleon, it originally stood outside Buckingham Palace. If Marble Arch figures high on the tourist's list of London sights, to native motorists it signifies little more than bumper-to-bumper traffic jams.

St. Christopher's Place, an alley so narrow you could easily miss it, leads off the north side of Oxford Street almost opposite New Bond Street and is lined with high-fashion, one-off boutiques, stores that sell just one example of a particular design. The Warehouse clothing store and the home-furnishing frippery store, the Reject Shop, are doing a roaring trade in the Plaza shopping mall. And running at a tangent to the mainstream traffic off the south side of the Bond Street tube station is super-chic **South Molton Street**, which is closed to vehicular traffic.

Manchester Square, north of Oxford Street behind Selfridges, contains the **Wallace Collection**. When the first marquis of Hertford started amassing 18th-century paintings and French furniture and artworks, the collection was housed in Paris, but by the time it had passed into the hands of Richard Wallace, five generations later, it was in England, opened to the public in 1900. (For the interesting area around the Wallace Collection, see Marylebone Road in the London North section.)

Regent Street

Take a sharp turn to the south at Oxford Circus, step down Regent Street, and you take a giant stride up the elegance scale. The street, laid out by John Nash in the early 19th century, was originally planned to run straight from the prince regent's home, Carlton House, north to the new Regent's Park, but Nash interrupted the tedium of the endless avenue approach with his unmistakable, lavishly expansive curves. Immediately attractive to the rich and famous (Nash himself lived at number 14; Lady Hamilton, Admiral Nelson's renowned mistress, resided down the road at number 25), Regent Street soon became an attractive proposition for shopkeepers as well.

Although large chunks have been reconstructed over the years, Regent Street, now controlled by the Crown Estates Commissioners, is enjoying a revival. The mock-Tudor Liberty's and the Dickins & Jones department stores, and the racks of trenchcoats at Burberry's on Lower Regent Street, for example, are still here, and the grim airline offices and fusty one-off stores are being gradually nudged out by a brigade of parquet-floored, marble-pillared designer newcomers like the U.S.–imported Gap, the middle-of-the-road Next, and the popular Laura Ashley fabric outlets. The world's biggest toyshop, **Hamley's**, is to be found on six floors on Regent Street. It's a paradise for children of all ages, with any and every toy you could possibly want, plus dozens you've never even heard of; all those working models you can see through the window are bound to lure you in. It opened as Noah's Ark in 1760 at Holborn, but moved to Regent Street in 1881. Just down the street is one of the most famous Stateside exports, the **Disney Store**.

Bond and Jermyn Streets

Window-shop, if nothing else, on Bond Street (Old Bond Street to the south, running up from Piccadilly, and New Bond Street at the northern end up to Oxford Street). A jewelers' lair for decades, the street has retained its sumptuous image, with sky-high rents and retail prices to match. The same applies to Jermyn Street, just south of and parallel to Piccadilly—where it helps to be rich *and* male because a large proportion of shops here (Bates, Harvie & Hudson, and Astley's, for example) cater exclusively to men with a whim for a jar of mustache wax or a badger-hair shaving brush.

The Piccadilly Area

Two of the West End's biggest shopping attractions are on Piccadilly: **Burlington Arcade**, built in 1818 as one of Britain's first covered shopping malls, for fine woollens, linens, jewelry, and the like; and the upscale **Fortnum & Mason** emporium. Even the royal family stocks up on groceries in the latter's frogs'-legs-to-*fines-herbes* food hall. While you are here, stop for a moment to notice the clock on the shop front, where the polite figures of the original Mr. Fortnum and Mr. Mason appear on the hour, turn, and bow to each other to a tune played by 17 bells. Weary shoppers who wander off in search of sustenance in the area can choose between two of London's most palatial afternoon tea haunts—the Soda Fountain in Fortnum & Mason and, a scone's throw away, down Piccadilly to the west, the Palm Court Room in the Ritz hotel. If they're both full, cross the road and listen to the harpist in the lounge of the Hotel Meridien.

Follow such heavenly delights with a visit to the **Royal Academy of Arts** in Burlington House, nearby on Piccadilly. The grand courtyard, filled with snaking lines at peak visiting times (especially on Sunday mornings during the annual Summer Exhibition), fronts a Renaissance-style building. Inside is a grand, sweeping staircase and galleries of treasures, including Michelangelo's *Madonna and Child*. The Royal Academy is such a London institution that most visitors don't realize it is devoted solely to temporary exhibitions.

At the back of Burlington House is the more modest, though equally Italianate **Museum of Mankind** (6 Burlington Gardens), whose exhibitions always focus on non-Western cultures. Within the same building is the British Museum's ethnographic collection, including a skull carved from a single piece of Mexican crystal.

Savile Row, also north of Burlington House, is famous throughout the world for having the finest tailors in London. Gieves & Hawkes at number 1, and Hardy Amies at number 14, are among the better-known names. Number 3 was the headquarters of the Beatles' company, Apple Corps.

London is at her most gaudy and flirtatious with tourists in **Piccadilly Circus**. (Piccadilly got its name from a large house built in the early 1600s on what is now Great Windmill Street. The owner, Robert Baker, made his money selling pickadils, stiff collars worn at Court—hence his house became known as Piccadilly Hall.) Walls of neon flicker day and night here, captured by a million cameras. As part of the Circus's general face-lift, the aluminum statue of Eros (officially the Angel of Charity), once marooned in the tawdry center of the Circus, has been renovated and is now back in the limelight on the south side. Approval of his new good looks is welcome: When

Eros was unveiled in 1893, *The Times* described him as the "ugliest monument in any European capital, more suited to the musical hall," while many simply frowned on his nakedness.

Piccadilly's newest entertainment venue is the **Trocadero Centre** on Coventry Street. Featured at this youth-oriented mall is the excellent Guinness World of Records, an exhibit that derives from the world's best-selling book. The rest of the complex is devoted to noisy, touristy shops and restaurants and video games. Adjacent is the **London Pavilion**, a similar mall that hosts Rock Circus, the latest brainchild of Madame Tussaud's. As you admire the details of the wax renditions of your rock and pop favorites, your short-wave headphones pick up their greatest hits.

The Theater District

The back doors of the Trocadero open onto **Shaftesbury Avenue**, the West End's evening breadwinner. More than 100 years old (its centenary was in 1987), the heart of London's theater district boasts six theaters and two cinemas. Shaftesbury Avenue was named after the the earl of Shaftesbury, the 19th-century philanthropist who carried out much of his alms-giving work in this area; its construction actually resulted in the demolition of several squalid Dickensian slums. The first theater to go up along the new avenue was the Lyric, in 1888. The Royal English Opera House on Cambridge Circus followed, but demand for fine singing was slack, as the music hall was in fashion, and the theater was renamed the Palace. Musicals are still the staple diet of London's theater, particularly if they're written by Andrew Lloyd Webber. The Palace, in fact, is currently owned by Lloyd Webber, and once housed his *Jesus Christ Superstar,* the second-longest-running musical in the history of British theater; the theater now has *Les Misérables,* which is in its eighth year.

The Apollo, the Globe, the Queen's, and the Shaftesbury complete the six. Originally the New Prince's theater, the Shaftesbury is most famous for its misfortunes: A gas explosion interrupted Fred and Adele Astaire's dancing in Gershwin's *Funny Face,* while later the musical *Hair* literally brought the house down when part of the ceiling collapsed. If your theatergoing plans are thwarted because the blockbuster shows are full, you'll usually be able to get a ticket to Agatha Christie's *The Mousetrap,* which opened at the Ambassadors Theatre in 1952 and is still running (it moved to St. Martin's Theatre, just off St. Martin's Lane, in 1974), making it the longest-running show in the world.

MAYFAIR

Between the West End and, to the west, Hyde Park you'll find Mayfair, which owes its name to a disorderly fair that was held every May between 1686 and 1764 where Curzon Street and Shepherd Market now are. The small, appealing parts of Mayfair are the rows of elegant brownstones that were the original *Upstairs, Downstairs* houses of London's upper (and lower) echelons. Concentrated chiefly on Mayfair's two most famous squares, Grosvenor and Berkeley, these brownstones boast former servants' quarters that today command some of the highest rents in town, while the mews houses, once the stable yards for the coach and horses (with upper-floor living accommodations for the driver), sell for small fortunes. **Grosvenor Square** also houses the embassy of the United States of America, the largest embassy in Great Britain, which covers one whole side of the square and is watched over by an American eagle with a wingspan of 35 feet.

The essence of Mayfair is its elegant shops and squares, though working Londoners are also aware that the city's most prestigious office buildings tower above it. Window-shoppers and those with plenty of disposable income should head for Brook Street, South Molton Street (one of the city's most elite pedestrianized precincts), New and Old Bond streets, and Savile Row (all discussed above). Smaller showrooms and galleries are to be found on Dover Street, also home to **Brown's Hotel** at number 22, London's renowned "gentleman's" hotel, founded by the husband of Lady Byron's maid and now owned by Forte Hotels. The hotel has worked hard to preserve its atmosphere of quietude and privacy, and it still attracts some of the city's most gentrified visitors. It also serves an excellent traditional tea.

In Charles Street is the **Chesterfield**, whose rooms are cheaper than—and as comfortable as—many in the grander international hotels along the more famous Park Lane, and whose two restaurants and bar (for the price of a gin and tonic you can browse through the day's newspapers and the week's magazines) are comfortable rendezvous. Curzon Street, part residential (number 19 marks the spot where Disraeli died in 1881) and part commercial, backs onto **Shepherd Market** (the name belies its wealth), a delightful "village" of narrow streets, period houses, and pubs like the Bunch of Grapes (referred to as Ye Grapes), cafés geared for alfresco dining, and tiny courtyards—the whole linked by a series of archways. The area is also noted for its prostitutes.

Thanks to the heavy traffic and plethora of motorcycle messengers in central London, a quiet stroll around **Berkeley Square** is possible only on a Sunday morning. Nevertheless, it's not difficult to appreciate the grandeur of its 200-year-old plane trees (all that remain of Berkeley Woods), which shelter some of the city's most beautiful architecture. Two buildings to look out for are number 45, the former home of Clive of India (where in 1794 the career colonialist committed suicide, although he had been vindicated by Parliament's investigation of the "East India Company scandal"), and number 50, where **Maggs Bros.**, the antiquarian book specialists, delights bibliophiles.

WESTMINSTER

Westminster is London wearing its most royal plumage and governmental robes. On the map, the area officially defined as the City of Westminster is vast, bordered by Camden to the north and the Thames to the south, but even Londoners rarely relate the name to its full territorial stake. Westminster really connotes the government buildings of Whitehall, the Houses of Parliament, Westminster Abbey, the prime minister's official residence at 10 Downing Street, and St. James's Park. And while it is a residential borough, its palaces and government offices, including the bulk of the ministry headquarters, overshadow the lives of its ordinary citizens.

Buckingham Palace

Buckingham Palace, built for the duke of Buckingham in 1703 and bought by King George III in 1761, is Westminster's prize showpiece. John Nash played a part in the building's restructuring in 1825, although many of the trimmings that you see today were the result of a face-lift in 1913 by Sir Aston Webb. Today's palace is yesterday's Buckingham House, a beautiful pillared and porticoed mansion house of white Portland stone overlooking a semicircular arc of manicured gardens. The grandeur continues inside, from the bedchambers to the state rooms; even the stable block is magnificent. **St. James's Palace**, on Pall Mall at the foot of St. James's Street (south from Piccadilly), was the official royal residence before

Queen Victoria moved to Buckingham Palace in 1837. The red-jacketed and bear-skinned guards in front of the palace at the foot of St. James's Street are much photographed. (See below for the Changing of the Guard ceremony.) St. James's Palace, Henry VIII's turreted gift to Anne Boleyn when they were married, is now virtually redundant as a royal house, though any announcement of a change of ruler is traditionally made from its Friary Court balcony.

Londoners' interest in **Clarence House**, between St. James's Palace and the Mall, was greatly enhanced during 1990 when, on August 4, the Queen Mother became 90. For many years this most popular member of the royal family (or "the firm," as the duke of Edinburgh refers to it) has appeared at the gate of the palace to greet well-wishers, rather than remotely from a balcony. Clarence House (Stable Yard Road, St. James's Palace) dates from 1828, and was designed by John Nash. During World War II it was the headquarters of the Red Cross and St. John Ambulance, and between 1947 and 1950, prior to her accession, it was the home of Princess Elizabeth.

If the gold Royal Standard flag is flying high above Buckingham Palace, the Queen is in residence. Occasionally, you may catch a glimpse of one or another of the royal family sitting rather anonymously in the back of a sleek black Daimler. The Queen Victoria Memorial right outside Buckingham Palace was not just erected for people to climb on to watch processions and ceremonials, though it is useful for that. The principal figure, of Queen Victoria, was unveiled in 1911; its creator, Thomas Brock, was knighted on the spot.

For the first time in its long history, Buckingham Palace opened its doors to paying visitors in 1993. For an eight-week period in August and September for the next five years, sightseers may buy tickets (£8 for adults, £4 for children) for a tour of the State Apartments and Picture Gallery. Most tickets are sold for same-day tours at the St. James's Park ticket office in front of the palace; lines may begin forming as early as 7:00 A.M. Information is available from any of the tourist offices in London.

A few thousand members of a more select public—aristocrats, sporting personalities, the higher echelons of local government, and the like—are invited to this inner sanctum for one of the Queen's summer garden parties. The even luckier, if that is the right word, are summoned here to investitures, in which knighthood and other hon-

ors are bestowed. The **Queen's Gallery**, just around the corner on Buckingham Gate, is open every day except Mondays for exhibitions of paintings from the royal collection. In the **Royal Mews**, on Buckingham Palace Road, are the family's Cinderella-like coaches, including the cherub-covered Gold State Coach, which carried Queen Elizabeth II from the palace to Westminster Abbey for her coronation. The Glass Coach, which transports royal brides, is also on show, as are some vintage royal cars, such as the 1901 Daimler built for Edward VII. Open Wednesday, Thursday, and some Friday afternoons during the summer; Wednesday afternoons only in winter.

Westminster is London's venue for pomp and circumstance. The **Changing of the Guard** at Buckingham Palace, a military pageant of horse guards and infantrymen dressed in black bearskins and red tunics, is the familiar image most often chosen to depict London on postcards and travel posters. At 11:00 every morning between April and July (alternate days, August to March—although in 1993 the alternate schedule crept up into July, so it's best to check), the St. James's Palace detachment of the Old Guard is inspected in Friary Court. Carrying the Colour (the regimental flag), it then marches off via the Mall, the wide formal boulevard between Trafalgar Square and Buckingham Palace designed by Charles II. At Buckingham Palace the palace detachment is lined up and inspected. The St. James's detachment enters by the South Gate and, together with the Buckingham detachment, awaits the arrival of the New Guard (at 11:30). Led by a regimental band, the New Guard marches into the palace forecourt via the North Centre Gate, having earlier assembled at Wellington Barracks on Birdcage Walk along the southern side of St. James's Park. By 12:05 it's all over for another day (except for the duties of the street cleaner).

The **Institute of Contemporary Arts**, with often obscure and controversial items featured among its contemporary exhibitions, is in Nash House on the Mall. It offers three galleries, as well as a cinema, a theater, and a restaurant.

St. James's Park and Green Park

For such a central city borough, Westminster supports a surprising abundance of greenery. Running along the south side of the Mall, with its fashionable promenades, lanes, and walkways, St. James's Park, the oldest royal park in central London, has been compared to the grounds at

Versailles. James I, a passionate lover of wildlife, stocked it with deer; Birdcage Walk, which runs along the park's southern flank, was named after a string of aviaries established by Charles II. The pelicans that reside in the park are descendants of a pair presented to Charles II by the Russian ambassador in 1665. Duck Island, in the middle of the park's elongated lake, is a private sanctuary for several species of birds. Stand on the small bridge that hoops over the lake and look across the water at the turrets and minarets of tree-fringed St. James's Palace and you might even feel as if you're in the middle of a Hans Christian Andersen story.

After a turn around St. James's Park, Charles II would habitually stroll up Constitution Hill, which cuts through neighboring Green Park north of Buckingham Palace. Although only the Queen Victoria Memorial separates them and both border on the Buckingham Palace grounds, Green Park has a completely different feel than St. James's. It's much smaller (53 acres in contrast to St. James's 93) and has rejected any attempts at floral trimmings, opting for just an ample ration of trees and grass. As its name suggests, it remains an expanse of simple, unadulterated green and is the ideal place to walk off a breakfast or a grander feast from the nearby Ritz hotel up on Piccadilly, Green Park's northern boundary.

The quarter of **St. James's**, east of Green Park and north of St. James's Park and including St. James's Square, is an almost exclusively male preserve, its domain defined by the entrenchment of some gentlemen's clubs, the most famous being Brooks's, Boodle's, White's, and the stuffy like. Walk down Pall Mall and step inside these inner sanctums of conservatism (subject to invitation, of course, and your sex), and the only event likely to disturb the status quo is the creak of a chubby leather-backed chair, the tinkle of ice against crystal, the rustle of the pink pages of the *Financial Times,* and the slow ticking of a grandfather clock. You can occasionally peek through the windows at such scenes, but only at that time of day when the inside lights have been fired and the curtains have yet to be drawn on the outside world.

London's finest surviving 18th-century private palace, **Spencer House** at 27 St. James's Place, overlooking Green Park, has been opened to the public after extensive restoration. Among the highlights are the Palm Room with its ornate palm-effect columns and decorative ceiling, the Painted Room with exquisite painted panels, and several important paintings and pieces of furniture. Open Sundays, 11:30 A.M. to 5:30 P.M. Closed August and January. Tours every 15 minutes; art tours by appointment (Tel: 499-8620).

Pall Mall, which runs from St. James's Palace east to Trafalgar Square, was also conceived by Charles II, in this case so that he could play *paille-maille,* a newfangled game he had discovered across the Channel that is similar to croquet. He leased a house here to Nell Gwyn, who poutingly insisted that she should own the freehold of the house—after all, her "services" to the Crown were given freely. Charles agreed, and 79 Pall Mall is still the only privately owned property on the broad avenue.

Trafalgar Square

The top (east end) of Pall Mall opens up into Trafalgar Square. Laid out by John Nash in 1820 as part of his grand design, the square is rather a hodgepodge of architectural styles. The focal point is its central area, with fountains by Sir Edwin Lutyens and the granite Nelson's Column by William Railton (with the statue of Lord Nelson on top by Edward Hodges Baily—contrary to common fallacy there is no eye patch—and four bronze lions by Sir Edwin Landseer forming the base plinth). Four cylindrical stone plinths stand at the corners of the square, each with a bronze octagonal lamp. The door on the one at the southeast corner is a later addition; a clue to its purpose can be seen in the observation slits. In the late 19th century it was set up as a secret observation post, just big enough to accommodate a man and a telephone, in order to monitor the political rallies that have traditionally congregated here. Adolf Hitler was one of those aware of the importance of Nelson's Column—he intended to move it to Berlin, after conquering Britain, as a symbol of world domination. Today the square is home to flocks of pigeons, as well as a huge spruce Christmas tree donated every year by Norway in gratitude for Britain's help during World War II. On December 31 New Year's revelers in a generally harmless alcoholic haze cheer Big Ben's midnight chimes here: not a bad place to be if you are alone in London then.

The **National Gallery**, by far the most beautiful building on Trafalgar Square, is backed by the National Portrait Gallery. Climb the steps to the National Gallery, a grande dame built in the Neoclassical style, and look back for a sweeping view of the square. Then get on with your exploration of the art inside. The gallery was opened in 1838 to house the nation's many art treasures (at the time the gallery shared its premises with the Royal Academy, but for reasons of space the latter has since moved to Burlington House, Piccadilly). Today all the great periods of European painting are represented here—works by Botticelli and Bellini hang in the Italian rooms alongside Leonardo da Vinci's *Virgin and Child with St. Anne* and *St. John the Baptist.* Constable's *Haywain* and Gainsborough's *Mr. and Mrs. Andrews* are also here, as are a great many Dutch and Flemish paintings. Recently opened (after ten years of controversy about its design) on the northwest corner of the square is the Sainsbury Wing, housing early Italian, Dutch, and German Renaissance paintings. The use of natural light in the bright, airy galleries provides an almost ethereal setting for the new wing's many treasures, and the brasserie and coffee shop afford superb views of Trafalgar Square.

The original aim of the **National Portrait Gallery**, around the corner in St. Martin's Place, was to portray Britain's history through paintings, sculptures, miniatures, and photographs of the country's historical personalities. With so many famous people now represented here, it has become a visual *Who's Who.* Start at the top and work your way down in chronological order.

At the northeast corner of Trafalgar Square is the church of **St. Martin-in-the-Fields**, the parish church of the sovereign and the best-loved work of Scottish architect James Gibbs. The first mention of it dates back to 1222, when it was a chapel serving Westminster Abbey, and it was later called St.-Martin-near-the-Cross (Charing Cross). The present church was built between 1722 and 1724 and was originally designed as a round church. (Although this design was rejected, it was later adopted for a church in Connecticut.) The tower, rebuilt in 1824, was very controversial at the time, rising centrally from behind the huge Classical portico, but this design was soon used in many churches, particularly in the United States. Here Francis Bacon and Charles II were christened, John Constable was married, and Nell Gwyn was buried, though the crypt has been divested of most of its tombs and is now the site of a restaurant. The church is the venue for the St. Martin-in-the-Fields Sinfonia and also hosts free lunchtime concerts by various artists on Mondays, Tuesdays, and Fridays (Tel: 839-1930).

Whitehall

From the square, a stroll down **Whitehall** takes you past some of England's most prestigious civil-service departments, including the Treasury, the gigantic headquarters of the Home Office and the Foreign Office, and the stark new Ministry of Defence building. On the left is the **Banqueting House**, a superb example of Palladian-style architecture built by Inigo Jones for James I in 1619, and still used for official receptions. Its ceilings are decorated with nine remarkable paintings by Rubens (they brought £3,000 and a knighthood to the artist). Thirty years after the hall was built, Charles I stepped from one of its windows onto the waiting scaffold, where he was executed.

Great Scotland Yard (the former office of the Metropolitan Police, as seen in a thousand B-movies) is also off Whitehall, though the headquarters have since shifted to Victoria Street. A military presence in the form of two Household Cavalry sentries who sit motionless, immune to the persistent flash of cameras (though they do change shifts every so often), is maintained at **Horse Guards Parade**, and a ceremonial guard is mounted daily at 11:00 A.M. (Sundays at 10:00 A.M.). A few yards farther down Whitehall is the Cenotaph, the simple Lutyens monument to Britain's war dead.

Britain's prime ministers have never had to walk far to work. Behind the famous black door and lion-shaped brass knocker of **10 Downing Street** is an eight-room top-floor apartment; state rooms used for official receptions and banquets on the middle level; and Cabinet room, anterooms, and offices opening onto private gardens on the ground floor. Downing Street is closed to the general public.

Located some 10 feet below Whitehall, the **Cabinet War Rooms** (entrance adjacent to the park end of King Charles Street), a secret bombproof headquarters during World War II, opened its doors to visitors as a museum a few years ago. Nothing has changed in this three-acre maze of rooms and corridors since the Blitz: According to the map room and various notices around the place, the war is still going on. Sir Winston Churchill's bed and the telephone cabinet from which he would phone President Roosevelt are just as they were.

Palace of Westminster (Houses of Parliament)

The Palace of Westminster, the official name of the Houses of Parliament, is an extravagant example of Gothic style. Its lean clock tower has four clock faces, each measuring 23 feet across, and its 13.5-ton bell, Big Ben, chimes on the hour. The palace is another one of London's most photographed sights; the familiar view is taken from across the river. The public is admitted to the Houses of Parliament only to hear the debates in the Lords or the Commons (usually the livelier of the two). Visitors may enter the House of Commons starting at 2:30 P.M. Monday through Thursday, and at 9:30 A.M. on Fridays. Admission to the House of Lords begins at 2:30 P.M. Monday through Wednesday, 3:00 P.M. Thursdays, and 11:00 A.M. Fridays. On Tuesdays and Thursdays, Prime Minister's Question Time in the Commons is always popular and busy. You can avoid standing in line for these sessions by applying to your home country's embassy for tickets well in advance.

Westminster Hall is the oldest and most historic part of the parliamentary complex and home to the original law courts before they moved farther north to their present site around Chancery Lane. These courts witnessed the kinds of state trials that have made history, including that of Guy Fawkes, the man who attempted to blow up the Houses of Parliament with kegs of gunpowder in 1605 and whose effigy now sits atop thousands of bonfires every November 5. Within the Houses of Parliament are the Royal Gallery, the Prince's Chamber, the Lords' Chamber (where every bill passed by the Commons or initiated in the Lords has to receive the Peers' assent before becoming law), the Members' Lobby, and the royal throne in the Peers' Chamber. The stationary figures in the Central Lobby are Prime Ministers Churchill, Lloyd George, Arthur James Balfour, Herbert Asquith, and Clement Attlee.

The highlight is the **House of Commons**, the arguments and debates of which are broadcast and now televised into British homes. This room full of green leather benches (in contrast to the red of the House of Lords) seats 437 M.P.s plus 15 Commons officials at any one time. (There are fewer seats than M.P.s entitled to them; this is a deliberate policy—instigated during Churchill's time as prime minister—with the intent of heightening the sense of occasion when the House is full.)

In the Norman Porch you can see samplings from a collection of some two million parliamentary records, including the original copies of all acts of Parliament, some dating back to the Middle Ages. A few yards away, in Victoria Tower Gardens, the bronze statue of Emmeline Pankhurst honors the leader of Britain's suffragist movement, who was on her deathbed in 1928 when the House of Lords first saw the bill for equal suffrage.

Westminster Abbey

Across the street from Parliament stands Westminster Abbey. It is the royal church, where monarchs are crowned on the ancient coronation chair, a piece of furniture that has served this regal purpose since Edward II's coronation in 1307.

The abbey was originally owned by a Benedictine monastery, one of the few that managed to escape Henry VIII's anticlerical wrath, which accounted for the destruction of much of ecclesiastical England. Today more than three million people visit the abbey each year, so if you come in search of spiritual peace and sanctuary you'll be a shade disappointed. Even the burial space is overpopulated with kings and queens, from Edward the Confessor, who founded the abbey in 1065, to George II, the last monarch to be buried here, in 1760. Such historic literary figures as Chaucer, Tennyson, Dickens, Kipling, Hardy, and Browning are buried in the Poets' Corner; Ben Jonson was buried upright in the nave—by choice, as it happens, but it certainly made a contribution toward alleviating the space problem.

Westminster School, founded at the beginning of the 13th century for clerks of the abbey, is one of the oldest surviving schools in London. Adjoining the abbey are the school's oldest sections, which were built as part of the monastic dormitory in about 1100.

Next to Westminster Abbey is **St. Margaret's**, the parish church of the House of Commons. Founded by Edward the Confessor in the 11th century, it was rebuilt in the 14th century, and that part is the core of the present building, with details dating from the 18th and 19th centuries. (In 1539 an attempt was made to raze the church and use its stones for the construction of the duke of Somerset's new house in the Strand, but the duke's men were fought off by parishioners.) The east window contains London's most important early-16th-century stained glass. The marriages of Samuel Pepys, John Milton, and Winston Churchill were performed here.

If you walk north along the river from **Westminster Pier**, adjacent to Westminster Bridge and very close to the Houses of Parliament, as far as Charing Cross Pier, you'll come in sight of another landmark: Cleopatra's Needle, the twin of the one that stands in New York's Central Park. Both originally stood beside the Temple of Heliopolis in Alexandria, but the bronze sphinxes at the base of the granite monolith date from the 19th century. The statue is across the street from part of the **Embankment Gardens**, which in the warm weather that seems increasingly to be a summertime occurrence in London pick up any stray breeze from the river. At certain times there are open-air musical performances in the bandstand.

Tate Gallery

One can only praise the Classical-style Tate Gallery, near the Pimlico tube station on Millbank, a section of the river's north shore upriver from Parliament between Lambeth and Vauxhall bridges. The gallery's origins date back to 1897, when the country was looking for a home for a national collection of British art. Sugar magnate Sir Henry Tate put forward the money, plus his personal collection of 64 paintings. Many a Londoner's Sunday afternoon is spent browsing its galleries. The original 64 paintings have been joined by continually changing exhibitions as well as a permanent collection of British works from the 16th to the early 20th century, Impressionist canvases, and, since 1916—when it was decided the Tate would not just be an extension of the National Gallery—many works of modern art from abroad. Matisse, Braque, Chagall, and Picasso share space with Jackson Pollock, Henry Moore, Barbara Hepworth, and Alberto Giacometti. In its Clore Gallery, the Turner Bequest contains more than 300 oil paintings. The entire Tate collection has recently been rehung and rearranged in chronological order, and the results are impressive. The Tate also has a good restaurant (lunches only) famed for its wine list, as well as a self-service cafeteria.

A minor detour across the Thames (at this point the "south" bank is to the east) will bring you to **Lambeth Palace**, a medieval building and the London residence of the archbishop of Canterbury for more than seven centuries. It's open to groups on Wednesdays and Thursdays by prior arrangement (apply to the palace secretary; Tel: 928-8282).

Dulwich Village

Though it is only a 12-minute train ride south across the Thames from Victoria Station and then a ten-minute walk (ask to be pointed in the right direction at the station), Dulwich Village is more like a leafy, well-preserved enclave in stockbroker country than a London suburb. It really would not be too surprising to see postchaises scooting along the mostly 18th-century main street through the village, past houses set back from the road behind wide grass verges, enhanced by white fence posts and fences. (Half close your eyes, and parts of it might remind you of Colonial Williamsburg.)

Opposite what was once known as the College of God's Gift, founded in 1613, stands the extremely attractive and welcoming **Dulwich Picture Gallery**, designed by Sir John Soane and opened in 1814. Its collection of old masters is impressive, and it is also famous for having been robbed more than its share of times, with pictures mysteriously reappearing in the back of taxis or on park benches a year or two after their theft. The gallery, the grandiose 19th-century buildings, and the impressive playing fields of Dulwich College are another ten-minute walk from the village. The college itself is sometimes open to the public by prior application in writing to the Master, Dulwich College, London, SE21.

London West

KNIGHTSBRIDGE – BELGRAVIA

Harrods

Think of Knightsbridge, and you inevitably think of Harrods. The two names seem to reinforce each other in a fragrant blend of high income and refined taste. No matter where in the world you normally do your shopping, Harrods, on Brompton Road, warrants a pilgrimage and at least a small spree.

In 1975, when he was governor of California, Ronald Reagan ordered a baby elephant from Harrods. Your own needs might be rather more basic, but whether you go to Harrods to buy or to browse, you can't fail to be bowled over by the sheer weight of its style, let alone its contents.

Harrods is the largest store in Europe, recently refurbished and restored to its former glory. It has its own bank, its own power station, and its own water supply (it draws its water from three wells—the deepest of which is 489 feet below the store). Just to reel off a few of its stock statistics, it offers 150 types of pianos, 9,000 ties, 450 kinds of cheese, 130 kinds of bread, 85 different brands of malt whisky, and more or less anything else that is made on the planet. No wonder its telegraphic address is still "Everything London." If you want just a taste, head for the Food Hall, a palatial, beautifully tiled, magnificently stocked emporium. The store's own-brand items, often packed in distinctive green tins with the Harrods label, make easy and popular presents.

Other Shopping

Nearby at Knightsbridge—the street as distinct from the area—and Sloane Street, the main intersection west of Buckingham Palace and the Palace Gardens, past where Piccadilly ends in a vast traffic interchange, is Knightsbridge's "other" department store, **Harvey Nichols**. Harrods may have its special Queen's entrance, but Harvey Nichols is the store where you're more likely to come across Princess Di casting an eye over the designer labels. Apart from the main shopping arteries of Brompton Road and Knightsbridge proper, another shopping mecca that caters to the wealthy is **Sloane Street**, which runs south from Knightsbridge and the Knightsbridge tube station. In fact, the very name has spawned its own London social type, whose style, in the words of *The Official Sloane Ranger Handbook* (by Ann Barr and Peter York), is all about "quality, conservatism, and classicism." And that's exactly what you can expect from the majority of stores on Sloane Street.

The tiny streets that lie in the elbow formed by Knightsbridge and Sloane Street constitute a neighborhood of expensive town houses and small, exclusive stores selling antiques, paintings, haute-couture gowns, and pretty frippery. Cross Sloane Street, and Belgravia's **Halkin Arcade**, in particular, which spans Motcomb and West Halkin streets, has more priceless items in its windows than you'd come across in a sheikh's palace—which is, indeed, the ultimate destination of many of the items on sale here. This entire area is also home to many of London's finest small hotels; see the Accommodations chapter, below.

Knightsbridge (the name may recall the time when French nobles took up residence here to escape the egalitarian consequences of the Revolution) is also home to **Beauchamp Place** (pronounced BEE-cham), off Brompton Road east of Harrods. Contrary to recent trends, Beauchamp Place has remained a refreshingly anachronistic oasis of small, independently owned boutiques and restaurants (some of the most interesting of which are in

unprepossessing basements). Originally a row of Regency houses, this narrow 400-yard-long street has more variety than many shopping streets ten times its length.

Belgravia

Those in search of Belgravia won't find a sign, but they've found it once they're in Wilton Crescent, Belgrave Square, Eaton Place, or Eaton Square. Belgravia, lying just east of Sloane Street, was a neat, early-19th-century development later rebuilt in Neoclassical style. Surprisingly, it is not the generously proportioned 18th-century Grosvenor Square, the Mayfair home of the U.S. embassy, but Belgravia's Chester Square that has earned the nickname "American Square in Mayfair," on account of its high proportion of expatriates in residence. In recent times they have included Henry Fonda, Tony Curtis, and Robert Wagner. Today's residents are likely to be seen in the area's top Italian restaurant, **Mimmo d'Ischia** (on Elizabeth Street), presided over by the flamboyant Mimmo and his lively team of waiters, or on the opposite side of the street in the **Ebury Wine Bar**, which specializes in steaks grilled before your eyes (if you sit at the counter, that is).

Hyde Park and Kensington Gardens

Knightsbridge is not only an elegant place to shop but an elegant place to live as well. After all, the Queen resides just around the corner. The sweeping crescents, anonymous mews, and manicured squares—with their smart Rollers, Jags, Bentleys, and Daimlers patiently waiting like faithful retainers at curbside—all lie within an easy stroll of high-quality shops and, to the north, Hyde Park, that vast, pool-table expanse of greenery, at 340 acres the largest of central London's royal parks.

Kensington Gardens, the royal gardens of Kensington Palace at the west side of Hyde Park and the London home of Prince Charles and Princess Diana, are worth a visit. See the bronze statue of Peter Pan, the Sunken Garden (to remind you of the formality of the original 1728 gardens), the monuments to William III and Victoria, and, for the children among us, daily puppet shows in the summer. The palace's state apartments are also open to the public.

Hyde Park, along with Kensington Gardens, is the London equivalent of New York's Central Park, a place to let off pent-up steam by jogging, hiring a rowboat, or renting a horse from Richard Brigg's stables on Bathurst Mews by Lancaster Gate station. If you opt for the latter, you can follow the hoofprints of the palace guards, who canter around a mile-long sandy track known as Rotten Row in the wee hours every morning. In addition to its before-work, after-work, and weekend activity, the park still lives up to its popular image: Nannies wheel perambulators along the Broad Walk; children throw crusts of bread to the ducks; model boats make their way sedately across Round Pond; brass bands play on Sundays; small-time politicos expound on a soapbox at Speakers' Corner (Britain's symbol of democracy, where anyone can express whatever opinion he or she may hold dear, within reason) in the northeast corner near Marble Arch; and Spartan swimmers plunge from the Lido into the Serpentine at 5:30 A.M., sometimes breaking a layer of ice to do so.

CHELSEA

Like the Roman Empire, ancient Greece, and the Weimar Republic, Chelsea has already wallowed in its golden era. Unlike the other three, however, its place in the annals of history is rooted not in its military supremacy or imperialistic acquisitiveness but rather in the ephemeral world of fashion. The Chelsea that attracted the attention of the world in the early 1960s was symbolized by the scantiest of all emblems: the miniskirt. Chelsea earned that attention by virtue of the creativity of its highly talented designers, as well as the scores of artists, writers, and musicians who came to live within its geographical and emotional boundaries. It was the birthplace of "Swinging London," a notion born of an alchemy of coincidences—an enormously attractive environment, proximity to central London, and the then-low rents.

The decade of the 1960s was not Chelsea's only period of creativity. Scores of famous people, particularly in the arts and literature, had lived in the village previously, among them Charles Kingsley, Dante Gabriel Rossetti, T. S. Eliot, Henry James, Oscar Wilde, and the so-called sage of Chelsea, Thomas Carlyle, whose Queen Anne house on Cheyne Row is open to the public Wednesday through Sunday during the summer. Other famous residents included Mark Twain (Samuel Clemens), who lived at 23 Tedworth Square, Chelsea, while in London in 1896. His visit was made during an extended tour of Europe, and it was here (in mourning for his daughter Susy, and because he shunned company) that accounts of his death began to circulate, reports that he later called "greatly exaggerated."

Chelsea, between Knightsbridge and Kensington (Kensington is the area just to the west of Knightsbridge, farther out along the southern side of Hyde Park) and, to the south, the Thames, still merits a visit today, and not just to mourn its passing glory. Chelsea is a delightful place to live or, as a compromise, to visit. Its terraces and squares, studded with trees and lined by rows of pretty, pastel-painted town houses that look like outsized dollhouses, seem more in keeping with a rural than an urban context. Chelsea's main drag, the **King's Road**, named after the path that Charles II took as part of his private processional route to Hampton Court Palace—is still an interesting shopping street, even though its heyday was long ago. The retail action now stretches from Sloane Square in the east along the New King's Road continuation and onto Fulham Road, which parallels the King's Road to the north.

Cheyne Walk

Don't miss the lovely 18th-century houses on riverside Cheyne Walk, and look for the blue plaques that tell you about former famous residents: George Eliot (pen name of Mary Anne Evans, 1819–1880) lived briefly at number 4; the Pre-Raphaelite painter Dante Gabriel Rossetti took number 16 with Algernon Charles Swinburne and George Meredith in 1862. Rossetti's pets included a bull, a raccoon, a wombat, kangaroos, armadillos, and peacocks. The noisy peacocks so upset the neighbors that a clause (still in existence) forbidding the keeping of peacocks was forced into future Cheyne Walk leases. Numbers 19–26 stand on the site of the former Chelsea Manor, where Queen Elizabeth I grew up and reputedly planted the mulberry trees over the wall by number 24. Rolling Stone Mick Jagger also had a house on Cheyne Walk in the 1960s.

Chelsea Harbour

Chelsea Harbour, on the border with Fulham, upstream from Battersea Bridge, is a new development on the river distinguished by the Belvedere Building with its bright-red ball. On the site once occupied by an old coal depot there are now luxury flats, offices, shops, cafés, and restaurants, including **Deals**, which is partly owned by Lord Litchfield and Viscount Linley.

At Chelsea Harbour, off Lots Road, you can also catch one of the **Riverbuses**, which run daily from here down-river through central London, making several stops before the last one at Canary Wharf, where you can catch a shuttle bus to the City Airport. No traffic jams here, just great views! Get your tickets from dispensing machines before you board. (For more information on Riverbus service, see "Boat Excursions" in the Getting Around section, below.)

Shopping and Eating in Chelsea

Once they lost their ability to shock, London's punks were adopted as a kind of tourist attraction, gracing many a postcard and poster. You can still see mohawks, safety pins, and studded leather on the King's Road most Saturdays, though other members of the Saturday crowd sport Paul Smith and Armani suits. They spend small fortunes in interior-decor stores like Conran's near the South Kensington Underground station and luncheon spots like the Habitat Café.

Clothing stores still predominate, but there are also plenty of antiques arcades and art galleries. If you happen to be partial to Victorian and Edwardian lighting, find your way to **Christopher Wray's** period light emporium at 600 King's Road. He stocks hundreds of models, mostly quality reproductions, some originals. The street is also heavily endowed with lighting stores of the modern-design type. **Antiquarius** is a covered 200-stall antiques market selling Art Deco and Art Nouveau designs, English porcelain, watercolors, and period jewelry and clothing.

In between is a generous sprinkling of pubs and restaurants, many having occupied the same site for more than two decades now. The most famous include the **Man in the Moon** and the **Markham Arms**; plant-filled and patioed, the latter hosts throngs of lager drinkers in summer. **The Pheasantry**, a popular 1960s meeting place with an unusual arched entrance and a historic blue plaque, now houses a cocktail bar, a brasserie, and a nightclub.

Perhaps the busiest eatery of them all, on account of its minute proportions, is the **Chelsea Bun Diner**, tucked down a side road on Limerston Street. Arrive anytime between 7:00 A.M. and 11:30 P.M. and you can be served a foaming cappuccino, a traditional English breakfast, a sandwich, or a burger. Everything's homemade, but the owners have no liquor license, so bring your own bottle.

Historic Chelsea

Places of historical interest in the neighborhood include
the **Chelsea Physic Garden**, 66 Royal Hospital Road on
the bank of the Thames, established by the Society of
Apothecaries in 1673, making it the second-oldest botanic
garden in England (after Oxford's, 1623). Its 5,000 plant
species include—as the name suggests—the medicinal
variety as well as Britain's biggest olive tree (there used to
be cannabis, too, until 1982, when a dedicated home
botanist jumped over the wall in the middle of the night
and took the specimen). Short courses for gardeners and
conducted garden tours can be arranged; open Wednesday and Sunday afternoons in summer.

The **National Army Museum**, which records the history
of the British military and exhibits, along with medals,
military badges, uniforms, and military paintings, themes
showing the human side of "The Story of the Army," is
also in Chelsea, as is the home of the Chelsea Pensioners,
the **Royal Hospital**, originally founded by Charles II as a
home for "men broken by war and old age." After Mary
Quant designed the miniskirt, originally sold on the
King's Road in her store Bazaar, uniformed pensioners
sharing the frame with pretty girls with dead-straight hair,
heavily made-up eyes, and lots of leg were the photographic cliché of London.

SOUTH KENSINGTON

You may feel that Chelsea falls short on serious culture, but
neighboring (to the north) South Kensington more than
compensates for it. **Exhibition Road**, running north off
Cromwell Road, a 20-minute walk to the north of Chelsea,
was Prince Albert's special project. As Queen Victoria's
consort he was able to wield enough power to open the
Great Exhibition in Hyde Park in 1851. It was such an
immense success that in 1856 all profits were used to buy
the Gore Estate, on which, he demanded, a collection of
educational establishments should be built. Judging by the
hordes of schoolchildren filing into the estate's grand
collection of museums, which spill down the Cromwell
Road west of Harrods and the Brompton Road, his wishes
have been well respected.

Victoria and Albert Museum

Queen of them all is the Victoria and Albert Museum,
home to a vast collection of fine and applied art. It's the
sort of museum best tackled by studying the plan, picking

your favorite handful of "theme" rooms, and ignoring the rest. In fact, those who decide to "do" all the galleries would be wise to invest in a pair of hiking boots, as they stretch a total of seven miles. At least the abundance keeps people coming back, discovering something new each visit. Don't miss the collection of Chippendale furniture, John Constable's landscapes on the first floor, or the Jones Collection, a riveting display of French interior decoration, painting, furniture, ceramics, and other decorative arts, including examples of Marie Antoinette's lavish tastes. The Dress Collection contains one of the greatest clothing collections in the world, popular with pencil-wielding fashion students. The rest of the museum's collections can only be hinted at: Japanese, Islamic, and British art and music, Raphael cartoons. . . .

Natural History Museum

Just west on the Cromwell Road is the Natural History Museum and its more specialized adjunct, the **Geological Museum**. From the outside the Natural History Museum resembles a grand sandstone church; the massive interior can be divided into five main departments: botany, entomology, mineralogy, paleontology, and zoology. It's also one of the city's most popular museums; most Londoners, even if they haven't visited, have at least seen pictures of the skeletons of the *Brontosaurus, Tyrannosaurus rex,* and other dinosaurs, formerly housed in the magnificent central hall, now all except one located in the new Ronson Gallery (*Diplodoctus* remains in the central hall). After that it's a question of which awe-inspiring sight to look for first. The ceiling of the Whale Hall in the west wing has to be seen to be believed: Skeletons and models of several species of mammals hang from it like spiders from their webs. There are also fossil collections, bird galleries, underwater creatures and coral, plants and minerals, plus a gallery devoted to simple ecology.

Science Museum

For fans of interactive displays, the Science Museum, just north of the Geological Museum on Exhibition Road, is unbeatable, with knobs to twiddle, lights that flash, and plenty of bleeping sound effects. Children make up a generous proportion of the museum's devotees—there's even a Children's Gallery on the lower ground floor devoted to teaching simple scientific ideas using dioramas and working models. Older visitors, having been mesmerized by the Foucault pendulum that hangs near the entrance on the ground floor (its slow deviation proves that the earth does indeed rotate), usually head straight for the Apollo 10 space capsule and simulated moon base in the new Exploration of Space Gallery. But the museum also caters to steam engine buffs (Puffing Billy, the world's oldest surviving locomotive, is in the road and rail transport wing) as well as lovers of astronomy, nuclear physics, modern technology (see the Challenge of the Chip display), photography, electronics, and navigation.

Royal Albert Hall

The Royal Albert Hall is north of the Science Museum on the Kensington Road, just across from Kensington Gardens. If it were in Spain you'd swear the hall was a bullring. A multipurpose venue, it hosts everything from regular Eric Clapton concerts to political conventions, graduation ceremonies of the University of London to boxing matches, but is perhaps best known as the site of the summer Promenade Concerts, or "the Proms." The hall, which seats about 7,500 people, was built as a memorial to Prince Albert and inspired by the Roman works in Provence. Guided tours are available from May through October, and include the Royal Box.

One final sight is number 14 Princes Gate, South Kensington, where John Fitzgerald Kennedy lived with his father, Joe, when the latter was U.S. ambassador to Britain after 1937.

RICHMOND

Identifying Richmond on most maps of London has never been difficult. At the region's heart lies a gigantic green expanse, Richmond Park, usually located near the map's bottom left-hand corner. If you fly into Heathrow from the east, this expanse appears as a sea of green floating below the left-hand windows. Richmond is a prosperous borough that not only has more open spaces than any other in London but also has hundreds of listed buildings (because of their historical value they cannot be drastically altered or demolished)—even the trees have preservation orders slapped on them. Though circumstances may not allow you to live in Richmond, there's no excuse for omitting it from a London visit.

Richmond-upon-Thames, to give the borough its full name and pertinent location, spans the banks of the river upstream from central London between Hammersmith Bridge and Hampton Court. Despite its proximity to central London (30 minutes by tube), it's actually a collection of small "villages": Barnes, Ham, Kew, Teddington, Twickenham, and Mortlake, all of which have managed to cling to significant shows of antiquity.

The name Richmond was inherited from a palace rebuilt by Henry VII, who had borrowed the name from his Yorkshire earldom. All that remains today of the original 12th-century building, whose foundations were laid by Henry I, is the **Gatehouse**, just off Richmond Green (the Gatehouse is not open to the public). During the 15th century Richmond Palace, originally called Shene, was a favorite Tudor retreat. Later, Shakespeare staged performances of his plays here, while the wardrobe that Queen Elizabeth I stored in the palace—it contained well over 2,000 dresses—would put Joan Collins to shame. Both Henry VII and Elizabeth I died here, and the palace's importance gradually declined until the structure was finally demolished in 1660, after the Restoration.

Despite its distinctive character, Richmond is just a half-hour Underground trip on the District Line from central London. From Richmond station it is a two-minute walk to the Green. You can also travel by British Rail from Waterloo Station in about 20 minutes. But the most scenic way to approach Richmond is aboard one of the boats that chug up from Westminster Pier in central London during the summer. Once you step ashore you'll find yourself in the middle of a completely self-contained village. There's likely to be a cricket match in mellow swing on the Green, the locals (anyone from barristers and bankers to writers and actors) toing and froing with liquid refreshments in hand between their patch of grass and the beery interior of the Cricketers pub.

Different styles of architecture jostle for position—Georgian, Palladian, Tudor, and Victorian—but the last definitely predominates. Minutes away are the Richmond Theatre and aging, narrow walkways and streets such as Old Palace Lane, which runs from Trumpeters' Court to the river, and **Maids of Honour Row**. The latter is a famous row of four tall 18th-century houses, complete with wrought-iron gates and railings, built in 1724 for the companions of Caroline, wife of the future King George II. But the name is now more synonymous with the **Maids of Honour Tearoom** on Kew Road near the famous Botanic Gardens. At the latter, you can either line up for a table and wallow in the cottagey ambience, or take out a bag of scones, cakes, and Maids of Honour curd tarts (made from a secret recipe) and eat them at your leisure down by the river. Sadly, it is closed on Sundays.

Summer is the best time for a **riverside walk** (in spring and autumn, heavy tides have been known to flood the walkway). Low tide in hot, dry weather reveals the river's steep, sandy banks. Low-slung trees trail their leaves in the water, and ducks, swans, and moorhens rock along on the wash left by motorboats revving past. The most hectic time for the Thames here (not to mention its wildlife) is March, when the **Oxford and Cambridge Boat Race** is held. Cutting through the waters from Putney to Mortlake, this is an amateur race for rowing "eights" and an important competition for the two universities. The best viewing points are on the Surrey bank above Chiswick Bridge, Mortlake, close to the finish line, or anywhere else along the towpath. To show your allegiance, wear either light blue (Cambridge) or dark blue (Oxford).

Richmond's stretch of river is also active during **Swan Upping**, an ancient and rather curious pageant held in late July/early August. The Worshipful Companies of Vintners and Dyers spend one week rowing their half-dozen Thames skiffs upstream from Sunbury to Pangbourne, ceremoniously catching swans, counting them, and nicking the beaks of the year's new batch of cygnets. The tradition dates back to the Middle Ages; its original purpose was to establish the ownership of these then-profitable, prestigious, and tasty birds. The Crown can still lay claim to any unmarked swans. At present only some 200 swans are to be seen in the entire Lower Thames, and the Swan Upping ceremony has become a crucial census for ecological reasons.

Richmond Park

The least urban of London's boroughs, Richmond contains Richmond Park, the largest of the royal parks. It covers 2,500 acres and was first enclosed by Charles I as a deer sanctuary. In fact, you might pack a pair of binoculars so you can examine the large herds of fallow and red deer that roam freely here.

The park's woodland gardens and Isabella Plantation are at their best from mid-April to the end of May, when the azaleas and the rhododendron dell are in full bloom. Historic buildings here include the King's Observatory; the White Lodge, built in 1727 as a hunting lodge for King

George II (open only in August); and Princess Alexandra's home, the Thatched House Lodge. Stop for tea at **Pembroke Lodge**, a restaurant and café with its own garden and terrace, found on the west side of Richmond Park, down the road through the park heading south from Richmond Gate. This place, ideal for pensive reflection, was the childhood home of the philosopher Bertrand Russell.

Ham House, in Richmond, is being restored by the National Trust to show what life was like for a 17th-century aristocrat; it will not be open to the public until mid- to late 1993. It has all its original furniture, as well as displays of costumes and paintings, including the famous miniature of Queen Elizabeth I by Nicholas Hilliard. The formal garden has been replanted as it was 300 years ago.

Kew Gardens

For years it cost only two pennies to pass through the turnstiles of the Royal Botanic Gardens, also known as Kew Gardens. The fee has now risen to £3.30. Take the District Line to Kew Gardens station, and follow the posted directions from there for the entrance. From May to September you can also take a riverboat from Westminster Pier. The 300 acres of landscaped gardens originally were made up from the combined estates of Richmond Lodge (now demolished) and **Kew Palace**. This small Jacobean mansion is the last of a group of royal residences, and was formerly known as the Dutch House. (The original Kew Palace was demolished in the early 18th century.) The three-story palace is open to the public daily from 11:00 A.M. to 5:30 P.M., April to September.

The Royal Botanic Gardens contain more than 25,000 species of plants from all over the world. The hurricane of October 16, 1987, wreaked havoc on Kew, toppling 800 trees and destroying in one night 150 years' worth of careful nurturing, but restoration of the gardens has been completed. The magnificent Palm House, built in the 1840s, is a fantasy in glass inspired by the classic Victorian greenhouse, and contains about 3,000 species of palms.

Aircraft heading to or leaving from Heathrow Airport fly overhead at the peak rate of one a minute, creating an incongruous din as visitors wander through groves, woodlands, and rock gardens, stopping to visit the Orangery, the four temples, the tall red Pagoda, or one of the plant houses. These fine Victorian conservatories, with such names as Alpine House, Water Lily House, Temperate House, and the new Princess of Wales Conservatory, are an architectural mélange of cast iron and glass. The 17th-century Dutch House, a sturdy red-brick and gabled building by the main gate, is one of the exceptions, and is all that remains of the original Kew Palace.

The Temperate House, one of the biggest hothouses, is dominated by a single giant palm whose towering leaves brush the ceiling. Visitors can walk along an upper balcony for aerial views of fountains and ponds full of ornamental fish. When visiting the houses be prepared for abrupt climatic changes—within the space of a few paces you can be transported from the tropical rain forests of South America to the arid desert of Arizona.

Richmond Environs

For the most delightful river walk to be had in these parts, head for the Hammersmith Bridge (a two-minute walk from either of Hammersmith's two Underground stations—one of which is served by the Metropolitan Line, the other by the District and Piccadilly lines) and walk along the north bank toward Chiswick. The best time for such a walk is early on a summer's eve, when you can buy a glass of "bitter" (ale) in any (or each) of four charming pubs—the **Blue Anchor**, the **Rutland Arms**, the **Ship**, and the **Dove**—and sit and sup in the open with a friendly crowd, idly watching the scullers whose boathouses line the banks below the bridge. **Hammersmith Terrace** is a delightful row of Georgian houses (several with their tiny gardens right above the river) separated from the homes by the towpath. William Morris used to live in Kelmscott House here.

Just before you reach Chiswick Square, step into the churchyard of St. Nicholas, where the painters James Whistler and William Hogarth are buried. Beyond lies **Syon House**—famous for Robert Adam's Great Hall—the London residence of the duke of Northumberland. The house is open to the public, although Syon's biggest draw is its gardens, the 18th-century handiwork of Capability Brown, who included a lake, conservatory, aviary, and aquarium in his designs. He had nothing, however, to do with the Heritage Motor Museum, which is also on the grounds and houses a collection of British cars from 1895 to the present day, nor with the London Butterfly House, which displays numerous species fluttering madly about in a tropical greenhouse. More energetic walkers can cross Hammersmith Bridge and follow the south bank as far south as the **Bull's Head** pub in Barnes, a mecca for jazz fans.

A couple of miles south of Putney Bridge is **Wimbledon Common**, an open parkland with a distinctive windmill, and on nearby Church Road the famous **All England Club**, home of the lawn tennis championships played every year in June and July. Overlooking the Centre Court is a museum housing a vast historical collection of tennis fashions and associated trivia.

HAMPTON COURT

When Henry VIII made Richmond Park the place to hunt, outsiders built hunting lodges nearby, and it became, at the same time, a popular stopping-off place for boats on their way upriver to Hampton Court Palace after Henry became its owner. Unlike other palaces that have stood empty as museums, Hampton Court has been lived in continuously since it was built by Cardinal Wolsey, the lord chancellor of England, in 1515. George III was the last sovereign in residence; today it is partly occupied by pensioners of the Crown, the "Grace and Favour" tenants. The palace is unique in that it represents the very best examples of English architecture of both the 16th and early 18th centuries. And the location, hard on the Thames, is stunning.

In March 1986 a fire caused severe damage to Hampton Court. Amazingly, although many works of art were destroyed or damaged, most of the palace's valuable contents, including an outstanding collection of 500 Renaissance paintings, were saved. The building itself, however, suffered enormously. The fire gutted the King's Audience Chamber, the Cartoon Gallery (named for the Raphael cartoons bought by Charles I and moved to the Victoria and Albert Museum more than a century ago), and State Apartments designed by Sir Christopher Wren for King William and Queen Mary. Restoration work is now completed; the King's State Apartments were opened by the Queen in July 1992. The Tudor kitchens illustrate the feast of St. John the Baptist as it was held on Midsummer's Day in 1542, when Henry VIII entertained his court on a lavish scale.

Although inhabited by a succession of kings and queens, Hampton Court is probably best known for its associations with Henry VIII, who, after he became its owner, extended the palace in earnest, including building the Chapel Court as a nursery for Prince Edward, his son and presumed heir. But by the time William and Mary came to the throne, the

Tudor style was considered rather passé, and they commissioned Wren, the architect of St. Paul's Cathedral, to demolish the entire palace and build a new, more symmetrical and spacious residence on a scale that would rival Versailles. Because the palace was fully inhabited, Wren could only work on a portion of it at a time, and, mercifully for posterity, the money ran out before he could implement his grand designs. Hence the uniqueness of Hampton Court: One of the most complete examples of a Tudor palace coexists harmoniously alongside buildings by England's greatest architect.

The most popular element of Hampton's horticultural displays is its **maze**, first planted in 1714. It may not look too challenging from the outside, but it can take up to an hour to get out of the half-mile labyrinth of yew-hedge. So don't postpone finding the way out till the main gates are about to close. Some visitors from abroad, it is said, have watched their homebound aircraft pass overhead, having taken off without them from Heathrow just down the road.

Hampton Court is easy to get to from central London. It is less than half an hour on British Rail from Waterloo Station, but you can also pick up that BR line at the Wimbledon station on the District Line of the Underground. Most people get on the District Line to Wimbledon at Earl's Court station. You can also get there by riverboat from Westminster Pier and other locations.

NOTTING HILL

The broad Bayswater Road, the continuation of Oxford Street that forms the northern boundary of Hyde Park, begins its westward journey at Marble Arch. Once past the western edge of the park, it almost immediately becomes the southern boundary of Notting Hill, a much-gentrified, ethnic area of town. Increasingly, professionals gravitate here, unable to resist the combination of ethnic color and the gentility of five-story houses on tree-lined avenues such as Elgin Crescent.

Notting Hill's August Bank Holiday Caribbean Carnival draws more than a million people into the area, in particular along Westbourne Grove and Ladbroke Grove. There are stalls, floats, and dancing in the streets to reggae and calypso. For a relief from the noise, walk south along Ladbroke Grove to find **Holland Park**, a delightful oasis of woods, a good café, and a new Japanese garden with a waterfall.

Saturdays at the **Portobello Road Market** (northwest of the Notting Hill Underground station), where you will find antiques, Victoriana, and a variety of secondhand items, are already on the tourist circuit. What you don't want to miss are the many small, specialized art and photographic galleries that have recently opened along **Kensington Park Road**, parallel to Portobello, as well as down various side streets.

If you'd like an American-style breakfast, start the day relaxing over your newspaper in the multilevel **Gate Diner**, also on Kensington Park Road. More serious eating, with a modern British approach to the cooking, takes place at **Leith's** at number 92. **192**, at number 192, is Italian with a new slant. **Julie's Wine Bar and Restaurant** opposite David Black Oriental Carpets on Portland Road also attracts the smart set; it serves an international cuisine but veers toward the highly traditional for its Sunday lunch. At the eastern end of Westbourne Grove, near the junction of Queensway, are a number of excellent and reasonably priced Indian restaurants, including **Khan's** (13–15), the **Standard** (21–23), and the **Kyber** (56). On Queensway itself the Edwardian department store called **Whiteley's** has been restored and transformed into a large mall with many individual stores, cafés, and a multiscreen cinema.

London North

MARYLEBONE ROAD

When Madame Tussaud, a French sculptor and one of King Louis XVI's tutors, arrived in London with her bizarre collection of wax facsimiles of heads that had rolled during the French Revolution, she could not have dreamed that **Madame Tussaud's Waxworks Museum**, the exhibition she established on the southern fringes of Regent's Park on the Marylebone Road in 1835, would eventually become London's most-visited admission-paid attraction. Today visitors line up far down the street to see lifelike figures of historical, political, royal, and show-business personalities. Some exhibits are remarkable, but by no means could all be confused with their originals. In the **Planetarium** next door there are permanent constellation exhibitions as well as, every evening from Wednesday through Sunday, laser shows accompanied by rock and classical music. Try to avoid the lines by going early and skipping Saturdays

altogether, when the ranks of tourists are swelled by British out-of-towners.

Marylebone Road (originally St. Mary-le-bourne; *bourne* meant "river" in the 18th century) is long and busy. It is also the location of St. Marylebone Church, most famous for its tiered tower and cupola. The church is wedged into the opening of Regent's Park's York Gate, one of the main entrances to the park, built in 1817. Marylebone Road's offshoots, stretching almost as far as Regent's Park in the north and Oxford Street to the south, include Harley Street, where the country's top physicians have clinics, and Wimpole Street, where Robert Browning courted Elizabeth Barrett.

Baker Street, the biggest and longest of these offshoots, is most famous as the fictional address of detective Sherlock Holmes. In his day, that part of Baker Street was known as York Place. Today, thanks to the renumbering of the street in 1930, the house at 221B is inhabited by the Abbey National Building Society, whose employees must every day reply politely to "Dear Sherlock Holmes" letters. For those determined to pursue the famous detective, he can be found at the **Sherlock Holmes** public house (formerly the Northumberland Arms Hotel) on Northumberland Street in Westminster. Upstairs, you will find a complete reconstruction of his study, and in the pub itself there are posters and photographs of various actors who have played the immortal detective.

The more interesting and prettier **Marylebone High Street**, parallel to Baker Street, is lined with shops and small cafés. **Maison Sagne**, at number 105, is one such refreshment stop. This Swiss pâtisserie and bakery, established in 1921, is still concocting pastries and cakes on the premises. Antiquities can be found in **Blunderbuss**, on Thayer Street (the southern continuation of the High Street), an eclectic shop full of pistols, helmets, swords, and other military bric-a-brac. The Wallace Collection (see the West End, above) is just west of Thayer.

Chiltern Street, parallel to and east of Baker Street, is interesting for its fashionable boutiques, its antiques stores and fabric shops, and its music and musical instrument shops stocking oboes, flutes, early-music instruments, and musical scores.

HAMPSTEAD

Hampstead Heath

Hampstead is London at its most rural. Drop strangers in the heart of the 800 acres of leafy, luscious Hampstead Heath, north of Regent's Park and Camden Town, and they will swear that they have been abandoned in some remote English shire, a verdant, bushy-tailed wilderness far from the madding crowds. Only when their ears turn away from birdsong to the distant hum of metropolitan traffic will they accept the heath's urban coordinates. Stuff them into a taxi and they can be in central London in 20 minutes.

As a place to live, Hampstead's tree-lined lanes and twisting alleys have long been favored by the wealthy and well known. Residents have included Robert Louis Stevenson, D. H. Lawrence, John Keats, John Galsworthy, George Orwell, William Blake, and John Constable. By the early 1900s Hampstead had become London's Montmartre, full of painters, their entourages, and hangers-on. Wander around the streets today and you'll see many of the distinctive blue plaques that mark the residence of a famous previous tenant.

Hampstead Heath is also one of the "lungs of London." Tranquillity and clean air (at least by city standards) are its stock in trade, and the lichen grows thick. Judging by the real-estate prices, which rank among the highest in the city, such virtues have much appeal today. Among its rich and famous current residents are Jeremy Irons, John Le Carré, and Glenda Jackson. Hampstead being what it is, no one bothers with a second glance after spotting a celebrity buying out-of-season asparagus at a local greengrocer, taking tea at **Louis Pâtisserie**, or sipping a cappuccino at the **Dôme Café**.

A Walking Tour of Hampstead

Despite the massive Heath, the appeal of Hampstead is all too easy for the London visitor to miss. Emerge from the Hampstead Underground station—London's deepest, at 192 feet below ground level—onto a busy intersection lined with unexciting shops and you'll immediately wonder what the fuss is all about. Turn down Hampstead High Street, though, and left again onto **Flask Walk**, and the prospect improves.

You'll want to slow your pace as you approach the **Flask**, one of Hampstead's many pleasant pubs. The very name Flask puts things into immediate historical context.

It is derived from the bottles of medicinal waters that once were filled from nearby chalybeate springs and sold here. The shops now go in for Perrier and other variations on the *eau* theme, but several are well worth a browse. Follow Flask Walk onto Well Walk, another place with watery associations, and pause at number 40, once the home of John Constable, England's finest landscape painter. From his house, after a few more minutes, you should come face to face with the Heath.

Hampstead is the one place in London where a map and compass are more useful to the tourist than a handful of currency. To experience the best of the greenery you need to walk in, around, and through the Heath, and, with luck, return to the point where you started. Take heart in the knowledge that even locals go astray.

The point to head for, out of sight but likely to be known to passing strollers, joggers, dog walkers, bird-watchers, and the like, is **Kenwood House**. A very large and very white house situated on the far side of the Heath northeast from the general location of Constable's house, Kenwood is a classic example of the 18th-century species of gentleman's country home. First owned by Lord Chief Justice William Murray, who employed Robert Adam to enlarge and embellish the property, Kenwood is now a bequest to the nation, and it contains a fine collection of paintings by Rembrandt, Vermeer, Rubens, and others. During the summer there is a series of open-air concerts on the grounds.

From Kenwood, walk through the rhododendron gardens, littered with the occasional piece of weathered sculpture, along the linden-shaded gravel path, and ask to be pointed toward the Spaniards Inn, where both Charles Dickens and Dick Turpin, the highwayman, drank. From there slip through the still-narrow gap between the inn and the tollhouse, both 18th century and famous for the part played by the landlord in 1780 in saving Kenwood House from the mob during the Gordon riots (the U.K.'s worst-ever riots, provoked by anger over the repeal of anti-Catholic legislation; according to local legend, the landlord plied the mob with so much free drink that by the time soldiers arrived they were too drunk to resist). Then head south along Spaniards Road (or, better still, follow a more rural course parallel to the busy thoroughfare) toward Whitestone Pond, whose dark waters mark the highest point in London (443 feet). Just before you reach the road you will catch a glimpse of the distant city

skyline rising out of the Thames valley, an especially spectacular sight when the afternoon sun is low on the horizon, striking gold against the city structures.

As this is the high point of the walking tour, you might like to take time out at **Jack Straw's Castle**, a white wooden eyesore of a pub named after one of the leaders of Wat Tyler's Peasants' Revolt of 1381 who was caught while trying to seek refuge near here and later hanged on the site where the pub now stands. The current pub was rebuilt in the 1960s after the original was destroyed in World War II. Or you can follow North End Way to the popular **Bull and Bush Tavern**, built on the site of a 17th-century farmhouse that was briefly home to Hogarth and was later made famous in 19th-century music halls. A still-popular song has the rousing refrain "Down at the old Bull and Bush."

Also, don't miss the **Vale of Health**, the only village *on* Hampstead Heath. It is likely that there were inhabitants here as early as a thousand years ago, but it wasn't developed in earnest until the late 18th century. In the hope of attracting new people to the village, it adopted its charming name. One such person was D. H. Lawrence; look for blue plaques. **Parliament Hill**, near South End Green, covers 270 acres and rises to 319 feet. From here the panoramic view takes in the whole city. The hill reputedly owes its name to the 1605 Gunpowder Plotters, who intended to meet here to watch the Houses of Parliament burn on November 5. These days it's a favorite haunt of kite-flyers. If you get too hot on the Heath, you can always cool off with a dip in the Hampstead Mixed Bathing Pond, open May to September. There is also the men-only Highgate Pond (for competent swimmers) and the female (over 8) Kenwood Pond, all natural bodies of water.

Hampstead has a few other landmarks well worth a detour before you return to more central parts of town. One is **Keats House** on Keats Grove (open to the public), set in the delightful garden where the poet composed "Ode to a Nightingale." Another is the 17th-century **Fenton House** on Hampstead Grove, with an interesting collection of paintings, furniture, and ceramics, as well as a highly regarded collection of early keyboard instruments. A third landmark is the remarkable 18th-century terrace of "brownstones" along **Church Row**. Planted with trees, and with the Church of St. John's (where John Constable is buried) at the end of the row, the scene is quintessentially English. Imagine it with a dusting of snow and you have the makings of a classic Christmas card. Look for number 99 Frognal, where General de Gaulle lived during much of World War II. In the **Freud Museum**, 20 Maresfield Gardens, six rooms remain as they were when Freud died here. In addition to the famous couch, you can see manuscripts, antiquities, books, and the original Viennese furnishings he brought with him when he escaped Nazi-occupied Austria in 1938.

If the day is fine, head northeast across the Heath toward the ponds to **Highgate**, another London hilltop village, which meets Hampstead on Hampstead Heath. Close to another **Flask** pub (this one, with its large courtyard and outside summer tables, looking unmistakably rural), a onetime haunt of Karl Marx and William Hogarth, where the latter would work depicting scenes of drunkenness, and where Dick Turpin is once supposed to have hidden, lies **Highgate Cemetery**. It is divided into two sections: The section to the east of Swains Lane is the newer half, and contains the grave and bold bronze bust of Karl Marx; the section to the west is a tangled, overgrown, rather bizarre yet beautiful world of vaults and other monumental masonry. The graves of George Eliot and Sir Ralph Richardson are also to be found in Highgate Cemetery.

In adjacent Waterlow Park stands **Lauderdale House**, which Nell Gwyn, mistress of Charles II, is said to have used as a summer residence. Now open to the public, it offers exhibitions of work by local art-college students as well as recitals. Among the 17th- and 18th-century houses in the Grove you will find number 3, where Coleridge lived for a short time.

Finally, of particular note on Highgate Hill (don't miss the views while you're looking for it) is the Whittington Stone, on the spot where Dick Whittington, the boy who came to London in search of his fortune and became lord mayor, is supposed to have heard Bow Bells (the bells of St. Mary-le-Bow, on Cheapside) summon him to "Turn again Whittington, thrice lord mayor of London." Incidentally, Whittington was mayor *four* times. And the position of *lord* mayor was created many years later. His legendary companion, the cat, who sits on the stone, was added in 1964.

CAMDEN TOWN

The charm of Camden Town, the lively district bang in the center of north London (southeast of Hampstead and a ten-minute Underground ride due north of Tottenham Court Road), lies mainly in its social and cultural mish-mash. Along Camden High Street, Chalk Farm Road, and Parkway, plant-filled wine bars and bistros, antiques shops, and smart clothing boutiques rub shoulders with disheveled discount stores, secondhand music retailers, and the pulpy droppings from the fruit-and-vegetable market on Inverness Street. Harmless down-and-outs, oc-cupants of the Arlington Road shelter for the homeless, are deep in inebriated conference on most street corners.

The slightly seedy, hippie ambience of **Camden Lock's weekend market** is famous throughout London. Its scale is generous, spilling from the cobbled lockside area sur-rounding the stagnant basin waters to Chalk Farm Road, almost as far as the former Roundhouse Theatre (located in an old brick-built railway locomotive shed). The blue-canopied stalls are surrounded by trendy shops and reno-vated haylofts and warehouses. The market has recently been significantly rebuilt, the central core now known as the New Market Hall.

Anyone wishing to sell his or her wares to the battal-ions of young professionals and punks lines up at nine in the morning and, if lucky, is allocated a stall. The market has everything from potted palms to pine furniture, hand-made jewelry to Hawaiian shirts, posters to pure-wool sweaters, antiques and bric-a-brac to high-tech gift items.

Two French-inspired restaurants almost justify an excur-sion to the area: the **Brasserie** (for some of the best french fries in town) on Camden High Street just south of the market, and **Café Delancey** on Delancey Street, open from breakfast (check the daily specials blackboard). Both draw the arts and media clientele, many of whom saunter over from the futuristic television studios build-ing, with its "egg cup" rooftop trimming, on Buck Street.

Camden Town is home to several music venues. The **Jazz Café** on Parkway often features visiting U.S. musi-cians, while the **Camden Palace** by Mornington Crescent as well as the **Electric Ballroom** on Camden High Street, just next to the Underground station, host up-and-coming rock bands. Many of the area's pubs, including the **Dublin Castle** (also on Parkway) and **Liberties Bar** (on Camden High Street), host live Irish music.

The 50 acres of **Primrose Hill**, an offshoot of Regent's Park to the west of Camden, are a voluptuous green hummock on an otherwise pancake-flat horizon. This area earned its name from its wildflowers, although in the

18th century the area blossomed with as many derelicts as blooms, and only the foolhardy would dare cross its boundaries once night had fallen. Today Primrose Hill's Regency terraces rank among the most salubrious and expensive in north London. On Sunday afternoons the grassy mound is busy with kite-flyers and walkers who climb to its summit to enjoy one of the best panoramas of London.

London Zoo

The function of the most prominent structure on the southern horizon viewed from Primrose Hill would be impossible for most visitors to guess. It is an aviary, designed by Lord Snowdon and, standing within the London Zoo in Regent's Park, one of the city's biggest tourist attractions. Open seven days a week, the zoo was founded by Sir Stamford Raffles (a name more immediately associated with the hotel in Singapore, the British trading colony he founded).

Apart from the aviary, other highlights of the menagerie, which is home to more than 5,000 animals, include a tropical house where hummingbirds freely commute between thick foliage and your head; an "open-plan" lion house; an insect and arachnid house; and a tigers' den, where only a pane of glass separates you from the toothsome beasts. There's also a rich-smelling elephant house, where the public can witness regular teeth-cleaning and toe-filing sessions; several high-octane monkey houses; and the Moonlight World, where nocturnal fauna are deceived into activity at hours that suit visitors.

Chalk Farm, the area tightly bordered by Primrose Hill, Regent's Park Road, and a main railway line, had been a fairly run-down precinct until gentrification occurred in the 1970s. The main thoroughfare here is Regent's Park Road; its lower portion is now a neighborhood of shops that seem to sell a blend of everything—wine and kitchen equipment included—that an affluent community could possibly need. There's also a smattering of restaurants, including the refined **Odette's**, for modern international cuisine, and the nearby **Lemonia**, a stylish Greek eatery.

Regent's Park

A large proportion of Camden is made up of parklands. During the British civil wars of the 17th century the future of Regent's Park, arguably London's most urban park, looked gloomy, as most of its trees were razed to

Regent's Park

```
0    yards   300

0    meters   300
```

be used as firewood for the needy. It was John Nash, backed by the prince regent, who at the end of the 18th century engineered today's triumph. Within the manicured hedges that line the Outer Circle road lie 500 acres of gardens, shrubbery, and bird life, all in a basic Victorian format, right down to an old-fashioned bandstand where tubas and trumpets entertain lunchtime and Sunday-afternoon picnickers.

More modern trappings include a boating lake (formed by damming the River Tyburn), a children's boating pond, the zoo, and ornamental bridges. There's also an open-air theater, where the New Shakespeare Company performs throughout the summer. The glades and woods provide the perfect setting, and the audience, sitting on tiered seats exposed to the elements, can move around with the scenes when necessary, clutching their plates and glasses of wine as they go.

Once you are inside the Queen Mary's Gardens, within the park's Inner Circle road, the sounds of London are reduced to that of an occasional airplane. This fragrant enclave is a mass of perfumed rosebushes grouped around a landscaped rock pool on the site where Nash originally planned to build a royal palace for the prince regent.

The Outer Circle road is lined with **Nash terraces**—smart, cream-colored, porticoed and pillared buildings that nowadays function as fashionable offices as well as private homes. The houses were originally built to raise money for the Crown and attracted the well known and well-to-do—Hugh Walpole lived at 10 York Terrace, for example; King Edward VIII's lover, Mrs. Simpson, was ensconced at 7 Hanover Terrace; and H. G. Wells lived at 13 Hanover Terrace.

The only significant dwelling within (as opposed to bordering) the park is Winfield House, once the mansion of Woolworth heiress Barbara Hutton. It's now the official London residence of the U.S. ambassador, and can be viewed only through the closely guarded gates at the bottom of the drive on the Outer Circle road. Almost opposite, straddling the south end of St. John's Wood High Street, is the Central Mosque, copper-domed and minareted, one of the most incongruous sights in the vicinity. At the end of the day it can be mistaken for the sun setting behind the trees.

Just outside the park, on the corner of Wellington and St. John's Wood roads, is **Lord's Cricket Ground**, recognizable by its white sails on the Mound Stand, completed to celebrate the Marylebone Cricket Club's bicentenary in 1987. Guided tours include "the Ashes," a trophy symbolizing the first time the England team lost to Australia in 1882, and the famous Long Room gallery containing, among other memorabilia of the game, a stuffed sparrow killed by a ball powerfully struck by Pakistani batsman Jehangir Khan in 1936. Visits by appointment (Tel: 266-3825 or 289-1611).

Regent's Canal
The Regent's Canal, part of the Grand Union Canal network, flows around the northern perimeter of the park (you can see some of the zoo animals from the water) before taking a dogleg up to Camden Lock. Its total length runs to eight miles, from the pretty core of **Little Venice** (west of the park and north of Bayswater near Warwick Avenue Underground station) east to Limehouse in the Docklands. Several longboats operate regularly in summer between Camden and Little Venice (the round trip takes just under two hours), including the *Jenny Wren* and *Jason's Trip*. The boat ride takes you along the still waters past rows of Georgian houses to Little Venice, where you can break your journey with a jar of ale in the tiny, low-ceilinged **Warwick Castle** pub (especially vital if, as an alternative, you cover the one and a half miles on foot). The London Waterbus Company operates regular service on the Zoo Waterbus between Camden Lock and the zoo. *My Fair Lady* serves lunch and dinner; nondining passage is not offered. You can catch these boats near either the Warwick Avenue (near Little Venice) or Camden Town Underground stations.

ISLINGTON
One of the first of London's "villages" to be gentrified by an influx of middle-class residents, Islington—east of Regent's Park and north of the City—suffers from a proliferation of real-estate agents whose windows advertise "bijoux" properties with quarter-of-a-million-pound price tags. Well-connected by the Underground (Highbury & Islington stop on the Victoria Line, the Angel on the Northern Line, a 15-minute trip from central London), Islington has come a long way since its days as one of London's seediest working-class boroughs.

The Domesday Book records Islington as a small settlement within the Great Forest of Middlesex, a largely rural, dairy-producing district supplying London. In the 17th century, when plague and fire caused a mass exodus from central London, Islington became a fashionable residence for the nobility and otherwise well-heeled (Charles and Mary Lamb lived here in the 1800s), who were attracted by its rejuvenating spas. By the 19th century Islington was a curious mixture—the construction of better roads and the introduction of railways resulted in the development of fine terraces and squares—but the central core had declined and was awash in grime, poverty, and working-class slum buildings. George Orwell, Walter Sickert, and Evelyn Waugh all made their homes here earlier in our century.

Today Islington is the undisputed territory of the intelligent socialist. Ruled by a council of liberal tendency, it's a borough that survives on meager finances but doles out welcome bowls of sympathy. Such a reputation has made it a place of refuge for struggling minority groups and has spawned countless voluntary self-help associations, among them the Islington Voluntary Action Council, designed to help those who would doubtless suffer discrimination elsewhere.

However, as is often the case with economically depressed areas (Islington is the eighth-poorest borough in London), its low real-estate prices have attracted an influx of the upwardly mobile. Rubbing shoulders with those relying on state support, the newcomers are buying the last of the borough's decaying properties and converting them into smart residences. And they buy all their fixtures and fittings on **Upper Street**, Islington's main thoroughfare, chockablock with wine bars, restaurants, designer kitchen-accessories shops, and all manner of other late-20th-century paraphernalia.

Of course there are antiques stores. Islingtonians frequent **Camden Passage**, north of the Angel tube station, a narrow, flagstoned, pedestrians-only street behind the miniature Islington Green, where wrought-iron shop signs advertise numerous emporiums: Franco's, the Furniture Vault, Gordon Gridley, Ark Angel, and Laurence Mitchell, to name a few, not to mention the **Angel Arcade**, a Gothic-style precinct of 20 shops selling silver, porcelain, rare books, and objets d'art. Finbar Macdonnell has a caged mynah bird whose chirruping will accompany your browsing through his old prints and engravings. And if you wind up in **The Mall**, on neighboring Islington High Street, you may never come out—it contains a bewildering 35 galleries filled with antiques and decorative arts. On Wednesday mornings and all day Saturdays there are also rows of antiques stalls set up in Camden Passage.

A large part of the borough of Islington is dominated by a district to the south called **Clerkenwell**, named after the Clerks' Well, which was discovered in 1924 in what is now the New Statesman/Society building. The well was christened after the medieval parish clerks of the City of London (south of this area), who performed miracle plays near here on the banks of the River Fleet. The **Charterhouse**, a beautiful, towered building near the Aldgate Underground stop and Smithfield market (see below), owes its construction in 1371 to Sir Walter de Manney, who recognized its potential as a center of prayer and place of refuge for plague victims. Since then the Charterhouse has been home to Carthusian monks, a palace visited by Elizabeth I, and a famous boys' school. Large parts of it were destroyed during the Blitz; what remains is home to the Charterhouse Pensioners and is open on Wednesdays for guided tours.

The fertile meadowland on which Clerkenwell was founded is alive with spouting wells. Some are still quite productive, such as the one under the **Sadler's Wells Theatre** on Rosebery Avenue. The purity of the local well water attracted beverage makers such as Gordon's, famous for its gin distillery, and Samuel Whitbread; both occupy their original sites. In fact, the Whitbread Brewery Shire Horses still clop along their morning delivery rounds to pubs in the City to the south and southeast and also turn out for the Lord Mayor's Show and other ceremonial occasions.

No wonder Islington's wine bars are so well stocked. **Mon Plaisir du Nord**, in The Mall, is a cool, conservatory-like brasserie. **The Dôme**, on Islington High Street, has a Parisian ambience, particularly when the windows are opened wide in summer and the smell of croissants drifts into the street. A glass of wine at these places is a good way to begin a night that may include a little theater: Many a West End box-office success has begun on the tiny stage at the back of the **King's Head** pub on Upper Street. Performances are held nearly every night. When the show ends, live music in the bar begins. The pub's old decor and gentrified spit-and-sawdust feeling is complemented by the staff's quaint habit of using a cash till that dates

back to the days before the decimal system went into effect, so keep your currency converter handy or be prepared to trust the change.

After the theater you can squeeze into **Minogues** on the corner of Liverpool Road and Theberton Street, one of London's few Irish pub/restaurants, for flowers on the table and traditional dishes ordered from a blackboard menu. **Young's** Chinese restaurant is a short distance away on Upper Street; the nearby **Upper Street Fish Shop** is bright, breezy, and a bit upscale, at least for a fish-and-chip shop.

You'll have to get up early to catch the market traders at **Smithfield Central Market**. This wholesale meat, poultry, and game market in the southern portion of Clerkenwell near the Barbican Underground stop, though of little initial attraction to the visitor, has been a London tradition since the tenth century. Located on the site of Islington's old Caledonian livestock market (in those days the cattle were alive), it extends over 10 acres, with 15 miles of rails and the capability of hanging 60,000 sides of beef. Smithfield is active Monday through Friday.

The Norman **St. Bartholomew-the-Great Church**, one of the oldest and most atmospheric churches in London, lies a few minutes' walk to the east. There is also a restaurant here called **Café du Marché** that looks as if it belongs somewhere on Paris's Left Bank. It's hard to find, though: Stand on Charterhouse Square, look north, and you'll see it tucked down a tiny alleyway.

London East

EAST END

London's East End is not an obvious destination for visitors. It is far from refined, short on interesting shops, relatively light on historic buildings, and lacking in greenery. But for anyone interested in London as a sociological phenomenon, the East End—located at the eastern end of the city, from about the Tower area onward, and hugging the northern bank of the Thames—is an essential detour.

Although London has nowhere near the same melting-pot alchemy that, say, New York City does, it has certainly welcomed its fair share of huddled masses. The first to stake a claim were the Huguenots in the 16th century.

Close on their heels came Sephardic Jews, Irish Catholics (who excavated the city's docks), Polish and Russian Jews escaping the pogroms, and later, though less concentrated as a group in this particular section of town, thousands of Central European Jews fleeing Nazi persecution.

In 1887 a sociological study described Whitechapel, the area between the City and the rest of the East End, as simply the "dwelling place of the Jews," where they practiced tailoring and other traditional skills. Today the East End is still steeped in Jewish history. For example, Bevis Marks, near Aldgate Underground station, is Britain's oldest surviving synagogue, built for the Sephardic community in 1701. Jewry Street is nearby, and there is even a Jewish soup kitchen on Brune Street. Cable Street is famous for the "battle" in which Jewish resistance to a march by Oswald Mosley and his Black Shirts stemmed the rising tide of fascism in Britain in the 1930s.

In recent years there has been a shift in the ethnic makeup of the East End. Many Jews have moved out, upgrading their properties and buying in more desirable parts of town (particularly in the northwest London suburbs of Golders Green and Hendon; most of the Orthodox have moved to Stamford Hill). Even the Great Synagogue of Duke's Place closed in 1978, and so have ten others in the neighborhood, as the Jewish population has declined from 125,000 in 1900 to around 12,000 today.

Their places have been filled by a fresh wave of immigrants from the Indian subcontinent, notably Bengal and Bangladesh, who have taken over the lower-priced real estate as well as the traditional sweatshops. There are now as many *halal* butchers in the main shopping streets as there are kosher. On one street corner, where Fournier Street meets Brick Lane, there is a structure that was built as a Huguenot chapel, later became a synagogue, and is now a mosque.

The East End has always been on the "other" side of the tracks, a tough, working-class district of crowded row houses and flats, outside lavatories, and communal baths. At the end of the last century its slums were notorious. They inspired, among others, the U.S. philanthropist George Peabody to finance the building of apartment blocks in an effort to alleviate the worst areas of overcrowding. Crime and prostitution flourished here, and the area was the setting of the macabre deeds of Jack the Ripper.

To place yourself in this famous and still slightly raw and intriguing corner of London, walk about half a mile north of the Tower of London or due east from the Bank of England. But before you venture east, try to catch an episode of Britain's most successful soap opera, "Eastenders." The show may pay only lip service to the truth, but it will familiarize you with the Cockney dialect. It is said that anyone born within the sound of Bow Bells (the bells of St. Mary-le-Bow, on Cheapside) is a true Cockney, and most of the East End's places of interest lie within earshot of their chimes.

Petticoat Lane

If your itinerary allows, save the East End for a Sunday morning. Do this not so much for any religious resonance—though many beautiful churches designed by Christopher Wren and Nicholas Hawksmoor are found in this part of town—but for its Petticoat Lane market. You won't find that name on a map, though; just take the tube to Aldgate and follow the crowds. If you prefer to trust a map, look for Middlesex Street and you'll find yourself in the heart of the action. (Less touristy and more ethnic and interesting are the Sunday morning markets on Brick Lane, mainly devoted to used and secondhand goods, and Columbia Road, with flowers and plants.)

At Petticoat Lane there are a few antiques and bric-a-brac stalls, but nothing to compare with, say, Portobello Road or Camden Lock. In fact, the market's name hails from the days when it was predominantly a clothes market. Today's wares, on the other hand, are as much a celebration of plastic and fly-by-night manufacturing as anything remotely tied to nostalgia. The real pleasure of Petticoat Lane is all about listening to the patter of the stall holders, barrow boys, costermongers, and fly-boys, the unlicensed traders always ready to flee at the first sign of a bobby. You should simply drift along with the crowd, soaking up the sheer vitality of the scene. This is an extremely popular market, almost an institution among local residents, so you'll find yourself mingling with just about all the Cockneys in London. Petticoat Lane is one of those classic markets where, wags say, you can find whatever was stolen from you the week before. Don't trust the irresistible prices, explained away by an unfortunate accident whereby the merchandise just happened to fall off the back of a lorry.

Elsewhere in the East End

In the shadow of the recently completed and massive Broadgate development, a complex of mostly offices plus shops at ground level, nestle some of the oldest and most atmospheric residential areas of London. In the area north of the now-closed Spitalfields Market are Folgate Street and Elder Street, with many beautiful 18th-century Georgian houses (number 18 Folgate Street, furnished in the style of the period, has limited opening times; Tel: 247-4013). Behind **Christ Church**—Hawksmoor's masterpiece, now sadly run-down—is Fournier Street, with more, also often run-down, Georgian houses. To the south of Spitalfields are Artillery Lane and Gun Street; Jack the Ripper's last and most grisly murder took place in nearby White Row, off Crispin Street. For a by now much-needed drink, head for **Dirty Dick's** (202 Bishopsgate), previously a house where recluse Nathaniel Bentley stopped washing on the death of his fiancée. The pub has authentic-looking cobwebs and mouse skeletons.

Other interesting sights in the East End are worthy of higher cultural esteem. On Whitechapel High Street, the **Whitechapel Art Gallery**, with its renovated Art Nouveau façade, is one of the best in London specializing in exhibitions devoted mainly to modern visual art. Opposite the Whitechapel Underground is the London Hospital, most notably the home of John Merrick, better known as the Elephant Man. The **Geffrye Museum** has an unusual, altogether charming atmosphere; contained within almshouses shaded by plane trees, and founded by a local benefactor, Sir Robert Geffrye, is a small but perfect collection of fully furnished rooms dating from the 1600s to 1939. The museum is located on Kingsland Road about a mile north of Liverpool Street Station. A great favorite for a family outing is the **Bethnal Green Museum of Childhood** on Cambridge Heath Road, with collections not only of children's toys but also of costumes and furniture; it lies a short walk north of Bethnal Green Underground station.

With all its ethnic character, you won't go hungry in the East End, but you may have to abandon your food prejudices. **Tubby Isaacs'** seafood stall on Greatorex Street is an East End institution, and the place to buy small plates of jellied eels, whelks, cockles, and winkles. The fine range of Indian and Bangladeshi restaurants, from small cafés to more upmarket establishments catering to nearby City gents, include **Nazrul** and **Clifton**, both on Brick Lane and both inexpensive. **Bloom's**, on Whitechapel Road, the East End's main artery, is London's best kosher restaurant. Takeout sandwiches or borscht followed by pastrami are the order of the day here.

DOCKLANDS

Visitors to London beware. The capital is changing faster than any other city in the world except perhaps Paris, Hong Kong, and Tokyo. But if you stick to the familiar haunts of the City and the West End, visiting only such popular landmarks as Westminster Abbey, the Houses of Parliament, St. Paul's Cathedral, and Buckingham Palace, you won't notice a thing. Even many Londoners are none the wiser—their typical reaction, when shown what's happening on their very doorstep, is amazement at just how much has already been altered.

Venture just five minutes or so east from the Tower of London and you'll discover a London that is undergoing redevelopment on a scale seen only on two previous occasions—after the 17th-century Great Fire and during the 1950s, when the city was busy repairing the ravages of war. Although work began here only in the early 1980s, the Docklands is on the way to becoming one of the most important and exciting inner-city developments in Europe.

The Docklands is a vast area of basins, locks, and canals where, during the peak of the country's imperial power, raw materials were unloaded from the colonies and manufactured goods were exported to the rest of the world. But with the gradual loss of empire and the undermining of England's commercial supremacy, as well as the growth of containerized traffic, the docks gradually dwindled in importance. Decline led to decay, and over time the area became a giant urban wasteland.

Canals in the Docklands that were filled in during the 1960s, having ceased to function as commercial arteries, are now being dug out for purely aesthetic considerations. With its eight miles of River Thames and 460 acres of retained water, the Docklands has been compared to Amsterdam and Venice—which is also where several architects have looked for inspiration.

In fact, top names in architecture, both British and foreign, have been recruited to renovate the area's structures (some of which survive from the 1790s although most are from the 19th century) and to design new residential and commercial buildings.

In a location as big as central London itself (a land area equivalent to that stretching from Marble Arch to the Tower of London and from Waterloo to Euston), old warehouses—some still smelling of the spices they once stored—are now being transformed into chic stores, wine bars, restaurants, exhibition centers, craft workshops, art galleries, museums, and hotels.

Immediately east of the Tower is **St. Katharine's Dock**, built between 1825 and 1828 despite 11,000 protesting inhabitants, and at one time providing warehousing for valuable commodities such as carpets, cigars, French perfume, spices, and ivory. (Hence Ivory House, which, at its peak, handled a grisly 22,000 tusks a year.) In this restored Docklands area you may still occasionally see a historic Thames sailing barge. Nearby, modern yachts anchor in a basin surrounded by arcaded warehouses constructed by Scottish engineer Thomas Telford. The **Dickens Inn**, a wooden warehouse now converted into a pub with a sawdust floor and two restaurants, is also nearby.

On the other side of the river, a short but breezy walk south across the Tower Bridge, is **Butler's Wharf**. Sir Terence Conran, fresh from revitalizing the high streets of Britain, turned this outstanding remnant of original 19th-century riverside warehouses (Quilp's Wharf, in Dickens's *Old Curiosity Shop,* was sited nearby) into shops, homes, restaurants, offices, and, notably, the excellent **Design Museum**. Established by the Conran Foundation, this collection of everyday objects explores why they look the way they do. Two new restaurants well worth considering here are the **Blueprint Café**, for modern British cooking and for outstanding views of the river (on the first floor of the Design Museum), and the even more stylish, modern French **Le Pont de la Tour** in the renovated wharf.

The Docklands Light Railway Route

The Docklands Light Railway (DLR) serves the new residents, workers, and visitors. Quite unlike the Underground, this high-tech system runs on a raised track some 20 feet above street level, using many of the original Victorian viaducts, from the Tower of London to the tip of the Isle of Dogs (see below), east along the Thames to the London district of Stratford, and now extends to Beckton, near the City Airport. (DLR operates only Monday through Friday; on weekends a bus runs along a similar route.) The best way to see the Docklands is to jump aboard one of the brightly colored, driverless trains at either the Bank or Tower Gateway stations (by Tower Hill, just opposite the Tower of London). The **Green Line**, which runs through Canary Wharf to Island Gardens, is of most interest to visitors: for the passing sights, which include historic churches, Victorian industrial scenery, and futuristic architecture; and because it terminates at the foot tunnel that leads under the Thames and emerges in Greenwich.

An early landmark to spot from the train's right-hand window—get off at Shadwell if you are a fan of ecclesiastical architecture—is Hawksmoor's **St. George in the East** on Cable Street. Trained by Wren, Hawksmoor would surely be shocked to his quills by the restored, modern interior; the original church was severely bombed in 1941.

Shadwell is also your stop if you want to enjoy two of London's best riverside pubs. The **Town of Ramsgate** on Wapping High Street was where the notorious "hanging" judge George Jeffreys was arrested in 1688 when the political tide turned against him (just along the river is Execution Dock, where various pirates were hanged). Though there is no access across the river at this point, on the opposite bank of the river, on Bermondsey Wall (from Shadwell take the East London Underground Line two stops to Rotherhithe), is the **Angel**, a 16th-century pub where diarist Samuel Pepys paused, lingered, procrastinated on his way to Deptford Dockyard, his place of employment. The *Mayflower* is also on the southern shore, on Rotherhithe Street, near where the Pilgrims set sail in 1611.

Back on the north bank, about a half mile walk through renovated warehouses, is the **Prospect of Whitby** pub on Wapping Wall. It is often crowded and, sadly, altered through renovation, but its wonderful terrace overlooks the river. Samuel Pepys, Charles Dickens, and the artist J. M. W. Turner all supped here.

Limehouse station is the stop for Hawksmoor's **St. Anne** church, topped by the highest church clock in London. Walk down to the river and Narrow Street for **The Grapes**, a small pub immortalized by Dickens as the Six Jolly Fellowship Porters in *Our Mutual Friend*. It has a fine view, and a good fish restaurant upstairs.

After Westferry station the tracks take a swing to the right to enter the **Isle of Dogs**, so called because Henry VIII kept his hounds in kennels here when the area was a bushy wilderness. The "isle" is in fact a kind of peninsula formed by an enormous U-bend in the river. You can hardly miss Olympia & York's **Canary Wharf**, the giant pride of the area's redevelopment, with its 800-foot tower capped by a silver pyramid, at night lit from the inside as a beacon dominating the new East London skyline. Most floors of the building (designed by Cesar Pelli) are devoted to offices, while at its base is **Cabot Place**, with shops, cafés, an exhibition, and often musicians entertaining passersby. Cabot Square, just outside, is the largest square built in London since Trafalgar was completed in 1850.

The train passes over two of the large basins of the West India Dock; at South Quay you can get out and wander along the quaysides. At Limeharbour you'll find the Docklands Vistors Centre with lots of information on the various attractions in the area. Nearby, the **Island History Trust**'s photographic display shows what life was like in the area during the 1880s. The Trust is at Island House on Roserton Street (afternoons only, Tuesday, Wednesday, and Friday; Tel: 987-6041).

Next stop is Mudchute, a 32-acre working farm with riding stables for local residents, created from the first dredgings of the docks in 1802. The end of the tracks is at Island Gardens opposite Greenwich, a view painted by Canaletto.

The DLR **Red Line** extends north to the London district of Stratford (no connection with Shakespeare and of no tourist interest). From here you can change for British Rail's North London Line, which heads southwest to London's City Airport. Just 15 to 20 minutes after collecting their baggage—less than half the time it takes to journey into central London from Heathrow—arriving travellers can be in the heart of the City, making the airport an ideal gateway for financiers and other businesspeople. From the City Airport, shuttle buses connect with Riverbus service at Canary Wharf.

From the visitor's point of view the most exciting aspect of the Docklands may be not what's new but what's old. Again, you can take the DLR Red Line north to Stratford and change for the BR North London Line to reach, at the end of the line (just past the City Airport), the North Woolwich **Old Station Museum**. Restored to its period glory, the Old Station, with its lovely old flagstone floors, exhibits railroad memorabilia from the Great Eastern Railway and the North Eastern Railway in the Booking Hall, the Ticket &

Parcels Office, and the Ladies and General Waiting rooms. The pride and joy of the museum, however, is the lovingly restored "Coffee Pot" saddle-tank engine, the only survivor of a class of engines regularly used to shunt goods about the area.

The neighboring Woolwich Ferry, still a free ride across the Thames, affords a fine view of the **Thames Barrier**, one of the most remarkable works of engineering in modern times. Built between 1975 and 1982, it consists of steel plates that lie flat on the riverbed, but pivot up to a vertical position when a flood threatens, reaching as high as a five-story house. There are six gates, between which are huge piers that house the operating machinery. There is an excellent visitors' center, with audiovisual displays and scale models explaining how it all works, plus cruises around the Barrier. (Access is via the south bank only.)

What's best about the Docklands is that this is a living environment, not an artificial stage set manicured for tourists. When the Docklands really was docks, high walls kept Londoners from seeing, let alone enjoying, their backyard acres of water. Today, with the building of scores of promenades along the Thames and the canals, an entire waterscape is opening up before their eyes.

GREENWICH

Greenwich, the historic maritime heart of London, lies some 5 miles (8 km) east of the center of town on the southern bank of the Thames, opposite the Isle of Dogs. Because its maritime traditions still shape its present-day appeal, it is especially fitting to arrive in Greenwich by boat from Tower Pier, Westminster Pier, or Charing Cross Pier (behind Charing Cross Station). Step off the pier at Greenwich and, within a few paces, you can be mounting the gangplank of the *Cutty Sark,* a magnificent clipper that plied 19th-century trade routes carrying cargoes of tea, the brew that oiled the cogs of an empire. Beautifully restored and resting in its own dry dock, it is an important piece of nautical history, and houses a fine collection of figureheads and scale replicas of ship's cabins of the period.

Just a few yards away, dwarfed by the soaring masts of the *Cutty Sark,* is the tiny *Gipsy Moth IV,* the yacht that carried Sir Francis Chichester on his solo circumnavigation of the globe in 1966 and 1967. Nearby is the Royal Naval College, inspired by Wren, Hawksmoor, and Sir

John Vanbrugh, and, just across the main road, the **National Maritime Museum**, which brings Britain's rich seafaring heritage vividly alive. Housed in a grouping of some of the country's finest 17th-century buildings, the museum displays paintings, models, and real-life boats, as well as exhibits that evoke some of the country's great naval battles and the voyages of discovery by Captain Cook and other adventurers. Within the museum is Inigo Jones's **Queen's House**, restored by the National Maritime Museum and opened by the Queen in 1990. It was once home to Queen Henrietta Maria, wife of Charles I.

After exploring these sights, hike to the top of Greenwich Park, where, from the ankles of the statue of General Wolfe, you'll enjoy a grand view of the river. Try to time your climb so you reach the summit by 1:00 P.M., when the famous ball drops from the top of the **Old Royal Observatory**. The moment marks the correct Greenwich mean time. The observatory, part of the Maritime Museum, houses the largest refracting telescope in the U.K., as well as an extensive collection of historical timepieces and astronomical instruments. A plaque marks the Greenwich Meridian, the spot that defines the zero line of longitude—stand astride it and you'll have one foot in the Eastern Hemisphere, the other in the Western.

An interesting alternative return route to central London is to follow the **foot tunnel** beneath the Thames from Greenwich to the Isle of Dogs. Built in 1902 to carry workers from south London into the docks, the tunnel is 1,200 feet long. Also here, on the north side of the river, are the **Island Gardens**, the last (or first) stop on the Isle of Dogs part of the Docklands Light Railway, and claimed by some to have the best view in London. After admiring the view of Greenwich south across the river (painted by Canaletto in 1755), you can catch the DLR (on weekdays; a bus on weekends) back to Tower Gateway.

LONDON MUSEUMS

"When a man is tired of London, he is tired of life," said Samuel Johnson. The same can be said of the museums that grace the present-day metropolis; in a lifetime of museum-going you will not tire of the riches to be enjoyed behind their doors.

The nearest Underground stop follows each address in parentheses. Regular closing days, if any, follow each entry. For special exhibitions, consult listings in current periodicals such as *Time Out* or *What's On*.

Apsley House: The Wellington Museum, 149 Piccadilly (Hyde Park Corner). Fine porcelain and silverplate, batons and swords, and paintings by British and Continental masters now fill the Duke of Wellington's aristocratic residence, designed by Robert Adam in the 1770s and remodeled by Benjamin Wyatt in the 1820s. Closed Mondays. (Closed since 1992, Apsley House is due to reopen in June 1994.)

Bethnal Green Museum of Childhood, Cambridge Heath Road (Bethnal Green). The old toys, games, and dollhouses are not the only attractions here; the upper floor is given over to historic costumes of the rich and poor. Closed Sunday mornings and Fridays.

British Museum, Great Russell Street (Russell Square). The Elgin Marbles and the Rosetta Stone are but two of the treasures in one of the world's largest collection of antiquities. The vast and diverse inventory also includes Chinese porcelains, European drawings, medieval timepieces, and the holdings of the British Library—due to be moved to new quarters in 1995—whose miles of shelves house one edition of every book ever printed in Great Britain. Closed Sunday mornings.

Buckingham Palace, Buckingham Gate (Victoria, Hyde Park Corner). In order to raise revenue to pay for damage sustained to Windsor Castle in 1992, the Queen is opening the **State Apartments** and **Picture Gallery** to the public for eight weeks each year from mid-August to mid-September. Guided tours begin at 9:30 A.M. (the line forms at least one hour earlier) and cost £8 for adults.

Cabinet War Rooms, Whitehall (Westminster). The Cabinet's bomb-proof World War II headquarters, including Winston Churchill's personal quarters, have been authentically preserved.

Carlyle's House, 24 Cheyne Row (Sloane Square, then bus 11, 19, or 22). The Scottish historian and essayist moved into this house in 1834 and lived here until his death in 1881; manuscripts, books, and furniture—and the sense of the comfortable life Carlyle led here—are perfectly preserved. Closed Mondays and Tuesdays, and from November through March.

Clink Museum, 1 Clink Street (London Bridge). The museum is located within what was the infamous Clink

Prison. Exhibits tell the story of the prison, which in its heyday housed malefactors from the seedy Bankside brothels.

Commonwealth Institute, 230 Kensington High Street (Kensington High Street). A colorful collection of arts and crafts—many for sale—from some 50 Commonwealth countries fills this dramatic circular building. Closed Sunday mornings.

Coram Foundation (Foundling Hospital Art Museum), 40 Brunswick Square (Russell Square). Thomas Coram, a retired sea captain, established a home for destitute children in 1739. Hogarth, Gainsborough, and other artists donated their works to raise funds, and many of these masterpieces have been bequeathed to the museum. Closed Saturdays and Sundays.

Courtauld Institute Galleries, Somerset House, The Strand (Aldwych or Temple). The mainstays of this sumptuous collection are the Impressionist paintings acquired by Samuel Courtauld—Manet, Degas, Bonnard, Gauguin, Cézanne, van Gogh. Here, too, are 30 paintings by Rubens, canvases by Tiepolo and Breughel, and works by Roger Fry and other members of the Bloomsbury Group. Closed Sunday mornings.

Design Museum, Butler's Wharf (Tower Hill). Salt shakers, typewriters, roller skates, and other trappings of everyday life are displayed as works of art in sleek galleries overlooking the Thames. Closed Mondays.

Dickens House Museum, 48 Doughty Street (Russell Square). The novelist was well-to-do by the time he bought this house, in 1837; little of the original furnishings remains, but there is a fine collection of manuscripts, portraits, and other Dickens memorabilia. Closed Sundays.

Dr. Johnson's House, 17 Gough Square (St. Paul's or Blackfriars). Dr. Johnson and his assistants compiled the *Dictionary* in the garret of this house; a first edition is displayed in the memento-filled rooms below. Closed Sundays.

Dulwich Picture Gallery, Dulwich (West or North Dulwich stops on train from Victoria Station). Edward Alleyn, one of the realm's greatest 16th-century actors, commissioned an elegant manor in what is now a south London suburb and filled it with paintings of his contemporaries. The collection has grown over the years to include works by Rembrandt, Poussin, Reynolds, and

Gainsborough, and is housed in a splendid Neoclassical gallery designed by Sir John Soane, completed in 1814. Closed Sunday mornings and Mondays.

Fenton House, Hampstead Grove (Hampstead). The oldest house in Hampstead is furnished with exquisite period pieces, porcelain, and an outstanding collection of musical instruments. Closed Thursdays and Fridays, April through October; open weekend afternoons only in March; closed November through February.

Freud Museum, 20 Maresfield Gardens (Finchley Road). The famous couch and other personal belongings fill the house where the father of psychoanalysis lived after he fled Vienna in 1938. Closed mornings and Mondays and Tuesdays.

Geffrye Museum, Kingsland Road (Old Street). Authentically furnished period rooms honor centuries of British furnishings. Closed Sunday mornings and Mondays.

Ham House, Ham Street, Richmond (Richmond). In this elegant mansion on the Thames near Twickenham, furniture, paintings, and architectural detail evoke all the grandeur of the Baroque. Closed Mondays and from October through March. (Closed for restoration until April 1994.)

Hampton Court (train from Waterloo Station). Henry VIII began the painting collection—which now includes Titians, Holbeins, and Brueghels—that graces this palace just outside London. The King's State Apartments, which reopened in late 1992 after six years of restoration, house the best collection of tapestries in the country.

Hayward Gallery, South Bank Arts Centre (Waterloo or Embankment). This vast space overlooking the Thames hosts temporary exhibitions organized by the National Arts Council.

Hogarth's House, Hogarth Lane (Chiswick Park). This exceptionally perceptive artist, who captured the essence of 18th-century British life in his engravings (many hanging here), called his summer home his "box on the Thames." Closed Sunday mornings and Tuesdays, and the first two weeks of September and last three weeks of December.

Imperial War Museum, Lambeth Road (Lambeth North). Weaponry and military equipment, decorations, and uniforms from the two world wars; the newest additions are two excellent multisensory exhibitions: the Trench Experience, which deals with the horrors of World War I, and the

Blitz Experience, in which visitors endure a vivid re-creation of a World War II air raid.

Institute of Contemporary Arts, The Mall (Green Park). The well-executed temporary exhibitions here provide a glimpse of the latest from the British avant-garde. Closed mornings but open till 11:00 P.M.

Jewish Museum, Woburn House, Tavistock Square (Euston and Russell Square). This small but fascinating collection of Anglo-Judaism and Jewish ceremonial art is due to move to larger premises at 129 Albert Street in May 1994. Closed Saturday mornings. To confirm opening date of new location, Tel: (071) 388-4525.

Keats House, Keats Grove (Hampstead or Belsize Park). The Romantic poet wrote "Ode to a Nightingale" in the garden of this small house, whose rooms are filled with his diaries and other memorabilia. Closed lunchtime, Sunday mornings, and Monday and Friday mornings in winter.

Kensington Palace State Apartments, West Side of Kensington Gardens (Queensway or High Street Kensington). This home to British monarchs from William and Mary to George II was the birthplace of Queen Victoria. Admission includes entry to the **Court Dress Collection**.

Kenwood House, Hampstead Lane (Golders Green or Archway, then bus 210). The hand of man intrudes gently into the natural splendor of Hampstead Heath: Robert Adam designed the Classical 18th-century façade of this Stuart-period mansion, which houses one of London's best picture collections, including works by Rembrandt, Turner, and others.

Leighton House, 12 Holland Park Road (Kensington High Street). Lord Leighton, the Victorian painter, built this house in 1866 to suit his tastes, which—as displayed in the tiled Arab Hall and in his paintings—were charmingly excessive. Closed Sundays.

Linley Sambourne House. 18 Stafford Terrace (Kensington High Street). Original William Morris decoration, as well as the bell pulls, greenhouses, and other trappings of Victorian life, remain beautifully intact. Open Sunday afternoons and Wednesdays, March through October.

London Toy and Model Museum, 21 Craven Hill (Queensway). Europe's finest collection of toy and model trains, boats, cars, airplanes, dolls, stuffed animals, and more. In the garden there's a working railway and a carousel. (Closed for renovation until 1995; for details of reopening, Tel: 071/262-9450.)

London Transport Museum, Covent Garden (Covent Garden). The old flower market of Eliza Doolittle fame now houses a vast collection of the vehicles Londoners have used to get around their great city over the years.

Lord's Cricket Ground, St. John's Wood Road (St. John's Wood). A real treat for cricket fans. The guided tour includes the Long Room and the museum, which brings the history of cricket to life. Advance booking required (Tel: 266-3825 or 289-1611).

↙ **Madame Tussaud's Waxworks Museum**, Marylebone Road (Baker Street). The wax figures made by this Frenchwoman, who learned her craft fashioning death masks during the French Revolution, are one of London's biggest draws. You can turn your sights to the stars at London's **Planetarium**, next door.

Museum of Garden History, St. Mary-at-Lambeth, next to Lambeth Palace on Lambeth Palace Road (Waterloo or Victoria, then bus 507). Exhibition of aspects of garden history, along with a collection of antique tools and a replica of a 17th-century garden. Closed Saturdays and mid-December to end of February.

Museum of London, 150 London Wall (Barbican or St. Paul's). The latest technology depicts London from its Stone Age beginnings to the present—re-creations of the first Thames settlements; a dramatically lit view into a remnant of the wall that surrounded Roman London; a model that shows the progression of the Great Fire; and entire 19th-century streets. Closed Sunday mornings and Mondays.

Museum of Mankind, 6 Burlington Gardens (Piccadilly Circus or Green Park). Arts from the Americas, Africa, and Asia fill this Victorian building, which serves as the ethnographical division of the British Museum; for lack of space, exhibits change on a regular basis. Closed Sunday mornings.

Museum of the Moving Image, South Bank Arts Centre (Waterloo). Fred Astaire's top hat and tails and Marilyn Monroe's shimmy dress are here, along with hundreds of other artifacts of the silver screen.

Museum of the Worshipful Guild of Clockmakers, Guildhall, Aldermanbury (Bank). There are 700 timepieces here, some quite extraordinary, among them a watch in the shape of a silver skull that belonged to Mary, Queen of Scots. Closed Saturdays and Sundays.

National Army Museum, Royal Hospital Road (Sloane

Square). A comprehensive history of the British army, with weaponry, campaign maps, and uniforms, all handsomely displayed.

National Gallery, Trafalgar Square (Charing Cross or Leicester Square). What is considered by many to be the world's finest collection of Western art hangs in what are probably the best-designed galleries anywhere. Rembrandt, Rubens, Botticelli, and other masters form the foundation of a collection that now includes some 2,000 paintings. Closed Sunday mornings.

National Maritime Museum, Greenwich (for Riverbus service, see "Boat Excursions" in Getting Around, below; or Maze Hill stop on train from Charing Cross Station). Royal riverboats, maritime paintings, ships' logs, and other relics pay homage to the era when Britannia ruled the waves. Closed Sunday mornings.

National Portrait Gallery, 2 St. Martin's Place (Charing Cross). Portraits—be they paintings, photographs, drawings, even caricatures—capture famous Britons from the Middle Ages to the present. Closed Sunday mornings.

Natural History Museum, Cromwell Road (South Kensington). The number of specimens here, including whales, dinosaurs, gemstones, Stone Age artifacts, and insects, is close to 50 million, and the remarkable collection is growing at the rate of about 350,000 objects a year. The vast and well-designed exhibits of the **Geological Museum** (in the same building) trace the geological history of the British Isles and the rest of the earth; the gemstone collection is arguably the world's best.

Old Royal Observatory, Greenwich (for Riverbus service, see "Boat Excursions" in Getting Around, below; or Maze Hill stop on train from Charing Cross Station). Telescopes, clocks, and other astronomical equipment are on display in a fine Wren-designed building. Closed Thursdays, Fridays, and Sunday mornings.

Old Station Museum, Pier Road, North Woolwich, Docklands (last stop east on British Rail's North London Line). A lovingly restored 19th-century Italianate station recalls the heyday of rail travel. Closed Sundays.

Operating Theatre, Museum, and Herb Garret, 9A St. Thomas Street (London Bridge). England's only example of an early-19th-century operating theater. Exhibits outline the history of surgery and herbal medicine. Closed Mondays.

Percival David Foundation of Chinese Art, University

of London, 53 Gordon Square (Euston). The Western world's finest collection of Chinese porcelains. Closed Saturdays and Sundays.

Pollock's Toy Museum, 1 Scala Street (Russell Square or Goodge Street). This collection of 19th- and 20th-century toys is sheer delight. Closed Sundays.

Public Record Office Museum, Chancery Lane (Chancery Lane). The Domesday Book, Shakespeare's will, Guy Fawkes's confession, and some of the other most remarkable documents of British history can be found here. Closed Saturdays and Sundays.

Queen's Gallery, Buckingham Gate (Victoria, Hyde Park Corner). There isn't room in this former chapel to display more than a fraction of the superb royal collection of art; exhibits change frequently. Closed Sunday mornings and Mondays. The **Royal Mews**, just down Buckingham Palace Road, houses state coaches. Open Tuesday through Thursday afternoons; open only Wednesday afternoons in winter.

Royal Academy of Arts, Burlington House, Piccadilly (Piccadilly Circus). Reynolds, Constable, and many other English artists have been members of this august institution. The great works of art the academy has accumulated over the years are on display as only part of the society's numerous and ambitious public exhibitions. Hours vary with exhibitions.

Royal Air Force Museum, Grahame Park Way, Hendon (Colindale). The trip out to this northern suburb is mandatory for aviation enthusiasts; this is one of the world's best collections of aircraft.

Science Museum, Exhibition Road (South Kensington). Seven acres of galleries chronicle mankind's mastery of scientific principles and technological achievement: Foucault's Pendulum, behemoth steam machinery from the 19th century, spacecraft, and countless other exhibits. Don't miss the **Wellcome Museum of the History of Medicine** on the fifth floor.

Shakespeare Globe Museum, 1 Bear Gardens, Bankside (London Bridge or Cannon Street). Exhibits recreate the theaters, such as the ones Shakespeare knew, that were concentrated in this area until the 18th century. Closed Sunday mornings.

Sir John Soane's Museum, 13 Lincoln's Inn Fields (Holborn or Chancery Lane). A wonderful jumble of artifacts—sarcophagi, paintings by Hogarth, Canaletto, and Turner, Piranesi drawings—runs riot in the home this prominent architect built in the early 1800s; the house is as much an attraction as the collections. Closed Sundays and Mondays.

Tate Gallery, Millbank (Pimlico). London's foremost collection of modern art begins with the Impressionists and runs through Pollock, Hockney, and other contemporary artists. The latest addition to the formidable British collection is the Clore Gallery, a temple to the paintings of Turner. Closed Sunday mornings.

Theatre Museum, Russell Street, (Covent Garden). Richly decorated displays capture several centuries of the British stage. Closed Mondays.

Tower Bridge (Tower Hill). Exhibitions in both towers explain the history and workings of the bridge, and glassed-in walkways provide spectacular views over London.

Tower of London: The Crown Jewels (Tower Hill). The glittering prizes here include the Koh-i-Noor diamond (109 carats); Charles II's crown; and the Royal Sceptre (containing a 530-carat diamond, the largest ever cut).

Victoria and Albert Museum, Cromwell Road (South Kensington). Once described as "England's attic," the V & A is a vast storehouse of decorative arts: French interiors, Chinese jades, Spanish altarpieces, Persian carpets—seven miles of galleries in all, devoted to textiles, costumes, jewelry, glass, ceramics, and all other manner of craftsmanship. Closed Sunday mornings.

Wallace Collection, Hertford House, Manchester Square (Bond Street). The marquises of Hertford accumulated what is perhaps the largest collection of French paintings and objets d'art outside of France, as well as works by Titian, Rubens, and other European masters. The Hertford mansion is now one of London's richest galleries. Closed Sunday mornings.

Whitechapel Art Gallery, 80 Whitechapel High Street (Aldgate East). The building, put up in 1897 by C. Harrison Townsend, a follower of the Arts and Crafts movement, is an attraction itself; the temporary exhibitions of modern art are much attended. Open only when exhibitions are on. Closed Mondays; open Wednesday evenings till 8:00 P.M.

William Morris Gallery, Lloyd Park, Forest Road (Walthamstow Central). The museum represents the decorative arts in general, with an emphasis on the Arts and Crafts movement led by Morris. Open Tuesday through Saturday, and the first Sunday of the month, 10:00 A.M. to 5:00 P.M.; closed lunchtime.

—Paul Murphy

GETTING AROUND IN LONDON

The telephone area code for inner London (roughly anywhere within a four-mile radius of Trafalgar Square) is, with one or two exceptions, (071). The area code for outer London is (081). Throughout this chapter we have given the area code only if it is (081); if it does not appear, you can assume that the area code is (071).

Main Airports

Heathrow (Tel: 081-759-4321; British Airways, 081-897-4000) is 15 miles (24 km) west of the city and can be reached in 50 minutes on the Piccadilly Underground Line from central London (one stop before the last for Terminal 4; last stop for Terminals 1, 2, and 3); trains run every five minutes, starting around 5:30 A.M. Monday through Saturday and ending around midnight. On Sundays the first train is around 7:00 A.M. and the last around 11:00 P.M. Airbuses pick up at several points throughout the main hotel areas of central London. **Gatwick** (Tel: 081-668-4211) is around 30 minutes from Victoria Station by British Rail Gatwick Express (every 15 minutes from 5:30 A.M. to midnight, hourly service throughout the night). Combined Gatwick Express/Underground tickets are available at any Underground station.

British Rail

London is served by several railway stations whose lines fan out like spokes on a wheel to various destinations of day-trip interest to the visitor. The best single source of information is the **British Travel Centre** at 12 Regent Street; open Monday through Friday, 9:00 A.M. to 6:30 P.M.; Saturdays and Sundays, 10:00 A.M. to 4:00 P.M.; Saturdays from May to September, 9:00 A.M. to 5:00 P.M.; no phone information. Inquiries about specific services can be directed to the various stations: Charing Cross (Tel: 928-5100); Euston (Tel: 387-7070); King's Cross (Tel: 278-2477); Liverpool Street (Tel: 283-7171); London Bridge (Tel: 928-5100); Marylebone (Tel: 262-6767); Paddington (Tel: 262-6767); St. Pancras (Tel: 387-7070); Victoria (Tel: 928-5100); and Waterloo (Tel: 928-5100). (For all of these numbers, a central stacking system ensures that phone calls are answered in strict rotation, so be patient and wait for a reply.) For information on the areas of England served by the main stations, see Useful Facts at the front of this book.

Visitor Information

The most detailed sources of information for visitors to London are the weekly listing magazines *Time Out* and *What's On,* of which *Time Out* is by far the better. These come out on Wednesdays and are sold at all newsstands. The *Evening Standard,* London's weekday evening newspaper, is also a useful source of information, particularly on entertainment. Major tourist-information centers include:

The **London Tourist Board,** 26 Grosvenor Gardens, London SW1W 0DU, will answer written queries; **London Tourist Information Centres** at the following locations: Victoria Station Forecourt, open daily, 8:00 A.M. to 7:00 P.M., with reduced winter hours; Selfridges department store (basement), Oxford Street, open 9:30 A.M. to 6:00 P.M. Monday through Saturday, 9:30 A.M. to 8:00 P.M. Thursdays; Liverpool Street Underground station, open Mondays 8:15 A.M. to 7:00 P.M., Tuesday through Saturday 8:15 A.M. to 6:00 P.M., and Sundays 8:30 A.M. to 4:45 P.M.; Heathrow Terminals 1, 2, and 3 Underground station, open daily 8:30 A.M. to 6:00 P.M.; **British Travel Centre,** 12 Regent Street, near Piccadilly Circus, open Monday through Friday 9:00 A.M. to 6:30 P.M., Saturdays and Sundays 10:00 A.M. to 4:00 P.M., Saturdays from May to September 9:00 A.M. to 5:00 P.M.

There are also Tourist Information Centres in Bloomsbury, Croydon, Greenwich, Harrow, Hillingdon, Hounslow, Lewisham, Redbridge, Richmond, Tower Hamlets, and Twickenham, as well as in St. Paul's Churchyard in the City of London. The two that carry the most comprehensive selection of booklets, maps, and the like are those in the Victoria Station Forecourt and on Regent Street near Piccadilly.

Moreover, the hall porter of your hotel probably knows as much as anyone at the information centers.

Guided Tours

London Transport (Tel: 222-1234) operates half- and full-day tours from Victoria Coach Station, Buckingham Palace Road. For information, maps, and brochures contact the British Travel Centre, 12 Regent Street, Piccadilly Circus (Tel: 730-3400). Other tours are operated by **Cityrama** (Tel: 720-6663), **Harrods** (Tel: 581-3603), **Evan Evans** (Tel: 930-2377), and **Frames Rickards** (Tel: 837-3111). Both *Time Out* and *What's On* give details of the numerous independent lecturers and walking-tours available. There are also taxi guide services; details are available from Tourist Information Centres.

You can take a one-hour helicopter flight over London for £125 per person; contact Cabair, Tel: (081) 953-4411.

Underground (Tube) and Buses

London Transport has a 24-hour travel-information telephone service (Tel: 222-1234; English only), and also operates **Travel Information Centres** at the following stations: Euston (BR concourse), Heathrow terminals 1, 2, and 3 Underground stations (and all airport terminals), King's Cross, Liverpool Street, Oxford Circus, Piccadilly Circus, St. James's Park, and Victoria (BR concourse).

For the first-time visitor the Underground presents a challenge, but in fact it is quite simple and much the quickest way to move around London, as there are nine lines and more than 200 stations, all interconnected. Just consult the London Underground map—a masterpiece of simple design—buy your ticket (which you must hand to the ticket collector at the *end* of your journey), and board the train on the platform indicated by the line's last stop in the direction you intend to go.

The first trains run from around 5:30 A.M. (7:00 A.M. on Sundays) and the last stop at approximately midnight (11:00 P.M. on Sundays). Children under five ride for free, and those under 14 ride at reduced fares, as do 14- and 15-year-olds with a Child Rate Photocard (available from post offices in the London area; be sure the child has a passport-size photo and proof of age). Free maps of tube and bus routes, a huge number of ever-changing leaflets describing various fares, and special passes are available at Underground and bus stations. The map of the city bus network is posted on tube station platforms, bus shelters, and main bus stations. Individual bus routes are detailed at bus shelters.

Travelling by bus means you can window-shop as you sit in traffic jams, but of course it is much slower. The system is more complicated than the Underground, as there are 129 central London bus routes. But with the aid of a bus map, and by looking at the relevant details posted on bus shelters, you will soon work it out. To stop a bus, hold your arm out horizontally when standing at a bus stop.

Fares on both tube and bus are computed according to stages and zones; therefore, a relatively short bus ride crossing three fare zones costs the same as or more than a much longer ride in a single zone.

Tourist Passes

The **London Visitor Travelcard**, available only outside Britain through British Rail offices and travel agents, offers more or less unlimited use of the Underground, all London red buses (except sightseeing tours), the Docklands Light Railway, and British Rail within London and suburban zones for three-, four-, or seven-day periods. The card comes with discount vouchers for a number of tourist attractions, such as Madame Tussaud's.

Available only in Britain is a one-day Travelcard; it can be purchased from London Transport offices in Underground stations.

Taxis

London's distinctively shaped black cabs (a few are maroon or some other color) are rated the best in the world. Any cab with its yellow "For Hire" sign lit should stop if you flag it, and, provided your journey is under six miles and within the borders of London, the cab must take you where you want to go. Tip 10 to 15 percent. You may telephone **Radio Taxis** for a black cab (Tel: 272-0272, round the clock).

A second form of taxi is the minicab. Unlike black cabs, drivers need no special qualifications and cars are generally unmetered with the fare being agreed upon in advance. Minicabs cannot be hailed in the street, and you should avoid drivers soliciting business, as this is illegal. (Less scrupulous drivers may not even be insured to carry fare-paying passengers.) However, over long distances a minicab may be cheaper than a black cab. Two reputable 24-hour companies are **Atlas Cars** (Tel: 602-1234) and **West One** (Tel: 560-5346).

Driving in London

Do not drive in London unless it is absolutely necessary: Traffic is extremely dense, traffic jams are the norm, and parking places—if you can find one—are expensive. **National Car Parks** (NCP) has several locations throughout London; two of the more central ones are on Cavendish Square (Tel: 629-6968) and on Brewer Street near Piccadilly Circus (Tel: 734-9497). The NCP at the National Theatre, Southbank (Tel: 928-3940), is less expensive. A free list of locations is available from NCP, 21 Bryanston Street (Tel: 499-7050). The North and South Circular ring roads of London are easily accessible from the city center (though generally very busy) and link up to all major motorways around London.

Rental Cars
Budget: central reservations (Tel: 0800-181-181; toll free); **Avis**: central reservations (Tel: 081-848-8733); **Europ Car InterRent**: central reservations (Tel: 0532-42-22-33 or 081-950-5050); **Hertz**: central reservations (Tel: 081-679-1799). It is best to pick up a car at one of the London airports, which has the added advantage of allowing you to become familiar with driving on the left before you hit the traffic in central London.

Boat Excursions
In summer boats leave from Westminster Pier and travel regularly up the Thames to Kew from 10:15 A.M. to 3:30 P.M. Trips upstream to Hampton Court leave at 10:30 A.M. and noon (Tel: 930-4712). **London Waterbus Company** runs trips to the London Zoo and along Regent's Canal, which depart from Little Venice, near the Warwick Avenue/ Camden Town tube stations (Tel: 482-2550); **Jason's Trip** also offers cruises along the canal from Camden Town tube (Tel: 286-3428). Riverboat Information Service, a recorded message giving the times and routes of river trips, can be reached at (0839) 123-432.

Riverbus service operates high-speed catamarans every 20 minutes (on weekdays) from Chelsea Harbour to Greenwich via Cadogan Pier, Charing Cross Pier, Festival Hall Pier, Swan Lane Pier, London Bridge City Pier, St. Katharine Pier (convenient for both Tower Bridge and the Tower of London), Canary Wharf, and Greenland Pier, with a shuttle-bus connection to the City Airport from Canary Wharf. Riverbus Explorer tickets also entitle the holder to discounts at selected riverside attractions. Riverbus is primarily a commuter service and originally ran only on weekdays. However, there is some (limited) weekend service; fares depend on the length of your journey; Tel: 987-0311.

Bus Excursions
Green Line buses leave from Victoria Coach Station for various places of interest in the surrounding area. For information on routes and fares (including the Diamond

Rover tickets, valid for one to three day's unlimited travel on the network) call 081-668-7261. Several companies also offer one-day tours, including **Harrods** (Tel: 581-3603), **Frames Rickards** (Tel: 837-3111), and **Evan Evans** (Tel: 930-2377).

—Paul Murphy

ACCOMMO-DATIONS

By Katie Lucas

Katie Lucas, the author of a best-selling book on walking tours of London, runs a specialized London-based British tours company.

Part of the pleasure of visiting London is staying in a hotel that is typically and eccentrically British. London is rich in just such places. Many London hotels occupy converted town houses full of hidden corners and great charm. Others are refurbished Victorian and Edwardian hostelries in which no two rooms are alike. Even new hotels in London often try to make each room different from the others.

The following list is far from comprehensive, but it includes some of the best in different price ranges. The rates given are projected 1994 prices for a double room, without breakfast, unless otherwise stated. As prices are subject to change, you should always double-check before booking. Keep in mind that London is crowded with visitors year-round, so it is always best to book well in advance. Also, because London is such a huge city, you should decide upon the area in which you wish to stay before you make your booking; there is no point in saving money on a hotel only to spend it on travelling to and from the places you wish to visit.

The telephone area code for inner London, including all accommodations listed here, is (071).

Tower/City

▶ **Tower Thistle Hotel**. Despite its ugly modern exterior and out-of-the-West End location next to Tower Bridge, the Tower Thistle Hotel does have its pluses: a most wonderful position on St. Katharine's Dock, unmatched views, and attractive rooms.

St. Katharine's Way, E1 9LD. Tel: 481-2575; Fax: 488-4106; in U.S., Tel: (800) 847-4358, Fax: (402) 398-5484. £135–£165.

Whitehall/Strand

▶ **Royal Horseguards Thistle Hotel**. Large but cozy, this pleasant hotel has taken over most of the elegant buildings of the old National Liberal Club, with its long political history. Magnificently situated on the Embankment overlooking the River Thames, it is shielded from the noise of both river and road traffic by leafy gardens, and is within easy walking distance of most of Westminster's historical sights. Because of its proximity to Parliament there is a Division bell in **Granby's Restaurant** to summon M.P.s to vote. The coffee shop serves light meals all day, and the cocktail bar also serves a selection of inexpensive food at lunchtime. There is a business-services center, which incudes the use of a personal computer, and, of course, 24-hour room service.

2 Whitehall Court, SW1A 2EJ. Tel: 839-3400; Fax: 925-2263; in U.S., Tel: (800) 847-4358, Fax: (402) 398-5484; in Canada, (800) 448-8355; in Australia, (008) 22-11-76. £110–£155.

▶ **Savoy Hotel**. Built on the site of the medieval palace of Savoy, this is probably London's best-known luxury hotel and is doubtless the one with the most fascinating history. It was built by the brilliant impresario Richard D'Oyly Carte out of the profits he made on his productions of the operettas of Gilbert and Sullivan, which were performed at his Savoy Theatre next door. When he took his productions of Gilbert and Sullivan to America he was so impressed by the standards of the luxury hotels there that he decided to build a comparable one in London. He certainly succeeded: The Savoy was the first hotel in Britain to provide private bathrooms and the first hotel in London to have elevators. Another brilliant advance in civilized life, but nothing to do with Mr. D'Oyly Carte, is the hotel's association with the 99.9 percent perfect dry martini. You can enjoy one in the **Savoy Bar**. Next to this popular gathering spot is the **Savoy Grill**, a favorite place for after-theater suppers.

The Strand, WC2R 0EU. Tel: 836-4343; Fax: 240-6040; in U.S. and Canada, (800) 63-SAVOY; in New York State, (212) 838-3110; in Sydney, (02) 233-8422; in the rest of Australia, (008) 22-20-33. £195–£260.

Bloomsbury

▶ **Hotel Crichton.** This 19th-century house across from the British Museum in Bloomsbury is a well-run hotel and understandably popular. The large breakfast (included in the price) is a good start to a day of sightseeing.

36 Bedford Place, WC1B 5JR. Tel: 637-3955; Fax: 323-0018. £46–£48.

▶ **Radisson Kenilworth Hotel.** This recently refurbished hotel on the edge of Bloomsbury close to the British Museum caters to business meetings and small conferences. Even so, it's well equipped for tourists.

97 Great Russell Street, WC1B 3LB. Tel: 637-3477; Fax: 631-3133; in U.S., (800) 447-7011; in Canada, (800) 333-3333; in Australia, (008) 22-11-76. £145–£186.

▶ **Euston Plaza.** Opened in the early 1990s, this hotel is close to the major railway stations of Euston, King's Cross, and St. Pancras, convenient if you are travelling to the north. It is large and beautifully decorated in the Scandinavian manner, and the rooms are well-appointed. The winter garden conservatory, The Terrace, offers light food all day, while the restaurant serves a wider choice during normal dining hours. A health and leisure area offers Jacuzzi, solarium, and saunas.

17–18 Upper Woburn Place, WC1H 0HT. Tel: 383-4105; Fax: 383-4106. £129–£147.

Covent Garden/Soho

▶ **Fielding Hotel.** If you are visiting London to wallow in opera or the ballet, this is the hotel for you, as it is situated in a quiet, gaslit alley one minute from the Royal Opera House. Even if the opera is not for you, the Fielding is still a delightful place to stay: Being in the center of Covent Garden is like stepping onto a set for *My Fair Lady*. The hotel is shielded from the noise of this exciting area of London by the bulk of Bow Street Magistrates Court, famous as the home of the Bow Street Runners, England's first detective force. The hotel is small, with lots of stairs and no elevators, modest-size rooms, and plenty of character. There is a breakfast room and bar.

4 Broad Court, Bow Street, WC2B 5QZ. Tel: 836-8305; Fax: 497-0064. £70–£93.

▶ **Hazlitt's.** Soho has always been renowned as the red-light district of London: raffish, sleazy, but also fun and crammed with restaurants of all types, good and bad, cheap and expensive. Over the last few years things have changed, and Soho has gained respectability. Created from three Georgian houses (one of which was the home of William Hazlitt, the great essayist whose father founded the Unitarian church in Boston, Massachusetts), Hazlitt's, on Frith Street, in the heart of Soho, is a rather higgledy-piggledy kind of place, with lots of corners, stairs, potted plants, and great charm. Breakfast (not included in the price) is served in your room, but for other meals there are all the restaurants of Soho to choose from. There are no porters and no elevators here, and although there are direct-dial telephones in the rooms, the switchboard is closed to incoming calls between 11:30 P.M. and 7:30 A.M.

6 Frith Street, W1V 5TZ. Tel: 434-1771; Fax: 439-1524. £135–£150.

North of Oxford Street

▶ **Berners Park Plaza Hotel.** This large and lavishly decorated Victorian hotel, which recently has been upgraded, is situated in the heart of rag-trade land, just north of Oxford Street and close to Soho. Its splendid marble entrance hall is a popular meeting place for Londoners.

10 Berners Street, W1A 3BE. Tel: 636-1629; Fax: 580-3972; in U.S. and Canada, (800) 448-8355; in Australia, (008) 22-11-76. £130.

▶ **Dorset Square Hotel.** This small, attractive hotel occupies several 19th-century town houses on the corner of two-and-a-half-acre Dorset Square, just to the southwest of Regent's Park (the square was the original site of Lord's Cricket Ground, created by Thomas Lord in 1787 and moved a few blocks north to its present location in 1811). Despite the discreet town-house atmosphere, the Dorset Square offers all the most up-to-date amenities: state-of-the-art security systems, 24-hour room service, and secretarial services.

39–40 Dorset Square, NW1 6QN. Tel: 723-7874; Fax: 724-3328; in U.S., (800) 543-4138. £110–£165.

▶ **Durrants Hotel.** This is one of the oldest hotels in London, having been built in 1789. Therefore it is hardly surprising that the service is efficient and considerate; the management has had plenty of time to get it right. The atmosphere is dignified yet cozy, with wood-paneled walls and leather-covered wing chairs in the many sitting areas. It has a very clubby atmosphere and a loyal following. Although most of the hotel has been refurbished, it is essential to specify exactly what you require when you make your booking, as not all rooms have private facilities. The rooms also vary widely in size, quality, and comfort. Durrants is situated around the corner from Marylebone High Street, with its excellent shopping. There are also several very good restaurants in the area if you don't wish to dine in the hotel restaurant, and the tiny bar is one of the most charming and Dickensian in London. If all else fails, 24-hour room service is available, as are fax, telex, and photocopying services.

26–32 George Street, W1H 6BJ. Tel: 935-8131; Fax: 487-3510. £95–£100.

▶ **Mandeville Hotel.** Tucked away in Marylebone north of Oxford Street near Wigmore Hall and the Wallace Collection, this attractive hotel is a favorite of busy executives who make use of its restaurant, coffeehouse, two bars, and comprehensive business services.

Mandeville Place, W1M 6BE. Tel: 935-5599; Fax: 935-9588; in U.S. and Canada, (800) 44-UTELL; in Australia, (02) 419-7111. £122 (includes Continental breakfast).

▶ **Merryfield House.** This small hotel is perfect for people who do not have much money to spend but want a comfortable, quiet, and convenient place to lay their heads. Each room has its own sparkingly clean bathroom, with plenty of towels. Located on a quiet side street in Marylebone, it is close to Baker Street, Madame Tussaud's, the London Planetarium, and the Wallace Collection. A full English breakfast (included in the price) is served in your room.

42 York Street, W1H 1FN. Tel: 935-8326. £48.

▶ **Mostyn Hotel.** Relaxing comfort, a welcome relief from the bustle of Marble Arch and Oxford Street, is what the Mostyn is all about. In 1740 Lady Black of George II's court commissioned John Adam to build her a grand house. Her home, which is now listed by the Historic Buildings and Monuments Commission, has been skillfully incorporated into the rest of the present building, but you can see part of the original structure as you enter the restaurant and cocktail bar. The grand staircase, superbly molded ceilings, wall paneling, and handsome fireplaces all exhibit the airy spaciousness of 18th-century design.

Bryanston Street, W1H 0DE. Tel: 935-2361; Fax: 487-2759. £130–£142 (includes full English breakfast).

▶ **Savoy Court Hotel.** In a quiet mews just moments from the noise and bustle of Oxford Street sits this small, unpretentious hotel. Maybe its greatest asset is that it is almost next door to one of the biggest Marks and Spencer stores in Europe, as well as being one minute from Selfridges. If you are intent on shopping it is a wonderful location, and the hotel has a cocktail bar and restaurant to revive you when you return exhausted with your purchases.

19–25 Granville Place, W1H 0EH. Tel: 408-0130; Fax: 493-2070; in U.S. and Canada, (800) 333-3333. £111–£118.

▶ **Seaford Lodge.** This stately Victorian house in Chalk Farm recently has been refurbished and converted into a small, pleasant, family-run hotel, with two ground-floor rooms fully equipped for disabled visitors. It also boasts a perfect location from which to stroll to the weekend market at Camden Lock and the antiques shops in the same area. The hotel does not have a liquor license. Breakfast is included in the price and other meals can be arranged.

2 Fellows Road, NW3 3LP. Tel: 722-5032; Fax: 586-8735. £65–£70.

Mayfair

▶ **Brown's Hotel.** In 1830 James Brown, a gentleman's gentleman who was married to Sarah, the lady's maid to Lady Byron, bought the first of the large Mayfair houses that make up this most understated but elegant hotel. Over the next 150 years another 11 houses on Dover Street and Albemarle Street were acquired, making the hotel a veritable rabbit warren but in no way detracting from the impeccable service that makes this one of the most civilized places to stay in London. The cozy, paneled public rooms are crammed every afternoon as people enjoy the delicious afternoon tea for which Brown's is famous. It was in this hotel, in 1876, that the first successful telephone call was made in Britain—between the youthful inventor Alexander Graham Bell and the young son of the landlord, Henry Ford. It was also from this hotel that Theodore Roosevelt walked to his wedding at St. George's Church in Hanover Square, and a few years later Franklin and Eleanor Roosevelt spent several days of their honeymoon in the same suite.

Albemarle and Dover streets, W1A 4SW. Tel: 493-6020; Fax: 493-9381; in U.S. and Canada, (800) 225-5843, Telex: 6852554; in Australia, (008) 22-24-46, Telex: AA121448. £205.

▶ **Chesterfield.** Created from a town house in the heart of Mayfair, close to Berkeley Square and Curzon Street, the Chesterfield is a gracious hotel. Named after the fourth earl of Chesterfield, who was a local landowner, this hotel is affiliated with the English Speaking Union, whose headquarters, Dartmouth House, are next door. The interior is warm and inviting, and the staff is very friendly and helpful. There's also an attractive interior terrace with tables where tea can be taken.

35 Charles Street, W1X 8LX. Tel: 491-2622; Fax: 491-4793; in U.S. and Canada, (800) 44-UTELL; in Australia, (02) 419-7111. £150–£170.

▶ **Claridge's.** This wonderful hotel in the heart of Mayfair, near New Bond Street, may remind you of the great transatlantic liners, and the service is comparable, too. Quite simply, Claridge's is the ultimate in luxury and discreet service, which is probably why guests of the royal family are frequently put up here. The rooms are among the most comfortable and best equipped anywhere, yet they still retain the grace and style of a bygone era. During World War II Claridge's became a haven for exiled royalty and heads of state. The story is told of a diplomat who telephoned Claridge's and, asking to speak to the king, received the reply, "Which king?"

Brook Street, W1A 2JQ. Tel: 629-8860; Fax: 499-2210; in U.S. and Canada, (800) 223-6800; in Australia, (008) 22-20-33. £270–£329.

▶ **Connaught.** This establishment near the U.S. embassy is more like a very select club than a hotel; most of the guests have been staying here—and eating at the renowned **Connaught Grill**—for years. The high standards maintained at this hotel are all the more appreciated these days, when they are so rare. Most of the staff has been here for years, providing impeccable service. Book well in advance for both the hotel and the grill.

16 Carlos Place, W1Y 6AL. Tel: 499-7070; Fax: 495-3262; in U.S. and Canada, (800) 223-6800; in Australia, (008) 22-20-33. £270.

▶ **Delmere Hotel.** Close to Paddington Station and Bayswater, this former town house is the best choice on a street of small hotels. With 40 attractive rooms, it caters not only to the vacationer but also to the business traveller, offering all the usual support services, including fax machines.

130 Sussex Gardens, W2 1UB. Tel: 706-3344; Fax: 262-1863. £91–£102 (includes Continental breakfast).

▶ **London–London Hotel.** This newly opened hotel has high standards, as well as all the usual amenities. Converted from several large houses on a quiet London square, it is close to Paddington Station, which serves the west of England as well as some of the nearer tourist destinations, such as Windsor. The hotel is also close to the Bayswater district north of Hyde Park, and, for those who like to shop, Oxford Street is within walking distance. Thatchers, the hotel restaurant, specializes in vegetarian food.

2–14 Talbot Square, W2 1TS. Tel: 262-6699; Fax: 723-3233. £90.

▶ **Le Meridien.** This fashionable hotel is once again the ultimate in opulence. Built in 1908 to serve the luxury end of the market, it gradually went downhill, becoming seedy and shabby. Happily, it has been rescued, and an immense amount of money has been spent on turning it into one of the best hotels in London. The Edwardian building not only survives, it glories in its own magnificence. The **Oak Room** is one of the best—and most expensive—restaurants in London, while the **Terrace Garden Restaurant** is less expensive, very pretty, and one of the few places open after the theater for supper. The health club also has exceptional health facilities, such as a 12-meter swimming pool, squash court, and sauna, plus a restaurant. The public rooms are what you would expect from a hotel of this quality, and the bedrooms are lovely—and air-conditioned. Of course, there is 24-hour room service.

Piccadilly, W1V OBH. Tel: 734-8000; Fax: 437-3574; in U.S. and Canada, (800) 543-4300; in Australia, (008) 22-13-07. £247–£270.

▶ **Park Lane Hotel.** This large, independently owned hotel opened its doors to the public in the 1920s, and the aura of that era still hangs over it. There are vast public rooms such as the Palm Court Lounge, which is an excellent meeting place, and the Art Deco Ballroom, which is often used for art and antiques fairs. Over the last few years a great deal of money has been spent on the hotel, and it shows, particularly in the 320 bedrooms (many air-conditioned) and bathrooms. The views from the top floors are spectacular, especially from the rooms on Piccadilly, which look over Green Park to Parliament and Buckingham Palace. Unusual for London, the hotel has a 180-car garage, much appreciated in the crammed streets of Mayfair. It also has all the usual public rooms, 24-hour room service, a business center, and a fitness center.

Piccadilly, W1Y 8BX. Tel: 499-6321; Fax: 499-1965; in U.S. and Canada, (800) 223-5652; in Australia, (008) 22-10-23. £175–£205.

St. James's

▶ **Dukes Hotel.** This small and attractive hotel off St. James's Street is tucked away in a courtyard brimming with flowers. With service that matches its comfort, no wonder it is recommended by regulars who wouldn't think of staying anywhere else.

35 St. James's Place, SW1A 1NY. Tel: 491-4840; Fax: 493-1264; in U.S. and Canada, (800) 525-4800; in Australia, (008) 80-25-82. £220–£290.

▶ **Ritz.** This is where the word "ritzy" originated, and everything about it is just that—from the service to the decor, from the opulent public rooms, the most beautiful in London, to the elegant guest rooms and suites. The **Palm Court** is probably the best place in London for afternoon tea; the magnificent, gilded dining room looks out onto Green Park. The Marie Antoinette Suite, next to the dining room, is where Winston Churchill, General Eisenhower, and General de Gaulle planned the invasion of Normandy.

Piccadilly, W1V 9DG. Tel: 493-8181; Fax: 493-2687; in U.S. and Canada, (800) 525-4800. £220–£280.

▶ **Stafford Hotel.** Reached from St. James's Street through a cobbled mews, Blue Ball Yard (although there is a more conventional entrance in the front of the hotel on St. James's Place), this is one of London's hidden treasures. The smallish Stafford occupies two converted 19th-century town houses just to the east of Green Park. Public rooms are formal but welcoming, and attention to detail is in evidence everywhere—comfort even extends to a tunnel leading from the hotel beneath nearby buildings into the park. The restaurant is likewise excellent and expensive. In the cellars, hidden away among the bottles of wine, is a small, private, and fascinating museum of wartime memorabilia, complete with sandbags and posters of the period; during World War II this was a bomb shelter for the U.S. and Canadian officers who used the hotel as a club.

16–18 St. James's Place, SW1A 1NJ. Tel: 493-0111; Fax: 493-7121; in U.S. and Canada, (800) 525-4800; in Australia, (008) 22-74-95 or (02) 954-5255. £220–£235.

Sloane Square/Victoria Station

▶ **Eccleston Hotel.** Within easy walking distance of Victoria Station and its trains to Continental Europe and Gatwick Airport, as well as Victoria Coach Station and the Underground, both with their links to Heathrow, this large and efficiently run hotel has an ideal location for the business traveller or for the vacationer who will be doing a lot of moving around. The Eccleston offers most of the amenities you would expect to find in a more expensive hotel. Office facilities can be arranged.

82–83 Eccleston Square, SW1V 1PS. Tel: 834-8042; Telex: 8955775; Fax: 630-8942; in U.S., (800) 223-6764 or (617) 581-0844; in Canada, (800) 223-6764. £78–£89.

▶ **Elizabeth Hotel.** Situated only a few doors away from one of the former residences of Sir Winston Churchill on one of the many garden squares of London, this small hotel has a loyal following among travellers. A full English breakfast is included in the price, and residents may use the tennis court in the communal gardens.

37 Eccleston Square, SW1V 1PB. Tel: 828-6812. £60–£80.

▶ **Goring Hotel.** Perhaps London's best small hotel, the Goring is still owned by the same family that built it in 1910. (The Goring claims to be the first hotel in the world to have central heating and private bathrooms in every room.) Much loved by regulars, it occupies a quiet location by the Royal Mews of Buckingham Palace and is close to Victoria Station. Many of the rooms, as well as the comfortable and pleasantly seedy lounge and bar, overlook a garden. The motto of the hotel is "There is no longer a Mr. Claridge at Claridge's, there is no longer a Mr. Brown at Brown's, but there will always be a Mr. Goring at Goring's!"

15 Beeston Place, Grosvenor Gardens, SW1W 0JW. Tel: 396-9000; Fax: 834-4393; in U.S., (800) 323-5463. £200.

▶ **Royal Court Hotel.** Sloane Square, where the famous King's Road begins, is the heart of Chelsea. Here, punks can be seen next to film stars, artists, authors, and other habitués of one of London's most interesting villages. One of London's very best department stores, **Peter Jones,** which on Saturdays is more like a club than a store, is situated on the square, as is the Royal Court Theatre, renowned for producing avant-garde plays. Between these two bastions of Chelsea life sits the Royal Court Hotel. Despite its location it is surprisingly peaceful, and justly popular. The restaurant, **No. 12**, is very pretty, and offers good international cuisine. Also on the premises are the Old English Tavern and Court's Café Bar, both very popular. There is 24-hour room service in the attractive and newly decorated rooms.

Sloane Square, SW1W 8EG. Tel: 730-9191; Fax: 824-8381; in U.S. and Canada, (800) 44-UTELL; in Australia, (008) 22-11-76. £145.

▶ **Rubens Hotel.** Built at the turn of the century to serve Victoria Station, this hotel situated opposite the Royal Mews has recently been refurbished. Included in its many facilities are five meeting rooms that can be rented for conferences or social occasions. Located close to excellent Underground and bus services, as well as Victoria Station, the Rubens is particularly convenient.

39–41 Buckingham Palace Road, SW1W 0PS. Tel: 834-6600; Fax: 828-5401; in U.S. and Canada, (800) 424-2862. £123.

▶ **St. James's Court.** Originally built at the turn of the century as grand apartments, by London standards this hotel is huge, with 390 bedrooms—but this does not mean it is without character; far from it. Recently upgraded, the St. James's is built around a landscaped central courtyard with a magnificent fountain. The building boasts an enormous brick frieze, which depicts scenes from Shakespeare, but for more modern tastes the facilities also include three very good restaurants, a health and leisure center, and a large business center. Considering its location, south of Buckingham Palace and close to St. James's Park, the St. James's Court is very reasonable.

Buckingham Gate, Westminster, SW1E 6AF. Tel: 834-6655; Fax: 630-7587; in U.S., (800) 458-8825. £152–£188.

▶ **Wilbraham Hotel.** This is another small, friendly hotel created from several converted town houses. The location, just off Sloane Street and Sloane Square in Chelsea, and close to many good restaurants, is excellent. Breakfast (not included in the price) is served in your room, as is early morning tea if you wish it. Tastefully decorated, with a genteel air and service to match, the Wilbraham is much recommended by London hotel aficionados.

1–5 Wilbraham Place, SW1X 9AE. Tel: 730-8296; Fax: 730-6815. £73–£80.

Knightsbridge/Kensington

▶ **Alexander Hotel.** Several of the large, terraced houses on this pleasant street in South Kensington have been converted into bed-and-breakfast hotels. The Alexander is one of the best, albeit among the most expensive. Recently renovated, it offers attractive bedrooms with good-size bathrooms and an attractive breakfast restaurant leading onto the garden, which is perhaps its greatest asset, as tea can be taken there on sunny days rather than in the sitting rooms.

9 Sumner Place, SW7 3EE. Tel: 581-1591; Fax: 581-0824. £128–£185 (includes full English breakfast).

▶ **Astor House Hotel.** Yet another of the small hotels on Sumner Place, Kensington, this one is very much family-run by Mr. and Mrs. Peter Carapiet. They stress that you are a guest in their home, with your own front-door key. Most of the rooms have been nicely refurbished and have private facilities. Breakfast, included in the price, is served in the newly built and attractive Orangery. There is also a garden. This is a no-smoking hotel.

3 Sumner Place, SW7. Tel: 581-5888; Fax: 584-4925. £68–£85.

▶ **Basil Street Hotel.** This wonderfully old-fashioned hotel has a large clientele that wouldn't think of staying anywhere else. Its excellent location in Knightsbridge off Sloane Street is perfect for shoppers and is very popular with affluent women from the country who come to London to shop. In fact, the whole hotel has a very clubby atmosphere and is furnished throughout with comfortable chairs and writing desks. The staff-client ratio is one of the highest in London, and the staff tends to stay.

8 Basil Street, SW3 1AH. Tel: 581-3311; Fax: 581-3693; in U.S. and Canada, (800) 44-UTELL. £156.

▶ **Beaufort.** On a cul-de-sac of very large, terraced houses near Harrods, this small hotel is privately owned and attractively decorated in country-house style. Guests are given their own key to the front door when they arrive, and come and go as though the hotel were their own home in London. Continental breakfast, included in the price, is served in your room or in the small sitting room, and there is a complimentary 24-hour bar, as well as use of a health club. Closed Christmas and New Year's.

33 Beaufort Gardens, SW3 1PP. Tel: 584-5252; Fax: 589-2834; in U.S., (212) 682-9191; in Canada, (416) 598-2693; in Australia, (02) 957-4511. £150–£220.

▶ **Berkeley**. This modern luxury establishment, close to Hyde Park and the shops of Knightsbridge, has all the old-fashioned qualities you expect from a great London hotel. Unusual for London, though, are its penthouse swimming pool, beauty and health center, and a basement garage (a great plus in a city where parking is such a problem). There is secretarial and valet service, and 24-hour room service.

Wilton Place, SW1X 7RL. Tel: 235-6000; Fax: 235-4330; in U.S. and Canada, (800) 63-SAVOY. £270–£310.

▶ **Blakes Hotel**. Owned and decorated by actress and designer Anouska Hempel, this hotel is like no other: It is completely original in every way. Each room is decorated in a different theme, and the public areas also show Ms. Hempel's flair for exotic decorations. The attractive restaurant is presided over by a Japanese chef, who produces some of the most imaginative food in town. Not surprisingly, this hotel in the deep fastness of South Kensington between Cromwell Road and the King's Road is a home away from home for many show-business people.

33 Roland Gardens, SW7 3PF. Tel: 370-6701; Fax: 373-0442; in U.S., (800) 926-3173; in Australia, (008) 25-16-64. £195–£330.

▶ **Capital Hotel**. Small, quiet, and beautifully decorated, not to mention just around the corner from Harrods and the bustle of Knightsbridge, this hotel is a gem. The restaurant (one of the best in London) is a favorite of gourmets.

22–24 Basil Street, SW3 1AT. Tel: 589-5171; Fax: 225-0011; in U.S., (800) 926-3199. £210–£260.

▶ **Cranley Gardens Hotel**. Among London's less expensive hotels, this one shines like a beacon. It is converted from four attractive adjoining houses and overlooks a private garden square in one of the most popular areas of the city. It is beautifully decorated, in both its public rooms and bedrooms, and members of the staff are pleasant and helpful. Continental breakfast is included in the price. The small restaurant serves only breakfast, but the area abounds with dining establishments of all types.

8 Cranley Gardens, SW7. Tel: 373-3232; Fax: 373-7944; in U.S. and Canada, (800) 44-UTELL. £89–£99.

▶ **Eleven Cadogan Gardens**. There is no sign on the door of this small hotel off Sloane Street south of Harrods to suggest that it is anything other than a private house. Nor is there a reception desk or a restaurant, just a visitor's book and room service. Ring the bell next to the front door and a manservant will let you in. Created from several Victorian houses, this hotel is much favored by diplomats and art dealers. Room service provides light meals, but for anything more substantial just venture down the road, where you'll find plenty of excellent restaurants.

11 Cadogan Gardens, SW3 2RJ. Tel: 730-3426; Fax: 730-5217. £132–£172.

▶ **Gore Hotel**. This pleasant small hotel across from Kensington Gardens, west of Royal Albert Hall, is very quiet yet close to all the activity of South Kensington. It has, in addition, a pleasant lounge and a bistro that serves light meals, as well as one of the most popular restaurants in this corner of London, **One Ninety Queen's Gate**.

189 Queen's Gate, SW7 5EX. Tel: 584-6601; Fax: 589-8127; in U.S. and Canada, (800) 528-1234; in Australia, (02) 954-8111. £142–£197.

▶ **L'Hotel**. This delightful small hotel on the street behind Harrods has an air of the country about it, perhaps because it is frequented by people who come up from the country to shop or attend meetings and who neither want nor need all the services of a larger hotel. The guest rooms are simple, but they are most attractive, with pine and brass fittings. There are no public rooms, but the bistro in the basement, **Le Metro**, is very popular with hotel guests and neighborhood residents alike. L'Hotel is a sister hotel of the Capital next door (see above).

28 Basil Street, SW3 1AT. Tel: 589-6286; Fax: 225-0011; in U.S. and Canada, (800) 223-5695 or (914) 833-3303. £125 (includes Continental breakfast).

▶ **Hotel George**. This attractively decorated and spacious hotel has grown over the years until it now occupies almost an entire terrace of 19th-century houses. Its position is marvelous, close to Earl's Court, one of the main Underground junctions, and the noisy cosmopolitan shops of Earl's Court Road. The excellent facilities include a fitness center with swimming pool, sauna, spa, and a garden and a free parking lot, rarities in London hotels.

Templeton Place, Earl's Court SW5 9NB. Tel: 370-1092; Fax: 370-2285. £79–£95 (includes Continental breakfast).

▶ **Hyde Park Hotel**. At 10:30 every morning you can see the Horse Guards riding past this stately hotel, one of London's oldest, on their way from the Horse Guards Barracks next door to the Changing of the Guard at

Whitehall. With a lovely dining room overlooking Hyde Park, and several bars and lounges, this member of the Forte Hotels group is a favorite meeting place for Londoners and visitors alike. All rooms have recently been redecorated and are partially furnished with antiques.

66 Knightsbridge, SW1Y 7LA. Tel: 235-2000; Fax: 235-4552; Telex: 6852554; in U.S. and Canada, Tel: (800) 225-5843; in Australia, (02) 299-7224. £277–£356.

▶ **Kensington Palace Hotel.** This is another of the Thistle Hotels, and, as with many of their group, it is conveniently located for shopping, sightseeing, and good local restaurants. It also has unequaled views over Kensington Gardens and Palace. Quite large, with 320 rooms, it has a pub, restaurant, bar, and coffee shop, as well as 24-hour room service and same-day laundry. But, of course, being large, it also attracts tour groups.

De Vere Gardens, W8 5AF. Tel: 937-8121; Fax: 937-2816; in U.S., Tel: (800) 847-4358, Fax: (212) 779-0732; in Canada, (800) 448-8355; in Australia, (008) 22-11-76. £100–£142.

▶ **Knightsbridge.** This is a small, cozy, unpretentious place, and one of the least expensive of several small hotels on this quiet cul-de-sac just west of Harrods, off Brompton Road. Don't expect much more than a bed, Continental breakfast, and a front-door key. Spend your money instead in the delightful restaurants on nearby Beauchamp Place.

10 Beaufort Gardens, SW3 1PT. Tel: 589-9271; Fax: 823-9692. £50–£90.

▶ **Lanesborough Hotel.** Following its opening in the early 1990s, this hotel quickly assumed a place in the top echelon of hotels worldwide. The magnificent building, constructed at Hyde Park Corner as one of London's major hospitals in 1828, has been completely restored and renovated with style and attention to detail. The great conservatory at its heart has become a popular lunchtime meeting place, as has the library bar. The dining room is elegant—and expensive. Each room has two personal direct-dial telephones and fax, VCR, compact disc player, and safe. Every floor has a butler who ministers to the guests and their special requirements, which are recorded for future visits. Attractive rooms are available for guests who wish to give parties.

1 Lanesborough Place, SW1X 7TA. Tel: 259-5599; Fax: 259-5606; in U.S., Tel: (800) 999-1828; Fax: (800) 937-8278. £258.

▶ **Lowndes Hotel.** With a wonderful location in Knightsbridge close to all the best shops and restaurants, this hotel has always had a loyal following. It is quiet, with attractive public rooms, and it has all the charm of a small hotel with the amenities of a large one, including business facilities and 24-hour room service.

21 Lowndes Street, SW1X 9ES. Tel: 823-1234; Fax: 235-1154, in U.S. and Canada, (800) 233-1234; in Australia, (008) 22-21-88. £211.

▶ **Number Sixteen.** Built in 1848, these four interconnected and charming town houses create a most agreeable ambience. They're well placed in South Kensington, too, south of the Victoria and Albert Museum and just south of the South Kensington Underground station. The hotel has two drawing rooms, in one of which tea and coffee are served throughout the day; the other is a delightful conservatory drawing room overlooking the attractive walled garden.

16 Sumner Place, SW7 3EG. Tel: 589-5232; Fax: 584-8615. £85–£135 (includes Continental breakfast).

▶ **Onslow Hotel.** Once upon a time this hotel was so genteel that you were frightened to cough, because all the retired spinsters doing their knitting would look up and frown. Then, because of its location in buzzing South Kensington, someone had the bright idea of doing it up, and now it is very popular. Pleasant public rooms, including bar and restaurant; 24-hour room service.

109–113 Queen's Gate, SW7 5LR. Tel: 589-6300; Fax: 581-1492. £120–£135 (includes Continental breakfast).

▶ **Pelham Hotel.** This hotel in South Kensington, a very popular corner of London that is close to many important museums as well as to the shops and restaurants of Knightsbridge, is a hidden treasure. Like numerous other London hotels, the Pelham comprises two very large converted houses, but the standard to which they have been converted is extraordinary. It is owned by Kit and Tim Kemp, who also own the Dorset Square Hotel (see above in the North of Oxford Street section), and the attention to detail is everywhere evident.

15 Cromwell Place, SW7 2LA. Tel: 589-8288; Fax: 584-8444; in U.S., (800) 553-6671. £140–£165.

▶ **Swiss House.** A small and inexpensive family-run bed-and-breakfast hotel, the Swiss House is situated in the heart of South Kensington, close to the Gloucester Road Underground station. There are just 16 rooms, 12 of which have private facilities. This attractive house, its frontage covered in trailing ivy and flower-filled window boxes, is a winner of the Best Value Bed and Breakfast award. Continental breakfast is included in the price.

171 Old Brompton Road, SW5 0AN. Tel: 373-2769 or 373-9383; Fax: 373-4983. £50–£60.

Notting Hill and West of Hyde Park

▶ **Abbey Court.** Elegantly converted from a large town house, this small hotel offers very personal and friendly service. Snacks and drinks are available around the clock, and a full English breakfast can be served in your room every morning, though it's not included in the room rate. This area of London (Notting Hill, just west of Bayswater and north of Kensington Gardens) abounds with restaurants of every kind.

20 Pembridge Gardens, W2 4DU. Tel: 221-7518; Fax: 792-0858. £130–£160.

▶ **Garden Court Hotel.** This family-run hotel is conveniently situated close to Queensway, a busy and cosmopolitan street with two adjacent Underground stations, Queensway and Bayswater. There are many restaurants of various types in the area. The hotel, which is in the process of being upgraded, has comfortable rooms and a pleasant and helpful staff. Not all rooms have private facilities. Breakfast is included.

30–31 Kensington Gardens, W2. Tel: 229-2553; Fax: 727-2749. £39–£52.

▶ **Halcyon Hotel.** Newly converted from two large houses on the corner of Holland Park (west of Hyde Park/ Kensington Gardens), the Halcyon is already popular with theater people. No doubt they are drawn here by the greenery beyond the front door and the tastefully decorated rooms, designed to make you feel like a guest in a country house. The restaurant is also highly regarded.

81 Holland Park, W11 3RZ. Tel: 727-7288; Fax: 229-8516; in U.S. and Canada, (800) 457-4000; in Australia, (008) 80-18-55. £235.

▶ **Holland Park Hotel.** This hotel in Notting Hill has 24 rooms, two of which are for families. Although small, the rooms are individually furnished and have en-suite facilities. There is an attractive sitting room with a fireplace, adjacent to a pleasant garden where tea or Continental breakfast, included in the price, can be taken in the summer.

6 Ladbrooke Terrace, W11 3PG. Tel: 792-0216 or 727-5815; Fax: 727-8166. £63.

▶ **Observatory House Hotel.** Campden Hill is an attractive hilly area of 18th- and 19th-century houses that stretches from Kensington to Notting Hill. Almost at the top of the hill, and equidistant between the Underground stations of Notting Hill Gate and Kensington High Street, is the Observatory House Hotel. The air is cleaner than in central London, the surrounding area most attractive, and the walk will do you good. This small bed-and-breakfast hotel is in an interesting 19th-century building built on the site of the old observatory of the astronomer Sir James South. Staying in this recently refurbished hotel is like staying in an exclusive London club, but at reasonable prices. Amenities include in-room safes and secretarial services.

37 Hornton Street, W8 7NR. Tel: 937-1577; Fax: 938-3585. £65–£80 (includes full English breakfast).

▶ **Pavilion Hotel.** Sussex Gardens is an area known for its small, and mostly cheap, hotels. Sadly, we can recommend few of these. An exception is the Pavilion, which has a slightly idiosyncratic but attractive atmosphere. The rooms have fairly basic en-suite facilities, and, because the hotel has no dining room, Continental breakfast is served in the guest rooms.

34–36 Sussex Gardens, W2 1UL. Tel: 262-0905. £50.

▶ **Pembridge Court Hotel.** This small, privately owned hotel on a quiet tree-lined street has 26 comfortable rooms, as well as a cozy lounge, restaurant, and bar. The Pembridge Court is close to the bustle of the Portobello Road antiques market, which takes over all the surrounding streets on Saturdays, and is also close to Notting Hill, with its many restaurants and pubs. The north side of Kensington Gardens is just a stroll away. The upper floors of this small hotel are served by an elevator.

34 Pembridge Gardens, W2 4DX. Tel: 229-9977; Fax: 727-4982. £115–£160 (includes full English breakfast).

▶ **Portobello Hotel.** Media people tend to frequent this easygoing hotel, situated in a hard-to-find corner of Holland Park, within a stone's throw of Portobello Road market and all the fun shops and restaurants of this corner of town, west of Hyde Park/Kensington Gardens. The bar/restaurant is open to guests 24 hours a day, and the whole place has a very relaxed atmosphere. Rooms range in size from a ship's cabin to very large, but they all have the necessary amenities. The hotel also is equipped with a special clean-air system developed in Scandinavia.

22 Stanley Gardens, W11 2NG. Tel: 727-2777; Fax: 792-9641. £100–£120 (includes full English breakfast).

Bayswater

▶ **Henry VIII.** The Henry VIII has a lot to offer. Its position is just north of Hyde Park, on a quiet shopping street just off Bayswater and very close to Queensway, one of the liveliest late-night streets in London. A Continental breakfast buffet and full English breakfast are served in the restaurant. Other features of this hotel include a heated indoor swimming pool, a sauna, and a gym. Full business facilities are also available.

19 Leinster Gardens, W2 3AN. Tel: 262-0117; Fax: 706-0472; in U.S., (914) 736-6181. £99.

▶ **Westminster Hotel.** Occupying several large converted houses in Leinster Square, close to the Bayswater and Queensway Underground stations, this hotel is in an interesting area: slightly raffish, with a cosmopolitan feel and restaurants of every type close at hand. The hotel's helpful staff create a friendly atmosphere, and the pleasant public rooms are popular with businesspeople. The bedrooms are adequately furnished and have en-suite facilities. Breakfast is included.

16 Leinster Square, W2 4PR. Tel: 221-9131; Fax: 229-3917. £102–£114.

▶ **Whites Hotel.** Looking like a beautiful white wedding cake, this recently restored, large hotel boasts a wonderful location overlooking Kensington Gardens and Bayswater. On weekends the railings of the park become an open-air picture gallery where artists hang their paintings in the hopes of making a sale. The hotel's public rooms are most attractive, and the bedrooms have been decorated in an unusual and luxurious style, with all comforts included. Office facilities can be arranged.

90–92 Lancaster Gate, W2 3NR. Tel: 262-2711; Fax: 262-2147. £170–£210.

Other Areas

▶ **Hotel Conrad.** There are no rooms at the Conrad, just suites, a new concept in Britain. Situated on the marina of fashionable Chelsea Harbour, just off the King's Road in Chelsea, with its exclusive shops and restaurants as well as luxury private residences, the hotel has a location that is among the best in London. Although expensive, the Conrad does have a lot to offer, with several restaurants, bars, and function rooms, as well as a health club with facilities such as steamrooms, saunas, and a lovely swimming pool. Each room has two telephone lines plus fax facilities, and individual air-conditioning and heating controls. Also on the premises is a fully equipped business center.

Chelsea Harbour, SW10 0XG. Tel: 823-3000; Fax: 351-6525; in U.S. and Canada, (800) 445-8667; in Australia, (008) 22-22-55. £229–£306.

▶ **Swiss Cottage Hotel.** Swiss Cottage is an area of North London close to Regent's Park that has a strong middle-European flavor to it. Many refugees from Central Europe have made their home here, and the main street, the Finchley Road, close to the Swiss Cottage tube station, reflects this with its wonderful Austrian and Hungarian pastry shops and cafés. This hotel, which from the outside looks like exactly what it is, namely four large converted London town houses, feels quite different once you step through the door. It is as though you have strayed into a Viennese sitting room. The hotel is family-run, and it certainly has a distinctive decor, with its heavy overstuffed furniture and intrusive wallpapers. But it has a loyal clientele that appreciates its eccentricities and undoubted character. It also has 24-hour room service, a dining room, and a bar.

4 Adamson Road, NW3 3HP. Tel: 722-2281; Fax: 483-4588. £85–£140 (includes full English breakfast).

Apartments

For those who'd rather look after themselves when they come to London, the answer is to rent a serviced apartment, of which there are many. Although they are not necessarily cheaper than hotels, you do get more space for your money. Here are some of the best.

▶ **Dolphin Square.** Not far from the Tate Gallery, this was the largest apartment complex in Europe when it was built in 1937, and it offers the widest range of apartments. They are perfectly adequate but definitely not in the luxury class, although the in-house facilities make up for this. There is a shopping arcade with butcher, grocer, ticket agency, two licensed bars, squash and tennis courts, gym, and a very good restaurant of the brasserie type that overlooks the large swimming pool. There is also a large central garden.

Chichester Street, Pimlico, SW1V 3LX. Tel: 834-3800; Fax: 798-8735. £115 per night.

▶ **Draycott House.** Just off Sloane Square, these exceedingly well designed apartments—always very popular—are temptingly close to the shops and restaurants of Knightsbridge and the King's Road in Chelsea.

10 Draycott Avenue, SW3 3AA. Tel: 584-4659; Fax: 225-3694; in U.S., (800) 448-4852. £840–£2,174 per week.

▶ **Durley House.** Excellently situated on Sloane Street between Chelsea and Knightsbridge, these apartments were taken over in 1989 by the ubiquitous Kemps of Dorset Square and Pelham Hotel fame, who are fast becoming the leading entrepreneurs in the small-hotel world of London. Refurbished to the Kemps' usual high standards, the formerly ramshackle Durley House is no longer recognizable. The only drawback to this sort of makeover is that such excellent service and comfort don't come cheap. (But included in these rates is the use of the tennis courts in Cadogan Square Gardens.)

115 Sloane Street, SW1X 9PT. Tel: 235-5537; Fax: 259-6977; in U.S., (800) 553-6674. One bedroom, £195–£300 per night; 2 bedrooms, £275 per night.

▶ **47 Park Street.** This is the place for those looking for unabashed luxury and privacy. Although Mayfair is synonymous with elegance, these sumptuous serviced apartments are the top of the tree. The entrance hall is commanded by a concierge who will look after you down to the smallest detail, and the in-house restaurant is none other than Michelin-starred **Le Gavroche**. Even breakfast, served in your suite, is a gastronomic delight.

47 Park Street, Mayfair, W1Y 4EB. Tel: 491-7282; Fax: 491-7282; in U.S. and Canada, (800) 637-7200. £284–£499 per night (suites only).

▶ **In the English Manner.** This firm offers more than 50 luxurious apartments in various areas and price ranges, in and around London. All are attractively furnished, and on arrival fresh flowers and breakfast provisions will be waiting for you.

Lancych, Boncath, Pembrokeshire SA37 0LJ. Tel: (02) 397-7444; Fax: (02) 397-7686; in U.S., Tel: (800) 422-0799, (510) 935-7065, or (213) 629-1811; Fax: (213) 689-8784; in Australia, (02) 957-4511. £360–£1,650 per week.

DINING

By Alex Hamilton and Susan Grossman

Alex Hamilton, formerly an executive in London's Central Meat Market, is now travel editor of the British daily The Guardian. *Susan Grossman is the editor of* The Best of Britain Guide *(American Express) and editor of* Upbeat *magazine.*

There is no single gourmet dining area in London, although Soho, shedding its red-light image, is becoming increasingly well endowed with decent eateries. Covent Garden, on the other hand, has more than its share of mediocre establishments that service a fast turnover of tired shoppers and hungry theatergoers.

Some of Britain's best chefs are firmly ensconced in the top hotels; others move around, taking with them a steady band of dedicated followers to unlikely backwaters of London. And while the city's ethnic restaurants have always been its most inexpensive, a number of Indian, Japanese, Chinese, Thai, and Lebanese establishments now offer some of the best food in the capital in fashionable designer settings. More than 100 national cuisines thrive in London restaurants, to the extent that some people say it is impossible to find native cooking. But that is not so.

As a rule, it is necessary to make reservations for good restaurants (and there is often an answering machine for the purpose). In a difficult economic period when it has been easier to list restaurants that have closed than to find new openings, some of the most expensive seem to be recession-proof. Top-line establishments such as Le Gavroche and One Ninety Queen's Gate, where you can

165

expect to pay £80 and £100 per person, respectively, are sometimes booked up to two, three, even six weeks ahead. However, cancellations tend to come through on the afternoon of the day itself.

The recession and fluctuations in currency exchange rates have made even more problematic the always difficult task of categorizing eating establishments by price. While prices at many London restaurants may seem unbelievably high to North Americans outside New York City, our categories reflect the way *the British* view the cost of dining out: A meal for one person (cover charge, appetizer, main course, dessert and coffee, tax and tip, but not wine) is "inexpensive" if the bill is less than £20; £20 to £40 is "moderate," and more than £40 is "expensive."

The following section describes London restaurants in all price ranges, serving all types of ethnic food, in all of London's diverse neighborhoods.

ENGLISH

Although plenty of restaurants, particularly in hotels, serve traditional British food of the roast beef and Yorkshire pudding variety, an increasing number offer a more modern approach, imaginatively combining ingredients and flavors and using the best of British produce.

Although they are listed elsewhere under Eclectic or Brasseries, Alastair Little's, Bibendum, and Kensington Place (all outstanding) also offer modern British dishes. The eponymous **Stephen Bull** does the same. Bull, one of London's most exciting chefs, changes his menu twice daily, and on it you will find some of the best examples of modern British cooking. Among outstanding dishes are fillets of John Dory (a white fish, brought in fresh from Cornwall) with a black olive butter; a twice-cooked goat's cheese soufflé; and a legendary "variations on a theme of chocolate." The simple decor—careful lighting and bare walls and floorboards—deliberately ensures there is no distraction from the food. For a lunch of, say, artichoke stuffed with anchovies, pork loin braised in milk, plus sweet, and coffee, estimate £30 a head. 5–7 Blandford Street off Marylebone High Street. Closed Saturday lunch and Sundays; dinner from 6:30 P.M. Tel: 486-9696.

Leith's occupies three Victorian houses knocked into one at 92 Kensington Park Road in Notting Hill. Prue Leith, the talented principal of Leith's School of Food and Wine, owns this establishment, which has been expensively equipped with French silver, English bone china, and Dartington glass. Swivel chairs make for relaxing dining, spotlights ensure that you can see how good the food is, and the Wagons Leith, trolleys for hors d'oeuvres and desserts, are outstanding. Dishes include charcoal-grilled rib of beef, ox tongue, and their unfussy like. There are also English cheeses, and herbs and vegetables from Prue's own farm in Gloucestershire, though the new chef, Alex Floyd, is trying to broaden the range and ever so gently to Frenchify the mix. Open 7:30–11:30 P.M. daily. Prices are moderate to expensive. Tel: 229-4481.

The **Tate Gallery restaurant** on Millbank, along the river near the north end of Vauxhall Bridge, is formal and rather expensive but well established. It serves lunch only (steak-and-kidney pie, roast beef, and various dishes made to old English recipes, such as trifle for dessert). Entrance is through the gallery (which is free); the restaurant is on the lower ground floor, with tables encircled by a Rex Whistler mural. The wine list has a fine reputation. Tel: 834-6754. Closed evenings and Sundays.

Roasts, bangers and mash (sausage and mashed potato), treacle tart, and spotted dick (suet pudding with raisins) are among the dishes to look for in the traditionally English establishments. No place does them better than the Connaught Hotel (part of the Savoy Group), on Carlos Place in Mayfair; see also the Savoy Grill in the Strand (both under Hotel Restaurants).

Simpson's-in-the-Strand (also part of the Savoy Group) has long been known—150 years—for its quintessentially English setting, club-like atmosphere, and traditional menu. There are several dining rooms with ornate ceilings, chandeliers, rich drapes, and original paintings, patronized by a host of civil servants. Roasts are carved from huge gleaming trolleys, and puddings include spotted dick and bread-and-butter pudding. 100 The Strand, WC2. Moderate; Tel: 836-9112.

Rules, 35 Maiden Lane, linking Bedford and Southampton streets just north of the Strand, is a venerable institution dating back some 190 years, with caricatures of celebrities across the years by such famous cartoonists as Spy and Deighton on the walls. There is a good choice of game in season (which begins August 12) and the traditional steak-and-kidney pie is swollen like a ripe melon. Prices are moderate. Open from noon to midnight; Tel: 836-5314.

In St. James's, **Green's Restaurant and Oyster Bar** on

Duke Street (Tel: 930-4566; closed Sunday evenings) is famous for its nursery food (bangers and mash, steak-and-kidney pie, fishcakes, and treacle tart) as well as for its oysters. Offers pre-theater suppers at moderate prices.

The chef at the **Greenhouse** (same ownership as the Capital Hotel), tucked away in a cobbled mews behind a privet hedge in London's West End, is Gary Rhodes, who won acclaim at the Castle Hotel at Taunton in Somerset. The food is of the salmon fishcakes, smoked haddock, Welsh rarebit, beef stew, and sticky toffee pudding variety, cooked with flair. Noisy, and popular with businesspeople for lunch. 27A Hay's Mews. Moderate; Tel: 499-3331.

At 21 Romilly Street in Soho, the **Lindsay House** attempts to make you feel as if you are a guest in a private town house: You ring the bell to enter, drink an aperitif in front of an open fire in the downstairs sitting room, and eat upstairs amid drapes, flounces, and flowers, from an elaborate and moderately priced 18th-century English menu that includes traditional English puddings. Even so, the place hasn't quite managed to exorcise the ghost of the Chinese restaurant that occupied these quarters before it. Open every day; dinner from 6:00 P.M. until midnight, 7:00 P.M. to 10:00 P.M. on Sundays. Moderate/expensive; Tel: 439-0450.

The Lindsay House has three sister restaurants: The **English House** (on Milner Street, off Cadogan Square; Tel: 584-3002) uses 18th-century recipes, with the emphasis on game. Moderate/expensive. The **English Garden** (on Lincoln Street, off the King's Road; Tel: 584-7272), in a terraced house on a residential street, with the main restaurant in a Victorian conservatory at the back, is somewhat less formal. Moderate. The third, **Waltons**, on Walton Street at Brompton Cross (Tel: 584-0204), is the flagship: an intimate, formal dining room, mirrored, draped, and filled with flowers. The food, like the waiters' accents, is English with a French influence. Moderate/expensive.

The **Dover Street Restaurant**, at 8 Dover Street in Mayfair, is neither fish nor fowl, neither restaurant nor wine bar nor jazz club, but a bit of each. They ask you to dress smartly and let you stay till 4:00 A.M., and the jive and jitterbug are lively enough to make the Anglo-Saxon meal acceptable. Prices are moderate. Music from 10:00 P.M.; Tel: 629-9813.

HOTEL RESTAURANTS

Some London hotels have excellent, if pricey, restaurants—though most are a better value at lunchtime. Recently there has been a considerable increase in the availability of prix-fixe lunches, and sometimes an option between the regular three-course menu and a less costly two-course offer. The following is a selection of the best.

The **Four Seasons**, at the Inn on the Park Hotel, overlooking Hyde Park near the western end of Piccadilly, is a palm-filled, rather fussy room in which the young Bruno Loubet offers *cuisine du terroir* (classic bourgeois cooking with modern touches) like his mother made back home in Bordeaux. He also highlights dishes that are low in cholesterol and sodium. Although the meals are expensive, there is a reasonable *menu du jour* at lunch. Tel: 499-0888.

Next door at the Inter-Continental on Hamilton Place, Peter Kromberg presides over the surprisingly small and intimate **Le Soufflé** restaurant on the ground floor. The menu is based on cuisines from around the world, and the dessert soufflés must be ordered in advance. Again, the set lunches represent good value. Moderate/expensive. Closed Saturday lunch; Tel: 409-3131.

Bernard Gaume, the resident chef at the Hyatt Carlton Tower, near Harvey Nichols at 2 Cadogan Place in Knightsbridge, is well respected for the French (but not nouvelle) cuisine he prepares for the **Chelsea Room**. The restaurant has a sunny conservatory overlooking the gardens of Cadogan Square, deep settees in an adjoining bar, and a moderately priced set lunch that includes half a bottle of wine (which is unusual for London). The **Rib Room** downstairs offers roasts and grills as well as a fine selection of seafood. Moderate/expensive; Tel: 235-5411.

When the Ladbroke Group acquired the Hilton chain it renamed its own hotels Hilton Nationals, distinguishing its new purchases as Hilton Internationals. London can now boast of having seven Hiltons, which vary in quality. Ladbroke has opened a big, new International, the Langham Hilton, to complement the one on Park Lane. The hotel is directly opposite the BBC's Broadcasting House on Portland Place. Eating here is a three-tier experience, from Continental breakfast in the **Palm Court**; a light but extravagant lunch on marble tables in the adjacent, crimson **Tsar's**, where they stock 40 kinds of vodka and specialize in caviars, smoked salmon, and Champagne; and dinner (which can be pre-theater from 6:00 P.M.) in the also adjacent **Memories of the British Empire**. Less British than Empire, it offers dishes from India, Malaysia, Hong Kong, and, rather strangely, Japan. Champagne and caviar apart, Memories is not too devastating in price: £30 per person might just see you through. Tel: 636-1000.

The **Oak Room** in the Meridien Piccadilly is a spacious and gracious dining room, almost overwhelmingly sumptuous in its decor, with huge gilt mirrors, chandeliers, and an accompanying pianist. Perhaps not the place for an intimate tête-à-tête, but the food is generally excellent (if pricey), and, again, at lunchtime there is an excellent *menu du jour.* Moderate; closed Saturday lunch and Sundays. Upstairs, the **Terrace Garden**, a split-level conservatory with huge glass windows overlooking Piccadilly, is one of the prettiest dining rooms in London. Here the varied menu includes vegetarian choices and simple salads as well as more expensive dishes, served to the accompaniment of piano music. Moderate/expensive. Open all day; Tel: 734-8000.

Probably the most consistently outstanding hotel dining room is the formal, wood-paneled, very English, and expensive **Connaught** on Mayfair's Carlos Place. Estimate £50 to £60 per person. The grill is closed on weekends; Tel: 491-0668. Over on the Strand, the **Savoy Grill** attracts businesspeople at lunchtime with a menu that includes English specialties such as jugged hare or Irish stew as well as French dishes. Pre-theater dinners from 6:00 P.M. A jacket and tie are the expected attire on weekends. Moderate/expensive. The hotel's **River Restaurant** is rather more ornate, with elaborate decor, classical columns, and lovely river views during the day. A band plays at night. The Grill room is closed for Saturday lunch and on Sundays. Expensive; Tel: 836-4343.

The more intimate **Claridge's** in Mayfair on Brook Street is popular with royalty. Here a Hungarian trio serenades waiting diners (take note if you hear "The Teddy Bear's Picnic"—it denotes the arrival of HRH The Princess Margaret). **The Causerie**, Claridge's other restaurant, is a lot less expensive and more informal (though you're just as likely to spot the royals), and offers an early buffet supper from 5:30 P.M., as well as a lunchtime smorgasbord. Expensive; Tel: 629-8860.

The French-Baroque Louis XVI dining room of the **Ritz Hotel** on Piccadilly at the northeastern edge of Green Park is an outstanding setting in which to dine, if rather formidable and expensive. It's also pleasant to take tea here. It has dancing, but only on Saturday nights. Tel: 493-8181.

On Park Lane at the eastern edge of Hyde Park, Forte's Grosvenor House Hotel boasts chef Nico Ladenis's creations at **Nico at Ninety**, a luxurious dining room filled with paintings and antiques and offering French cuisine of the highest quality that very nearly justifies the high prices. Couples may feel more comfortable dining here in the evening, as women are scarce among the expense-account crowd at lunch. Expensive. Closed Saturday lunch and Sundays; Tel: 499-6363.

The autumn of 1990 saw the reopening of the Dorchester Hotel next door, now owned by the sultan of Brunei, who has spent many millions on the renovations. Anton Mosimann's sous chef (Anton now runs his own club/restaurant) is in charge of the **Terrace** (live band nightly except Sundays) and the **Grill Room**, and the hotel has a new restaurant serving Cantonese food. Expensive. Tel: 629-8888.

The **Halkin** (Tel: 333-1000), just off Belgrave Square in Belgravia, is one of the few new arrivals on the scene, with cooking by Gualtiero Marchese from his own three-starred restaurant of that name in Milan. He strikes the middle way between French and Italian cooking, and offers Milanese specials like breaded veal and risotto with saffron. Closed Sundays. Initial impressions are good, based on a three-course set menu at £21.

The **Capital**, near Harrods on Basil Street, has a small (12 tables), French-style, highly regarded dining room with a set lunchtime menu that is a good value at £20. In the evening last orders are at 11:15, just about manageable for after-theater dinners. Moderate; Tel: 589-5171.

Of the rest, the Westbury's **Polo Room** on the corner of Bond Street and Conduit Street in Mayfair, is intimate and elegant, and good for people-watching, especially at lunch. Moderate/expensive; Tel: 629-7755. The St. James's Court Hotel, south of Buckingham Palace on Buckingham Gate, has several restaurants, including the French **Auberge de Provence**. Modeled after the Oustaù de Baumanière in France, the restaurant is unfortunately a somewhat drab re-creation (white-washed vaulted ceilings and tiles), but the food imaginatively captures the flavor of Provence. The Auberge has dropped its à la carte menu in favor of an amplified choice of prix-fixe menus at £24. Closed Saturday lunch and Sundays. Tel: 834-6655. In Hyde Park you can see Rotten Row from the elegant **Park Room** of the

Hyde Park Hotel. The menu is Mediterranean; tea is also served. Moderate/expensive; Tel: 235-4552.

Over in Holland Park, the Halcyon Hotel's dining room—**Room at the Halcyon**—is an airy lower-ground terrace, with a golden York stone floor. Excellent value set menus, with breakfasts from 7:00 A.M. and a Sunday brunch from 7:00 A.M. to 4:00 P.M. Moderate; Tel: 221-5411.

The Conrad, London's first all-suite hotel, opened in 1989. On the river at Chelsea Harbour, it offers a good Champagne Sunday brunch buffet (with amplified live music) at which you can help yourself to anything from sausage and eggs to an excellent fish stew or roast beef and Yorkshire pudding. Generally the style is international, with three-course weekday set lunches in the **Brasserie** at £18, and access to tables outside on the terrace with lovely harbor views. Moderate; Tel: 823-3000.

FISH

Restaurants that specialize in fish are becoming increasingly popular in London. A south-of-France atmosphere prevails in Pierre Martin's fish restaurants (he also has one in Villefranche on the Côte d'Azur). The simple, crowded **Le Suquet**, 104 Draycott Avenue at Brompton Cross in South Kensington, is popular with celebrities who don't mind rolling up their sleeves and tucking in to £30's worth of seafood centered on the vast *plateau de fruits de mer.* Open every day of the week. Tel: 581-1785.

La Croisette, 168 Ifield Road (running past the cemetery into the Old Brompton Road—look for the awning), was the first of Martin's London restaurants to open. Ring and you will be ushered into a crowded basement where London's French come for the prix-fixe menu and to socialize over the enormous cork platters loaded with crab, langoustines, winkles, oysters, and mussels. La Croisette is 100 percent French, down to the youthful staff in Cannes tee-shirts, the paintings of the Mediterranean, and the unsalted butter. Closed Sundays, Mondays, and Tuesdays and throughout August. Moderate; Tel: 373-3694.

At Martin's **Le Quai St. Pierre**, 7 Stratford Road just off the Earl's Court Road, you can sit at the counter under a huge umbrella or at a table in the only slightly more formal dining room up the spiral staircase. What this place lacks in finesse it makes up for in atmosphere. Closed all day Sunday and Monday lunch. Moderate; Tel: 937-6388.

La Croisette is best for an intimate evening, Le Quai St. Pierre more fun if you're with a group, Le Suquet if you like star-spotting. All are excellent value for the money.

Manzi's, on Leicester Street on the north side of Leicester Square, is an old favorite that's always busy and always noisy. The fish is of the freshest, and arrives largely unadorned other than with tartar sauce and a basket full of chips. Dinner is served from 5:30 P.M. Moderate/expensive. Tel: 734-0224.

With its long, narrow room reminiscent of a turn-of-the-century railway carriage, and its marble-topped oyster bar (popular at lunchtime) and discreet cushion-filled alcoves divided by etched-glass screens, the Savoy Group-owned **Wilton's**, on Jermyn Street opposite Hilditch & Key, is a London institution. In the oyster season, which starts September 1, about 500 oysters a day are consumed on the premises, either at lunch or as a pre-theater snack, and most are washed down with Champagne. Dishes are simply cooked and dispensed by matronly, rather awe-inspiring waitresses in long white overalls. Wilton's specializes in game in season and traditional English "savouries" such as anchovies on toast and Welsh rarebit. Expensive; Tel: 629-9955.

Another famous oyster-and-Champagne bar is **Green's Restaurant and Oyster Bar**, on Duke Street off Jermyn Street in St. James's. The **Greenhouse** oyster-and-Champagne bar, 16 Royal Exchange (next to the Bank of England in the heart of the City), is a sibling of Green's. It is the smallest restaurant in London, like a front room, a mere 18 × 16 of square footage. Out of season it keeps its oyster-mad City patrons going with cultivated Irish rock oysters (at £4.20 a half dozen) until September brings in the native bivalves at £10 to £15 a half dozen. It is open weekdays only from 11:00 A.M. to 8:30 P.M.; Tel: 929-3131.

Of course, the majority of London restaurants, large and small, cheap and expensive, have a fish element on their menu, leading with Dover sole, cod, finnan haddock, and scampi. The preparation in recent times has become both more sophisticated and healthier, except, that is, in the fish-and-chip shops (known as chippers or chippies), where the batter still oozes the oil in which the cod, plaice, rock salmon (another term for dogfish), and haddock are fried. But these, plus a bagful of chipped potatoes, remain a cheap (£2 or £3) staple for many, along with the breaded chicken joints, saveloys (battered sausages), meat pies, and fish croquettes that share their display space. Rare in the very heart of the city, genuine fish-and-chip shops can still be found on, to name a few locales, Cleveland and Baker streets in the West End, and off such central street markets as Rupert Street, Brewer Street, Exmouth Market, and Portobello Road. They tend to close in the early evening. A cut above the rest is **Fryer's Delight**, at 19 Theobold's Road, opposite the corner of Lamb's Conduit Street. It makes no difference to the Englishness that most of the fryers are Italian, and a good piece of fish can be had for £2.50. Also try the **Upper Street Fish Shop** in Islington, at 324 Upper Street; it's a bit more expensive at £5, but there are good, strong benches to sit on. Open from 5:30 to 10:00 P.M.

FRENCH

A few of London's restaurants regularly receive the highest accolades from the food critics. As well as several in hotels (see Hotel Restaurants), the following are among the outstanding: **Le Gavroche**, 43 Upper Brook Street in Mayfair (Tel: 408-0881), owned by the famous Albert Roux (whose brother Michel has the Waterside Inn in Bray) is very expensive. You can spend a minimum of £60 for a meal without wine, and other choices go to £200, but £80 per person is a fair average. There is a more affordable lunch menu. Book two weeks in advance and, if frustrated, try again on the day you hope to go. **La Tante Claire**, 68 Royal Hospital Road, in Chelsea (Tel: 352-6045), is run by Pierre Koffmann (famous for his £23 dish of pig's trotters, which he stuffs with wood mushrooms) and offers a good set lunch for the same money. **Nico Central**, 35 Great Portland Street, a stone's throw from Oxford Street near Oxford Circus, with its largely classical French menu, has been satisfying its discerning followers for years. The food here is simply outstanding and presented flawlessly. A meal is an almost theatrical experience, and the prix-fixe lunch menu at £27 is an especially good value. Expensive, but the menu is à la carte, so you could just order a main dish and a glass of wine. Tel: 436-8846. (Chef Nico Ladenis now holds court primarily at Nico at Ninety in the Forte Grosvenor House Hotel; see Hotel Restaurants, above.)

All three of the above places are expensive, are closed weekends, and need booking well in advance.

Nico's original premises at 48A Rochester Row in Westminster are now **Simply Nico**, which offers an informal brasserie-style experience with a reasonably priced set menu (£24). Open every day except Sunday, with dinner served from 6:00 P.M.; Tel: 630-8061.

Le Bistro Carapace was until recently Le Mazarin. It consists of a series of alcoves leading off a main dining area in an elegant pink basement at 30 Winchester Street, just beyond Victoria Coach Station. The new owner has retained some of the former kitchen staff, who prepare exquisite sauces from quality ingredients, and a Mediterranean style accentuates the bistro presentation. The menu has been shortened and prices reduced to a moderate level. Closed Sunday evenings; Tel: 828-3366.

Le Boulestin, in the basement of 1A Henrietta Street, Covent Garden (south of the Piazza and opposite the Jubilee Market), opened in the 1920s. While the food is classic French, the decor is Edwardian country home, with banquette seating, heavy drapes, marbled pillars, and horsey paintings. Service is formal (the sommelier even makes a fuss over the mineral water), it has recently introduced a good prix-fixe menu at £19, and it stays open late for after-theater dining. Closed Sundays; Tel: 836-7061.

Worth trying if you're in the Southwark area, is **La Truffe Noire**, 29 Tooley Street, which, in a change of ownership to M. Ahmed, acquired Pascal Lucas and his Belgian cuisine in this formerly Parisian-styled dining room, opposite the gruesome London Dungeon, near London Bridge. The prix fixe is £15. Closed Sundays; Tel: 378-0621.

The St. Quentin restaurants in Knightsbridge are owned in part by the Savoy Group. The **St. Quentin**, a bustling, elegant French establishment on two floors at 243 Brompton Road (opposite the Brompton Oratory), serves a reasonable prix-fixe lunch at £15. Moderate; Tel: 589-8005. The **Grill St. Quentin**, 2 Yeoman's Row off Brompton Road (past the Bunch of Grapes pub), occupies a huge, bright, and warmly lit basement reminiscent of La Coupole in Paris. Open all day for snacks. Closed Sundays but the brasserie stays open. Moderate; Tel: 581-8377.

You can also eat inexpensive French food in London's numerous brasseries (see Brasseries and Cafés).

ITALIAN

Italian food is becoming increasingly fashionable in London, and as a consequence more expensive. Currently the Italian restaurants not only to be seen in, but also to experience authentic cooking in, are Cibo, Orso, and the River Café.

Cibo, in a backwater of Kensington west of Holland Park at 3 Russell Gardens (use Kensington Olympia Underground station), opened in September 1989 and met with immediate success. Authentic peasant food (in enormous quantities) is served on colorful earthenware pottery against a backdrop of modern art, which includes a three-dimensional "Giorgioni" look-alike. Cibo is noisy, somewhat cramped, and fairly expensive (about £30 per person). Try the risotto and the *zabaglione alla frutta*. Closed Sunday evenings; Tel: 371-6271.

Orso, 27 Wellington Street in Covent Garden, a sister to Joe Allen's around the corner, is a dimly lit, noisy, cavernous basement, vaguely 1950s in design, that is popular with media people. Pizzas and pastas are served here along with risottos and pork dishes. The £10 suckling pig offer is hugely popular and tends to run out by 9:00 P.M. The entrance is a dark doorway just north of the Aldwych. Open noon to midnight every day; no credit cards. Moderate; Tel: 240-5269.

It is well worth the effort to find the **River Café**, on Thames Wharf, Rainville Road, between Putney and Hammersmith bridges. Part of a complex of converted warehouses, it overlooks a relatively undeveloped stretch of the Thames. Run by Rose Gray and Ruthie Rogers, the kitchen is open to the dining area, the tables are black and square, and the chairs wicker and steel. The food is authentic regional Italian, with an emphasis on Tuscan cuisine. There are tables outside in summer. Open for dinner weekdays only, with last orders at 9:30 P.M., also Saturday and Sunday lunch. Moderate; Tel: 381-8824 or 385-3344.

There are any number of old-school Italian trattorias in London. One of the most fashionable is **San Lorenzo**, around the corner from Harrods at 22 Beauchamp Place, popular with Princess Di and others, who eat pasta among the potted plants and exchange the sort of gossip that columns are made of. Estimate £45 per person; closed Sundays. Tel: 584-1074. **Santini**, 29 Ebury Street near Victoria Station, attracts businesspeople at lunchtime with its set menu at £19. It is ultrasmart, quietish, and airy; the menu hovers around the Veneto. Tel: 730-4094. Santini's newer sister restaurant, **L'Incontro**, 87 Pimlico Road in Belgravia, also specializes in the cuisine of the Veneto at similar prices (set lunches £19; average with à la carte £35). Closed Sunday lunch. A pianist plays every evening except Sundays. Tel: 730-6327.

San Martino, on Chelsea's fashionable Walton Street, is unusual in that Martino grows his own vegetables and herbs (at home and in the restaurant's window boxes), including black cabbage for the minestrone and arugula for the salads. He also makes his own *bresaola* and specializes in his native Tuscan dishes as well as game in season. The place is small—only 12 tables—and can be as inexpensive as £12 a head. From about August 15 Martino makes a point of offering game, successively grouse, partridge, snipe, and woodcock. Reservations only on the day. Tel: 589-1356.

Few London restaurants offer more than a couple of tables for eating outside in summer, but **La Famiglia**, opposite the World's End pub on Chelsea's Langton Street, has a large, plant-filled courtyard (seating 100) strung with lights. It is cheerful and popular with Chelsea residents, but there is no awning—if it rains the water may get in your soup. Last orders at 11:45 P.M. Inexpensive; Tel: 351-0761.

Bertorelli's, on Floral Street opposite the stage door of the Royal Opera House in Covent Garden, offers reasonably priced regional dishes, pasta, and light snacks in a café/wine bar downstairs. Average for three courses, £18. Open for lunch and dinner until 11:30 P.M. Closed Sundays; Tel: 836-1868.

Don't let the refined Edwardian atmosphere fool you: **Kettners**, at 29 Romilly Street, is actually a branch of Pizza Express. The Champagne bar, a fashionable Soho meeting place, is open until 11:00 P.M. Prices average around £15, with a nice house wine at £7.50. There is a cocktail pianist every evening and on Thursday and Friday at lunch. Tel: 734-6112.

The other members of the same chain, **Pizza Express** on Dean Street, Soho (Tel: 437-9595), **Pizza on the Park** at Hyde Park Corner (Tel: 235-5550), and **Pizza Condotti** in Mayfair, at 4 Mill Street, off Conduit Street (Tel: 499-1308), have live jazz, which is otherwise not very common (see Pubs, Nightlife, and Entertainment).

AMERICAN

Many of what are assumed to be standard American dishes, such as T-bone steaks and ribs, are incorporated into general menus in London, especially at the proliferating chains of steak houses. Again, the American influence is widespread among the fast-food outlets and the fried chicken and hamburger counters, which are cheap, efficient, hygienic—and mundane. If you're in the mood for a less routine hamburger, the place to go is the **Hard Rock Café**, at the Hyde Park Corner end of Old Park Lane—that is, if you can stand loud music and don't mind sharing a table or lining up to get in. In Soho, **Ed's Easy Diner**, a small, neon-lit café wedged into the corner of Old Compton Street and Moor Street, serves quick, 100 percent additive-free burgers and soda. In the jukeboxes on the counter, 5p buys 1950s rock and roll. There is also a branch on the King's Road at number 362.

Joe Allen's, in a brick basement at 13 Exeter Street just behind Covent Garden, livens up with a theatrical crowd late at night. Tel: 836-0651.

The **Rock Island Diner** on the top floor of the London Pavilion at Piccadilly Circus is a huge 1950s-style eatery with a Chevy suspended over the bar. The DJ plays period music, there's a roller-skating mâitre d', and food is of the meatloaf and steak sandwich variety. Open seven days a week, 11:00 A.M. to 11:30 P.M. No need to reserve ahead, but you may have to stand in line. While you're here you might want to visit the Rock Circus, Madame Tussaud's newest animatronic homage to well-known stars of the rock-'n'-roll era, though you have to be well over 30 really to enjoy it.

Adjacent to the London Pavilion is the Trocadero Centre, now home to **Planet Hollywood**, which opened in 1993 amid a blaze of publicity guaranteed by its brawny owners, Sylvester Stallone, Arnold Schwarzenegger, and Bruce Willis. The food is all-American in the Hard Rock Café tradition, and, also in the Hard Rock fashion, you'll have to wait on line to get in.

Old Orleans, 29 Wellington Street, the Covent Garden branch of a chain of 14 restaurants, is perkier than this fact suggests, and attractively offers such fare as ribs, alligator dips, and gumbo. Estimate £10 a head; Tel: 497-2433.

All the above are inexpensive. Definitely expensive, though, is **Christopher's—The American Grill**, at 18 Wellington Street in Covent Garden, opened in 1992 by an Englishman with a passion for New England food. Maine lobster, clam chowder, and "New England Boiled Dinner" of salt beef and vegetables are permanent features on the menu; Tel: 240-4222.

At **Clarke's**, 124 Kensington Church Street, you don't get a choice on the evening menus. However, whatever comes out of the basement kitchen, which you can view from the dining room, is good. The menu, which changes nightly, leads with dishes from California, France, and Italy, supported by Sally Clarke's homegrown fruit and vegetables. Expensive. Closed weekends; Tel: 221-9225.

BRASSERIES AND CAFÉS

Brasseries and cafés are usually cheaper than more formal restaurants, and many serve meals—which tend to lean toward French cuisine—from breakfast onward.

Currently popular with Londoners is **Kensington Place**, 201–205 Kensington Church Street, west of Kensington Gardens, the noisy Continental sister of the more formal Launceston Place. Revolving doors lead to a high-tech glass-fronted brasserie that specializes in exciting and unfussy European dishes featuring the freshest of ingredients. It is moderately priced (estimate £20 per person) and always crowded. Open every day from noon to midnight; Tel: 727-3184.

The Continental-style **Soho Brasserie** at 23 Old Compton Street offers typically French dishes such as fish soup, as well as snacks at the long bar (which is a popular drinking venue). On summer evenings when the restaurant gets crowded, the full-length doors are opened and patrons spill out onto the sidewalk. Open noon until 11:30 P.M.; on Sundays there is a special offer of Norfolk oysters at £3 a half dozen. Inexpensive/moderate. Tel: 439-9301.

Off Piccadilly, **Langan's Brasserie** on Stratton Street near Green Park is always crowded (but it's big so you can usually get in). The two floors are jammed with splendid paintings, lots of large round tables, and a regular influx of conversation stoppers, including the occasional entertainers (Michael Caine is one of the owners). Upstairs is quieter but doesn't serve their famous spinach soufflé—it would go flat on its journey up from the basement. To compensate, the upper floor has its own exclusives. The extensive menu offers dishes, including daily specials, of variable quality, and the service can be interminably slow. But you shouldn't leave London without eating here at least once. Moderate/expensive. Open Monday through Friday, 12:30 P.M. to 2:45 P.M. and 7:00 P.M. to 11:45 P.M.; Saturdays, 8:00 P.M. to 12:45 A.M. Live band after 9:00 P.M.

Tel: 493-6437. Booking ahead up to six weeks is encouraged, but call on the day you want to go, as some bookings may have been cancelled.

Le Caprice, on Arlington Street in Mayfair, is chic, stylish, and frequented by stars. Reserve well ahead, unless your name alone will get you in. The decor features lots of black, white, and chrome, with David Bailey photos on the walls. Simple snacks and meals for the diet-conscious are served from 6:00 P.M. until midnight; brunch on Sundays until 3:00 P.M. Open every day of the year, including bank holidays. Moderate/expensive; Tel: 629-2239.

Joe's Café, on Draycott Avenue at Brompton Cross, opposite the Conran Shop, is very stylish and about as far removed from an ordinary café as you can get. Waiters sport black waistcoats and white shirts that match the black-and-white decor and black-and-white tagliatelle. The lunch menu includes salads, bagels, and a few hot dishes. Evening meals are more formal, though still quite inexpensive. The bar is open weekdays from 6:00 P.M. to 9:00 P.M.; otherwise, you have to eat. It also serves Saturday breakfast and brunch on Sundays. Moderate; Tel: 225-2217.

The **Emporio Armani Express**, 191 Brompton Road, a couple of blocks down from Harrods (Tel: 823-8818), is as smart as the clothes it sells. Armani worked closely with his architect on the design, hence the elegant bone-handled monogrammed cutlery and the Armani eagle on every table. Long and thin like a railway carriage, the moderately priced restaurant serves modern Italian dishes, snacks such as *crostini* or *foccaccia*, as well as cakes, teas, and espresso during store hours: Monday through Saturday, 10:00 A.M. to 6:00 P.M. (7:00 P.M. Wednesdays).

Casper's Restaurant at 6 Tenterden Street off Hanover Square (Tel: 493-7923) is a gimmick that works. Modern European food is served (warm, not hot) in Chinese-style wicker *dim sum* baskets stacked high, dishes piled one on top of the other. Try the monkfish casserole with fennel potatoes or the salmon carpaccio with guacamole. If you can't decide, choose a five-course "multi-storey" at £14. For children there's a three-course "fairy storey" at half price (and even a "baby storey" at £4). Moderate prices and an animated, lively atmosphere. Open seven days a week from noon to midnight; Tel: 371-9673.

The **Café Kensington** (Tel: 938-2211), on the site of the former barracks in Lancer Square at the bottom of Kensington Church Street, is a good stop for lunch. The head chef is from Clarke's up the road. Guitar, blues, or jazz background music, and a cruise-liner feel; there are tables outside for dining in fine weather. Open daily until midnight. Moderate.

In St. James's, south of Piccadilly, **Fortnum & Mason's Fountain Restaurant** (entrance on Jermyn Street) has always been popular for tea. Frequented by elegant shoppers, the restaurant is open all day and also serves salads, ice cream, grills, and light meals until 11:00 P.M. (closed Sundays). There is also a more formal restaurant on the fourth floor that is open during store hours. Moderate.

Visitors to the British Museum should search out the tiny, reasonably priced, but unlicensed **Museum Street Café**, a few hundred yards south of the museum. It's unlicensed, so you can bring your own wine. The menu is short and the dishes mostly char-grilled or roasted without sauces. It doesn't take credit cards and isn't open on weekends. Tel: 405-3211.

The **Blueprint Café** on the first floor of the Design Museum at Butler's Wharf on the south bank of the Thames is too expensive to be a real café, though the atmosphere is stylishly informal. Owned by Conran, Blueprint has a menu that changes daily. There are stunning views of Tower Bridge and the Thames from the highly sought-after tables on the outside terrace in summer. Lunchtimes are packed. Estimate about £20 a head and another £10 for the house wine. Closed Sundays; Tel: 378-7031.

ECLECTIC

A growing number of London chefs take their inspiration from several countries; on the same menu you may find dishes from Europe, America, and the Far East.

One of London's most accomplished yet modest chefs is Alastair Little, who runs a stylized, simple, monochrome café to which he's given his name on Soho's Frith Street. With its black lacquered tables, bright lighting, and rather stark decor, at first glance **Alastair Little's** looks like a Japanese restaurant. Actually, you might get something vaguely Chinese from the menu . . . or French, or Danish, or modern British—whatever captures the chef's fancy. Little changes his menu twice daily, and his imaginative dishes are considered to be some of the most exciting in London. Estimate £50 per head plus drinks. Lunch from noon to 3:00 P.M., dinner from 6:00 P.M. to 11:30 P.M.

Closed Saturday lunch and Sundays. There's also a small downstairs bar where patrons can order lighter meals. Tel: 734-5183.

The Ivy, 1 West Street just off the Charing Cross Road on the western edge of Covent Garden, is wedged into a corner opposite the St. Martin's Theatre, where Agatha Christie's play *The Mousetrap* is in its 42nd year. New chef Nigel Davis, whose pedigree includes Le Manoir de Quat' Saisons, is restoring some of The Ivy's former glory with his Cumberland sausages, salmon fishcakes, and braised oxtail, and at much lower prices (three courses at about £25). Open seven days a week; last orders are at midnight. Moderate; Tel: 836-4751.

Renowned chef Simon Hopkinson, who has no patience with nouvelle cuisine, is at the helm of the spacious, bright dining room of **Bibendum**, on the first floor of the Michelin Building on the Fulham Road in South Kensington. Elegant and fashionable in an Art Nouveau building, Bibendum attracts serious food lovers and celebrities. The menu is mostly expensive (estimate £40 per person but with a set menu at £24, though lunch is more of a bargain—try the fish and chips), and spans the cuisines of France, Italy, and Britain. Tel: 581-5817.

One Ninety Queen's Gate, near the Albert Hall, was conceived as a restaurant/club for chefs and is now a gourmet club run by a committee of famous chefs. Open to the public, it is discreetly hidden behind an elegant stuccoed façade. Inside, there are cherubs on the ceiling in the entrance hall, a comfortable wood-paneled bar on the ground floor, and several intimate, slightly decadent boudoir-style dining rooms downstairs. The food is "gutsy" and the portions generous. Chef Anthony Worrall-Thompson may offer stuffed pig's trotters or tripe, as well as unusual combinations such as mullet served with white beans and duck foie gras. Prices are very high—perhaps £95 to £120 per person—but the ambience makes it ideal for a romantic dinner for two. The restaurant also offers a remarkably cheap executive lunch. Worrall-Thompson is also cooking for the cheaper **Bistrot 190** on the ground floor of the newly revamped Gore Hotel next door (see Early and Late). Worrall-Thompson has opened yet a third restaurant in the same location, **Downstairs at 190**, specializing in fish at moderate prices. Downstairs is closed Sundays; the Bistrot is open 7:00 A.M. to midnight seven days a week; the restaurant closes for Saturday dinner and Sundays. Expensive; Tel: 581-5666.

Dell'Ugo, at 56 Frith Street, another Worrall-Thompson creation, was one of the most acclaimed openings in recession-hit London last year. It offers a mixture of all the styles of the Mediterranean, sometimes on the same plate, with very generous portions. Inexpensive to moderate; Tel: 734-8300.

With the backing of 13 shareholder friends, chef Bryan Webb bought **Hilaire's** at 68 Old Brompton Road, opposite Christie's, from Trusthouse Forte, and has installed highly imaginative modern British as well as European dishes on his menu. The upstairs street-level room is small and has cool green walls, paddle fans, and deferential service. The downstairs basement area is more intimate. The set menu is reasonably priced at £20 for lunch and £26.50 in the evening. Closed Saturday lunch and Sundays; Tel: 584-8993.

Also see the South of the River section below, and Stephen Bull in the English section above for other eclectic selections.

EARLY AND LATE

Apart from brasseries, which serve meals all day, most London restaurants don't start serving until 7:30 P.M. and stop at 11:00 P.M., so you have to make plans if you want to eat before or after the theater, unless you fancy Chinese and ethnic food (many of these restaurants often stay open very late). In most theaters the curtain goes up at 7:30 or 8:00 P.M. and comes down at around 10:30.

Some theaters and concert halls have their own restaurants. These include Ovations, with meals before and after performances in the South Bank Centre (Tel: 928-3531), the Mermaid, the Barbican, the Palace Theatre, the Young Vic in Lambeth, and the Camden Arts Centre. Theater menus are usually inexpensive, but there is often enough range of offerings to build up an impressive bill. Many theaters have sandwiches and coffee available in the bar, and the Royal Opera House offers moderately priced buffets at curtain fall.

In Covent Garden, the French **Café du Jardin**, 28 Wellington Street, serves a pre- and post-theater supper from 5:30 P.M. to 11:30 P.M. Royal Opera House patrons, rather more formally attired than the rest of the clientele, wander in clutching their programs, and waiters wend their way between tables balancing trays of Cognac. Choose the ground floor to be seen, downstairs to get on with it.

The food, though inexpensive, is as erratic as the service. Tel: 836-8769.

Magno's, around the corner on Long Acre, is rather more formal but also relatively inexpensive, and its pre-theater menu of simple, quick dishes that change weekly is an especially good buy. Tel: 836-6077. On nearby St. Martin's Lane, the enormous and inexpensive **Café Pelican** (Tel: 379-0309) stays open until after 1:00 A.M. Almost next door, **Café Flo** has an excellent menu and attracts the early dining set. Inexpensive; Tel: 836-8289.

Rules (see English), 35 Maiden Lane, just north of the Strand, serves traditional English food in a decor to match, and is open from noon to midnight. Moderate; Tel: 836-5314. **Le Boulestin** (see French), 1A Henrietta Street, also welcomes late diners. Moderate; Tel: 836-7061.

The **Savoy Grill**, in the famous luxury hotel off the Strand, is within walking distance of the theaters and offers a pre-theater menu. Moderate/expensive. After the show you can go back for dessert and coffee in the Thames Foyer. Jackets and ties are required in both places. Closed Sundays; Tel: 836-4343. If you don't meet the dress code at the Grill, **Upstairs at the Savoy** will serve you relatively inexpensive snacks, oysters, Champagne, and vintage wines by the glass from noon to midnight weekdays, and 5:00 P.M. to midnight Saturdays (closed Sundays). You can sit at the marble counter or at one of the tables along a narrow corridor, from which you'll have a fascinating view of people arriving at the front entrance. It also offers a breakfast buffet on weekdays (8:00 A.M. to 10:00 A.M.). Also handy for theaters with early evening curtains are: **Alastair Little's** bar (see Eclectic); **Orso** (Italian); and **Manzi's** (Fish).

Le Caprice, on Arlington Street in Mayfair, is open from 6:00 P.M. to midnight daily, even on holidays, as is **Kensington Place** (see Brasseries and Cafés, above). The **Causerie** at Claridge's in Mayfair has an early buffet supper from 5:30 P.M. You can get reasonably priced snacks at **Fields**, a restaurant/coffee bar in the crypt of St. Martin-in-the-Fields church on Trafalgar Square until 8:30 P.M.

The **Terrace Garden** at Le Meridien hotel is open every day from 7:00 A.M. to 11:30 P.M. for an inexpensive breakfast, lunch, or dinner, a light French snack, or tea. In this spectacular conservatory overlooking Piccadilly, a harpist plays at tea, a pianist most evenings (see Hotel Restaurants).

The **Limelight**, previously a disco and nightclub on the

site of a former church at 136 Shaftesbury Avenue (near Cambridge Circus; Tel: 434-0572), is now four separate dining, dancing, and drinking areas. The Late Supper Club has live music from 10:30 P.M. to 3:00 A.M. There is also the Gallery Bar serving cocktails and lighter dishes.

Brown's in Albemarle Street, behind Bond Street, is one of the Forte hotels. It serves tea or high tea from 4:15 P.M. to 5:45 P.M. (salmon fishcakes, griddles, and scones with clotted cream). Moderate; Tel: 493-6020.

Bistrot 190, an elegant high-ceilinged room on the ground floor of the Gore Hotel on leafy Queen's Gate, around the corner from the Albert Hall, stays open until midnight. The "Mediterranean"-style food (charcuterie with homemade pickles, *bollito misto,* Toulouse sausages with mashed potatoes) is prepared by chef Anthony Worrall-Thompson, who also owns the successful One Ninety Queen's Gate next door. The room is bright, airy, and faintly colonial in style; there are vases of herbs and virgin olive oil on each table and you can help yourself to bread and olives. Expensive; Tel: 581-5666. (See Eclectic, above.)

Across Waterloo Bridge on the South Bank, **RSJ,** in a converted hayloft behind the National Theatre at 13A Coin Street, is a restaurant that offers imaginative French dishes. Prix-fixe menu or à la carte. Open for lunch and from 6:00 P.M., with last orders at 11:00 P.M.; closed Sundays. Moderate; Tel: 928-4554.

Lakorn Thai at 179 Rosebery Avenue (north of Holborn) opens at 6:00 P.M. for pre-theater meals, particularly for Sadler's Wells, which is just up the road; in fact, the restaurant used to be called the Ballerina. Moderate; closed Sundays. Tel: 837-5048.

ETHNIC

Indian

Some of London's best Indian restaurants are also some of its most unpretentious, but those of the new school have turned up the lights, spruced up the decor, and begun to offer cocktails as well as beer with their curries. Heading the list of these upscale Indian restaurants are the **Last Days of the Raj** at 22 Drury Lane, which has North Indian cooking, reinforced with vegetarian dishes from the south (Tel: 836-1628), and **Lal Qila** nearby at 117 Tottenham Court Road (Tel: 387-4570). Both are moderately priced and offer North Indian cuisine.

A real find for the vegetarian who likes curries: the scrupulous and imaginative cooking at **Rani**, at 7 Long Lane, near Smithfield Market. Moderate; closed Saturday lunch. Tel: (081) 349-4386. For South Indian cooking of the state of Kerala at unpretentious prices, it is hard to improve on the **Ragam**, a small, fairly recent arrival with a friendly, busy atmosphere at 57 Cleveland Street, which runs parallel to and west of Charlotte Street. Tel: 636-9098.

At the **Bombay Brasserie** in Bailey's Hotel on Courtfield Close, 140 Gloucester Road in South Kensington, the decor is impressively colonial in style—chandeliers, ferns, a conservatory, paddle fans, and a white piano. You can sample food from all over India here; Tandoori dishes are the real strength, and, as at many Indian restaurants, the buffet lunches are a good value. Moderate/expensive. Tel: 370-4040.

Chinese

London's Chinatown, where you'll find most of the city's best Chinese restaurants, is south of Shaftesbury Avenue on and around Gerrard Street, in Soho. **Fung Shing** on nearby Lisle Street (Tel: 437-1539) and **Wong Kei** on Wardour Street (Tel: 437-3071) are authentic old-school Cantonese establishments. Wong Kei is inexpensive, and Fung Shing offers, in addition to a very full à la carte miscellany, a six-dish menu for two at £21, seven dishes for three at £35, and eight dishes for four at £46.

You can get some of London's best wind-dried food (a Chinese process of hanging out food to dry naturally) at the ever-popular **Poons**, 4 Leicester Street (Tel: 437-1528), as well as at the vast **Chuen Cheng Ku**, 17 Wardour Street (it's been there 20 years or so; Tel: 437-4433), and **New World**, on Gerrard Place (Tel: 734-0677). **Yung's**, on Wardour Street, is open from 4:00 P.M. until 4:00 A.M. (Tel: 437-4986). No need to reserve a table at any of the above. Each of these restaurants offers a choice of items that can make for an inexpensive or a moderate bill.

London's first formal Chinese restaurant was **Ken Lo's Memories of China**, on Ebury Street near Victoria Station; Tel: 730-7734. A second branch with the same name overlooks the boats in Chelsea Harbour and, unlike most other Chinese restaurants in the city, offers a varied menu, an inexpensive brasserie, and Sunday brunch. Two floors, with "Ming dynasty" gold-and-blue decor. A pianist plays on Friday and Saturday, and jazz has been introduced on Sundays. Estimate £25 per person. You can arrive by Riverbus (from the Embankment) or via Lots Road. Moderate; Tel: 352-4953.

For beautifully presented Chinese food and a backdrop of cascading water, try **Zen** in Chelsea Cloisters on Sloane Avenue (Tel: 589-1781) or **Zen Central**, 20 Queen Street off Curzon Street in Mayfair (Tel: 629-8089). Both attract a fashionable clientele, including many Chinese. (There's a third branch in Hampstead; see below.) All have fountains and set menus at £28, with set-price big feasts at £33.

Thai

It's well worth the journey out to the Fulham Broadway (south of Earl's Court on the Underground District Line) for a meal at the **Blue Elephant** restaurant, which is almost opposite the Underground station at 4–5 Fulham Broadway. Here, in an exotic setting of ferns and bamboo, an ever-smiling staff expertly presents moderately priced Thai dishes and beautifully sculpted fruit. It calls its big feast, at £28, the Royal Banquet Menu, and Bangkok could hardly do better. Tel: 385-6595.

Popular Thai restaurants in Soho include **Chiang Mai** at 48 Frith Street, with a set menu for two at £34 (Tel: 437-7444), and the rather gloomy **Bahn Thai**, where you can choose from hundreds of dishes, on the opposite side of the street at 21A. There are no set menus, except for large groups; reckon a fair average at £25 per person. (Tel: 437-8504). Both closed for Sunday lunch.

Japanese

Some of London's most expensive Japanese restaurants are found in the City near St. Paul's. **Miyama** on Godliman Street (Tel: 489-1937) caters to businesspeople on expense accounts and is closed on weekends.

Elsewhere in London, the expensive **Suntory** at 72–73 St. James's Street (south of Piccadilly) is popular among discerning Japanese (Tel: 409-0201); the **Miyama** at 38 Clarges Street (Tel: 499-2443; closed Sundays and Saturday lunch), off Piccadilly near Green Park, is much less expensive, especially at lunchtime; and the prix-fixe meals at **Shiki Restaurant**, 27 Davies Street in Mayfair (Tel: 409-0750), which is closed on weekends, are also a good value at between £16 and £28 for lunch, £33 for dinner. The basement **Ikkyu**, 67 Tottenham Court Road near Goodge Street Underground station, is handy for shoppers. Closed Sunday lunch; Tel: 636-9280.

Greek

Greek restaurants aren't currently in vogue in London, but the old standbys do a brisk business. Among these is the **White Tower**, 1 Percy Street (off Tottenham Court Road), which has been offering Greek and Continental dishes since 1938. Moderate/expensive. Closed weekends; Tel: 636-8141. The less expensive **Beotys**, 79 St. Martin's Lane (near the theaters), has been around for more than 40 years; it starts serving pre-theater dinners at 5:30 P.M.; Tel: 836-8768. For a livelier atmosphere, you can watch plates being thrown around and dance on the tables in **Anemos** (now also owned by the White Tower), 32 Charlotte Street. Moderate; Tel: 636-2289. Still lively but a lot less raucous is the cavernous, candlelit, and usually crowded **Mega-Kalamaras** on Inverness Mews, an alley behind Queensway in the Bayswater area just north of Hyde Park. The Greek owner often plays the bouzouki for diners. Open until midnight. Closed Sundays and at lunch; Tel: 727-9122.

One of the longest-surviving Greek establishments, with a seemingly changeless, homey atmosphere and welcome, is the **Hellenic** at 30 Thayer Street, east of Baker Street. Diners will find white tablecloths, Cypriot wines, and a menu split between such Greek staples as *moussaka, sheftalia,* and *kleftiko,* and English dishes like oxtail casserole. Either way estimate £15 per person unless you indulge in the specialty, suckling pig. Inexpensive. Tel: 935-1257.

Mediterranean and Middle Eastern

The Lebanese **Al Hamra**, 31 Shepherd Market, Mayfair, offers sophisticated Middle Eastern fare. The tables are set close together, so if you're not sure what to eat you can follow the example of a neighboring diner. You'll be safe, however, if you stick with the hot and cold starters (wiped up with pita bread) and the salads, which come in huge baskets and include plenty of chunky raw vegetables. The menu is 60 percent vegetarian. Early evening estimate £25 per person; after 10:00 P.M., when a show begins, the minimum is £33. Open until midnight every day. Moderate/expensive. Tel: 493-1954. Insomniacs can find Middle Eastern solace at **Al Maroush II**, 38 Beauchamp Place just southwest of Harrods, until 4:30 A.M. (Tel: 581-5434), as well as at the slightly less expensive **Al Maroush**, 21 Edgware Road near Marble Arch, until 1:00

A.M.; Tel: 723-0773. **Al Maroush III**, nearby at 62 Seymour Street, is open until 12:30 A.M. Moderate; Tel: 724-5024.

Of Jewish places, there is no question which name reverberates most familiarly in kosher quarters: **Bloom's**. There are two, both at the heart of Jewish enclaves. In the East End, the waiters at Bloom's, 90 Whitechapel Road, dispense chicken soup and gefilte fish with the minimal grace that suggests they know they are indispensable; Tel: 247-6001. In the Jewish residential headquarters, Golders Green, find the other Bloom's, 130 Golders Green Road, open 9:30 A.M. to 11:30 P.M., purveying the *latkas* and pot roast. Inexpensive/moderate; Tel: 081-455-1338.

Turkish cooking entered the consciousness of London diners when the **Topkapi**, 25 Marylebone High Street, won a Restaurant of the Year Award in 1984. They still celebrate the win, with their chicken breast (secret recipe). The spitted *doner* kebab turning in the window and the row of tall-hatted Turkish chefs tell you that you've arrived; the long list of *mezeler* (hors d'oeuvres) and general theatricality of the bistro communicate that you may as well settle in. Moderate; Tel: 486-1872.

VEGETARIAN

London's strictly vegetarian restaurants are few and far between, but numerous restaurants cater to non-meat eaters and most can produce a choice of suitable vegetarian dishes, especially the brasseries. Ethnic restaurants are usually the best bet, however. *The Vegetarian Good Food Guide,* available in bookshops, is useful.

Of the more formal restaurants, **Leith's**, 92 Kensington Park Road, has a vegetarian menu; many of the herbs and vegetables are grown by Prue Leith (she runs her own cooking school) on her farm in the Cotswolds. Moderate; Tel: 229-4481. In Soho, **Mildred's**, 58 Greek Street, is a remarkably good value with three courses possible at about £10. Apart from the odd shrimp skulking in a pie, it is wholly vegetarian, and usually has two or three strictly vegan dishes on the menu—cabbage parcels, mushroom and courgette (zucchini) pie, and so forth—with an array of vegetarian supports. No microwaves, everything cooked fresh daily, and it has an alcohol license. Open midday to 11:00 P.M. every day except Sundays; Tel: 494-1634.

Other less-expensive restaurants include **Cranks**, a chain that was among the first to offer "health" food in London. The various branches (including Marshall Street, near Oxford Circus, and the Market in Covent Garden) offer a selection of salads and hot dishes at very reasonable prices, but they are café-like in design and don't encourage lingering. Also in Covent Garden, you can get vegan dishes, pastries, pizzas, and a few hot dishes at **Neal's Yard Bakery** (it closes at 6:15 P.M. Monday through Friday and 4:30 P.M. on Saturdays), or try **Food for Thought** around the corner on Neal Street, which offers reasonable prices and high-quality food. It closes at 8:00 P.M. Monday through Saturday and 4:30 P.M. on Sundays.

The purist and the whole-fooder can enjoy an interesting meal at the **East West Centre** in Old Street (the eastern continuation of Clerkenwell Road): a health warren in an 18th-century building that was formerly the site of a plague pit. Here Nigel Walker, boss of one of the very few tour operations dedicated to vegetarians, demonstrates natural cookery. Inexpensive; Tel: 608-0300.

London's oldest vegetarian restaurant is on Primrose Hill in North London. **Manna**, 4 Erskine Road, offers huge portions of home cooking to devout locals as well as intrepid visitors. Inexpensive; Tel: 722-8028. Walkable from the Chalk Farm tube station. Closed Sundays.

FAMILIES

Most London restaurants don't take kindly to young children, but the few that do are worth knowing about. Apart from pizza places (Pizza Huts are possibly the best; they have high chairs and give kids coloring sheets and crayons) and the coffee shops in the smarter hotels, the following are worth considering:

TGI Friday's (Thank God It's), located on Covent Garden's Bedford Street, is a noisy, fun place that specializes in pizzas, burgers, and alcohol-free "cocktails" for children—as well as the real thing for adults. Under-12s qualify for a very cheap menu before 7:00 P.M. Balloons on weekends. Inexpensive; Tel: 379-0585.

Smollensky's-on-the-Strand (Tel: 491-1199) serves up the fundamental junior diet of the Western world: fish sticks, burgers, and funny-colored beverage concoctions, with a main-course price of £3.85. On weekends they have magicians and clowns and toys, but they all go away at 4:00 P.M. A milder and slightly more expensive version of this, **Smollensky's Balloon**, can be found on Dover Street (Tel: 499-1199), up the road from the Ritz Hotel. No toys, despite the title, but they do have entertainers until 4:30 P.M.

Just south of the John Lewis store on Oxford Street is the **Chicago Pizza Pie Factory** in Hanover Square, a good place to rest with youngsters if you're mid-shopping, though they don't put on anything special. Or try the equally inexpensive **Chicago Meat Packers** (near Foyles Bookshop), 96 Charing Cross Road, which offers a children's menu at £4.50 until 8:00 P.M., as well as a model railway. Magicians do their tricks on Sundays at lunchtime. Tel: 379-3277.

OUTER LONDON: THE NORTHERN SUBURBS

Camden Town
Camden Town is a bustling cosmopolitan area with lots of Greek restaurants (try **Nontas** on High Street, Tel: 387-4579, except Sundays, or **Daphne's** on Bayham Street, almost behind it, Tel: 267-7322) and several brasseries. All are inexpensive.

Hampstead
Le Carapace, up the hill on Heath Street (near Whitestone Pond), serves an enormous basket of crudités (hard-boiled eggs and artichokes among them) with peasant bread and garlic mayonnaise. Charcoal grills are the specialty, as are huge individual *tartes* for dessert. There is an open fire in winter, a few tables outside in summer, and a nonsmoking area. In addition, the set menus are a good value at £15. Lunch only on Sundays; Tel: 435-8000. Next to the post office you'll find **Zen W3**, the designer Chinese restaurant (and sister of the two Zens in town). Water cascades down the banister, and the large floor-to-ceiling windows overlook the bustle of High Street. Moderate; Tel: 794-7863.

Islington
Camden Passage browsers (for antiques) and City businesspeople frequent **Frederick's**, a much-loved, though somewhat inconsistent, French conservatory-style restaurant of long standing where the menu includes vegetarian dishes. Fixed-price menus at £18. Open at 6:00 P.M. for theatergoers. Closed Sundays; Tel: 359-2888.

One of a crop of new openings in this bustling neighborhood is **Ruby in the Dust**, at 70 Upper Street, with English and Creole dishes and plenty of enhanced fast food in a noisy, cheerful environment. Open noon to midnight Monday through Thursday, till 2:00 A.M. Friday and Saturday, 11:00 P.M. Sunday. Inexpensive; Tel: 359-1710.

OUTER LONDON: SOUTH OF THE RIVER

Some restaurants south of the river can be quite difficult to get to. Those listed below are well worth the effort.

Wandsworth

Harvey's, 2 Bellevue Road, is one of the very best restaurants in London, and its location, some miles from the center of town among a small parade of shops opposite Wandsworth Common, is no obstacle to serious food lovers. Marco Pierre White is an inspired cook, his bright street-level dining room an attractive blend of pastels. Each dish is a masterwork of creativity (some have up to 25 different components) to be savored slowly. Harvey's also offers set menus (£48), and lunch in particular (£24) is an exceptional value. Closed Sunday and Monday; Tel: 081-672-0114.

Battersea

The atmosphere at **L'Arlequin**, 123 Queenstown Road, just over Chelsea Bridge, is serious but understated; Christian Delteil, the chef/owner, has little time for pretension. Madame Delteil looks after the restaurant's patrons, many of whom are journalists from *The Observer,* just up the road. Again the set-lunch menu is reasonably priced (£22), but evening meals are expensive (£45). The restaurant is on the 137 bus route from Knightsbridge. Closed weekends; Tel: 622-0555.

INFORMATION

Restaurant Services, a "restaurant advisory and reservation service," offers advice and suggestions on thousands of restaurants, hotels, and wine bars in the London area and in Greater London, and can even be used to make reservations. Tel: (081) 888-8080.

The Good Food Guide, edited by Tom Jaine, is the British foodies' bible, with restaurants recommended by its readers. *The Vegetarian Good Food Guide* is an offshoot of *The Good Food Guide*. Both are available in bookshops.

RESTAURANTS BY GEOGRAPHICAL AREA

Bloomsbury
Museum Street Café (Brasseries and Cafés)

Chelsea
Brasserie (Hotel Restaurants)
La Croisette (Fish)
La Famiglia (Italian)
La Tante Claire (French)
San Martino (Italian)

The City and the East End
Bloom's (Mediterranean and Middle Eastern)
East West Centre (Vegetarian)
Greenhouse (Fish)
Miyama (Japanese)

Covent Garden Area
Beotys (Greek)
Bertorelli's (Italian)
Le Boulestin (French; Early and Late)
Café Flo (Early and Late)
Café du Jardin (Early and Late)
Café Pelican (Early and Late)
Christopher's—The American Grill (American)
Cranks (Vegetarian)
Fields (Early and Late)
Food for Thought (Vegetarian)
Fryer's Delight (Fish)
The Ivy (Eclectic)
Joe Allen's (American)
Magno's (Early and Late)
Neal's Yard Bakery (Vegetarian)
Old Orleans (American)
Orso (Italian; Early and Late)
River Restaurant (Hotel Restaurants)
Rules (English; Early and Late)
Savoy Grill (English; Hotel Restaurants; Early and Late)
Simpson's-in-the-Strand (English)
Smollensky's-on-the-Strand (Families)
TGI Friday's (Families)
Upstairs at the Savoy (Early and Late)

Fulham/Hammersmith
Blue Elephant (Thai)
Casper's Restaurant (Brasseries and Cafés)
River Café (Italian)

North and West of Hyde Park
Cibo (Italian)
Hellenic (Greek)
Leith's (English; Vegetarian)
Manna (Vegetarian)
Mega-Kalamaras (Greek)
Ragam (Indian)
Room at the Halcyon (Hotel Restaurants)
Stephen Bull (English)
Topkapi (Mediterranean and Middle Eastern)

Kensington
Bibendum (Eclectic)
Bistrot 190 (Eclectic; Early and Late)
Bombay Brasserie (Indian)
Café Kensington (Brasseries and Cafés)
Clarke's (American)
Hilaire's (Eclectic)
Joe's Café (Brasseries and Cafés)
Kensington Place (Brasseries and Cafés; Early and
    Late)
One Ninety Queen's Gate (Eclectic)
Le Quai St. Pierre (Fish)
Le Suquet (Fish)

Knightsbridge
Capital (Hotel Restaurants)
Chelsea Room (Hotel Restaurants)
Emporio Armani Express (Brasseries and Cafés)
English Garden (English)
English House (English)
Grill St. Quentin (French)
Al Maroush (Mediterranean and Middle Eastern)
Al Maroush II (Mediterranean and Middle Eastern)
Al Maroush III (Mediterranean and Middle Eastern)
Park Room (Hotel Restaurants)
Pizza on the Park (Italian)
Rib Room (Hotel Restaurants)
St. Quentin (French)
San Lorenzo (Italian)
Waltons (English)
Zen (Chinese)

Mayfair and St. James's
Brown's (Early and Late)
Le Caprice (Brasseries and Cafés; Early and Late)
The Causerie (Hotel Restaurants; Early and Late)
Claridge's (Hotel Restaurants)
Connaught (Hotel Restaurants)
Dover Street Restaurant (English)
Fortnum & Mason's Fountain Restaurant
    (Brasseries and Cafés)
Four Seasons (Hotel Restaurants)
Le Gavroche (French)
Greenhouse (English)
Green's Restaurant and Oyster Bar (English; Fish)
Grill Room (Hotel Restaurants)
Al Hamra (Mediterranean and Middle Eastern)
Hard Rock Café (American)
Langan's Brasserie (Brasseries and Cafés)
Memories of the British Empire (Hotel Restaurants)
Miyama (Japanese)
Nico at Ninety (Hotel Restaurants)
Oak Room (Hotel Restaurants)
Palm Court (Hotel Restaurants)
Pizza Condotti (Italian)
Polo Room (Hotel Restaurants)
Ritz Hotel (Hotel Restaurants)
Shiki Restaurant (Japanese)
Smollensky's Balloon (Families)
Le Soufflé (Hotel Restaurants)
Suntory (Japanese)
Terrace (Hotel Restaurants)
Terrace Garden (Hotel Restaurants; Early and Late)
Tsar's (Hotel Restaurants)
Wilton's (Fish)
Zen Central (Chinese)

Soho
Alastair Little's (Eclectic; Early and Late)
Anemos (Greek)
Bahn Thai (Thai)
Chiang Mai (Thai)
Chicago Meat Packers (Families)
Chicago Pizza Pie Factory (Families)
Chuen Cheng Ku (Chinese)
Dell'Ugo (Eclectic)
Ed's Easy Diner (American)
Fung Shing (Chinese)

Ikkyu (Japanese)
Kettners (Italian)
Lal Qila (Indian)
Last Days of the Raj (Indian)
Limelight (Early and Late)
Lindsay House (English)
Manzi's (Fish; Early and Late)
Mildred's (Vegetarian)
New World (Chinese)
Nico Central (French)
Pizza Express (Italian)
Planet Hollywood (American)
Poons (Chinese)
Rock Island Diner (American)
Soho Brasserie (Brasseries and Cafés)
White Tower (Greek)
Wong Kei (Chinese)
Yung's (Chinese)

Near Victoria Station
Auberge de Provence (Hotel Restaurants)
Bistro Carapace (French)
Halkin (Hotel Restaurants)
L'Incontro (Italian)
Ken Lo's Memories of China (Chinese)
Santini (Italian)
Simply Nico (French)
Tate Gallery restaurant (English)

Outer London (North)
Bloom's (Mediterranean and Middle Eastern)
Le Carapace (Hampstead)
Daphne's (Camden Town)
Frederick's (Islington)
Lakorn Thai (Early and Late)
Nontas (Camden Town)
Rani (Indian)
Ruby in the Dust (Islington)
Upper Street Fish Shop (Fish)
Zen W3 (Hampstead)

South of the Thames
L'Arlequin (Battersea)
Blueprint Café (Brasseries and Cafés)
Harvey's (Wandsworth)
Ovations (Early and Late)
RSJ (Early and Late)
La Truffe Noire (French)

PUBS, NIGHTLIFE, AND ENTER-TAINMENT

By Alex Hamilton

PUBS AND BARS

PUBS

Publicans, who may be addressed as "landlord" or more familiarly "guv'nor" (but never "friend," without giving offense), know a lot about beer, rather less about spirits, and hardly anything about wine. This probably reflects the amounts they sell of each. Distillers and winegrowers do not own pubs, but brewers do, with a consequent overwhelming influence on their stock, their appearance, and their staff. At least, brewers own the majority; pubs are known as "tied houses" when they principally sell beers from the brewer that owns them. The rest, which offer a fine miscellany, are known as "free houses." However officious a brewer may be, though, it is the personality and style of the publican—himself or herself—that make the vital difference. Though publicans are bound to observe the laws that protect the consumer and maintain the peace, they have one important freedom: They can bar whomever they wish, and without giving a reason.

Another, more recently acquired freedom—by no means universally popular—allows them to decide their own open hours, which must fall between 11:00 A.M. and 11:00 P.M., except on Sundays, when the hours are reduced to noon to 3:00 P.M. and 7:00 to 10:30 P.M. After a period of experiment and uncertainty, the practical effect of this liberation is that most pubs feel obligated by competition to stay open all that time, and the nonstop drinker can seem as much a fixture as the sign warning minors (under 18) off alcohol. The ritual shouts of "Last orders!" and "Time, gentlemen please—your glasses!" sometimes emphasized by a ship's bell or a barking dog, with a 10-minute allowance of "drinking-up time," are still followed by "chucking-out time," which in rougher neighborhoods is not the most sensible moment to be sauntering along the sidewalks.

To read the catering trade weekly the *Morning Advertiser* on a Monday is to feel that the whole pub network is under imminent threat of collapse. There are columns of vacant tenancies and pubs for sale. Stiff increases in rents and taxes and the many other entertainment options that have been created for a more affluent society have been a severe test. But some purging was needed; too many pubs were slovenly and dispiriting. And not to worry: There are still between 5,000 and 6,000 serving London.

Many old pubs have quaint names. The Frog & Nightgown and the Dog & Overdraft are journalistic fictions, but the Bag of Nails (derived from Bacchanales), the Elephant & Castle (from Infanta of Castile), and the Ferret & Firkin (located at the new Chelsea Harbour development) are real, and there are four called the Pig and Whistle. Indeed, the visitor should be aware that some popular pub names are adopted many times over. In London there are 25 pubs called the King's Head and 12 called the Queen's Head; there are 22 Railway Taverns; the ancient emblem of spring, the Green Man, is used 19 times, as is the George. The Coach and Horses, the Crown, the Rising Sun, the Red Lion, and the Blue Posts are each to be found in all sorts of incarnations, so in asking directions or instructing a taxi it is wise not only to give the name of the pub but also to specify the street.

It goes without saying that the discovery of London pubs is an intoxicating experience, but it is also important to add that the drinking-and-driving laws are now being enforced with much greater severity than ever, with the result that all pubs now serve low- and non-alcohol beers and lagers (such as Swan Light and Kaliber). All pubs also sell a range of bottled beers, chilled lagers (very light, European-style beers), and stouts (very dark, even black, malt brews), of varying tastes and strengths. At the upper end are such as Worthington White Shield, a unique bottle-conditioned beer with a sediment that the barman may leave you to pour for yourself; Gold Label; Export Special; and what the Scots call "wee heavies," a concentrated barley product. The most common foreign beers are Danish Carlsberg lagers, the Australian Fosters, and the American Budweiser. The quality of draft beers, pumped from the cellar, has been saved by CAMRA, the Campaign for Real Ale.

Draft beers are usually labeled on the pump handles, including Irish Guinness and dry cider, and are ordered in measures of pints and half pints. If you want a glass with a handle, ask for your beer "in a jug" or "with a handle." There are still a few pubs, though not in the center of London, where habitués keep their own tankards hanging on nails. A rare exception is the **George** on Mortimer Street with a hundred or more, sold at £10 each by the pub itself and actually holding a pint and a quarter (but the owner pays only for a pint). As a very rough benchmark: £1.60 will buy a pint of bitter (the traditional British form of draft beer, with a barley and malt base and a strong flavor of hops; it should be clear and golden-hued).

The earnest student of beer with a long swallow can repair to the **Sun**, northwest of Gray's Inn and opposite the children's hospital on Great Ormond Street in Holborn, which has the largest selection of cask-conditioned ales in the world: 187 at last count (not, obviously, all on tap simultaneously), with oddities such as Oy Vay, weissbier (a wheat beer), Merrie Monk, and Old Scrap Cyder. (An early-evening tour of the 1688 cellar can be arranged by calling the landlord; Tel: 405-8728.)

Pubs change, if slowly. Fine summer weather prompts tables and chairs to appear on the sidewalks, Continental style, but that cannot always be relied on. The big difference in London is the disappearance in many pubs of the old divisions between the plush saloon bar and the more basic and lower-priced public bar. The printed notices you will see warning workmen not to come in with dirty boots and overalls are an indication both of gentrification and of the amount of construction work going on in London these days. But, rejigged, upholstered, and smartened as many pubs may be, they adhere to the traditions of dark wood and paneling, heavy furniture, brass rails, and etched glass. The bric-a-brac that festoons the walls is reminiscent of the clutter of Victorian households: sporting prints, old advertisements, bellows and warming pans, pictures of thespians and royals, theater bills, cigarette cards, painted plates, Toby jugs, horse brasses, heavy double entendres burnt in wood, tea caddies, artificial flowers—the Rabelaisian profusion is a cleaner's nightmare, all reflected back through the smoke by huge etched mirrors.

In the current brewers' dispensation, the carpets are patterned and fitted, the lighting either dim or harsh, the toilets basic, the heating from gas-fired imitation coal grates, the cigarettes from vending machines, the Muzak from speakers, and the food from a lunch counter. That food tends to be starchy and filling, an unconscionable volume of pies, sausage and mash, steak and kidney, Cornish pasties, chips and beans, baked potatoes, cold meat and salads, and none of it expensive: £4.50's worth will anchor you to the seat.

All this is the norm. The pubs below score a notch or two higher.

Central London

By Central London we mean Soho, the West End, and Marylebone.

Just as time begins for the British at Greenwich, so distances are measured from Trafalgar Square. The precise center of the universe is the statue of Charles I at the entrance to Whitehall. Appropriately, one of the pubs against which others measure themselves can be found at one of its corners, where St. Martin's Lane leaves it, a dart's throw from the statue of poor Edith Cavell (a British nurse executed as a spy by the Germans in 1915). This is the **Chandos**—spacious, good beer, quick service, and a slightly more dashing menu than most that includes such items as beef olives, steak-and-pepper pie, and smoked mackerel. The pub is very much a meeting place, with six ground-floor cubicles, like little chapels with their stained glass windows looking out onto the square, and the Opera Lounge upstairs (the English National Opera is housed a few doors up the road) with its deep leather armchairs and blessed freedom from Muzak.

Farther up St. Martin's Lane, past an eclectic shopping alley called **Cecil Court** (which travellers should note as the collectors' hub for original Baedeker guides, as well as for old prints, out-of-print books on music, collectibles, and golf, and more), are two unusual places. The **Green Man & French Horn** is very long and narrow, like a cul-de-sac with a ceiling, the result of joining two pubs together. Victorian prints on the walls here illustrate the gloomy story of the decline of a drunkard and his family. Opposite, the **Salisbury** is much more ample, an island bar set in an ocean of rococo decoration and kitsch. The food is good, though the prices are a bit above average.

Among the plethora of pubs around Piccadilly Circus and the great shopping arteries nearby (the electronics stores of Tottenham Court Road, the rag trade and shoe-leather stores of Oxford Street, and the travel, fashion, ceramics, and silver emporia of Regent Street) it is hard to finger many of real distinction. But there are a few shining exceptions. On Beak Street, off the Soho (east) side of Regent Street, the **Old Coffee House**, with its burnished brass and copper fittings, comfortable furniture, and crimson carpet, offers a relaxed ethos and an amiable staff serving a wide range of bottled and hand-pumped beers. By contrast, the **John Snow**, farther into Soho, has substituted varnish for its former lugubrious charm and is now a pathetic memorial to the great Victorian who discovered the source of cholera in the then-contaminated water conduits of Broadwick Street. Likewise, the **Blue Posts** on Ganton Street suffers from the bane of tied houses: inattentive barmen.

Carnaby Street, that magnesium flare of the Swinging Sixties, offers the **Shakespeare's Head** at the corner of Great Marlborough Street, with wooden floors, good hot food, and an upstairs restaurant, but otherwise nothing to write home about. In Soho, choose the **Dog & Duck** on Bateman Street (a small street between Dean and Greek streets). Go not for the food but for the company of the flotsam and jetsam of bohemian society, a pleasant contrast to the monogrammed gear of the staff. Small and rowdy, the D & D has an upstairs snug (a small private room) with saucy cartoons and postcards and cozy casement tables from which to look down on the street action. The **French House**, at 49 Dean Street, with a somewhat raffish clientele and a staff that knows more about wine than most, has a reputation that dates from World War II, when it was the off-duty rendezvous of the Free French Army in Britain. In 1992 its French *patron* retired, and the pub was taken over by a corporation. Its bohemian regulars were relieved to learn the new guv'nor would be Daniel Farson, litterateur and publican, a man of their own kind.

If you penetrate the hinterland north of Oxford Street into Marylebone, you will see great swarms of young office workers, men and women alike in uniform charcoal-gray suits, gathered like colonies of seals outside such places as the **Lamb & Flag** on the corner of James and Barrett streets.

Coming west off Baker Street, you find, on the corner of Wyndham Place and Crawford Street, the brilliant front of the **Duke of Wellington**, worthy of an award with its shelves of china soldiers and mugs of the Napoleonic era. There are tables and benches on the sidewalk, and the Union Jack flies over all. Inside are more figurines, including a bust of the great man—not a square foot of wall space remains uncovered by paintings and cartoons of the period. You feel you should drink Napoleon brandy here, but it's one item they don't stock.

But the year-round special in Marylebone is the **Prince Regent** on Marylebone High Street. The portrait of the prince himself is a complete fantasy, not the corpulent Prinny we think of but a handsome Young Lochinvar. The pub has a strong miscellany of regulars, drinking under cartoons, prints, and its celebrated collection of cheese plates. On the bar, many now-deceased regulars from the 1890s onward are commemorated with small brass plaques, and one who is still alive, Jimmy Green, has presented the establishment with a box now waiting on a high shelf to receive his ashes when Bacchus calls the final "Time, gentlemen please!" on him.

In cobbled Weymouth Mews, west of and parallel to Portland Place, you'll find one of the oldest pubs in London, the **Dover Castle**, a former coaching inn on the first stage from the City en route to Oxford. It has a company management style unsuited to it, but the lounge and pleasant back room of this house are nonetheless crowded at lunch and in the early evening with media, design, and advertising people.

After 25 years a change of tenant at the **Queen's Head**, on the corner of Wheatley and Westmoreland, in the Marylebone district, has freshened up this attractive small pub. The new couple have the art of being lively but unpretentious, relaxed while busy. They offer a good line in salt beef, too.

East of Tottenham Court Road and across Gower Street, the **Museum Tavern** stands opposite the British Museum on Great Russell Street. With so many scholars and literati restoring their parched gray cells here, plus the pub's eccentric practice of serving afternoon tea, it is not surprising that a neighboring publisher has issued a book on its history, which dates from 1723. Ceiling fans turn above the tables, and there are waitresses, professional bartenders, a well-stocked cellar (although prices are on the high side), and a generally good-natured crowd.

Heading north and east across Southampton Row, stop for a quick one at the **Queen's Larder** in the Cosmo Street alley leading into Queen Square (there are hospitals of all sorts in this area and therefore doctors and nurses, too) on the way to the always fashionable **Lamb** on Lamb's Conduit Street, where you'll find hospital people at midday and theater people at night. Brass rails around the tables stop the drinks from falling off, and the strange old pivoting panels at the bar were apparently installed to prevent the staff from hearing private conversations. An even rarer feature is a nonsmokers' cubbyhole. On the walls hang rows of faded pictures of theatrical divinities alongside Hogarth prints and *Vanity Fair* cartoons.

The City

A jungle by day, a desert by night, the City has always had different hours and rules for its pubs—and its own police force to see them observed. The tendency is to close by 8:00 P.M., and not to open at all on weekends. Still, the old, heavy-beamed pubs like **Olde Wine Shades** on Martin Lane (near the junction of Cannon and King William streets) and **Ye Olde Mitre** on Ely Place off Holborn Circus do a brisk enough business with the stockbrokers, financiers, and conveyancers (real estate lawyers) to compensate for the shorter hours. The beer fancier curious to know what happens when a pub brews its own stuff can try the **Market Porter** on Stoney Street, south of the Thames across London Bridge and off Borough High Street.

The name of the latter suggests the great wholesale food markets that once pulsed within the City precincts and provided special indulgences for thirsty early-morning traders. The last significant example of these markets, still operating on its original site, is the Central Market, which has stood at Smithfield since the tenth century. The license to operate from 5:30 A.M. is still exercised by some pubs here; two in particular are recommended for their lively, humorous trader talk and hearty breakfasts with ale. The first, the **Cock Tavern**, is in a basement down steps from the second archway; the other, the **Fox & Anchor**, is adjacent to the entry to serene Charterhouse Square. Market porters critical of the beef served in local cafés sometimes bring in their own steak to fry, but that isn't necessary at the Fox & Anchor. One of the historical curiosities of Smithfield is the **Castle** on Cowcross Street, where King William IV, pressed for cash, called in and left his watch as a pledge for a loan, later granting the pub a pawnbroker's license in perpetuity.

The southern neighbors of Smithfield are St. Bartholomew, London's busiest hospital, and the Old Bailey, the central criminal court. Opposite Bart's is the **White Hart**, a serviceable and friendly establishment. The **Magpie & Stump**, formerly a ferment of gossip and good low-life stories spun by a clientele composed largely of lawyers and journalists, was dissolved in redevelopment for three years but has reappeared in one corner of an immense office building opposite the Bailey; now grand and glittering, as if the magpie had gone respectable and moved away from the stump, it is still ready to lubricate wagging tongues. It has rather more sophisticated dining than before, with exotic starters like deep-fried Brie cheese, main courses like grilled swordfish with anchovy butter, and good old English bread-and-butter pudding.

A find north of Smithfield is the **Crown**, a 17th-century inn on a small, attractive square called Clerkenwell Close. The square's great feature is the Marx Memorial Library, a storehouse of Socialist literature, from seething tracts and compassionate novels to stolid economic analyses, assembled to honor the author of *Das Kapital,* who labored on his seminal work at the British Library. Apparently apolitical, the pub nevertheless still separates the plusher saloon area from the public bar; it also has a back-room restaurant.

A short walk south of Smithfield at 22 High Holborn—a relatively dry area, which makes its discovery even more welcome—is the **Cittie of Yorke**. A pub has stood on this site since 1464, though it was rebuilt in the 1890s. The rebuilders kept many of its intriguing bits and pieces; within the cavernous long barroom, with its trussed roof, you find two beguiling rows of stalls with tables and padded chairs, and a triangular free-standing coal stove. There is cask bitter beer in a row of vats of between 500 and 1,100 gallons, and an international range of whiskeys. The only caveat: The edibles do not match the potables.

Chelsea

The pub crawl, an increasingly meandering walk punctuated by pints at a succession of pubs favored mainly by younger men, has a nearly perfect track in the King's Road, where, between the Royal Court Theatre on Sloane Square and the S-bend of the World's End to the southwest, no fewer than ten pubs await the crawler, not to mention several in adjacent streets, including the **Queen's Head** on Tryon Street, which has long attracted a gay clientele, and the **Front Page** on Old Church Street, perversely renamed after having been the Black Lion for 300 years (the same brewing company has renamed the Red Anchor, on Camera Place, the **Sporting Page**).

After the demise of the famous Markham Arms, the **Chelsea Potter** is now the favorite resort of gossip columnists looking for a story. Its very young clientele chatter like starlings, though the pub is so dark it looks closed from the outside even when it's not.

The Six Bells by the Town Hall (on the King's Road) has been renamed **Henry J. Bean's** ("but his friends all call him Hank") and transformed into a cocktail zoo with heavy-metal sounds, fast food, and fancy drinks. The hundreds of customers in this grand old barn average age 19, but the big garden in the rear remains a great, if crowded, romantic asset. At the **Cadogan Arms** on the corner of Old Church Street you'll find another young and lively but less frantic crowd, a jeans-and-sweater bunch swarming over its split levels. From here on west the pubs have lately taken to offering breakfast from 9:00 A.M. and sometimes earlier—the full-scale bacon, eggs, sausage, tomato, toast, and marmalade meal. The **Man in the Moon**, at the corner of Church Walk, is a free house with heavy maroon drapes, caramel-colored lighting, throbbing music, and its own theater club upstairs (see Fringe Theater, below). Then, at the S-bend at the Thames and Putney end of the King's Road, comes a cluster: upholstered leather seating and Denise's Kitchen serving bubble and squeak and turkey-and-corn pie in the **Water Rat**; a bar-and-billiards saloon downstairs and early breakfasts in the **Magpie & Stump** (no relation to the one in the City); the impersonal modern brick of the Riley Arms (enough said); and, finally, the harshly lit saloon, high ceilings, and slot machines of the World's End Distillery. Its name is the best thing about it, and, indeed, you may as well make the Man in the Moon the last drink on the route; anyway, six or seven pints are a skinful.

North of Hyde Park

This area covers the Paddington, Bayswater, Notting Hill, and Holland Park districts.

The visitor who on a fine day saunters about the great expanse of Hyde Park, watching the antics of the sunbathers and swimmers around the Serpentine Lido, dropping in on its art gallery, admiring the style of the wealthy horse riders along Rotten Row, and enjoying all those little dramatic cameos of the human comedy that evolve in a large green and public open space, may find himself or herself, as the sun sets, having walked much farther than seemed possible and feeling as dry as a newt in a curtain rod. It may then come as something of a shock to leave the park at, say, Lancaster Gate on the northern side, and realize that very little has been provided to refuel the poor human creature or let it put up its feet. In these circumstances, then, it is imperative not to stand on ceremony; one must be grateful for the discovery of any kind of hostelry, regardless of quality.

There stands—as it has for 200 years—on the Bayswater Road, which skirts the northern edge of the park, the **Swan on "the Water"** (the phrase has been used for decades by those who sink or swim in this melting pot of a district). Were it not for its longevity, seeing the pub pulsing with polyglot sing-alongs led by a sweating pianist you might say the Swan had been built solely for tourists.

Sharing the Swan's virtue of selling drink in an area that seems to favor weathered hotels that sport their stars and crowns and credit-card affiliations like campaign ribbons is the **Leinster**, reached by turning off "the Water" opposite Lancaster Gate into Leinster Terrace.

The situation eases somewhat in the bizarre hinterland of Bayswater and Paddington, though you are often liable to come across whole tracts where seemingly no brewer has ever been granted a visa. What is odd about this stretch west of the Edgware Road (the great artery that runs north out of London from Marble Arch and the Speakers' Corner of Hyde Park) is its residential mixture, sedate and even grand apartment terraces giving way to a hotel and bed-sitter land of long- and short-stay visitors, and of every conceivable provenance. With a few exceptions, pubs rarely thrive either in areas dominated by the very rich or, naturally, where most of the business is immigrant, and the housing here is largely occupied by people with Muslim, Hindu, or Chinese backgrounds.

Together with African, Caribbean, and Asian presences, each having its own sphere of influence as you proceed west through Paddington, Bayswater, and Notting Hill, the variety of trading interests provides surprising juxtapositions, and the conventional British pub often appears to be the odd one out.

Typical of the busiest thoroughfares is **Queensway**, running north from Black Lion Gate out of Kensington Gardens, the western extension of Hyde Park, and connecting with another vital street, **Westbourne Grove**. On Queensway, where the first coin-operated launderette in Europe (1949) spins the wash among tax-free stores and pizzerias, and an exotic cocktail bar offers the "Mega Fishbowl for four persons" near a shop specializing in videocassettes for Arabic-speakers, can be found the **Texas Lone Star Saloon**, a sort of honky-tonk 5,000 miles from home, and the **Prince Alfred**, unkempt and disheveled among the apartment-finding agencies, and flaunting its loaded ashtrays and cigarette-burned carpets cheek by jowl with Marco Polo's "Mongolian barbecue." At the junction of Queensway and Westbourne Grove, the **Redan**, commemorating the fall of Sebastopol to the British in 1855, is marginally better. Around the corner, the ebony frontage of **Piers** *looks* promising, but the interior, decorated with tired fake vegetables, is less than enchanting. Nevertheless, for the student of the British pub, these enduring places are important. The landlord may be as neurasthenic as Oblomov, his staff a band of terrorists *manqué,* the clientele as detached and motionless as if they were on opium, not beer, but in each case the pub is for some Londoners "the local," a comfort as deep as Mother.

And so, buoyed by this consideration, plod in a curve into the prosperous crescent of Pembridge Villas until, on the corner of Portobello Road, the **Sun in Splendour** rises into view—aptly named in the circumstances. In 1967 it was the *London Standard*'s "Pub of the Year" and now, as a "vintage pub" with a beer garden, a Saturday barbecue, and a list of wines posted, the flavor of a Mayfair saloon still hangs about its pale-green furnishings. With mindless tunes plonking out of its music machine, and a barmaid who has never heard of the label you call for, it will do— but no more than that—as a port of embarkation for the Portobello Road.

On that celebrated stretch of antiques merchants there is a pub on practically every corner, presumably as a restorative after strenuous discussion with a dealer in furniture or collectibles. **Portobello Gold**, facing Denbigh Terrace, is a hybrid of restaurant and pub, with a good selection of beers. The main recommendation for the **Earl of Lonsdale**, at Westbourne Grove, is its games room with bar billiards, while for those who really fancy the game in a genuinely scratched and dilapidated pub, the **Warwick Castle** on the corner of Westbourne Park Road is the place.

On the corner of Talbot Road, opposite Marc Saint's famous tattooing studio, is a very distinctive pub, plain as a canteen but with jazz every Saturday night, a Courage pub apparently without a name at the moment. The pleasantest of the Portobello Road pubs may be the paneled and partitioned **Wellington** on the corner of Elgin Crescent (one of the Finch's chain, which in London generally can be relied on for both the beer and some character). But the one that tends to attract the business is the **Market Trader** on the corner of Lancaster Road, despite its unprepossessing exterior with rusted nameplate and two Pan figures protruding like gargoyles from the outer wall. Inside, iron-backed chairs stand on a wooden floor, with illumination from a row of huge candlesticks on the bar that have shed their wax until they look like mops. Here you will find good beer and interesting company.

Leaving the markets behind again, and heading for the Notting Hill Gate Underground station via Ladbroke Grove and Holland Park Avenue, keep an eye out at the junction of those two for a great sprawl of a place on two levels called **The Raj**—big enough indeed to have prompted the management to set up internal signposts pointing the way to the food. A thoughtful addition is the bar stool in the rest room.

By the Notting Hill hub itself there is the **Old Swan**, a bit hearty with its photographs of "Old Swan Pissheads" and the like; for something a little more genteel try the **Macaulay Arms**, a short distance down Kensington Church Street, or, a little farther on at the corner of Campden Street, the **Churchill Arms**. The relationship of both to the great men whose names they bear is minimal, though Macaulay did live and work in the area, and Mellor & Baxter, antiquarian booksellers, do display Churchill's history of World War II in the window. As for the rest, under the aegis of Churchill there is excellent East Asian cuisine with a Thai chef in the pub. In the Macaulay Arms there are open bookshelves for patrons, full of works by authors whose main impact was made over half a century ago, including John Buchan, Michael Arlen, Van Loon, and A.E.W. Mason. The literary aspirations of this comfortable lounge are emphasized by a sententious quote from Mark Twain that hangs over the bar: "What marriage is to morality a properly conducted liquor traffic is to sobriety." What can he have meant?

WINE BARS

The closer association of Britain with Continental Europe has not yet, from the wine drinker's point of view, had any very noticeable effect on prices here, but the reductions must surely come now that the European Community has dropped trade barriers. Knowledge and appreciation of wines and places dedicated to their drinking have already improved, resulting in an increase in the number of wine bars, which have been taking some of the trade from the pubs.

The expansion has had two styles: The older is the *masculine* manner, leaning heavily on tradition and characterized by oak beams and rampart-like counters, clumsy, comfortable furniture—big casks often standing in for tables—a sprinkling of sawdust on the stone floors, a full-dress battalion of high-quality Champagnes such as Veuve Clicquot, and cumulus clouds of cigar smoke. Many of the best examples are to be found among the 40 owned by Davys, as well as among the chain run by Balls Brothers. There is, not surprisingly, a strong concentration in the City, among which the **Bottlescrue** in Bath House on High Holborn, the **Pulpit** on Worship Street (north of Liverpool Street Station), and the **Boot and Flogger** on Redcross Way (across London Bridge in Southwark) will wrap you in a dark and dignified ethos suitable to conversation about the bottom line.

The ancestor of them all is the **Olde Wine Shades**, on Martin Lane off Cannon Street, which opened in 1663 and was the only such establishment to survive the Great Fire three years later. Its owners have another, even more celebrated, place, **El Vino's**, on Fleet Street, which proffers a similar choice of fine wines, Ports, and Sherries drawn from a great parade of casks. Although the national newspapers are now scattered away from Fleet Street, something of the former mood persists, with fire-brigade journalists reminiscing about the good old days. The rule here barring women has been abrogated, but it is still preferred that women sit at a table rather than stand at the bar, and wear skirts, not trousers. The dress rule for men at the Olde Wine Shades and El Vino's is particularly strict: In the absence of jacket and tie you will be asked to leave. (A few doors down, opposite the ancient and also vinous **Olde Cheshire Cheese** pub, is a Tie Rack shop.)

An entrepreneurial New Zealander, Don Hewitson, has established himself with a slightly lighter version of this style, putting French art posters on the walls and white cloths on the tables, and offering tasty meals at around £10. His little empire comprises **Shampers**, on Soho's Kingly Street (parallel to Carnaby Street); the **Cork and Bottle**, in a cramped basement on Cranbourn Street off Leicester Square—nevertheless a Pub of the Year in the mid-1980s; and the much ampler flagship, the award-winning **Methuselah's** on Victoria Street, which is much liked by younger people (and not merely the trendies).

The other style of wine bar, which we will call the *contemporary* style, has had to adapt to designer-fashion currents, merging at the one end with restaurants—the **Soho Brasserie** is an example—at the other with cocktail bars, such as the **Long Island Iced Tea Shop** on Cranbourn Street, or with tourist-oriented places that have exotic themes, such as the *tapas*-bar whirl of **Brahms and Liszt** in Covent Garden. Generally they do not serve beer, but instead offer a wide range of wines, among them French, Alsatian, German, Italian, Spanish, and, occasionally, Australian vintages, with prices starting at £7 a bottle and commonplace Champagnes at £17 to £20 a bottle.

A valiant new opening, considering that on the opposite side of the street were no fewer than nine empty (recently bankrupted) restaurant and shop fronts, is the **Dock Blid**, at 50 Blandford Street in the West End. It is a wine and steak bar, in a cool basement, enhanced by interesting offerings like jugs of Port from the barrel. They decant vintage Ports daily and offer true-blue English food like game pie (lead shot hazard) and treacle tart with Devonshire clotted cream. Wine by the bottle: £10–£30.

An interesting hybrid, where you get two atmospheres for the price of one, is the **Edgar Wallace**, on the slope at 40 Essex Street, off the Strand. Downstairs it is a pub, upstairs a wine bar. Remember the old adage about not mixing grape and grain, although the great journalist and thriller writer whose name the place bears seems not to have troubled about that.

There is no such phenomenon in London as the North American singles bar scene, but it is fair to say that some bars, like **Le Cochonnet** in outlying Maida Vale (northwest of Paddington), which has a wine list as long as a telephone directory, are chummier than others. Among a relaxed miscellany that stand out for their individual appeal and amiability are **Morgan's** on Soho's Ganton Street, which offers reasonably priced meals and a barman with both a genuine delight in wine lore and a wish to lead his patrons in the right direction; **Volkers**, handily sited off Trafalgar Square on the Haymarket, and the place to drink pink Champagne from a bottle clamped in a pewter cuirass while you are sitting at the bar on a copper milk churn filled with Champagne corks; and the **Metro**, by Clapham Common Underground station, a conservatory-style meeting place that is popular with neighborhood cats.

COCKTAIL BARS

American bars and cocktail bars are as close to being synonymous in the British mind as Coke and Pepsi. An excellent choice with discretion and style, where a woman on her own may pause without discomfort, is the bar in **Brown's Hotel**, on Albemarle Street in Mayfair. On the same wavelength, with senior barmen who know what goes into a daiquiri or a Tom Collins, a whiskey sour or a planter's punch, are the nookeries of **Durrant's** on George Street in Marylebone, the **Connaught** on Carlos Place in Mayfair, and, through a door on an inner courtyard off St. James's Street, the **Stafford** on St. James's Place—all have that pukka (first-class) tone. And, in another secluded courtyard off St. James's, compare the skills of barman Gilberto Preti at **Dukes Hotel**. It's an old-fashioned-style bar, and he mixes an old-fashioned killer cocktail.

The dazzling white counter and Art Deco of the **Savoy Bar** conjures up the spirit of the 1930s, when the creative barman Harry Craddock expanded the cocktail range way beyond the confines of its original definition—a concoction of any spirit with water, sugar, and bitters. The period decor persists, though the menu lacks imagination. Nevertheless, with its Champagne cocktails, sharp old-fashioneds, Moscow mules, and knockouts such as brandy Alexanders and black Russians for nightcaps, the Savoy keeps the faith, and martini addicts swear that today's incumbent, Peter Morelli, measures up to the Craddock legacy. Expect to find similar standards prevailing in the **Ritz Bar** and **Claridge's Bar**. And, after a two-year overhaul of the hotel, the **American Bar** in the Dorchester Hotel has returned to its former position as a watering hole for visiting celebrities.

The luxurious old favorites just mentioned have their

counterparts in new branches of several chain hotels—the Hilton International, by the BBC on Portland Place, which opened in 1991 as the Langham; the Mayfair; and St. George's Hotel, opposite the new Hilton, with a bar on the 15th floor high above the spire of All Souls' Church—but the character of the bars in these newer establishments fluctuates with the changing tides of customers.

A cocktail lounge with a difference is that of the **Bombay Palace**, in a smart residential area on Connaught Street at the corner of Hyde Park Square. The special atmosphere may come from the mixtures of spices that go into the curries, which seem to suffuse the whole ethos.

Curiosities in vogue include the basement-art-gallery effect of **Freud's**, at the High Holborn end of Shaftesbury Avenue, and—a current phenomenon—the bar that suddenly changes its style on the whim of the owner, one example being **Efes II**, formerly the Manhattan, on Great Portland Street north of Oxford Circus. The bar now looks down on a kebab restaurant, but it still serves the cocktail that has lately been mandatory, and after which another busy house, on Cranbourn Street off Leicester Square, has renamed itself: the **Long Island Iced Tea Shop**.

NIGHTLIFE AND ENTERTAINMENT

DISCOS AND LIVE MUSIC

Believe no disco recommendation until you're in. Being admitted to a disco is generally a matter of matching its style and paying its admission price, but in the case of a few, whose attraction for an older set is their exclusivity, introduction by a member is needed and a hefty entrance fee is exacted. Remember, too, that as soon as a place makes it into print, one part of the crowd is ready to say it's history. **Annabel's**, on Berkeley Square, has lasted a few years and is entitled to be called semipermanent. It is notorious for its un-disco-like patrons, entry fee of £25, and annual membership (via an introduction) of £500. **Stringfellow's**, on Upper St. Martin's Lane, is another place for celebrities, though membership is not necessary. Admission is £8 Monday through Thursday, £15 Friday and Saturday.

The **Hippodrome** on Charing Cross Road is similarly

expensive but gets good repeat business. The **Hammer-smith Palais** (now just Le Palais) has been here forever, opening at least 20 years before Granddad came here to jive during World War II; now restyled, it is a good, modern disco near the Hammersmith Broadway tube station. The **Wag Club** on Soho's Wardour Street attracts a truly young crowd at the leading edge of streetwise.

But while **Gossips** on Dean Street in Soho, **Limelight** on Shaftesbury Avenue, and the cheerfully extroverted **Empire Ballroom** on Leicester Square all have their regulars and deserve them, some of the best disco action is a movable feast, like the crap game immortalized by Damon Runyon. Look for strangely dressed people on line buzzing with anxiety as they try to impress the men at the door with their street smarts and rightness for this evening's session.

Country-and-western music has its own special havens, most often arts centers or pubs like the **King's Head** out at Crouch End (in north London beyond Islington), the **White Horse** in Hampstead, and the **Swan** in Stockwell (south of the river and east of Clapham). Its temple, however, is the old Art Deco **Astoria Theatre** on Charing Cross Road, where people can also dance on the two floors that once were the stalls and the dress circle.

JAZZ

London is not Copenhagen or Chicago when it comes to jazz. **Ronnie Scott** seems to have propped it up in his club on Soho's Frith Street since almost before the big band became obsolete, distributing the foreign strains through an unrivaled sequence of eminent player-guests (Tel: 439-0747). More recently arrived, but thoroughly established among aficionados for their nightly variety as well as quality, are the **Bass Clef** on Coronet Street, Islington, and the **100 Club** at 100 Oxford Street.

A pleasant venue for listening while eating is the **Jazz Bistro**, alongside **Simply Sausages**, at 340 Farringdon Street, where they offer live jazz every Thursday night, and scrumptious sausages and pizzas every day (Tel: 236-8112).

After **Pizza Express** on Dean Street and the **Dover Street Wine Bar**, the dilettante is left clutching at straws of the Sunday-Jazz-Brunch-at-the-Hotel-Russell kind, which must be a contradiction in terms, but farther out there are a couple of good jazz pubs, namely the **Bull's Head** in Barnes, a Thames-side district in the west of London, and the **Prince of Orange** on the Mile End Road. Some 25 years ago Philip Larkin suggested that as jazz increasingly became a composer's art, it would move from the club to the concert hall, but that transition has not yet been realized in London.

The newly developed complex at Chelsea Harbour by the Thames has been encouraging jazz on weekends, but until the Harbour itself gathers strength, it's likely to remain a thin strain.

CLUBS, CABARET, AND CASINOS

The term "clubs" covers a multitude of sins and, no doubt, as many virtues. There are three main types, in addition to the residential kind that are run by the social, political, sporting, and artistic networks of the country and are joined only through introductions, and then generally for life, such as the Oxford & Cambridge, the Travellers, White's (Tory politics), the Garrick (publishers and literary intellectuals), and the Caledonian (Scottish regiments).

The first kind of club is of the same caliber as those mentioned above but is open to all, or has reciprocal arrangements with certain clubs overseas, such as the American Club in Piccadilly (Tel: 499-2303) or the Royal Overseas League (Tel: 408-0214) on St. James's Street. The Sloane Club (Tel: 730-9131) on Sloane Street, Knightsbridge, was founded as a ladies-only club but now accepts men as well. Peter de Savary's St. James's Club (Tel: 629-7688) is also unrestricted in its membership, but a night there can be as expensive as a life subscription to many other clubs.

The second kind of club is the nonresidential members' club, often with a restaurant and spacious bar, such as the Groucho Club, a media enclave on Dean Street, and the ad world's rendezvous, the Moscow Club on Frith Street. (If you want to join either of these you must be nominated by a member.)

The third kind usually switches on after nightfall. It may be quite demure, like the **Spanish Garden Club** off Maddox Street west of Regent Street, or somewhat raunchy like the **Pinstripe** on Beak Street, where drinks are served by topless French maids. Women accompanying men into cellar drinking clubs with topless entertainers such as are found in the **Gaslight Club** on Duke of York Street must be prepared for stony stares from the regulars.

Two clubs that depend on old-fashioned "glamour,"

with cabaret, sophisticated trappings, food and drink, and hostesses (but with an easy welcome for couples), are **Churchill's**, near the Royal Academy in Piccadilly, and the **Director's Lodge** in Mason's Yard off St. James's. Both offer erotic cabaret as a staple, but licensed striptease clubs with pretensions to Continental quality are few. Girls whose bodies seem to have been turned on a lathe show them off on the stage of the durable **Raymond's Revuebar** on Brewer Street (a 30-year Festival of Erotica, but, thank goodness, with a changing cast). The same Raymond also runs the adjoining **Madame Jo Jo's**, a campier and more louche venue.

The **Clubman's Club** on Albemarle Street (Tel: 493-4292) offers membership to selected clubs all over Britain for an annual fee.

Casinos

The style of London gaming houses is quite unlike that found elsewhere. You must apply for membership 48 hours in advance, and the dress code of suit and tie for men is strictly enforced. There is no cabaret and no drinks or tips at the gaming tables. The settings, however, are generally grand, the meals good, and the level of play interesting to international gamblers. The picture cards, so to speak, are **Crockford's** (Tel: 493-7771) and **Aspinall's** (Tel: 629-4400), both on Curzon Street. Less exalted but still decent are the **London Park Tower Casino** (Tel: 235-6161) and the hotel casinos of the Ritz and the Hilton.

There are some 20 casinos in London, and the **British Casino Association** (Tel: 437-0678) in Leicester House, Leicester Street, will provide callers with venues, rules, and regulations.

DINNER AND DANCING

Ballroom dancing has become more of a sport or a hobby these days than a social accomplishment, but the traditional dance rhythms are still to be heard accompanying diners in the great hotels, particularly at the **Savoy**, the **Ritz**, and the **Park Lane Hilton**. However, there are a number of ethnic restaurants—Greek, Italian, Spanish, Portuguese—with live music and small dance floors where couples who are a little rusty on the steps will not feel shamed by their performance. Among these are **Barbarella 2** (Italian) on Thurloe Street in South Kensington, **Costa Dorada** (Spanish) on Hanway Street in the West End, the **Grecian Taverna & Grill** on Percy Street in

the West End, and **Os Aquanos** (Portuguese) on Por-
chester Road in Bayswater. In the discos Latin American
rhythms such as the salsa and the samba, formerly the
taste of more mature dancers, are being discovered by
the young.

DINNER ON THE RIVER

By night, with the reflection of the city's lights on the
river, the Thames takes on a different character, and many
people like to take a dinner cruise or hitch up to one of
the many pubs that give on to the water. The most frequently cruised stretch runs from Greenwich in the east
to Kew Gardens in the west, with the departure point
most often at Westminster Pier. Which direction the boat
travels varies and is generally the decision of the captain
of the day. **Catamaran Cruises** sails into (or away from)
the sunset every evening except Saturdays (Tel: 839-
3572). **Romance of London** operates three-hour cruises
on Sundays only (Tel: 620-0474). **Tidal Cruises** offers a
disco with supper (Tel: 839-2164).

There is no company as yet that sets passengers down
at any of the river pubs; these have to be reached by road.
Those that are particularly worth the effort are the **Doves**
in West London's Chiswick; the **Samuel Pepys** in an old
tea warehouse on Brooks Wharf, Upper Thames Road
near Blackfriars Bridge; the **Anchor**, a creaking warren on
the south bank of the Thames near Southwark Bridge
(resonant with echoes of Dr. Johnson); and the medieval
George, off Borough High Street near London Bridge,
whose cobbled yard is the occasional summer setting for
Morris dancing and Shakespeare plays. (Take the Underground to the London Bridge station for Brooks Wharf
and Bankside.) The **Dickens Inn** on St. Katharine's Dock
is a lively and popular place in this burgeoning area,
though it has no historical pedigree.

THEATER

Periodic crises threaten to darken one theater or another
as developers encroach or the art houses find their subsidy
inadequate even when they are booked solid. Nonetheless, nearly 50 commercial playhouses soldier on. The
Royal Shakespeare Company performs seasonally in the
Barbican complex in the City—home also of the London
Symphony Orchestra. The **Royal National Theatre** in the
South Bank Arts Centre comprises three separate stages;
the whole complex includes the Royal Festival Hall, the

Queen Elizabeth Hall, the National Film Theatre, and the Museum of the Moving Image (MOMI). That other stalwart of the classical repertory, the **Old Vic**, lies just south of Waterloo Bridge. The venue for much serious modern work, the **Royal Court Theatre**, dominates Sloane Square in Chelsea. In the summer, defying the vagaries of the weather, the **Open-Air Theatre** in Regent's Park has mounted a season of Shakespeare for 60 years. The citadels of popular entertainment are the **Drury Lane Theatre** (musicals) and the **London Palladium** in Soho (celebrity shows).

Newspaper listings are rarely comprehensive enough to satisfy either film buffs or theatergoers. The best service is provided by two weekly magazines: *Time Out* and *What's On* (both published on Wednesdays); these publications also include information on productions at outlying theaters.

The largest ticket-selling organization in Britain, for live events and sporting occasions as well as theater, was the Keith Prowse agency, which ceased trading in the fall of 1991 after 200 years, a victim of the recession. However, like the conclusion of a pantomime, there was a spectacularly happy ending. The Prowse Agency was bought by Wembley Holdings and has returned like a giant refreshed. Wembley Holdings owns the stadium that features not only international boxing and other sporting events, pop concerts by such as Tom Jones and Michael Jackson, and the annual preseason tryouts for major National Football Conference teams (who travel over from the USA for the battle, in an event called the American Bowl), but innumerable conventions and corporate hospitality events. With 4,000 employees and a new company called the Ticketing Group, which handles promotions, corporate hospitality, etc. (Tel: 240-7200), it has revivified its subsidiary, which offers a variety of programs through Keith Prowse Londoners (Tel: 0800-88-18-82).

A new service for last-minute theater bookings, **Theatre Tonight** makes telephone reservations between 11:00 A.M. and 6:00 P.M. for major West End theaters. Callers pay by Access or Visa credit cards, at normal prices with no booking fee, and collect tickets at the theater. Tel: 753-0333.

For half-price tickets (plus booking fee) to same-day performances in West End theaters, apply to the **ticket booth on Leicester Square** between 2:30 P.M. and 6:30 P.M. Ticket limit of four seats per customer; cash only. Turning this idea on its head, a new charity venture with impeccable theatrical sponsorship, **West End Cares**, sells tickets at twice their face value for the best seats in the house at sold-out smash hits (Tel: 976-6751).

Fringe Theater

Innumerable elements make up the lively phenomenon of the London fringe theater: one-act plays, satirical revues, stand-up comedy, bravura solo acts, dramas that passionately argue political causes, expressionistic shows with no discernible argument, a local playwright working the parish pump, and a foreign import in translation for the first time. The fringe is a sprawling network that includes the by-products of established theaters near the middle of town, like the **Theatre Upstairs**, part of the Royal Court Theatre on Chelsea's Sloane Square, as well as very successful venues that, properly speaking, are not in London at all, like the **Warehouse** in Croydon.

Among the many fringe theaters, some of which have a transient, fitful career, half a dozen are worth mentioning. In Islington they are the **King's Head** and the **Old Red Lion**; in Hammersmith, the **Lyric Studio**; in Chelsea, at the opposite end of the King's Road from the Royal Court, the **Man in the Moon**; at Shepherd's Bush Green, the **Bush**; and in Notting Hill, the **Gate**. One of the longest-established fringe theaters, with consistently high standards, is the **New End** in Hampstead.

The Gate is particularly loved by the critics for its habit of staging unknown foreign plays, but as a rule fringe managements do not have settled policies of commitment and prefer a varied diet. However, the **Drill Hall** in Camden prides itself on supporting gay and lesbian culture, the **Tricycle** in Brent on backing new plays and black and Irish writers. The fact that many fringe venues are advertised as clubs is not often a bar to entry. Election to membership generally can be purchased at the door, and the fee is rarely a serious deterrent. Comfortable seating is not the strong point of such theaters; people like them for more important reasons that include an interest in discovering new talent and enjoying the camaraderie that can develop in their casual atmosphere.

Children's Theater

Aside from the pre-Christmas season, when the playhouses break out in a rash of pantomimes, not a great deal is done on the London stage for children. However, there are a few specialists who fill their schedules with a range that runs from classics to mixed-media entertainments involving slides, film, modern rap, and music hall. The principal pillars are the **Unicorn Theatre** on Great Newport Street and the **Polka** on the Broadway, Wimbledon, the only theater in Britain designed specifically for children. The **Little Angel Marionette Theatre**, on Dagmar Passage off Cross Street in Islington, puts on performances for the very young as well as for older kids, and in the same vein there is the **Puppet Theatre Barge**, moored in Little Venice near Paddington Station. Some public libraries have also taken to putting on children's shows, notably Willesden Green Library. Children's cinema, incidentally, can be found at the Barbican. **Theatre Line** advises on the availability of children's shows (Tel: 0836-43-09-63).

CLASSICAL MUSIC, BALLET, AND OPERA

From cinema to theater to concert hall to opera house, the prices rise in geometric progression, and at the top end patrons can feel pressure to make a commensurately heavy investment in their personal wardrobes. However, neither tickets nor clothes need be too extravagant in the "gods," or highest seats, of the showcase of opera, the **Royal Opera House**, Covent Garden (but demand heavily exceeds supply). The classic repertoire is sung in translation at the London Coliseum on St. Martin's Lane, home of the **English National Opera**. Both of these regularly include ballet in their schedules, but the heart of the balletomane lies in **Sadler's Wells Theatre**, at the northern end of Rosebery Avenue north of Farringdon Road where it runs into St. John Street, a cultural enclave as remote as a desert fort (it can be reached on the number 38 bus from Piccadilly; the nearest Underground stop is Angel).

The principal concert halls are those in the **South Bank Arts Centre**: the Purcell Room, Queen Elizabeth Hall, and the Royal Festival Hall, overlooking the River Thames. There is also the **Royal Albert Hall** in Kensington (where the annual Promenade Concerts are held) and the **Barbican Arts Centre** in the City. At the same level of intimacy as the Purcell, **Wigmore Hall** on Wigmore Street in Marylebone schedules recitals and chamber music and has had a long and continuing record of successful debuts. In the summer **St. John's** (formerly a church), on Smith Square, off Millbank, offers a huge and daily variety of lunchtime and evening recitals and concerts (for the box office, Tel: 222-1061; open seating).

Also in summer, open-air concerts, some with fireworks, are held by the lake on the grounds of **Kenwood House** on Hampstead Heath. Take a blanket, a thick sweater, and picnic (proper plates and glasses, please). No other advice on dress is needed for audiences of serious music; the majority of listeners at the great concert halls tend to dress formally but not competitively.

GOING HOME

The last Underground trains leave central London on weekdays at varying times between 11:30 P.M. and 1:00 A.M. (the Piccadilly Line), but midnight (and 11:00 P.M. on Sundays) is more the average. In the larger railway terminals, the first editions of the next day's newspapers, led always by the popular tabloids, begin to go on sale around 10:00 P.M. Night buses have Trafalgar Square as their hub—look for the prefix N on the route number and on the bus stop. (*Note:* The one-day and multizone London Transport bus passes are not valid on N buses.) About a third of London's 16,000 taxis are in action on the night shift, which is considered anything from 8:00 P.M. onward. The worst times for finding cabs are around 7:00 P.M. (when the day shift is going home, the night shift is not yet on the scene, and everyone else seems to be leaving the office or heading out to dinner and the theater) and at 11:00 P.M., when there is a general exodus from theaters, pubs, and restaurants. But at 1:00 A.M. there is often quite a fair supply, particularly near bridges where cabs are coming back into the center (such as Parliament Square or Aldwych). Oddly enough, though there is a small supplement after 8:00 P.M., the fare at night tends to be lower because of the relatively traffic-free streets.

A law on seat belts that came into force in 1991 requires passengers in the back seats of all cars, including taxis, to wear them, when provided. (Older taxis do not have seat belts.) The risk you run in ignoring this law is a £100 fine.

SHOPS AND SHOPPING

By Alex Hamilton

A "nation of shopkeepers" should be able to look to its capital city to be the catalogue and complete repository of any commodity one could wish to buy. Just as a character in a Jane Austen novel travels up from the country with the sole object of getting the haircut his provincial town could not manage, so it has been the practice for many to excuse a visit to London on the grounds that it is the only place to buy, say, a shoehorn a yard long, or a container to carry an egg uncracked up a mountain, or an umbrella that is also a swordstick (all available today). Not to mention objects of daily use, such as a sachet of Japanese tea.

Despite the speed of modern merchandising, which allows many regional high streets to reflect the latest lines in an echo of metropolitan style, and despite the crippling effect of new taxes and policies that force many businesses to go out or go under, the notion that London is the lodestone for shoppers still prevails.

In the early nineties some of the shine is taken off by the depressing effects of the most serious recession since the 1930s. These are evident not only in the mien of those who fear they may join the casualties already in the hands of the receivers, but in empty shop fronts and ramshackle temporary substitutes, even on such world-famous commercial arteries as Oxford Street. Visitors finding a gap where they thought a thriving enterprise was located should not, however, conclude that it has gone out of business. It may be simply that the huge increases in

221

rentals and local taxes have driven it to transfer to a less demanding town.

The usual response of merchants to sticky trading conditions and a public that has decided that saving is almost as good as earning is to form partnerships and mergers, cut staff, and offer discounts. All these measures have been taken, with the result, first, that the power and presence of many kinds of chain stores have been enormously increased at the expense of small businesses; second, that it sometimes seems impossible to find anybody working in a store willing and able to take money, let alone give advice on a purchase; and third, that "sales" are now ubiquitous and continuous rather than seasonal. Formerly there were two periods when genuine bargains could be anticipated—the New Year sales and the summer sales—but now there is literally no week in the year without its rash of special events, labeled New Year, Winter, Spring, Summer, and Autumn, and between times Shoulder, Closing Down, End of Line, Super, Amazing, Everything Must Go, and, when all passion is spent, simply Sale. This can be counterproductive: Buyers come to mistrust sellers who are not able to calculate the true value of their goods. People shopping for bargains should remember that inferior merchandise is often brought in from wholesalers in the hope of unloading it on customers trawled in by the genuine bargains on display in the window. Also, although it is illegal, it is fairly common for some shopkeepers to attach stickers advertising reductions from a high price that had never existed.

People often shop not merely to satisfy their needs but as an emotional episode, a mental and physical exercise. During such window-shopping they are flexible and float through an ambience of seductive and competing claims on their senses. But when they are in pursuit of a definite and coveted article, these same people want to track it efficiently to its authentic source. To accommodate the two distinct approaches—of the window-shopper and the hunter-gatherer—this chapter is in two main sections. The first describes the town in terms of general shopping, character, and atmosphere, and the topographical centers where it makes most sense to saunter and allow surprises to happen and unexpected acquisitions to be made. The second, leaving serendipity behind, homes in on the particular, with suggestions under classified headings of where to go if you have a shopping list already sketched out. The chapter closes with information on the current rules governing tax allowances, and ways and means of getting the booty home.

As a rule, in the West End shopping hours are 9:00 A.M. to 5:30 P.M. Monday through Saturday, with an extension to 8:00 P.M. on Thursdays; in Knightsbridge and Chelsea the late-hours bonanza comes on Wednesdays. There has recently been some relaxation in the Sunday trading laws; nevertheless, so far generally only supermarkets and souvenir shops have taken advantage of this to open on Sundays.

GENERAL SHOPPING
The Institutions

At the apex of London shopping are three magnificent stores: Harrods, Selfridges, and Liberty. Their reputation for supremacy over other emporia parallels that of the Ritz, Claridge's, and the Savoy over other hotels. It would not please any of them to be called one-stop shopping, but for people with deep purses they come close. They are flagships without fleets, self-contained and independent, with no clones or trailing appendages, bar some small Liberty concessions in other stores. Granted, this year Harrods took an unusual and extraordinary step in opening a large branch at Heathrow airport, and it is impressive—but not to be regarded as a substitute for the headquarters.

Harrods is on the Brompton Road, four blocks west of Knightsbridge Underground station. (Patrons might be expected to arrive by chauffeured limo, or at least a taxi, but it's not the law.) Harrods' sale, which takes place in August, is the only one in London that still means anything. It is not only that Harrods will sell you anything, or at any rate acquire it for you, but also that it provides services. It will sell you a piano, and send you a tuner to keep it in good fettle; it sells books as well as lending them from its library; it can sell you a dog and also provide a vet to see it through distemper and other canine disorders. It runs its own London sightseeing tours on open-top double-decker buses, as if the buildings along the way were themselves part of the Harrods stock. There was at one time a van with the sole purpose of delivering a loaf of bread daily to a woman 30 miles away in Kent, an arrangement that came to an end only when she died.

The other two stores are not quite so grand nor so all-encompassing; you do not hesitate before entering to check faults in your dress. In fact, **Selfridges** is downright bourgeois, so much so that many people feel it is more magnitude than magnificence that allows it to dominate Oxford Street, but both Selfridges and Libertys justify a cab ride. What Selfridges has is an exaggerated spread of what is offered by a routine big store, and a department for everything. Its food store has nothing like the chic of Harrods, its hampers have not the style of Fortnum & Mason in Piccadilly (see below), its fashions are not nearly as provocative and exciting as those of **Dickins & Jones** (Regent Street), nor its lingerie so deliquescent as **Fenwick's** (New Bond Street). None of them matches the refurbished glamour of **Debenham's** (1 Welbeck Street in the Marylebone district); nevertheless, the action provided by the customers at Selfridges, the traffic and bustle of the store, gives it a character that sets it apart.

Liberty opened as East India House in 1875 on Regent Street, with one façade on Great Marlborough Street, and was rebuilt just after World War I in a mock-Tudor vein, using the timbers of a couple of the last Royal Navy sailing warships. The orientation toward Oriental goods persists to this day. Liberty's strength lies in its leadership in British arts and crafts, its silks and prints and fabrics, its antiques, and an upper story devoted to furniture backed by a useful export division. Its comestibles display is negligible, except in the sensuous interface where teas and jams meet pomades and scents. Most staff, cashiers and clerks included, must have some formal training, preferably a degree, in arts and crafts. (The official seal that designates British design, which can be used as a barometer of ideas in vogue, can be viewed in a permanent exhibition at the **Design Centre Shop**, a retail outlet at 28 Haymarket, just south of Piccadilly Circus. For a continually updated display of the notions of scores of young British fashion designers, check out **Hyper-Hyper** on the High Street, Kensington.)

Knightsbridge

From Harrods it is a short step east along the Brompton Road to a variety of flossy, glossy upmarket fashion stops such as **Episode** (classics in natural fibers) and **R. M. Williams** (riding gear) and, on the corner with Knightsbridge, the **The Scotch House** (tartan romanticism and cashmere). This is fashion-magazine territory. At the more affordable east end is a big Knightsbridge store popular also for its accessories, **Harvey Nichols** (a Debenham's subsidiary), and, on the other side of Harrods, the boutiques of such high-style designers as **Caroline Charles** and **Bruce Oldfield**, strung along Beauchamp Place among interesting restaurants and night spots. This terrace in particular is the parish pump of modish gossip.

Oxford Street

The prospect from Selfridges (on the corner with Orchard Street) is less enticing. A walk the length of Oxford Street from Marble Arch east to Tottenham Court Road, ricocheting among the crowds on the sidewalks, is a long, hard grind for a poor return. Every passing year seems to bring the street's style down a further notch. There remain more than a score of shoe shops, most under the same ownership, among them **Lilley & Skinner** (one of the world's largest vendors of footwear, at number 360), and **Olympus Sports**, at 134, outstanding for its training shoes and shooting boots and bouncing young staff. Big department stores whose integrity and quality lift them above the general hustle include the two branches of **Marks & Spencer**, at Marble Arch and its Pantheon Store at 173, east of Oxford Circus, and **John Lewis** near the midway point just west of Oxford Circus. The other two big guns are audio stores, of which **HMV**'s two branches, one near the Bond Street tube station, the other east of Oxford Circus, are in every way better laid out, and more comprehensively stocked on both classical and pop sides, than their more vulgar rival near the Tottenham Court Road tube station, **Virgin Megastore**.

It is more rewarding (aesthetically, if not financially) to discover the fancier shops on the tributary roads here. There is little point in roaming the hinterland north of Oxford Street, except for the small fancy businesses that have taken over **St. Christopher's Place**, though the Marylebone district does have some interesting highly specialized shops, such as **Blunderbuss** for militaria, at 14 Thayer Street (a short strip within the southern part of Marylebone High Street); a model shop called **W&H Mod-**

els, at 14 New Cavendish Street; and, at 105 Marylebone High Street, **Maison Sagne**, one of England's most famous patisseries, where they make little marzipan (almond paste) animals. However, to the south a parallel to the high-fashion leaders of Beauchamp Place can be found in **South Molton Street**, where names like Gaultier, Hamnet, Lacroix, and Rifat Ozbek rule at **Browns**, and the Ali Baba's cave for fashion jewelry is **Butler & Wilson**.

Regent Street

From Liberty on Great Marlborough Street, the excursion south, around the corner and down Regent Street, is more cheering, beginning with a cheer for the fluttery, flattering, flowery patterns of the women's clothes and home furnishings of **Laura Ashley** at number 256. The ambience of the street is improving, particularly since the big effort made in 1992 to restore some of the elegance first lent it by its architect, John Nash. Like Piccadilly, it tends to overload on airlines and national tourist offices, dead zones from the viewpoint of a window-shopper, but otherwise there are enough good displays and variety to warrant spending an extra hour on your feet taking it in.

While Knightsbridge is the heart of money fashion and Oxford Street is strong on street fashion for the young, Regent Street focuses on pragmatic, sensible clothing. It has been thoroughly infiltrated by the wool industry. At number 149 is the **Woollen Centre**, at 184 **London House** for wool and cashmere, at 99 the **London Textile Co** (also wool); at 163 is the **House of Cashmere** for knitwear and suiting (one of many nearly the same), and almost next door at 169 is **Regent's**, for high-class ready-made suits, jackets, and capes for men and women. At 184 there is a reprise of the **Scotch House** (see above in Knightsbridge) for mohair stoles with a Scots slant, not to mention its kilts and clan stuff, badges of allegiance, and kilt pins. Kilts less classy but cheaper can be found at **British Designer Knitwear Group**, in the Quadrant Arcade, 80 Regent Street. This last also basically features wool, having been started by a group of five designers before handmade designer knitwear took off in the 1980s. Today you find handmade all-British cotton and woollen sweaters, and unusually embroidered sweatshirts as sort of higher-class souvenirs.

You could also buy a wool suit at **Burberry's** (165).

Today raincoats are not all they give their name to. Indeed practically all the clothes they sell now carry the Burberry name, and you pay for the privilege—embroidered on a woman's cotton sweater for £82.50, a three-quarter jacket for £260, a silk handkerchief for £11.50, kids' jeans for £35, and a plain white tee-shirt for £15.

Then there is a companion shop to R. M. Williams (in Knightsbridge), called the **Original Bushmen's Outfitters,** which offers otherwise authentic Australian clothing— boots, hats, jeans, weskits—endorsed with chatty ha-ha poems in the window from grateful longtime clients in the Outback.

But back to British clothes with traditions of the sturdi-est kind. **Aquascutum** at 100 is grand and expensive, with men's and women's raincoats at £350, a man's summer-weight suit at £380, a woman's summer suit at £600, a man's suede blouson at £275. **Jaeger** (200) is also for both sexes, quietly fashionable, nearly as pricey. **The Highlands** deals in country squire gear, mainly rural out-doors clothes. At 103 you'll find the byword for the English club gentleman, with the tailoring of understated good taste, **Austin Reed** (though, like some gentlemen's clubs, they also now admit women).

Aside from clothing and an emphasis on china, glass, and pottery (see below), Regent Street proffers an alluring miscellany in the **Pen Shop,** at 199, directly opposite Hamley's Toy Shop, and **Henry's** on the corner of Conduit Street, which specializes in purses and cases; **Godiva Chocolatier** on the corner of Prince's Street; a giant toy-shop at 188 called **Hamley's** (see below), plus two names that reverberate through social history for their trade in silverware and jewelry, **Mappin & Webb** (170) and **Garrard Crown Jewellery** (112).

In addition to a couple of examples of the **Chinacraft** chain, which deals in cheap lines, at 203 on the corner of Conduit Street, is **Villeroy & Boch,** a firm that has dealt in European china (mainly of German and Luxembourgish provenance) since 1748. They have tableware and gift items, all dishwasher safe and almost all microwave safe.

Wilson & Gill (137) deals in china and cutlery, and features lines from Rosenthal and from Thomas. A seven-piece cutlery place setting is priced from £80 to £200, a five-piece china setting from £20 to £120. They will order and ship anything for you, with prices going up to £250 for a single plate.

At **Waterford Wedgwood** (158; branches also on Piccadilly and Oxford Circus) the top seller is the traditional Peter Rabbit nursery line; its blue-and-white Wedgwood Jasper remains a favorite for gifts. Those who find their prices daunting can always come away with a Wedgwood metal caddy of specialty teas, at about £6.

Finally, **Lawley's**, almost adjacent, is probably the most successful at combining fun with serious buying. The gift stuff on the ground floor may make it seem as if the shop has been vulgarly changed from its old style, but upstairs there is still a very large range of British china and crystal. They stock Royal Crown Derby, Minton, the ever-popular Royal Bunnykins nursery china, Portmeirion tea sets, and Royal Doulton crystal sets. Ornaments and gifts include Caithness paperweights that look like giant marbles and Staffordshire Enamels.

Piccadilly

There are few other arteries that will properly challenge a real window-shopper. There is plenty to look at in Piccadilly, though, starting with the Royal Academy and continuing with automobile showrooms, airline offices, hotels, and the crowded French National Tourist Office, but for the shopper it really boils down to three or four high-style ports of call. **Fortnum & Mason**, in business since the mid-18th century, is in the grocers' pantheon. The Fortnum hamper, an egregious extravagance used, for example, for a picnic at a sports event or Henley regatta, costs about £100 for four people (Tel: 734-8040; order 24 hours ahead). **Simpson's**, 100 yards west of Piccadilly Circus, remains one of the great fashion department stores. Farther west, past Fortnum & Mason, **Hatchard's**, the bookseller, does a marvelously efficient job with a huge stock, though its attempts to acquire a modern look and lose the image of catering only to the carriage trade have deprived it of some of its original ethos.

It can be argued that the streets off Piccadilly make up for the deficiencies of Piccadilly itself. That is true up to a point. On parallel **Jermyn Street**, a name to conjure with in custom tailoring, where the young cub went to be fitted up for a career in foreign climes, are **Church's Shoes** at 112, and **Turnbull & Asser** at 70, for shirts that fit better than your skin. On the other (northern) side of Piccadilly is another provider of shirts more eloquent often than their wearers: **Airey & Wheeler**, with two branches, one at 44 Piccadilly that fits men with chests below 44 inches, the other nearby at 8 Sackville Street for those whose thoraxes expand up from 45 inches to opera-singer class.

The Arcades

The word "arcade" has been dragged down in recent times by the spate of complexes featuring computer games, slot machines, and virtual-reality adventures, but to the shopper it still describes a small pedestrian enclave off a main street with a walkway between small, almost intimate, specialty shops. The two smartest, with an ethos most worth inhaling, are the **Royal Arcade**, a late-Victorian alley running off Albemarle Street (which itself runs north from Piccadilly) in the West End, and nearby **Burlington Arcade**, created in 1819, which becomes **Piccadilly Arcade**, added in 1910. There are beadles about, empowered to prevent you from singing, running, cycling, carting heavy loads, and in general conducting yourself in an improper fashion. Almost incidentally, the shops sell—expensive stuff like sculpted, perfumed toiletries, Cuban tobacco, West African chocolate, Irish linen, cashmere sweaters, brocaded waistcoats.

Bond Street

Running south from Oxford Street as New Bond Street, growing grander all the way and becoming Old Bond Street as it approaches Piccadilly, Bond Street has a very high density of glamorous properties, particularly with its galleries for sculpture, painting, and prints, such as **Wildensteins** at number 147, **Ackermann & Johnson** at 33 (sporting prints), and the **Leger Galleries** (English painting) at 13. **Cartier** (175) and **Asprey** (165) provide some of the world's greatest displays of gold, jewelry, and antiques. Much the same is done for porcelain and silverware at **Georg Jensen**. These are all down at the Piccadilly end, along with the fashion houses of **Chanel** (26 Old Bond Street), **Lagerfeld** (173 New Bond Street), and **Saint Laurent Rive Gauche** (137 New Bond Street), while more affordable and various attractions in women's clothes can be toured in the street's only big store, at the other end, **Fenwick's**.

The King's Road

Even before the mini-skirted Mary Quant alighted with her liberating fashion messages and John Stephen dramatically altered men's styles on Carnaby Street, the King's Road was the strip where the young peacock and the ambitious talent flaunted their splendors. The fashion parade on the sidewalk is often more dazzling than in the great muster of boutiques.

The bohemian character of the artists' colonies of an earlier time—the Victorian era through World War II—is still reflected by a fair number of art galleries; the most interesting and modestly priced is **Stephen Bartley** at 62 Old Church Street, which runs to the north off the King's Road. Two old established art shops on the Road itself are **Chelsea Art Stores** at number 314, stocking everything for the painter, including smocks, and **Green & Stone**, framing specialists, at 259.

The top names for fabrics, furnishing, and linen are **Designers Guild** at 227, **Liberty Prints** at 340A, and **Osborne & Little** at 304. The long-established **Givan's** at 207 is the place for fine bedroom and bathroom linens and cotton. Nor should the local souk be ignored: The **Peter Jones** department store on Sloane Square at the Road's eastern end yields linens, fabrics, and household goods as well as clothing and much more. It is also a favorite registry for brides, as is the more exclusive and upmarket **General Trading Company**, a few steps away around the corner at 144 Sloane Street. More specialized for table- and kitchenware is **David Mellor**, across the square at number 4.

For outrageous, avant-garde clothing the first stop must be at 430, chez **Vivienne Westwood**, and for classical elegance (example: Princess Diana) **Chelsea Design Company**, a few paces off at 65 Sydney Street. Fashion boutiques pour on the price, but last year's sensations come a little less expensively. At 241, **Designers Sale Studio** offers last season's factory surplus from the output of such as Jenny, Byblos, and Christian Lacroix. (Another branch with the same name makes similar offers in St. John's Wood, at 78 The High Street.)

SPECIAL INTERESTS
Antiques

Some of London's antiques businesses and their owners seem even more ancient than their goods, though the goods are for the most part old enough. The great concentrations turn up at auctions and street markets (see below for both), as well as covered markets like **Gray's Antique Market** at 58 Davies Street in the West End. Above all other neighborhoods for antiques there is Chelsea, which is littered with antiques shops, mostly grand ones, including markets with several dealers under one roof. Two of these are on the King's Road, the massed stalls of **Antiquarius** at number 131, and the rather older **Chelsea Antique Market** at 253. More than 200 dealers are represented at 535: **The London and Provincial Antiques Dealers Association**.

But essentially the business has been trailing west—for example, to **Christopher Wray** at number 600, and north of these onto the Fulham Road, where one of London's last old-fashioned repositories of treasure is **Stephen Long** at 348, dearly beloved of interior decorators seeking chic and reasonably priced clutter, with **David Gill** at 60 for Art Nouveau and **L'Odeon** at 173 for Art Deco.

The other long stretch, practically a constitutional as walks go, is **Kensington Church Street**, heading north from Kensington High Street and lined with dozens of antiques shops all the way up to Notting Hill Gate. Two good stops among so many are **Pamela Teignmouth** at number 108 for 18th-century furniture, and **Raffety** at 34 for old clocks.

Auctions

In London, auctions bid up from a low or reserve price to whatever it takes. There are at least a score of regular events, with dealers and yourselves all in there pitching together. Almost always it is better to attend such early-day viewings as are offered, in order to ponder and to avoid the difficulties of seeing the goods when there are crowds. Aside from those mentioned under the specialized headings below, a couple worth a trip are **International Wine Auctions** at 40 Victoria Way (Tel: 081-293-4992; use the Embankment tube station) and **R. F. Greasby** at 211 Longley Road, Tooting Graveney (Tel: 081-672-1100; use the Tooting Broadway tube station), a mass turnout at which anything under the sun may come under the hammer, as it consists of goods disposed of by London Transport or bankrupt factory stock auctioned at the direction of the courts.

There are four internationally famous salesrooms, where the spectators' blood sometimes runs cold as the bidding climbs to stratospheric prices. These are the first names that occur to people coming on a putative masterpiece while rummaging in their attic: **Sotheby's** at 34 New Bond Street (for advance details, Tel: 493-8080), **Christie's** at 8 King Street off St. James's Square (Tel: 839-9060) and at 85 Old Brompton Road, **Phillips** at 101 New Bond Street (Tel: 629-6602), and **Bonham's** on Montpelier Street in Knightsbridge (Tel: 584-9161).

For high-value acquisitions, an export license may be necessary.

Books

There is no VAT (Value-Added Tax) on books, either new or secondhand. A law on retail price maintenance requires booksellers to sell at the prices marked by the publishers on the books, though educational titles are excepted and there is some minimal discounting for particular books. Nevertheless the main shopping arteries show many piles of bargain-book offers, which are generally remaindered stock or new editions published specifically for the cheap book market.

The bookstore chains, the most important by volume being **W. H. Smith**, **Dillons**, **Waterstones**, and **Books Etc.**, have in general improved their stock control and altered their appearance to become bright, sterile environments, a great help to the shopper who knows what he wants but not very appetizing to the browser. Even **Foyle's** on Charing Cross Road, at its corner with Manette Street—formerly famous for having a copy of everything and not being able to find it—has recently given itself a colossal overhaul. You now can cast your eye over 30 miles of shelving and pick out your title from the 5 million in stock.

London is riddled with bookshops. **Hatchard's** on Piccadilly and the **Dillons** branch on Malet Street at the University of London, east of Tottenham Court Road, are the grandest productions, but Charing Cross Road is still the backbone. At number 80, **Zwemmer's**, for instance, is the fountainhead of photographic books, new and secondhand: the history and the art, as well as techniques for pros, advanced amateurs, and fans. (Do not confuse it with **Zwemmer's OUP**, a few doors away, which has the same ownership but whose stock is exclusively made up of books from the Oxford University Press.) Next door, **Alhod** is all books on the Middle East and Muslim world. Meditating southward, you find **Silver Moon**, at number 68, claimed to be the largest women's bookshop in the world, with an entire wall of lesbian books, from ideology to thrillers. Another shop with a cause is **Books for a Change** (52), a project of CND (Campaign for Nuclear Disarmament) with Friends of the Earth and War on Want.

The higgledy-piggledy warrens of secondhand and antiquarian books on Charing Cross Road include **Shipley** (70) for art and jazz, and **Pordes** (58), with a general list. An excellent antiquarian cave, with burrow succeeding burrow and sallow bibliophiles on stools squinting at their finds, is **Quinto** (48A).

Powerhouse among antiquarians is **Maggs Bros.** of Mayfair, at 50 Berkeley Square. They will not only serve your special interests but also go in for "creative bookselling"—devising themes for collectors to build on.

The traveller wanting to peruse more travel has four excellent specialists to choose from. **The Travel Bookshop**, some way west in Holland Park at 13 Blenheim Crescent, is a long, narrow shop with an informed and enthusiastic owner. **Travellers' Bookshop**, in the pedestrian alley Cecil Court off Charing Cross Road, is full of antiquarian interests and has its own cache of arcana in the shape of the largest collection in the world of Baedeker guides. The most recent arrival on the travel book scene is **Daunt Books** at 83 Marylebone High Street, in huge elegant premises the size of a barn; its young owner is determined to stock at least one copy of every travel book published. Finally, the biggest and best source of maps, often covering places you might not suppose have been charted, is **Edward Stanford** at 12 Long Acre, near Covent Garden. Another with a very large stock is **Geographia**, at 58 Ludgate Hill, near St. Paul's Cathedral.

Two interesting shops for antique maps are the **Map House**, 54 Beauchamp Place, near Harrods, and **Jonathan Potter**, at 21 Grosvenor Street in Mayfair.

For official documents, surveys, and transcripts of government White and Green Papers (proposals for legislation), parliamentary proceedings, and much more, use one of the many branches of HMSO (**Her Majesty's Stationery Office**). For business and law studies, first try **Hammicks** at 119 Fleet Street, 100 yards from the Law Courts.

Clothes

Women's wear is featured in stores described throughout this chapter, but it would be a shame not to mention **Bradley's of Knightsbridge** (at 85 Knightsbridge) for the lingerie that promotes inner confidence, **Janet Reger** at 2 Beauchamp Place (in the same district) for dramatic creations associated with silken (or satin) dalliance, and **David Shilling** at 5 Homer Street, near where Marylebone Road meets the Edgware Road (by appointment only; Tel: 487-3179) for his cartwheel hats and freewheeling headgear fantasies to turn other heads at Ascot Races.

For men the various intriguing possibilities start conservatively at **Austin Reed** at 103 Regent Street, stepping up to chic power suits from **Antony Price** at 34 Brook Street in Mayfair. **Cecil Gee** is a chain, with branches in Long Acre, the King's Road, and New Bond Street, that offers up-to-date styles. For custom tailoring, along with an appetizing panorama of silk shirts, pajamas, and dressing gowns, the devotional murmurs are exchanged mainly on Savile Row and Jermyn Street. On the former, parallel to and west of Regent Street, a tailor's measure from each other, are **Huntsman** at 11, and **Henry Poole** at 15. At 7 Dorset Street in Marylebone, **Grey Flannel** is anything but, its stock including smart shirts, jackets, pullovers, and brilliant casuals.

Younger men gravitate toward **Yves Saint Laurent** at 137 Bond Street, while for gear in which to cruise the clubs they go to **Slot Machine** at 103 Oxford Street, finding there what is fashionable but not exclusive designer wear. And for desirable tee-shirts the cynosure is **Daniel James** on South Molton Street (south of Oxford Street, just west of New Bond Street). For feeding-frenzy clothes shopping among the young, the time is Sunday and the place **Camden Market**, where streets and streets and streets, from Camden High to Chalk Farm Road, are packed with loaded stalls and swarming youth.

Those of all ages who go on growing a little longer than the rest may find help from **Long Tall Sally** at 19

Dorset Street (east off Baker Street, south of Marylebone Road), with beautiful clothes for tall women. They can complete the ensemble at the **Small and Tall Shoe Shop** at 71 York Street (a few blocks to the northwest), where small means British sizes 13 to 2½, tall 8½ to 11. Branches of the **High and Mighty** chain do their best for the frustrated man-and-a-half. Among their branches are those at 83 Knightsbridge and in The Plaza at 120 Oxford Street.

Children's Clothes

Mothercare at 461 Oxford Street (the western, Marble Arch, end) is the headquarters of a chain of stores that, besides selling clothing, tries to cope with everything new parents need, from a huge maternity tee-shirt to a shield for VCR controls, and a babywalker. You'll find baby floats for swimming and baby sunglasses for being mysterious in, not to mention minute sandals, prams, cots, and mobiles.

The clothes offered for smaller children (up to about 10 years) at **Hennes** at 123 Kensington High Street (and two branches on Oxford Street) are low-priced and good value, basically in plain colors, though with some stripes and fantasy for toddlers. Expensively educated children in Britain often wear school uniforms, and this is the style of **Slick Willies**, a short distance away at number 41. There you'll also find roller skates and parka-like jackets. For kiddies' soldier uniforms and soldier dressing gowns, seek out **Dragon's** at 23 Walton Street in Chelsea. Two branches of **Please Mum** sell exclusive and expensive children's wear, as you might expect from shops on such prime sites as 15 Orchard Street (near Selfridges) and 69 New Bond Street.

On Elizabeth Street near Victoria Station, the exotic and the homegrown are neighbors: **Inca** at 45 and **Young England** at 46. This is the flowery, protected world of the pre-teen as it would like to manifest itself in England: on the one hand, South American cotton and dramatic costume jewelry; on the other, Laura Ashley-cum-royal affectations. Here the 19th-century sailor suit survives, and we meet our first waistcoat.

Gold, Silver, and Jewelry

The street named **Hatton Garden**, running from the eastern end of Holborn across to Clerkenwell, is given over almost entirely to the precious stones and metals business, wholesale and retail, where the valuer and the vendor, the cutter and the elderly itinerant salesman in yarmulke and white beard are all to be seen in action.

Even this apparently bottomless source of wealth has been affected by the economic problems that beset the rest of the country—the erosions are visible in the increased number of sale notices and declarations of bankruptcy and movings to addresses out of town. The damage as yet is only slight, however. For antique and modern jewelry, for old gold and rolled gold and Krugerrands, for silver and platinum, bullion and pearls, for pearl stringing, remodeling, wedding rings and engagement rings and eternity rings and just rings, for watches, clocks, chains, bracelets, pendants, for silver-plated book jackets and filigree brooches and jeweled earrings, Hatton Garden is still the place.

Buy diamonds on scales where the second pan is balanced with silver weights; have your initials carved on a gold-filigree brooch; find shops where a whole room may be devoted just to solitaires; check the daily bullion prices at 9 carat, 18 carat, and 22 carat. In the window of **King Solomon's Mine** a lapis lazuli cat is mounted on a crystal ball, in **Gerrards** a silver nymph swings in a silver arbor, at **Vingt Trois** some 500 rings are individually priced at sums between £250 and £6,000. In the **Garden Workshop**, where the blooms are in gold and silver, and interest-free credit is given on purchases over £125, a platinum Christ suffers on an agate cross; at **Classic Jewels** earrings go for between £115 and £1,125; at **Bernstones** a round-cut diamond, weight 2.75 carats, is available in the window at £15,250, and a round brilliant of 12.11 carats valued at £138,000 available for inspection inside.

At any of the above or at **Elite Gems**, **Ullmann**, **Hatton Diamonds**, **Fine Jewels**, **Hamilton's**, **Solitaire**, and many others on the Garden or on the roads running off it, you can negotiate to your heart's desire at a price not even to be whispered outside. On Thursdays there are nice, cozy lunchtime (1:30 P.M.) clearance sales at **Hatton Garden Auctions** (number 36; for viewings, Tel: 242-6452).

Hatton Garden does not have a monopoly. The most famous names in the retail business are a long way across town on Bond Street: **Cartier** and **Asprey**, whose fantasies in gems and precious metals sparkle on the ears, bosoms, and fingers of the glitterati, providing all the advertising they need.

And to learn just how little even really good silver can make, try selling your heirloom spoons and teapots at the **London Silver Vaults** on the other side of High Holborn in Chancery House, 53 Chancery Lane, where many dealers work in a catacomb of shops to offer a staggering cache of argentine creations, mundane and fantasy.

Music

For many instruments, teaching manuals, and classical sheet music, the publishers **Boosey & Hawkes**, at 295 Regent Street, and **Chappell**, 50 New Bond Street, are the best bets. (Other music publishers operate retail outlets; check the telephone directory.) For shops selling instruments, wind instruments in particular, Chiltern Street in Marylebone is a civilized strum. At the corner of Dorset Street is **All Flutes Plus**, where "plus" means mainly piccolos. Within earshot is **Howarth of London**, for saxophones, clarinets, and oboes. On the other side of Baker Street, at 106A Crawford Street, the leading brass dealer is **Phil Parker**.

For recorded versions of classical music, see in particular **HMV** on Oxford Street. Well established also is **Chimes** at 44 Marylebone High Street (the north end).

Stamps and Coins

Collectors may be tempted to kill in order to complete a set of whatever. These passions are held in check at the auctions and dealings of the world's leading philatelic dealer since 1856, **Stanley Gibbons** at 399 The Strand. The absence of any mailbox, so postmen can deliver only during opening hours, is a hint that a piece of paper the size of a butterfly wing and not half as pretty can be a very big deal. The rack of catalogues, with just the South America section reaching Part 20, indicates the vast and universal sprawl; the models of postmen and postboxes in a glass showcase represent the democratic awareness and welcome the amateur. Auctions are held monthly except in July and August.

The Strand is, in fact, the philatelic focus of London. **Strand Stamps** (opposite Stanley Gibbons, see above) is egalitarian and enthusiastic, with plenty of low-priced offers, while the neighboring **Stamp Centre** is more upmarket, with scores of dealers.

Coin auctions are held by **A. H. Baldwin**, with **Glen-**

denning's, at 7 Blenheim Street in Mayfair (Tel: 493-2445), and another good option is **Seaby's** at 8 Cavendish Square (northwest of Oxford Circus). The questing numismatist can otherwise try his luck on Saturdays at **Cutler Street Market** by Middlesex Street (north of the Tower of London) or head for the small streets opposite the British Museum to retailers like **Robert Johnson** at 15 Bury Place, whose stock begins with 400 B.C. and where Roman coins as well as proof sets of British coins from the Royal Mint can be had.

Street Markets

They battle on, a dwindling band that looks increasingly scruffy, their goods hardly worth the house room. Their interest lies not in the shopping but in the activity of the traders hustling their gimcrack lines in clothing, belts and purses and slippers, household goods, and books at their last gasp.

The stalls on **Portobello Road** (use Notting Hill tube station) are licensed only on Saturdays, all day, when they tend to obscure the scores of art and antiques galleries on either side that are open all week. For antiques **Camden Passage** is open Saturdays and Wednesdays (use Angel tube station). The most enjoyable is **Camden Lock** on weekends and public holidays (use Camden Town tube station), for its color, variety, and holiday feel.

Operating on Sundays until 2:00 P.M., **Petticoat Lane**, as Middlesex Street is called, today hardly lives up to its former reputation as a feisty rogues' gallery of picturesque characters who sold cheap items of dubious provenance under cover of some memorable waggishness (use Aldgate tube station). But way down river at **Greenwich** is an open-air market with a growing reputation, featuring all the usual bric-a-brac and saucy repartee, and some special lines in Oriental china and pottery (open 8:00 A.M. to 4:00 P.M. on weekends).

Toys and Games

For everything from conventional dolls, and railways with tracks, and machines for going into space, to the most extravagant fantasies and miniature Mercedes Benz roadsters, the fatally seductive place is **Hamley's**, six floors on Regent Street packed with the stuff of dreams. Many stores have their toy departments, but nothing else is remotely comparable. They claim, in fact, to be the biggest toy shop in the world.

Nevertheless, it is worth noting that **Just Games** at 71 Brewer Street in Soho has a useful stock of backgammon, Cluedo, Monopoly, spirographs, vast chess sets, and 4,000-piece jigsaw puzzles. For computer games try **Virgin Games** at the east end of Oxford Street, where these and board games are sold in addition to jigsaw puzzles. The Dungeons and Dragons fancy is also well served here with hundreds of lead figures, and boards and books are sold as well.

For games involving muscle—and bats, swords, rackets, or clubs—for children and sports people of all ages, there is a parallel to Hamley's, **Lillywhite's** on Piccadilly Circus. With the best of equipment and clothes and occasionally some professionals about, this is the serious but not quite clinical end of fun. **Multi-Sports** on High Holborn has a standard range of track suits, training gear, and bats and balls of all kinds, from table tennis to cricket.

For something impenetrable by the worst British weather, for the Berhaus couloir jacket and backpacks, not forgetting the Karrimor Diddy for kiddies, for camping stoves and tents, gadgets and compasses and suction plugs, start the trail at any one of several branches of **Black's** (for example, at 53 Rathbone Place, just north of Oxford Street, near Tottenham Court Road, and at 10 Holborn). Similarly excellent is the **YHA Adventure Shop**, 14 Southampton Street in Covent Garden.

Credit cards strike more sparks than traveller's checks in London, but as this is a buyers' market, most vendors will bend in your direction. To avoid paying VAT (Value Added Tax) of 17.5 percent, fill out a form at British Customs, attach a sales receipt for the goods, and mail the form back to the relevant shop for a refund. (Many advertise this mandate of law as a service.) For American tourists, the minimum amount eligible varies, from £50 to £150. (Check this out with the store concerned.) The law requires every vendor to write out a full, itemized receipt for every transaction over £10, if asked to. (Check the electronically generated slip first, as the full description may be contained thereon.) Food, books, and children's clothes are exempt from VAT.

Alternatively, at Heathrow Airport visitors can reclaim VAT paid on purchases in Britain and in Europe. The refund may be in cash or by check, or as a credit to a credit-card account. The booths, near Customs points, are open 6:00 A.M. to midnight.

To ship material of any weight, either inland or overseas, there are many organizations. For example, HR Embassy Freight Services, at 25 Goodge Street (Tel: 580-6059), works Monday through Friday collecting anywhere; they will package, band, and insure. Some large West End retailers will perform these services for you.

DAY TRIPS FROM LONDON

*By Frank Victor Dawes, Bryn Frank, Anthony Burton,
Angela Murphy, and David Wickers*

Most places in the southern half of England can be a day trip from London, by car, train, or bus. We have selected 19 destinations from the area—including the nearby coasts of France and Belgium—as being of the most general interest, and we discuss each in enough detail to help you choose the one or ones that appeal to you, and to let you get the best out of the destination in a day.

At the end of each section (south of London; west; northwest; north; and the French–Belgian coast) we discuss the logistics of getting to each, as well as the time involved. Some of the day trips—for example, Warwick and Stratford-upon-Avon—can be combined to make a single, if rushed, day out of London. Others, such as Canterbury and Boulogne or Calais (via Dover), could be combined for a two-day/one-night excursion.

There are plenty of tour operators in London who package most of these day trips, as well as special train excursions and cheap day-return tickets providing discounts on admissions to various tourist attractions; check with your hotel hall porter or with a London travel agency for details.

To make these trips even more leisurely, we also suggest one or a few overnight accommodations in most of

the destinations; for booking details see the Accommodations Reference listing at the end of each section.

MAJOR INTEREST

South

Canterbury: cathedral and other medieval historical sites

Royal Tunbridge Wells: 18th-century and Victorian spa town

Brighton: lively seaside ambience and shopping

Arundel: medieval castle town

Portsmouth naval museums and historic ships

West

Windsor castle, Eton, and Runnymede

Winchester cathedral and college

Salisbury cathedral

Stonehenge

Bath: 18th-century town

Northwest

Oxford

Warwick castle and medieval town

Stratford-upon-Avon

North

Cambridge

The Coast of France and Belgium

Boulogne: medieval old town

Calais: dining and shopping

Dunkirk seaside resort: Flemish atmosphere

Dieppe seaside resort: beach and dining

Bruges: medieval city

SOUTH

Canterbury

Although a large portion of this world-famous city about 58 miles (93 km) east-southeast of central London in Kent, on the way to Dover, was razed in the German firebomb attacks of 1942 and later rebuilt in unromantic 20th-century style, medieval Canterbury survives within stretches of Roman and Norman town wall and is easy to explore on foot. A visitor from a bygone age would instantly recognize, for example, the High Street, because

instead of fighting a gradually losing battle against motor
traffic Canterbury banished it entirely from the heart of
the city. Canterbury may be a place of great antiquity, but
it is also home to one of Britain's newest centers of
higher education: The University of Kent stands on a hill
named for Wat Tyler, who led the Peasants' Revolt of 1381.

MAJOR INTEREST

Canterbury Pilgrims Way exhibition
The cathedral
The King's School
Old Weaver's House
Canterbury Heritage Museum
City walls and castle
St. Augustine's Abbey
Roman pavement

All the sights mentioned below are within easy walking
distance of each other, and most are accessible to wheelchairs.

CANTERBURY PILGRIMS WAY EXHIBITION

Geoffrey Chaucer wrote "from every shires end of Enge-
lond, to Caunterbury they wende," and the permanent
Pilgrims Way exhibition on St. Margaret's Street near the
Tourist Information Centre, an easy walk from either the
east or west railway stations and parking lots, transports
the present-day pilgrim back in time to the "Tabard Inn"
in London's Southwark. From there a guide in period
costume leads the way through representations of medieval Kent. The "journey" is enlivened by the tales of
Chaucer's "verray parfit gentil knight," the bawdy miller,
the blowsy wife of Bath, the nun's priest, and the par-
doner. At journey's end is a replica of Trinity Chapel and
Becket's fabulous gold tomb—which was pillaged by
Henry VIII when he broke with Rome over his divorce.

THE CATHEDRAL

The exhibition serves as an introduction to the heritage
of centuries behind Christchurch Gate, just a few blocks
away, whose carved oak doors are shut every night at
9:00 P.M. following the ringing of the curfew bell, safe-
guarding the security of the mother church of England.
The cathedral was begun in 1070, and rebuilt after a fire a

century later with stone shipped from Caen in Normandy. The 235-foot-high "Bell Harry" rises above the four other towers. A single bell at the top tolls only for the death of a monarch or an archbishop of Canterbury, who is primate of all England.

The first view of the interior is breathtaking, with a fan-vaulted ceiling soaring over 150 feet, hundreds of paintings and sculptures, and richly colorful stained glass windows known as the "Poor Man's Bible."

On December 29, 1170, four knights who had over-heard their king, Henry III, call out in despair "Who will deliver me from this turbulent priest?" waylaid Arch-bishop Thomas à Becket in the cathedral and murdered him. He was recognized as a martyr by the Church, and canonized as Saint Thomas; the spot where he was cut down became a shrine. Everyone asks: "Where was Becket murdered?" A 1986 metal sculpture, with the sin-gle word "Thomas" carved into the stone paving beneath it, marks the spot in the northwest transept.

Becket's tomb itself is no more, destroyed by the great fire shortly after his murder, but near where it stood in the mosaic-paved Trinity Chapel is the tomb of Edward, the Black Prince, with a superb brass effigy of the hero of Crécy and Poitiers in full battle armor. Opposite is the only tomb of a king to be found in the cathedral, that of Henry IV, who lies beside his wife, Joan of Navarre. Surveying the presbytery and choir, the crossing of the nave and transepts under the central tower, and the full perpendicular sweep of the nave is St. Augustine's Chair, carved from Purbeck marble in the 13th century and used for the enthronement of every new archbishop.

The Norman crypt beneath the nave and transepts is vast—230 feet long and 130 feet wide—with daylight streaming in on columns that bear the distinctive marks made by the masons who carved them 900 years ago. The heraldic shields of more than 800 families are displayed in the intricate vaulting of the cloisters, and the chapter house has a barrel-vaulted roof of Irish bog oak. It was here that Prime Minister Margaret Thatcher and President Mitterand of France signed the treaty to build the Channel Tunnel, thus realizing a dream of two centuries.

THE KING'S SCHOOL

North of the cathedral cloisters is Green Court, which lies at the heart of the King's School. Refounded in 1541 (its origins are claimed back to Saint Augustine in 602), the school's former pupils include the Elizabethan dramatist Christopher Marlowe, son of a Canterbury shoemaker, and, more recently, Somerset Maugham, who bequeathed his library to the school in 1961 and whose ashes were scattered on the roses outside. The rosebushes face an external staircase that leads to the oldest schoolroom; this staircase is a gem of Norman architecture. Palace Street, on the far side of Green Court through Mint Yard Gate, is full of interesting shops selling antiques, sports and country wear, period postcards, toys and posters, china, and jewelry.

From Palace Street it's a short walk to the **West Gate** via St. Peter's Street. Those who climb the spiral staircase to the battlements of this Norman tower (rebuilt in the 14th century) are rewarded with a fine view of the city. Through this gate Chaucer's pilgrims plodded and Henry V rode after his victory against the French at Agincourt. Ports for ancient cannon survive. Until Victorian times the tower served as a jail, but today it's a museum of arms and armor.

THE OLD WEAVER'S HOUSE

The black-and-white gables of this old house overhang the River Stour, a narrow stream flowing through the city and under St. Peter's Street. The house took its name from the Protestant weavers who settled in medieval Canterbury, having fled from religious persecution in Continental Europe. The jetty where their wool was unloaded from barges is today crowded with tourists embarking in boats and taking photographs of the ducking stool formerly used to silence nagging wives. The house itself is now a coffee shop and souvenir store, and stocks good local craftware.

CANTERBURY HERITAGE MUSEUM

Holograms and computers are used here in the 13th-century Poor Priests' Hospital on Stour Street, near the junction of the High Street and St. Peter's Street, to create a "time-walk" from Roman times to the Blitz of 1942. The treasures on display include silver spoons used by the Romans, the original Canterbury Cross—a symbol of Christianity recognized throughout the world—a fully threaded loom tended by a model of a Huguenot silk weaver, and the writing desk of Joseph Conrad, who spent the last years of his life at Bishopsbourne nearby and is buried at Canterbury. But the prize exhibit is the

"Invicta," the engine that hauled the world's first regular passenger steam train from Canterbury to its port of Whitstable in 1830.

THE CITY WALLS AND THE CASTLE

A walk reached by a ramp near the castle (southeast of the museum on Castle Street) runs along the parapet of the city walls, which were begun by the Romans and extended and strengthened by the Normans. The walk encircles Dane John Gardens, which probably takes its name from the Norman *donjon,* or castle keep.

The keep of the castle, whose 11-foot-thick walls have survived, overlooks the gardens, which are themselves surrounded by houses of a later period. This little park is dominated by a grassy mound and has a charming monument to Shakespeare's rival, Christopher Marlowe. The Marlowe Theatre near the cathedral stages a varied program of opera, ballet, drama, and classical music, as well as light entertainment.

What little remains of **St. Augustine's abbey**, which Saint Augustine (the *other* Saint Augustine, the first archbishop of Canterbury) founded in 602, lies outside the city wall on the opposite side of the busy Upper and Lower Bridge Street and Broad Street loop, on the east side of the city. Its most impressive feature is the 14th-century Fyndon Gate at the top of Lady Wootton's Green.

ROMAN TESSELLATED PAVEMENT

Hitler's bombs may have destroyed many historic buildings, but they also revealed the remains of even earlier settlements, such as this fine example of mosaic and under-floor heating (hypocaust) from a Roman villa of A.D. 100. It is to be found eight feet beneath the new Longmarket shopping precinct, off Burgate between the abbey ruins and the cathedral. During 1990 it underwent extensive restoration and, together with a collection of coins, pottery, jewelry, and other finds from Durovernum (the Roman name for Canterbury) is well worth visiting. The contrast with the late-20th-century shopping mall above, where street musicians and buskers entertain throngs of visitors, is intriguing.

SHOPPING AND SNACKING IN CANTERBURY

Canterbury is accustomed to coping with two million visitors every year—all of them packing into the medieval heart of the city where everything is located. As well as shops to suit every taste and pocketbook—from the secondhand emporia of Northgate to the **Chaucer Bookshop** on Beer Cart Lane and **Canterbury Pottery** in the Buttermarket on Burgate opposite the cathedral—there are numerous teashops and taverns. The **Tea Pot** on St. Peter's Street is a good place for a relaxing cuppa, while **Morelli's** ice cream parlors are dotted around the city. Antiques and collectors' markets are held on Saturdays in the **Sidney Cooper Center** on St. Peter's Street and at **Latimer's** on Ivy Lane during the week. The Kingsmead Road Market takes place on Wednesdays.

STAYING AND DINING IN CANTERBURY

For those who decide to stay overnight so as to get a start on the crowds, the ▶ **County Hotel** is in the most central of locations on the High Street and has an excellent restaurant called **Sully's**. The ▶ **Falstaff**, which has stood on St. Dunstan's Street since the days of Chaucer's pilgrims, has been modernized without sacrificing its character. Indeed, both establishments offer the solid, if somewhat staid, comfort of the traditional English hotel, while providing amenities such as color television in the bedrooms.

—*Frank Dawes*

Royal Tunbridge Wells

The natural setting amid the green hills of the High Weald of Kent, with outcrops of sandstone such as Toad Rock and High Rocks, and 250 acres of gorse-covered common adjoining the town center, gives Tunbridge Wells, 36 miles (58 km) southeast of London, its distinctive style. The wells, fed by an iron-impregnated spring discovered by Lord North while out riding in 1606, soon became famous as the English answer to the Belgian spa waters. Queen Henrietta-Maria gave them the stamp of royal approval when she took the waters during her pregnancy in 1629, and two centuries later Victoria, as a young princess, referred to the town as her *"Dear* Tunbridge Wells." But it was left to her son, when he became King Edward VII, to bestow the "Royal" prefix on the town in 1909.

During the Victorian era, when the prosperous middle class made Tunbridge Wells its own, the town acquired a reputation for snobbery and starchiness that has been a long time dying. Its archetypal residents were retired colonels of the Indian Army who wrote letters to *The Times* signed "Disgusted, Tunbridge Wells." Only now is it coming to terms with newer lifestyles, and development goes on apace.

MAJOR INTEREST

The Pantiles
Church of King Charles the Martyr
The Common
Trinity Arts Center
Calverley Park

Virtually every English country town today boasts its pedestrianized shopping precinct, but only Tunbridge Wells has one laid out three centuries ago during the reign of Queen Anne. By then many houses, shops, and taverns had been built around the common and on the surrounding hills, named Mount Ephraim, Mount Sion, and Mount Pleasant by the austere Dissenters. This group of settlements formed a new town, one that developed coffeehouses, lottery and hazard rooms, apothecaries, and bowling greens during the Restoration period.

THE PANTILES

The town square called the Pantiles is just a short walk from the train station. It took its name from the square clay tiles with which it was originally paved, which were replaced after almost a century by the large flagstones we see today. The last of the original tiles were removed in recent renovations. In one corner of the square, under a canopy supported by iron columns, is the original Chalybeate Spring, with the "dipper" traditionally used to dispense medicinal sips of the water on hand from Easter to September. Victoria took the waters every day during her visit in 1834, and walked with her mother, the duchess of Kent, in the Pantiles afterward. The square leads on to the colonnaded Upper Walk and then the Lower Walk, which is paved with red bricks and shaded by a row of lime trees. The Bandstand is used for regular evening performances, ranging from military and Kentish town bands to New Orleans jazz and old-time music-hall entertainment.

The former Corn Exchange, one of the fine old buildings lining the Pantiles, houses "A Day at the Wells," a heritage center opened in 1990. It re-creates with sights and sounds the Georgian elegance of the Tunbridge Wells where Beau Nash, as master of ceremonies, decreed in the early 1700s that "All should learn—according to my Rule—to live in Society." It was a town of sedan chairs and coffeehouses, grand balls and gaming halls, where the fashionable took the waters and strolled among the Tuscan columns in order to see and be seen.

By the mid-1980s, however, the Pantiles was beginning to look rather shabby, and a much-needed restoration has made over not only the Corn Exchange but also the Assembly Rooms, formerly used for weekly auction sales, and the Royal Victoria Inn, where Queen Victoria stayed. The face-lift has preserved historic façades while providing modern facilities for leisure, entertainment, high-quality shopping, and restaurants. **Todd's Vintry**, which has been in the Pantiles since 1768, sells a staggering variety of wines, cheeses, and confectioneries, while **Binns** is *the* place for afternoon tea in Tunbridge Wells. The **Duke of York** pub, occupying converted stables, serves good lunches with cask ales.

In Chapel Place, just off the Pantiles, is the church of **King Charles the Martyr**, completed in 1696. With its white weatherboarded belfry and clock, it is strongly reminiscent of numerous counterparts in New England, but it is chiefly noted for the ornately decorated plaster ceiling inside, said to be the finest example of its kind in any church outside London.

THE COMMON

It is possible to step from the Pantiles into a rural scene simply by going through a passageway beside the Swan Hotel and crossing Eridge Road. A steep 200-yard path up through the woods leads to the Old Race Course, where young Victoria and her mother would watch the races from a carriage protected by a special awning. The grassy track is still traceable, although no longer used for horse racing. A little farther on is the Higher Cricket Ground and, to the right, Wellington Rocks, a favorite place for children's games.

TRINITY ARTS CENTER

Another steep footpath leads down across the common to Church Road, where the former Holy Trinity Church, whose foundation stone was laid by the duchess of Kent

on her birthday in 1827, now serves as an arts center. In
the late 1970s the church commissioners were, mercifully, thwarted in their plans to demolish the Gothic-style
Trinity to make way for further development. The finely
carved faces at the terminations of the roof are one of its
most intriguing features. The center provides a venue for
plays, concerts, dance, and exhibitions—a welcome complement to the town-center complex just across Mount
Pleasant Road, which houses the Tourist Information Centre, museum, art gallery, and library, as well as the Assembly Hall on Crescent Road, which is the major theater and
concert hall for the High Weald.

CALVERLEY PARK

Holy Trinity Church was, in fact, the first building of the
"new town" that the great Georgian architect Decimus
Burton was commissioned to design (in 1828) to rival the
Pantiles. The style he chose was Greek Revival, and he
used blocks of Wealden sandstone for his colonnades,
pavilions, and pilasters. Calverley Parade and Calverley
Terrace opposite the church were demolished in the
1930s to make way for the Civic Center buildings mentioned above, but **Calverley Park Crescent**, just up the
road, rivals anything in Bath or around Regent's Park in
London, while the villas in Calverley Park still conform to
the self-contained village plan of the original design. No
two structures are the same, but their bow windows and
towers are in perfect harmony. Much of the surrounding
park is open to the public, with tennis courts and a
bowling green, a children's paddling pool, and a cafeteria. Calverley Park is near the train station, with the
Pantiles and the common a short walk away. But Tunbridge Wells is very hilly, and so not the most ideal
destination for the not-so-fit.

SHOPPING IN TUNBRIDGE WELLS

Tunbridge Wells is a major shopping area, able to fulfill
almost any requirement from a lobster pick to a lawn
mower. There are, in addition, ten parking garages, some
multistory. The major chain stores are to be found in the
pedestrians-only Calverley Precinct between Calverley
Road and Mount Ephraim. Behind it, **Monson Road**, with
its curving, balustraded row of storefronts, has good
shops for china, ornaments, and jewelry, as well as many
varieties of tea and coffee at **Importers**. Nearby Camden

Road has numerous antiques shops, including **Sawdust and Lace**, which sells dolls and dollhouses, rocking horses, and teddy bears.

Along Mount Pleasant Road and the High Street running from Calverley Precinct to the Pantiles are shops of every description. **Hooper's Department Store** stocks designer fashions and high-quality men's and women's clothing at competitive prices. The china department has a wide range of imports as well as British porcelain. The **Great Hall** is an attractively restored glass-roofed arcade with furniture shops, boutiques, and a branch of Hatchard's bookshop. Antiquarian bookshops, art galleries, and antiques dealers are concentrated on Chapel Place and Nevill Street. Tunbridge Ware, a type of inlaid woodwork, is much sought after, and the best places to find it are the antiques shops on the streets mentioned above. A special room at the Museum and Art Gallery at the Civic Center is devoted to exhibits of Tunbridge Ware.

STAYING AND DINING IN TUNBRIDGE WELLS

Before the first large houses in Tunbridge Wells were built on the heights, royalty and aristocracy had to camp on the common while they took the waters. Some of those first mansions are still in use as hotels, alongside other, newer buildings. ▶ **The Spa** is probably the most comfortable, and provides its guests with an indoor heated swimming pool, tennis courts, and a children's play area. The ▶ **Periquito**, formerly the Wellington, has been restored with extremely colorful fabrics and furnishings while retaining the original Regency-period wood-carving and staircase, large windows, and high ceilings. The ▶ **Royal Wells Inn**, dating from the 1830s, boasts a vast coat of arms on its parapet, and its glass-enclosed balcony is a good place to have a drink while admiring the grandstand view of Tunbridge Wells. Its 22 rooms have been modernized and are air-conditioned.

Tunbridge Wells also has its associations with literary figures. E. M. Forster grew up here. A Regency house in London Road that was for a time the home of William Makepeace Thackeray is now a good restaurant called— simply enough—**Thackeray's House**. It has built a reputation for serving high-quality English fare at moderate prices, but is closed on Sundays and Mondays.

—Frank Dawes

Brighton

Queen Victoria was not amused by Brighton; on the other hand, George IV, as Prince of Wales ("Prinny" to fashionable Regency society), adored the place, which he first visited one Sunday in September 1783 when it was just a small fishing town called Brighthelmston.

Although it was known as early as the mid-18th century, when a local doctor published a pamphlet recommending the "oceanic fluid" as a curative, to be taken both by bathing and by drinking, Brighton, situated 53 miles (85 km) due south of central London, is a town built on misbehavior. Prinny installed his morganatic wife, Mrs. Maria Fitzherbert, here in a house at the center of town. (Today the house is a YMCA hostel.) In less permissive times it was an open secret that unmarried couples, or at least couples who were not married to each other, slipped down to Brighton for an illicit weekend of pleasure.

Fifty years ago Graham Greene used the resort as the backdrop for *Brighton Rock,* a novel about sleazy crime, day-trippers, and the racetrack in the hills above the town. The "rock" of the title is not a geographical feature but a stick of rainbow-hued candy, very hard on the teeth, with "Brighton" spelled out in red sugar all the way through its white core. Greene's boy-gangster, Pinkie, would have no difficulty recognizing Brighton—and its rock—today.

Less than an hour from London by train, which puts it within easy commuting distance, Brighton is a smart place to live, much favored by creative people such as the late Lord Olivier. Not so long ago kippers could be had for breakfast on the Pullman service to town but, alas, the *Brighton Belle* is no more. Frankly, the steeply shelved beach of large round pebbles is nothing to write home about, except that a section of it just west of the marina is reserved for nudists. But Brighton still revels in naughtiness and is always fun to visit, even for a day—though it has enough to keep you entertained and occupied for much longer. It is an extensive walk from the train station to the places of major interest listed below; better to take a cab or hop on a bus.

MAJOR INTEREST

Royal Pavilion and the Dome
The Lanes (antiques shopping)

Palace Pier views of the coast
The Aquarium
Volk's beachside railway

THE ROYAL PAVILION

Trim suburbs climbing inland up the grassy slopes of the
Downs, manicured public lawns, and bright ribbons of
flowers give no hint of the centerpiece that, when revealed, hits the visitor smack in the eye. It is a palace
seemingly from the hills of northern India, complete with
minarets and onion domes, magically transported and set
down in the midst of an English garden. The Royal Pavilion was built not by a Mogul emperor but by the extravagant, debauched, lecherous, eccentric George IV. About
the time of his father's terminal bout with madness,
George hit upon the idea of transforming the mansion he
had built in Brighton into an Eastern fantasy palace. His
architect was John Nash, who laid out London's Regent's
Park and Regent Street and redesigned Buckingham Palace. No expense was spared. The result, the Royal Pavilion, convinced some people that insanity ran in the royal
family. Among some of the more polite remarks: "This
pot-bellied palace, this minaret mushroom. This gilded
dirt pie, this congeries of bulbous excrescences. . . ."

The interior was no less exotic than the exterior, satisfying the prince's taste for chinoiserie, which can still be
viewed today, together with marvelous Regency furniture,
porcelain, glass, silver, and gold plate. Many of the pieces
are on loan from Queen Elizabeth II. The lavishly decorated Music Room, in which the 70 members of a royal
orchestra played while Prinny sang a popular song called
"Life's a Bumper," was gutted by a fire in 1975. The room
was restored, then wrecked again when a three-ton minaret crashed through the roof during the great windstorm
of 1987 (which also devastated the lovely central parks of
Brighton). Once again, however, the Music Room has
been returned to the original spendor of its design. So
has the Banqueting Room, still used for guests and looking much as it did when George IV last set eyes on it in
1827.

By the time the Pavilion was completed, the prince
regent had become king and lost interest in it. But the
fashion he had started rolled on. **Regency Square**, just
across the promenade from West Pier and planned as the
Royal Pavilion neared completion, provides the grandest

examples of the bay windows, balconies, and wrought-iron tracery that graced the houses of the period.

Before he built the Pavilion, George commissioned William Porden to build stables and a riding school in the style of a Muslim mosque. Today the **Dome** is the home of the Brighton Philharmonic Orchestra and is also used for events as varied as rock concerts, trade-union conferences, and the degree-conferring ceremonies of Sussex University, whose campus, designed by Sir Basil Spence in the 1960s, is situated high on the Downs outside of town. The adjoining stables fronting Church Street serve as Brighton's public library, art gallery, and museum.

THE LANES

Nowhere is the atmosphere of Brighton, a heady mixture of colorful history and present glamour, more in evidence than in what remains of Brighthelmston, a square mile of small weatherboarded houses and twisting alleyways called the Lanes, close to the Royal Pavilion and The Dome. Book and antiques shops, jewelers and junk dealers, pubs and restaurants are crammed into these pedestrians-only byways, the entrances to which are clearly marked in the wider streets surrounding them.

At the center of this medieval enclave is **Brighton Square**, a traffic-free 20th-century shopping precinct; the open-air cafés lend it a Continental atmosphere. Certainly you will hear a variety of European tongues here, and not only from tourists—Brighton is a busy center for English-language schools.

There is no need to confine your shopping to the Lanes, of course—the Gardner Street bric-a-brac market is nearby and Brighton has more than its share of stylish emporia, which have earned it a reputation as "London by the sea." Among the many fine stores on North Street, the department store **Hannington's**, the oldest (1808), prides itself on its knowledgeable and courteous staff. **Wyn Gillett**, 34 Upper North Street, sells antique linen and lace in pristine condition. **Graham and Jo Webb**, 59 Ship Street, specializes in antique music boxes, some of which play whole operatic overtures. Even farther off the well-beaten tourist track, in a narrow lane off Gloucester Road near the railway station, is **Pyramid** (at 9A Kensington Gardens), which has a wide range of Art Deco pieces, from tea services and lampshades to telephones and mahogany-cased radios.

THE ESPLANADE AND PIERS

It would be unthinkable to visit Brighton without taking a sniff of sea air and a stroll along "the front," which is as gaudy a promenade as you'll find at any other popular seaside resort. Between Brighton's two piers are fast-food joints, fish-and-chip cafés, cockles-and-whelks stalls, amusement arcades, bumper cars, paddling pools, putting greens, and sleazy shops selling a range of especially awful kitsch. Among the crowds taking the air are the inevitable dropouts, eccentrics, and aging punks, whose purple hair and safety-pin adornments have become as passé as bell-bottomed trousers.

The view from the end of **Palace Pier**, stretching a third of a mile into the sea from Grand Junction Road and Marine Parade, takes in a wide section of English Channel coast, including the start of the white cliffs to the east. Admission and deck chairs are free, and the diversions and amusements offered include karaoke in the Offshore Bar and video games in the Palace of Fun. Although it celebrated its centenary in 1991, this is the younger of the two Victorian piers. Local enthusiasts recently saved the **West Pier** from demolition, but it is no longer open for visitors to enjoy the slot machines that were shown in Richard Attenborough's film *Oh, What a Lovely War*. (Incidentally, Brighton and adjoining Hove were centers for movie-making before Hollywood set eyes on its first hand-cranked camera.) Built in 1866 by Eugenius Birch when the English seaside pier was at the zenith of its popularity, this is a Victorian masterpiece in form, style, and elegance of proportion. It now has an air of ravaged beauty, but the Brighton West Pier Trust plans to restore it to its original glory by the end of 1999. Brighton's **Aquarium**, next to Palace Pier, is well past its centennial and still displays sea lions, seals, and turtles, as well as thousands of fish. Also at hand is Britain's first public **electric railway**, Volk's. Opened in 1883 and travelling for a mile along the edge of the beaches (including the one for nudists), it carries passengers in little yellow wooden cars with open sides. The service runs from Easter to October and is inexpensive. At the farthest end of Brighton is one of the town's newer attractions, the largest yachting marina in Europe, opened by the Queen in 1979.

THE BRIGHTON INTERNATIONAL FESTIVAL

In 1967 Lord Olivier brought this arts festival to his home town. Held every year through most of May, it is now one of Europe's liveliest, rivaling the more famous one in Edinburgh, and encompasses theater, jazz, classical music, big bands, opera, rock, cabaret, poetry, fireworks, and such eccentric experiments as a conducted tour of the sewers and the world's smallest theater—an actor on a motorbike with an audience of one in the sidecar. On the first Sunday in November fans turn out for the London-to-Brighton Veteran Car Run.

DINING AND STAYING IN BRIGHTON

The best-known seafood restaurants in Brighton are **English's** and **Wheeler's**. Lesser known, and less expensive, is **D'Arcy's** on Market Street, where the plaice and other fish are fresh from the Channel. The **Eaton Garden Restaurant** in Eaton Gardens, Hove (which adjoins Brighton to the west), also serves excellent fish and good old-fashioned English fare such as steak, kidney, and mushroom pie. For those seeking a traditional English tea, the **Mock Turtle Restaurant** at 4 Pool Valley serves a good pot of tea with lashings of homemade cakes and jams on Wood's blue-and-white willow china. Brighton has numerous first-rate French restaurants, too, among them **La Marinade** in Kemp Town and **Le Grandgousier** on Western Street, where rich sauces, garlic, and *l'escargot* provide a whiff of the land just across the Channel. Of course, new restaurants are always opening even as others fade away.

Between the Lanes and the sea is the newly built
▶ **Hospitality Inn Brighton**, boasting a four-story plant-filled atrium, two restaurants, and a fully equipped health club and swimming pool. Its 200 rooms, many with sea views, are furnished and equipped to top-class international standards. It sits in stark contrast to its neighbor, the ▶ **Old Ship Hotel**, which is more than four centuries old. Thackeray stayed at the Old Ship while writing *Vanity Fair*, Charles Dickens gave public readings of his works in the ballroom, and Paganini gave a recital here in 1831. More recently the late poet laureate Sir John Betjeman was a habitué. Locally caught seafood is an Old Ship specialty, and the cellars are extensive. The accommodations have been comprehensively modernized, and all 154 bedrooms are *en suite*. Less historic but just as comfortably placed and very comfortable is the ▶ **Royal Al-**

bion, located in the heart of Brighton between the Royal
Pavilion and the seafront.

Just a short walk westward along King's Road, facing
the sea, are Brighton's fanciest hotels: the ▶ **Brighton
Metropole** and the ▶ **Grand**. Stately neighbors, they
have been extensively renovated, and both feature indoor swimming pools. Accommodation in either one
includes well-appointed suites as well as rooms with all
the modern amenities. For less-expensive lodgings, the
Brighton Accommodation Bureau is available to help;
Tel: (0273) 327-560.

—Frank Dawes

ARUNDEL

This small country town, set between the lush, green hills
that are the South Downs and the Channel coast, just 20
miles (32 km) west of Brighton and 58 miles (93 km)
south of London, is a perfectly preserved piece of old
England. It takes its name from that most famous of
Sussex rivers, the Arun, which flows through a gap in the
Downs at this point and on down to the sea at Littlehampton 4 miles (6½ km) to the south. The Downs are
at their most glorious around **Amberley**, a thatched village dating back to the Saxons that is located just before
Arundel on the railway from London.

Arundel boasts not only a magnificent castle—ancestral
home of England's foremost Roman Catholic family, the
Fitzalan Howards, dukes of Norfolk and earls Marshal—
but also the cathedral, which they built in honor of a faith
that survived the Reformation and centuries of anti-
Catholic discrimination. Apart from sightseeing, this area
has much to offer artists and photographers, bird-watchers
and botanists, anglers and hikers. Tour boats ply the Arun
among Littlehampton, Arundel, and Amberley (Tel: 0903-
82-26-34). Arundel itself is a town of steep ascents and
descents, and a cab from the train station to the castle or
cathedral is recommended.

MAJOR INTEREST

Arundel Castle
Cathedral
Wildfowl reserve

Amberley Castle
Amberley Chalk Pits Museum

THE CASTLE

The massive battlemented towers and keep overshadow the little town and valley of the Arun—which they were of course built to defend. Although the castle's origins are Norman, most of the present building is Victorian mock-baronial. Its story is entwined with that of the dukes of Norfolk, whose home it has been for 500 years, but goes back much further, to 1067, when Roger de Montgomery was created earl of Arundel and given a third of Sussex for taking care of things back home while William of Normandy was busy conquering England. It was Roger who built the original motte-and-bailey castle of timber, replaced in the 12th century by the round keep of Caen stone, which survives, open to the sky, atop a grassy mound at the heart of the much extended castle you see today.

The Lower Lodge, through which the visitor enters the castle precincts, was part of the late-19th-century reconstruction by the 15th duke. A drive leads up through the wooded park (decimated during the great storm of October 1987) flanked by a turreted curtain wall; the castle is entered over a wooden drawbridge and through a barbican dating from 1295. Above the archway can be seen the marks of cannonballs fired by Cromwell's artillery during the siege of 1643. The inner gateway is original 11th-century and the quadrangle, with its expanse of striped emerald lawn, occupies what was once the lower bailey. From the gatehouse in one corner a stairway leads up the walls of the keep, which commands views over the town to the coast as well as the gap in the hills through which the River Arun wends its way. When the duke is in residence a banner flies from the top of this tower.

The buildings around the quadrangle contain much of interest, and include a Victorian private chapel with columns of polished Purbeck marble, the Barons' Hall with a soaring hammerbeam roof of oak harvested from the estate, the **picture gallery** with its chronologically ordered portraits of the dukes and duchesses of Norfolk as well as some of the earls of Arundel, and the **library**, fitted out in carved Honduras mahogany and containing 10,000 books, a collection particularly rich in Catholic history. These and other rooms are packed with priceless treasures: medieval armor and swords, heraldic insignia, fine tapestries, and furniture (including the elaborate gilt bed made specially for Queen Victoria and Prince Albert when they visited Arundel castle in 1846). Paintings by Van Dyck, Gainsborough, and Reynolds hang beside recent photographs and mementoes of the family—to whom the castle is still home.

The tombs and monuments of the earls of Arundel and the dukes of Norfolk may be seen in the **Fitzalan Chapel**, partitioned from the rest of the 16th-century Anglican parish church of St. Nicholas and accessible only from the castle grounds.

THE CATHEDRAL

The pinnacles of the cathedral soar above the London road car park, between it and the castle. Despite its impressive Gothic lines, a pleasing counterpoint to the battlements dominating town and river, it was built only in the 1870s by the 15th duke to plans drawn up by none other than Joseph Hansom, the inventor of the Victorian horse-drawn cab of that name who was also a noted architect. It became the Cathedral Church of St. Philip Neri with the formation in 1965 of the Roman Catholic Diocese of Arundel and Brighton.

The cathedral would have been more dominating still, but the original plan to build a spire 280 feet high came to nothing. Its chief attraction is the shrine, in the north transept, of the 13th earl of Arundel, Philip Howard, who steadfastly refused to renounce his faith despite being incarcerated for 11 years during the Tudor period. He was canonized in 1970, almost four centuries after his death in the Tower of London.

The Catholic feast day of Corpus Christi is celebrated in the cathedral every June with a unique carpet of blooming flowers covering the long central aisle.

ARUNDEL TOWN

Attractive and well-preserved old buildings such as the
► **Norfolk Arms**, an 18th-century former coaching inn that still welcomes visitors and looks after them with style, grace the streets of the town clustered below the castle walls.

An interesting **Toy and Military Museum** at 23 High Street (Tel: 0903-88-31-01) is open most days from Easter to October, but the Georgian building itself is barely larger than a dollhouse, and with anything more than half a dozen visitors at one time it is overcrowded. It contains the Henderson family's private collection of teddy bears, dolls, toy soldiers, puppets, models, rocking horses, money boxes, games, and novelties gathered over several generations.

The town, once a thriving port, is rich in architectural styles from the 16th century onward, with particularly handsome Georgian terraces, packed with antiques shops. In complete contrast to its Old World surroundings, **Pogey's**, on Tarrant Street, serves an inventive menu in an Art Deco setting.

WILDFOWL RESERVE

North of town the River Arun swings across a wide, flat plain, part meadow and part marshland, that often floods. The Wildfowl and Wetlands Trust leases 64 acres from the duke of Norfolk that comprise the habitat of a great variety of flora and fauna, including Bewick swans (which fly in from Siberia every winter), sandpipers, snipe, king- fishers, and reed buntings. In spring, dozens of families of tiny ducklings wander about. There are seven hides (blinds), all of them suitable for physically impaired visi- tors, and wheelchairs can be borrowed without charge.

The reserve's Visitor Reception Centre (Tel: 0903-88- 33-55) is on Mill Road less than a mile north of the castle; look for the signs. The facilities include a gift-and-book shop, cinema, exhibition area, viewing gallery, and li- censed restaurant. Dogs are not allowed into the reserve, which is open year-round except Christmas Day.

AMBERLEY CASTLE

The wetlands are overlooked by another historic castle 4 miles (6½ km) to the north of Arundel in the village of Amberley, which can be reached by cab or bus from Arundel or from Amberley train station. For 900 years this castle has stood hidden from outsiders on the South Downs facing the flat plains of the Wildbrooks. Then, in 1989, it became a country-house hotel, also called ▶ **Am- berley Castle**. Its great walls, battlements, and oak portcul- lis are intact, yet every room (each named after a different Sussex castle) has its own Jacuzzi. Amberley Castle was attacked by Cromwell and twice visited by King Charles II. A mural of the latter, with Queen Catherine of Bra- ganza, is a notable feature of the hotel's 12th-century barrel-vaulted restaurant, the **Queen's Room**, together with lancet windows and French cuisine. Head chef Nigel Boschetti offers such unusual dishes as roast saddle of lamb with wild mushroom ravioli and cutlet of squab pigeon in puff pastry.

AMBERLEY TOWN

No two cottages are the same in this village that invites you to linger (the **Black Horse pub** is a further inducement). Extinct rural industries are recalled here in building names such as the Old Brewhouse, the Old Malthouse, and the Old Bakehouse. More formally, some 36 acres of idled chalk pits have been turned into an open-air museum with its own narrow-gauge railway and a collection of industrial steam and diesel engines dating from the 1880s. The **Chalk Pits Museum** (Tel: 0798-83-13-70) also has a collection of vintage Southdown buses as well as a working blacksmith, boatbuilder, printer, and potter. Open Wednesday through Sunday, Easter to October, it brings to life the sights, sounds, and smells of all those smoky, roaring workshops of the past, and has even managed to give an eight-ton, 1925-vintage steamroller a new lease on life crushing aluminum beverage cans brought by visitors. Funds raised by selling them to a scrap-metal dealer for recycling are plowed back into the museum.

—*Frank Dawes*

Portsmouth

Portsmouth, whose harbor has been the home base and fortress of British sea power since the 15th century, has been known as "Pompey" to generations of sailors. Today, with Britannia ruling the waves no longer, there are fewer warships on active service than ever before, and Pompey has at last fallen to an invasion of tourists. And why not? With its restored ships and maritime museums (not least the one commemorating the D-Day invasion that was launched from here in 1944), as well as the adjoining seaside resort of Southsea, there is something to interest almost everyone in this historic haven only 71 miles (114 km) south and west of central London.

MAJOR INTEREST

Old Portsmouth
Birthplace of Charles Dickens
Her Majesty's Dockyard: *Mary Rose, Victory,* and
   Warrior
Royal Navy Submarine Museum

Southsea Castle
D-Day Museum (including the Overlord
    Embroidery)

OLD PORTSMOUTH

The huddle of little streets on the east side of the harbor mouth in the vicinity of the **Round Tower**, built by King Henry V to guard the narrow entrance to the harbor from Spithead, the stretch of water just offshore, is best explored on foot. (There are convenient car parks at Clarence Pier and King's Terrace, and Portsmouth Harbour train station is within easy walking distance of all points of interest in the old town.) Seagulls wheel and cry overhead, and there's a salty tang to the air. Broad Street, which runs past the Round Tower and Sally Port Gate (where naval officers came ashore or embarked), used to be filled with pubs and brothels and was nicknamed "Spice Island." The pubs remain, many with colorful names such as the Lively Lady, the Still and West, and the Seagull. The first fleet to the convict colony of Australia sailed from Portsmouth in 1788; today's voyages from the ferry terminal are to the nearer destinations of Le Havre and Cherbourg, Caen and St. Malo, Guernsey and Jersey. The best place to watch the maritime traffic is from the tip of Portsmouth Point at the bottom of Broad Street.

CHARLES DICKENS'S BIRTHPLACE

Even the modest terrace house in which Charles Dickens was born in 1812 has a military connection appropriate to the Portsmouth area: His father was a navy pay clerk. The house is in Landport, a northern suburb of the city that has been largely redeveloped since World War II, when heavy bombing destroyed much of it. Originally number 1 Mile End Terrace, its address is now 393 Old Commercial Road, and it is preserved as a museum (signposted off the A 3 highway, or take a cab from Old Portsmouth) and furnished in period style. The mementoes on display include the novelist's inkwell and the couch on which he died at Gads Hill. (The family moved to another house only a few months after his birth.)

HER MAJESTY'S DOCKYARD

Victory Gate, a mile (1½ km) from the High Street down St. George's Road and a five-minute walk from the Portsmouth Harbour railway station and the Hard, as the ferry terminal is called, gives access to the Dockyard and the finest evocation of British seapower from the 16th to the 20th century. The story begins with Henry VIII's warship **Mary Rose**, raised from the waters of the Solent in 1982 in a remarkable salvage operation led by Prince Charles, himself a former naval officer. The ship is far from fully restored, but many of its Tudor timbers are preserved for inspection in a fine spray of water inside a special hall. Many of the artifacts carried on board, from bronze cannon to cooking utensils, a pewter tankard, and a pocket sundial, are displayed in the exhibit next door.

The masts of Admiral Nelson's flagship, **Victory**, still dominate the Dockyard. Visitors are guided through the reverently preserved vessel by modern successors of the "Jack Tars" who lived and died cheek by jowl below deck. They will point out the spot where Nelson fell fatally wounded in 1805 after bringing the Battle of Trafalgar against Napoleon's navy to a decisive conclusion. *Victory* represents the end of the era of the man-o'-war, wooden ships under sail firing their cannon at each other broadside on.

The trio of historic ships is completed by the **Warrior**, berthed at the quay just inside Victory Gate, the world's first ironclad, her sails supplemented by a Penn steam engine and her guns breech-loaded with rifled bores. The ship has been restored to her former glory as the showpiece of Queen Victoria's navy. Quartermasters in 1860s uniforms are on hand to answer questions, and visitors are encouraged to sit at a mess deck table, handle a Colt .45 revolver, climb in a hammock, and examine a cat-o'-nine-tails. Many other relics of the days of sail and steam are on display in the **Royal Naval Museum**, which is housed in one of the 18th-century dockyard buildings.

Refreshments are available in the heritage area of the Dockyard, but for an authentic taste of "Pompey" fare it is worth stepping outside the gates to the **George Tavern**, dating from 1781, on Queen Street. The bar food here is good and the dessert puddings are a specialty of the house.

Royal Navy Submarine Museum

A four-minute ferry ride from the Hard to Gosport, on the opposite, west, side of the harbor (13 miles/21 km from Portsmouth by road), brings you to a more recent piece of naval history. The Submarine Museum traces the story of underwater weapons, from a replica of the *Turtle*, the one-man sub built to attack the British fleet off New York in 1776, to today's roomier nuclear vessels. The museum's centerpiece is the submarine *Alliance,* completed in 1947.

Southsea Castle

On the east side of Old Portsmouth, the seaside resort of **Southsea** has long esplanades backed by green commonland and many of the handsome terraces built when the town became a watering place in the 19th century. (It's a couple of miles, about 3 km, so take a cab or bus unless you are a dedicated walker.) Its dominating feature is the castle built by Henry VIII to improve his coastal defenses. On a fine summer's day in 1545 the king stood with his entourage on these newly constructed battlements watching his fleet sail out to engage a French invasion force off the Isle of Wight. The watchers recoiled in horror as the pride of the fleet, the *Mary Rose,* suddenly keeled over for no apparent reason and went down with all 700 hands.

The castle is today open to visitors year-round and houses yet another **museum of military history**. High on the walls where Henry VIII stood a swivel-mounted cannon points across the Solent.

Southsea "prom" (promenade) has its piers and lifeguards and lots of diversions, including the Sea Life Center with a special ocean-reef display behind walls of toughened glass.

The D-Day Museum

An important attraction along Clarence Esplanade in Southsea is the D-Day Museum, which includes reconstructions and film of the invasion (in which a million and a half British, Canadian, and U.S. troops were transported across the Channel) as well as numerous exhibits and a gallery containing the **Overlord Embroidery**. It took 20 needlewomen five years to reconstruct this saga of our times in 34 panels, 41 feet longer in total than the famous tapestry at Bayeux.

Portsmouth's military history doesn't end at Southsea, however. On its outskirts, a mile or two farther east along the coast, is the suburb of Eastney, which was developed in the 19th century, and the Royal Marines' barracks. The splendidly ornate Victorian officers' mess is now the

Royal Marines' Museum. The corps was instituted in 1664 as a force for fighting at sea as well as on land, and also has a strong musical tradition. Silver memorial drums and trumpets commemorate the Marine bandsmen who died in two world wars.

STAYING IN PORTSMOUTH

Despite the growth in the numbers of visitors, Portsmouth is not well endowed with good hotels. A good bet is the ▶ **Portsmouth Marriott**, but it's beside North Harbour at Cosham, nearly 4 miles (6½ km) north of Old Portsmouth. It offers a high standard of comfort, with amenities that include air-conditioning in the rooms, a fitness center with heated indoor pool, and squash courts.

The ▶ **Posthouse Hotel** is one of the newest and best hotels along the front in Southsea, and apart from sea views offers an indoor swimming pool. Some of its rooms are reserved for nonsmokers.

—Frank Dawes

GETTING AROUND

Canterbury

Canterbury, 58 miles (93 km) southeast of London, has two railway stations, East and West, reached respectively from Victoria (1 hour, 20 minutes) and Charing Cross (1 hour, 30 minutes) with a train approximately every hour from each. By road it is via the A 2 and M 2.

Royal Tunbridge Wells

Tunbridge Wells, 36 miles (58 km) southeast of London, is reached by train from Charing Cross in 48 minutes, with a train every hour, and more at peak commuter times. By car, use the A 21. National Express buses run from Victoria Coach Station.

Brighton

Brighton, 53 miles (85 km) south of London, is reached in a mere 51 minutes by express trains, which run hourly from Victoria Station. Gatwick Airport lies midway between London and Brighton. By car, use the A 23/M 23. National Express buses run from Victoria Coach Station.

Arundel

Arundel, 58 miles (93 km) south of London, is reached by train from Victoria (Amberley Station, before you reach

Arundel, is on the same line) in around 1 hour, 15 minutes. It's an hourly service and stops at Gatwick Airport midway. There are also connections from Brighton, but these usually involve changing trains. By car, use the A 24, A 29, and A 284.

Portsmouth

Trains to Portsmouth, 71 miles (114 km) southwest of London, leave Victoria Station at 20 minutes past the hour and arrive at Portsmouth Harbor Station 2 hours, 15 minutes later. From Waterloo is faster. By car, A 3.

ACCOMMODATIONS REFERENCE

Rates are projected 1994 prices for a double room with breakfast, unless otherwise indicated. As prices are subject to change, always double-check before booking.

Canterbury

▶ **County Hotel.** High Street, **Canterbury** CT1 2RX. Tel: (0227) 76-62-66; Fax: (0227) 45-15-12. £70–£100.

▶ **Falstaff Hotel.** 8–12 St. Dunstan's Street, **Canterbury** CT2 8AF. Tel: (0227) 46-21-38; Fax: (0227) 46-35-25. £85–£95.

Royal Tunbridge Wells

▶ **Periquito.** Mount Ephraim, **Royal Tunbridge Wells** TN4 8BU. Tel: (0892) 54-29-11; Fax: (0892) 53-75-41. £37.50–£64.

▶ **Royal Wells Inn.** Mount Ephraim, **Royal Tunbridge Wells** TN4 8BE. Tel: (0892) 51-11-88; Fax: (0892) 51-19-08. £75.

▶ **The Spa.** Mount Ephraim, **Royal Tunbridge Wells** TN4 8XJ. Tel: (0892) 52-03-31; Fax: (0892) 51-05-75; in U.S. and Canada, (800) 528-1234. £88–£110 (breakfast not included).

Brighton

▶ **Brighton Metropole.** King's Road, **Brighton** BN1 2FU. Tel: (0273) 77-54-32; Fax: (0273) 20-77-64. £156–£164.

▶ **Grand Hotel.** King's Road, **Brighton** BN1 2FW. Tel: (0273) 32-11-88; Fax: (0273) 20-26-94. £168–£236.

▶ **Hospitality Inn Brighton.** King's Road, **Brighton** BN1 2GS. Tel: (0273) 20-67-00; Fax: (0273) 82-06-92; in U.S., (212) 689-9284; in Canada, (800) 668-1513; in Australia, (008) 22-11-76. £145–£165.

▶ **Old Ship Hotel**. King's Road, **Brighton** BN1 1NR. Tel: (0273) 32-90-01; Fax: (0273) 82-07-18. £75–£135.

▶ **Royal Albion**. 35 Old Steine, **Brighton** BN1 1NT. Tel: (0273) 32-39-72; Fax: (0273) 239-72. £115.

Arundel

▶ **Amberley Castle**. **Amberley** (near Arundel) BN18 9ND. Tel: (0798) 83-19-92; Fax: (0798) 83-19-98; in U.S., (800) 346-8480 or (800) 525-4800. £130–£225.

▶ **Norfolk Arms**. 22 High Street, **Arundel** BN18 9AD. Tel: (0903) 88-21-01; Fax: (0903) 88-42-75. £60–£70.

Portsmouth

▶ **Portsmouth Marriott**. North Harbour, **Cosham**, Portsmouth PO6 4SH. Tel: (0705) 38-31-51; Fax: (0705) 38-87-01; in U.S. and Canada, (800) 228-9290. £105–£115 (breakfast not included).

▶ **Posthouse Hotel**. Pembroke Road, **Southsea**, Portsmouth PO1 2TA. Tel: (0705) 82-76-51; Fax: (0705) 75-67-15; in U.S. and Canada, (800) 225-5843; in Australia, (008) 22-24-46. £53.50 (breakfast not included).

WEST
Windsor

From a plane approaching London's Heathrow Airport, or across the fields from a car on the M 4, the crenellated walls of Windsor Castle and its one big, round, hollow tower topped by a crown look like a child's dream of a heavenly sand castle. Sadly, in 1992 fire destroyed a large part of the buildings, including the Great Hall.

Closer, from the three-mile-long double avenue of trees called Long Walk, it seems to belong in Camelot rather than in this world of airports and freeways. Yet Windsor Castle, just 21 miles (34 km) west of London on the banks of the River Thames, is uniquely a part of both: the home and fortress of nine centuries of English monarchy and of the present helicopter-hopping, polo-playing royal family.

MAJOR INTEREST

Windsor
Royalty and Empire Exhibit
The Guildhall (Wren, royal portraits)

The Castle
St. George's Chapel (Chapel of the Order of the
    Garter)
The State Apartments
Queen Mary's dollhouse

Windsor Great Park
The Royal Mausoleum at Frogmore House

Around Windsor
Eton College
Runnymede

When Queen Elizabeth I commanded William Shakespeare to write a play for her court, this town of red-roofed houses became the setting for *The Merry Wives of Windsor*. The **Garter Inn** pub stands on the site of the very inn where Sir John Falstaff and his cronies roistered. (It was rebuilt much later as the Harte and Garter.) At the Victorian (1849) Central Railway Station, the **Royalty and Empire Exhibit** evokes a later period: the precise moment on June 19, 1897, when Queen Victoria stepped off the train with her entourage in readiness for the celebration of her diamond jubilee the following day. The **Guildhall** is a handsome 17th-century colonnaded building designed by Sir Thomas Fitz and completed by Sir Christopher Wren. It houses a small museum of local history, but its main attraction is its collection of royal portraits. Next door the Elizabethan **Market Cross House** leans as perilously as the Tower of Pisa.

Visited by nearly three million tourists each year, Windsor cannot begin to provide car-parking spaces for them all. Go by coach, train, or, even better, by boat. The royal borough is overshadowed by the huge castle, which is perched on a chalk ridge above the River Thames and dominates the approaches from London.

THE CASTLE

It is not difficult to picture Henry VIII, bloated with excess and age, dragging his ulcerated leg through the cloisters of Windsor, where courtiers plotted and whispered of heresy and treachery. It's even said that his halting steps can still be heard here. It was to Windsor that Henry fled in August 1517 when the "sweating sickness" struck the capital. But the epidemic followed the king, carrying off some of the royal pages who slept in His Majesty's chamber. Henry's coat of arms, along with the Tudor rose and the pomegranate of his first wife, Catherine of Aragon, are engraved in stone above the entrance gate named after the king. But Henry is only one of 41 monarchs who have added to and altered the castle that William of Normandy began just four years after he defeated Harold at the Battle of Hastings.

Henry II's Round Tower, which surveys the Thames as it winds through its green valley, is surrounded by other towers, walls, courts, lodges, and chapels built by successive royal dynasties. Plantagenets, Tudors, Stuarts, and Hanovers have added to the castle over the years. (The only interruption in the near millennium of royal residence at Windsor was the bitter decade of the Civil War in the 1640s.) The most recent occupants, the Windsors, so renamed their House of Saxe-Coburg and Gotha in 1917, when anti-German feeling was high. A new addition to the grounds is the Tudor-style mansion that the duke and duchess of York built for themselves after their marriage in 1986.

Tradition rules here at Windsor, the heart of the system that from an island of warring barons created a nation and an empire over which, it was later said, "the sun never set." British tradition is glorified every morning from Monday through Saturday at 11:00 with the elaborate rituals of the changing of the guard. Soldiers in their red tunics and black bearskin helmets stamp their boots and make the ancient walls ring. The same troops, in flak jackets rather than scarlet, are available for a combat role in NATO or farther afield. At Combermere Barracks on St. Leonard's Road, just a few blocks from the castle, is the **Museum of the Household Cavalry**. (The Household Cavalry can also be seen mounting the guard daily at the Horse Guards opposite Whitehall in London.) The museum tells the story of the Blues, who, confusingly, wear red plumes in their helmets, and the Life Guards (white plumes) from 1685 to the present. The two regiments are being merged in a planned reorganization of defense forces.

Chapel of the Order of the Garter

Also known as St. George's Chapel, this is the first building you see when you pass through the Henry VIII Gate. Carved choir stalls in the chapel include those of the Knights of the Garter, an order that, according to romantic legend, Edward III founded in 1348 after he picked up a garter the countess of Salisbury dropped while they were dancing. He rebuked the tittering courtiers with the words "*Honi soit qui mal y pense*" ("Evil be to him who evil thinks"), and this is the motto inscribed in gold letters on the dark-blue velvet garter that to this day members wear beneath the left knee.

Edward IV began building the present chapel where the processions and ceremonies of the Knights of the Garter are enacted. Their banners are hung in the choir. The chapel was completed by Henry VIII, who shares a tomb here with Jane Seymour, his favorite among his many wives. The body of Charles I, beheaded after the Civil War and brought secretly to Windsor, was found nearby in the chapel vault when it was opened by George IV in the early part of the 19th century. Apart from Henry and Charles, eight other kings of England, including three from the present century, rest in peace beneath the chapel's fan-vaulted ceiling.

The State Apartments

When, in 1820, George IV came to the throne late in life (he was prince regent for years during his father's madness), he transferred the family apartments from the dank north wing to the southern and eastern sides of the castle. He then had the Grand Corridor built to connect them with the State Apartments. These richly furnished quarters are used for royal ceremonies and receptions but are otherwise open to the public. The Queen's Presence Room is still as Charles II decorated it; the Neapolitan artist Antonio Verrio was commissioned to paint the ceiling. The walls are adorned with late-18th-century Gobelins, other tapestries, and royal portraits. In the sequence of rooms with majestic titles there are carvings by Grinling Gibbons, etchings by great masters, priceless porcelain and furniture, and paintings by Rubens, Rembrandt, Van Dyck, Canaletto, Dürer, Holbein, Reynolds, and others. The aptly named Grand Staircase is dominated by a vast, gleaming suit of armor made to measure in 1540 for a gouty Henry VIII. The Waterloo Chamber, created by George IV as a memorial to those who brought down Napoleon, has a seamless carpet 80 feet long and 40 feet wide. It was made in India for Queen Victoria and is probably the largest example of its kind in the world.

Everything in Windsor Castle is on a regal scale—everything, that is, except the **dollhouse** that was presented to Queen Mary in 1923 by the architect Sir Edwin Lutyens. It is built on a scale of 12:1, and so is everything in it, including works of writers such as Chesterton and Kipling and paintings by Orpen and Munnings, down to the electrical and plumbing fixtures of Lilliputian proportions. Like the State Apartments nearby, it is open to the public.

WINDSOR GREAT PARK

The 4,800-acre park, lying on the far side of the castle on a wide loop of the River Thames, was a hunting ground for William the Conqueror. In fact, herds of deer roam here still. At the farthest end of Long Walk is the Copper Horse, an equestrian statue of George III dressed as a Roman emperor—a suitably sardonic memorial to the king who lost the American colonies.

On the grounds of Frogmore House, a royal residence in a quiet corner of the park dating from 1697, is the **mausoleum**. A masterpiece of mosaic and monumental masonry, it is a reminder of the Victorian way of death, open to visitors only on occasional days in May. Victoria, the Widow of Windsor, had it built for her beloved consort, Albert, whom she mourned for 40 years before she joined him. In the burial ground outside lie the remains of the king of the briefest reign, Edward VIII, and of the woman for whom he gave up the throne of England, Wallis Simpson.

ETON AND RUNNYMEDE

Eton College, that oldest of old schools which molded no fewer than 18 British prime ministers, stands modestly beside the High Street of the little town from which it takes its name, just across the river from Windsor. Some of the buildings, including the exquisitely painted chapel, date from the school's founding in 1440 by Henry VI when he was only in his late teens. A tower completed by Roger Lupton in 1520 looks down on the cobbled schoolyard and the playing fields beyond, on which, according to the duke of Wellington, himself an old Etonian, the Battle of Waterloo was won. The younger boys still wear the inimitable Eton jacket and stiff collar, and the "Eton Boating Song" is still sung. (Ask at the Tourist Information office about when the school can be visited.) The founding charter, preserved in the college archives, provided for 70 "poor and indigent" scholars to be clothed, fed, and educated. Five and a half centuries later, there are still 70 "King's scholars" on highly prized scholarships. The other 1,200 pupils, called Oppidans, pay high fees for the privilege of an education at what Prime Minister Gladstone called "the queen of all schools of all the world."

One summer's morning in 1215 John and his entourage rode out from Windsor Castle to meet the king's disaffected barons, assembled on the open field of Runney Mede. Here King John was compelled to put his seal to a charter curbing royal power by insuring the feudal rights of barons, the freedom of the church, and the customs of towns. This document—the first in British constitutional history—later became known as the Magna Carta, or great charter. The water-meadows of **Runnymede**, 2 miles (3 km) northwest of Egham on the A 308, remain virtually untouched by the passing centuries. A small Classical-style temple was erected in 1957 by the American Bar Association, and nearby a memorial to President John F. Kennedy stands at the foot of Cooper's Hill. At the summit is another memorial, commemorating the 20,456 Allied airmen who died in World War II and have no known graves. Their names are recorded in the cloister.

ROYAL WINDSOR HORSE SHOW

The Royal Windsor Horse Show is held in Home Park in mid-May, a month ahead of the premier horse-racing (and high-fashion) event of the year at nearby Royal Ascot. Members of the royal family play an active part in the former event, whether it be show jumping or driving. The best way to see the show, which is done while drinking Champagne and eating smoked-salmon sandwiches, is to become a member. Write to the Secretary, Mews, Windsor Castle, Berkshire. For those who would rather listen to Baroque music than compare the finer points of horseflesh, the **Windsor Festival** runs from late September through October.

DINING IN WINDSOR

A good place to dine in Windsor is **The Castle**, a Georgian coach inn opposite its namesake that offers a plain à la carte menu. However, to escape the crowds it is worth taking a half-mile walk across the pedestrians-only bridge to the town of Eton (see above). **Christopher**, on Eton's High Street (closed Saturday lunchtimes and at Christmas), is fashionable and not terribly expensive. If you want to splurge and sample some of the finest food in Britain, head 6 miles (10 km) upriver to Bray for a meal at the **Waterside Inn**. The restaurant, run by the celebrated

Roux brothers of France, has views of smooth lawns and summerhouses, weeping willows, boats, and swans on the river. Book in advance; Tel: 0628-206-91.

—*Frank Dawes*

Winchester

Winchester is very much on the day-trip agenda for many visitors, though no commercial long-distance bus company includes it on conducted day tours. Perhaps this is because the city is well within commuting distance from London; if you take one of the sometimes cramped commuter trains in the afternoon you'll rub shoulders with office workers coming back from the capital. There is also regular bus service from Victoria Coach Station.

As so often happens, the walk from the train station to the city center is unexciting and promises little—which makes your arrival in the partly traffic-free High Street all the more enjoyable. But do make your way directly to this, the heart of the ancient city and the site of the great public school, the castle, and the riverside walks, as quickly as possible.

MAJOR INTEREST

Castle
Cathedral
Winchester College
River Itchen walk

THE CASTLE

At the western end of the agreeably compact city center is the 700-year-old **Castle Hall**. Built by Henry III on the site of a Norman fortress, it runs like a thread through English history. Henry V received the French ambassador here in 1415 before launching the campaign that ended in the English victory at Agincourt. Sir Walter Raleigh was sentenced to death here in 1603, Oliver Cromwell destroyed part of the building during the Civil War in 1645, and Judge Jeffreys held one of his "Bloody Assizes" here—200 victims were sentenced to be hanged, drawn, and quartered, and 1,000 sent as slaves to the West Indies—following the failed Monmouth Rebellion in 1655, in which the Protestant duke of Monmouth attempted a coup d'état against James II.

All this is much more historically reliable than the

supposed association with King Arthur. The first thing you see on entering the great echoing Castle Hall is the famous Round Table on the west wall, according to legend dating back to 1152. But the romantic appeal is not a 20th-century phenomenon: The table was repainted and restored in 1522, when Henry VIII entertained Emperor Charles V in Winchester.

If the castle is missed by many visitors, the unusual **Westgate Museum** is probably seen by only one in a hundred. Housed in the 13th-century Westgate, literally the city's west gate, it is really just one room housing Tudor and Elizabethan armor and weapons. You can reach out and touch the history here.

THE CATHEDRAL

Many people know before they even get as far as the spacious lawns that set it off so effectively that at 556 feet Winchester cathedral is the longest in Europe. They may also know that St. Swithin is buried in the churchyard, and that the manner of his burial made St. Swithin's Day part of English folklore. When Swithin, a humble man who was bishop of Winchester, died in 862 he was buried at his own request in the churchyard, where the rain would fall on him. On July 15 of that year, however, his remains were reburied inside the cathedral, and legend says this angered the saint so much that if it rains on July 15 it will rain every day for 40 days.

Among the many cathedral treasures that can be seen even in a short visit are the illuminated 12th-century Winchester Bible, and, in the transept, two wooden benches thought to be Norman; they are certainly the oldest pieces of oak furniture in the nation. There are, in addition, chests said to contain the bones of Saxon kings, including Canute and Ethelwulf. Jane Austen's grave is marked by a stone, but, curiously, no reference is made to her as a novelist. Another curiosity is that some windows contain 13th-century stained glass that was originally in Salisbury cathedral.

WINCHESTER COLLEGE

The cathedral is very impressive, but probably the favorite corner of Winchester is to be found to its south, in the quiet and comparatively little-frequented lanes that lead to and around Winchester College, one of several public schools—which are anything but public, of course—that claims to be the oldest in the country. (Most historians grant it the status of second-oldest, after King's School in Canterbury.) The atmosphere here (visitors are allowed) is a cross between that of a monastery and an Oxford or Cambridge college. Pupils at the school, which was founded in 1382 for poor scholars, are known as Wykeha-mists, after founder Bishop William of Wykeham. If you have time to explore only one of the streets behind the cathedral, make it Kingsgate Street, which takes its name from one of the medieval gateways to the old walled town.

The **River Itchen** runs close to the grounds of the school, and it is easy to find paths alongside it. These paths are extremely pleasant when Winchester is crowded and hot; as always in major tourist destinations, try to avoid summer Saturdays, especially if you do not have a hotel in which to escape the melee.

If you really want to get close to history, you can still call at the **Hospital of St. Cross**, founded in 1137 by a grandson of William the Conqueror, for "the Wayfarer's Dole" of a token amount of bread and ale. In so doing you will be part of an 800-year-old tradition, though the admission charge (currently £1.50), in place since 1911, might surprise the founder.

ELSEWHERE IN WINCHESTER

A number of other, lesser points of interest are worth looking out for if you are on foot, places that are some-times missed by the car-bound visitor who takes in only the cathedral and perhaps a couple of Winchester's several interesting bookshops (among which are **Gilbert's**, 19 The Square, and **Peter Daly**, 20A Jury Street, though you'll find other bookshops—for used and antiquarian volumes— around Kingsgate Street). For example, search out the bronze statue of King Alfred, erected in 1901, that gazes down from the High Street in the direction of Westgate. Also look for the Gothic High Cross, on the High Street, and, a few yards away, close to the cathedral precinct, the **city museum**. It is particularly strong in Roman remains (including glass and mosaics), and its Victorian shops— real, not reconstructed—are very popular.

DINING AND STAYING
IN WINCHESTER

Should the Wayfarer's Dole at the Hospital of St. Cross give you a taste for something more substantial, try a lunchtime snack or bar meal in one of Winchester's ancient pubs, which tend to be tucked away down the back lanes. One of these, the **Royal Oak**, off Royal Oak Passage, is a contender for the oldest pub in the country. The **Eclipse**, in the Square, is a very pleasant place to sit outside on a summer day, with sidewalk benches under the pub's jettied black-and-white half-timbered upper stories. Originally the rectory for the little church of St. Lawrence, the building predates the cathedral itself. The Eclipse offers traditional English food such as toad-in-the-hole (sausage cooked in batter) and kedgeree (fish, rice, eggs, and spices). Both the Square and Royal Oak Passage are near the northwest corner of the cathedral. For Itchen trout or pork in cream and cider sauce, with a better-than-average glass of pub wine, look for the **Wykeham Arms** on the corner of Canon Street, which is a westerly extension of College Street, running between the cathedral and Winchester College.

You may be lucky enough to find local venison—from New Forest deer—in some of the restaurants in and around Winchester; the spacious and well-run restaurant of the ▶ **Forte Crest Hotel**, considered Winchester's best hotel, is one such source. Another nice place to stay is the ▶ **Lainston House**, just west of town in the village of Sparsholt (a short taxi ride from Winchester). This luxurious retreat, which occupies a 17th-century country house surrounded by many acres of grounds, offers an elegantly served table d'hôte lunch (those who are not guests of the hotel are welcome).

—*Bryn Frank*

Salisbury and Stonehenge

Neither the train journey to Salisbury nor the walk from the station, past small, functional shops and snack bars, is very inspiring. But do not despair, for this small city with a very impressive cathedral indeed, as well as lots of history that often gets overlooked because of the cathedral, is always worth the trip.

This is the rare case of a tourist attraction that may be best seen as part of a guided day trip by bus from London. Evan Evans, for example, will take you to Stonehenge as well as Salisbury, saving you a lot of bother in the process. Stonehenge can also be seen during a day trip by rail to

Salisbury; see the end of the Salisbury section for information about buses from Salisbury to Stonehenge.

A recent major fire failed to spoil an unusually attractive approach from a huge car park into the city center— a fine riverside arrangement of shops and a few offices; renovations were skillfully done. Salisbury has an immediate charm, and there is much to see even in a short space of time.

MAJOR INTEREST

Well-preserved shops and houses
Salisbury cathedral and cathedral close
Stonehenge

AROUND IN SALISBURY

The River Avon does not dominate Salisbury, but its presence is definitely felt: A good and popular place to get oriented early in the day is beside the County Hotel, where swans bob on the Avon and friends meet to go off for lunch in one of several local hostelries—and sometimes in the good fish-and-chip shop called **Stoby's.**

Note that this is *not* Shakespeare's Avon, the one that flows (also with swans) through Stratford-upon-Avon, but the one that rises north of Salisbury Plain, runs close to Stonehenge, and reaches the sea near Bournemouth, due south of Salisbury. John Constable painted Salisbury cathedral most memorably from the river's banks near Harnham—and even in the course of a day trip you can walk to the mill there, which doubles as an unpretentious restaurant; see below. Though the trees have changed, it is not hard to re-create, through your camera lens or on your sketch pad, the scene that Constable knew.

Salisbury's original symmetrical medieval layout, which is roughly intact, has been compared with that of American cities, and makes orientation easy for visitors. A good point at which to begin a tour of the city, which even on a day trip can easily be coupled with a thorough inspection of the world-famous cathedral, is the parish church of St. Thomas Becket, which has a rare 500-year-old carved roof and a most impressive painting called *Doom*—a kind of day-of-judgment study—probably given by a parishioner who had made a pilgrimage to Canterbury.

A very well known bakery called **Snells**—also known for its many packaged coffees and its boxes of handmade chocolates—may provide the makings of a memorable picnic within sight of the cathedral. Just around the corner is the public library, which stands on the site of the Cheese Cross (where cheese was traded) that once stood here. Of all the medieval market crosses where trade was carried out in Salisbury only one, Poultry Cross, tucked away behind one corner of the marketplace, still exists.

If you visit Salisbury on a Tuesday or Saturday you'll find the lively open-air market in progress. A charter drawn up in 1227 permitted a daily market, but objections from local towns reduced these to twice-weekly affairs. Among other things, the marketplace is still associated with the great feast held for the coronation of Edward VII in 1902, when 4,000 people sat down to an open-air meal of roast beef.

On the opposite side of the market from the library and St. Thomas's lies **Cross Keys Chequer**, a small precinct of interesting shops, including a good bookshop. The "chequer" is based on a medieval layout from c.1225. Close by is the John A'Port House, officially a shop selling china and glass—quality souvenirs here—but equally well known for having been the home of a six-time mayor of Salisbury in the 15th century.

Behind the marketplace you will find Fish Row (no need to explain its origin) and Salisbury's tourist information center. Walk along Fish Row and you'll come to Butcher Row and then to Poultry Cross. There's a good pub, the **Haunch of Venison**, close to Poultry Cross, with better-than-average bar food and a restaurant, too.

Pick up New Canal Street and then Milford Street, where you'll find the **Red Lion Hotel**, an ancient inn whose heyday was probably in the early 18th century, when stagecoaches left for London at 10:00 every night. The moderately priced if not exceptional restaurant and, particularly, the bar offer lots of atmosphere.

On St. John Street (via Milford Street) you'll find another, slightly more genteel, more comfortable hotel that also serves good hot bar meals. This is the **White Hart**, whose handsome sign was put up in 1827 in response to a sign erected by a rival establishment. On October 9, 1780, on his way to negotiate a treaty with the Dutch during the American War of Independence, Henry Laurens, a former president of the Continental Congress, was captured at sea and kept overnight at the hotel before being taken to London and incarcerated in the Tower. (He was exchanged for General Cornwallis in 1782.) The **Rose & Crown** on

Harnham Road also has bar food and a restaurant. (See below for these last two places as accommodations.)

Here you are on the edge of a particularly interesting, quiet, and architecturally appealing quarter of the city. First is St. Ann Street; note the impressive carved exterior of Joiner's Hall. From the end of St. Ann Street cross St. John Street and walk through St. Ann's Gate, perhaps the nicest approach to the **cathedral close**; it is much less touristy than the more frequently used High Street Gate. Built in 1333, when the close was first laid out around the almost 100-year-old cathedral, the gate still has traces of late-Norman carving.

The houses in the close itself are full of interest. Near St. Ann's Gate, at number 14, is where Henry Fielding wrote *Tom Jones,* and, on the far side of the cathedral, Myles Place was the home of the distinguished historian Sir Arthur Bryant, whose ashes are interred in the cathedral. On the same side of the close, in the King's House, are the impressive **Salisbury and South Wiltshire Museum** (which includes in its varied collections a reconstructed country doctor's surgery and a giant figure that used to be carried at the head of parades in Salisbury) and a building known as the Wardrobe, which houses the Museum of the Berkshire and Wiltshire Regiment. Facing the cathedral from another side of the close, near these museums, is lovely **Mompesson House**, a National Trust property. It is a fine 18th-century building, with period furniture, objets d'art, and an unusual lived-in atmosphere.

Though it is not open to the public, look at the exterior of the College of Matrons, just inside the close near the High Street Gate. It was built in 1682 to house "twelve poor widows," and it still does, though the original means test is no longer applied.

It is said, by the way, that Trollope modeled his Barchester on Exeter, but it was while sitting in Salisbury's cathedral close that he conceived the idea of an intricate "cathedral society."

On the High Street do not miss one of provincial England's biggest and most interesting secondhand and antiquarian bookshops, **Beach's**, where the assistants wear uniforms. From the High Street turn into Crane Street and walk as far as Queen Elizabeth Gardens, from where you can follow the Town Path—so marked—to **Harnham Mill**. The mill, mentioned above, dates from

1135, and was used to house cathedral artifacts during the move from the Old Sarum cathedral site to the new one.

THE CATHEDRAL

Old Sarum was probably an Iron Age settlement before the site was taken over for defensive purposes by the Romans. It had grown up around the ancient church of St. Osmund and a castle on a hillside site, but it was later deemed unsuitable because it was affected by "too much wind and too little water," and the population was beginning to move south onto the more fertile plain. The move was made official by papal sanction to build a new cathedral. Tradition holds that the bishop declared a new cathedral would be built a shot-arrow's distance from the old cathedral. Some arrow: Salisbury cathedral is about 3 miles (5 km) away.

Many people are surprised by how light and spacious the cathedral (which was consecrated in 1258, only 38 years after the first stone was laid) seems inside. It belongs to a very distinctive period of cathedral construction; those of Lincoln and Amiens date from the same period. The nave is the longest in England after Winchester's, and there is much in the cathedral that is outstanding: the oldest piece of working machinery in Britain, and possibly the world, for one thing, in the form of a clock dating from 1386. The cathedral is also the repository of one of only four contemporary copies of the Magna Carta of 1215. This treasure has been kept in the cathedral continuously since 1225, except when it was hidden in a nearby quarry between 1940 and 1945 to protect it from German bombing. The spire was erected in about 1330, as it had not been part of the original plan.

Do not miss the cathedral's **cloisters**, which are the largest in area of any English cathedral, and a place of calm even when the cathedral is thronged with visitors— which does seem to be almost all the time. That last fact is an argument for visiting Salisbury during poor weather or during the winter months, especially now that there is central heating (the place was once well known for the number of people who brought hot-water bottles to carol services).

Even within a one-day trip it is possible to visit Stonehenge from Salisbury. Guided tours operated by Guide Friday leave the Salisbury train station three times a day, and the fare for the almost two-hour round trip is about £9. Further details are available from the tourist information center; Tel: (0722) 33-49-56 or from Guide Friday's headquarters at Stratford-upon-Avon (Tel: 0789-29-44-66).

Staying in Salisbury

If you decide to spend the night in Salisbury, the ▶ **White Hart Hotel** on St. John Street has an imposing façade and pleasant and spacious public rooms. It is also a favorite rendezvous of Salisbury's well-heeled citizens. For atmosphere, try the ▶ **Rose & Crown Hotel** on Harnham Road, which overlooks the river and has a well-known rose garden. Part of the building dates from the 14th century.

—*Bryn Frank*

STONEHENGE

Stonehenge, at the southern edge of Salisbury plain, just 8 miles (13 km) north of Salisbury, probably looms larger in your imagination than it does in actual fact. As has often been pointed out, its 162 stone blocks—unadorned, undressed, and only about 35 steps from one side to the other—would fit into the Library of Congress rotunda or within the dome of St. Paul's Cathedral. This most famous of all Britain's stone circles is one of Europe's greatest enigmas: Each year it inspires approximately three quarters of a million people to make a pilgrimage. These numbers are swollen by modern-day Druids, pop fans, and latter-day hippies who crowd onto Salisbury Plain for the summer solstice (as well as for the illegal rock festivals held to coincide with it). It is mainly on account of these celebrants that Stonehenge is now subject to a four-mile "exclusion zone" that applies for several days surrounding the summer solstice. Usually visitors can walk within 12 feet of the monument, separated from the stones only by a rope.

A thousand years before the Egyptians built the pyramids, Neolithic farmers lived on the windswept chalk plateau of Salisbury. There was little wood and less stone, yet they built burial chambers around which Stonehenge eventually grew—first as a cemetery, then as a temple. Over the years it was put to many uses, which is one of the reasons Stonehenge has so puzzled later generations.

As trade routes became busier and the population increased, Stonehenge and similar burial grounds took on the role of meeting places, not only for traders but also for participants in seasonal fertility rituals.

Among the earliest of all visitors to Stonehenge were the Druids, Celtic priests who came over from the Continent about 300 B.C., by which point Stonehenge already had lain abandoned and unused for more than 1,000 years. They took it over for ceremonial purposes (though not, as fancifully used to be supposed, for ritual slaughter).

In 1130 Henry of Huntingdon, a dean at Lincoln Cathedral, was commissioned to write a history of England, and he included Stonehenge. He borrowed from an even earlier chronicle—largely fictitious—that claimed Merlin, seer and prophet to King Arthur, had the stones removed from Ireland and reconstructed on Salisbury Plain. James I was utterly intrigued by Stonehenge, and commissioned John Aubrey, best known for his *Brief Lives,* to produce a thorough survey. But Aubrey was much more impressed with nearby Avebury Stone Circle, and his work at Stonehenge was skimpy. Among all the dross was the probably correct suggestion that this was a residential site of early British tribes.

Charles II was among the "great and good" to be fascinated by Stonehenge, and he commissioned Inigo Jones, the superb architect of St. Paul's, Covent Garden, and the Banqueting Hall in London, to solve the mystery. Jones concluded that as "those ancient times had no knowledge of public works, either sacred or secular, for their own use or honour of their deities, they could not be responsible for such an impressive structure." It must, ergo, have been Roman in origin.

People seem to have great difficulty counting the stones. A legend from Elizabethan times has it that no ordinary mortal can count the stones twice and arrive at the same figure. *Gulliver's Travels* author Jonathan Swift and Celia Fiennes, the 17th-century traveller and diarist, were among those who made a stab at it. Each came up with a different number, and Swift hedged his bets— "either 92 or 93."

Samuel Pepys took a day trip from Salisbury to Stonehenge but found the cost of his party's saddle horses rather high. Of the site itself he was characteristically blunt: "Worth going to see. God knows what their use was."

The Layout of Stonehenge

As you approach Stonehenge, you first come upon a ditch and a bank about 100 feet from the first stones. Inside this are the 56 Aubrey holes, found to contain remains of cremated human beings, and what is effectively a gateway to the site known as the Slaughter Stone, now fallen. The Heel Stone, a so-called sarsen stone, stands outside the entrance. (The word *sarsen* probably comes from *saracen,* or, simply, "strange" or "alien"; the term "Heel Stone" is derived from a mark on the surface that resembles a man's heel.) The Heel Stone is the only one to have survived from the first circle of stones that appeared here around 1800 B.C., and was erected exactly in line, along with other stones, with the point at which the sun rises above the horizon during the summer solstice.

Between 1700 and 1600 B.C. the construction of the second stage of Stonehenge began. Blue stones were transported from Wales and erected in two concentric circles. This was the work of the so-called Beaker Folk, farmers from the Continent whose name derives from their excavated drinking vessels. The construction of Stonehenge III began after 1600 B.C., when the blue stones were moved and 80 huge sarsen stones were transported here from the Marlborough Downs. These were formed either into a ring of upright stones, connected by carved lintels, or an inner horseshoe shape.

Later (also part of Stonehenge III) an oval arrangement of blue stones was erected within the sarsen horseshoe, and a block of sandstone, also from Wales, was erected in the center. It became known as the Altar Stone. Finally, sometime around 1300 B.C., the residents rearranged 19 blue stones into their current configuration.

A word of advice: As with Salisbury cathedral, try to visit Stonehenge when the rest of the world has decided to skip it. Dull, even rainy, days are good; misty or foggy ones are better still. It all helps to get the imagination working. Even when the site is closed, however, it is possible during daylight hours to see a certain amount of Stonehenge from the road. For further information contact the shop-cum-information center at the site; Tel: (0980) 62-31-08.

—*Bryn Frank*

Bath

The only sad faces you'll see in Bath are those belonging to people who have allowed themselves only one day to see the city. It's worth a whole week, but it *is* possible to get the flavor of the city in a day. Train travellers will find that the station is close to the heart of things. Just walk

north along Manvers Street until you see the **abbey**, which is famous for its light, bright interior and its delicate fan-vaulting. The mainly 16th-century structure was restored in the 17th century. The Pump Room and the Roman Baths are virtually adjacent to the abbey, and you get to Pulteney Bridge, for example, from the abbey by walking east toward the river and then left along Grand Parade. On a day trip you will have to resist the temptation to linger over lunch in one of Bath's elegant restaurants, though this genteel and self-conscious city has plenty of fast-food restaurants and pubs with food to keep you from flagging.

MAJOR INTEREST

Roman Baths
Royal Crescent
Pulteney Bridge

Even in history-rich Britain few places offer such an imme-diate hands-across-the-centuries link with the past. The Romans are omnipresent. It was they who first exploited the health-giving qualities of the water that fell on the nearby Mendip Hills about 10,000 years ago and now bubbles up from the earth at the rate of 240,000 gallons a day. The grateful Romans created a temple to Sulis Mi-nerva: Sul was an ancient Celtic deity and Minerva the Roman goddess of healing. The **museum** created around the excavated remains of the **Roman baths** (which came complete with the equivalent of today's Jacuzzis, saunas, and Turkish baths) is exceptional.

But it was the 18th century that created the Bath that today has such a powerful hold on visitors. The influx of outsiders looking for the elixir of life made massive redevelopment possible, and the soft, crumbly local stone was ideal for a comparatively quick transformation of the place, which was completed with skill and a keen aesthetic sense. Jane Austen, when she first came, disliked the squeaky-clean look of the new buildings, but these have now mellowed to form one of the handsomest cities in Europe.

Of course, the city is best seen on foot—unless you take a horse-drawn carriage (these are found at the bot-tom of Milsom Street) or an open-top bus tour. Because it takes you right out of the city into the surrounding hills, one advantage of the latter is that it offers distant views down into and across Bath. These buses are highly visible and can be picked up at several points.

The city is indeed friendly to walkers. If time is limited consider a conducted walking tour, best joined at the Pump Room; tours are free. Tickets for bus tours can be bought from the Tourist Information Centre, the Colonnades, 11–13 Bath Street; Tel: 0225-46-28-31. You can ask your guide all sorts of questions to help you get the most out of the limited time at your disposal: about pubs, restaurants, and shops, especially antiques shops, many of which are high class but nonetheless sell good-quality pieces that will not have you calling your bank for an urgent cash transfer.

Should you want an interesting angle on the city without walking, consider an hour-long riverboat trip from the Pulteney Bridge as far as Bathampton Weir. This fits well into a day-trip schedule. The boats leave every hour on the hour between 10:00 A.M. and 6:00 P.M., with evening trips in July and August.

A WALKING TOUR OF BATH

A walking route covering places not to be missed might start at the **Royal Crescent**, an elliptical terrace of imposing private houses created by John Wood the Younger between 1767 and 1775 and probably inspired by Bernini's Colonnade around the Piazza San Pietro in Rome. The **Royal Crescent Hotel** is right in the center of the elegant crescent: Lunch here is elegant as well. With or without lunch, you'll experience the elegance of a Royal Crescent interior at **Number 1 Royal Crescent**, a museum maintained in great style by the Bath Preservation Trust.

To the east via Brock Street, the handsome stone houses of the **Circus**, a symmetrical circle of fine houses also designed by Wood, are in the classical 18th-century tradition. A few yards away are the 18th-century **Assembly Rooms**, once the haunt of Bath's high society, and now housing an exceptional costume museum that reopened after major renovations in 1991. One contemporary costume is added to the collection every year.

There is good antiques hunting in and around **Bartlett Street**, and as you walk down Milsom Street you will hear echoes of Jane Austen, who referred to this street in *Northanger Abbey*. Actually, she referred to "the prettiest little hat you can imagine" in a shop window here, but you are also likely to notice the excellent bookshops—useful for souvenirs and guidebooks. In *Persuasion,* Sir Walter Elliott "counted eighty-seven women without there being a tolerable face among them." Also in Milsom Street, it's worth seeing the **Octagon Chapel**, famous for being so comfortable that some pews even had their own fireplaces. It is now the headquarters of the Royal Photographic Society, where exhibitions are regularly held in several different rooms, so there is usually something worth seeing. Tel: (0225) 46-28-41 for details.

From the bottom of the street you can hail a horse-drawn carriage; the usual route goes via **Pulteney Bridge**, built between 1769 and 1774 (perhaps the single most photographed structure in Bath, and the second-oldest surviving river bridge in Britain, after Lincoln's, to have houses built on it), to the **Holburne of Menstrie Museum**. Inspired by the works of Italian Renaissance architect Andrea Palladio, Robert Adam designed the bridge in 1770. The Holburne of Menstrie Museum is named after Sir Thomas William Holburne, who amassed a collection of fine paintings—among other things—with works by Gainsborough, Stubbs, and Turner, including his much-loved *Pembroke Castle*. There's also a fine permanent collection of 20th-century crafts, including more than 100 examples of Bernard Leach pottery.

A short walk from here, at the end of North Parade Passage and then into York Street, you'll find the house of Ralph Allen, who bought several stone quarries and organized much of the development of the city. Do not miss quiet, tree-shaded, and often-overlooked Abbey Green, nearby, which is close to the Roman Baths. The **Crystal Palace** pub on Abbey Green is convivial and has good food: The shepherd's pie and the steak-and-kidney pie are especially popular.

Unfortunately, the restoration of the city's 17th- and 18th-century baths (Cross Bath, Hot Bath, and the Beau Street Bath) has been suspended, and they can only be seen from outside. (Go via Bath Street, past the Tourist Information Center.)

Retrace your steps up Bath Street and you'll find the best souvenir hunting around Northumberland Place and Union Passage—a fascinating traffic-free rabbit warren of small shops and cafés. Turn left at the top of Union Street into Upper Borough Walls and you'll come to the Theatre Royal. Almost next door is the house once occupied by Beau Nash's mistress, Juliana Papjoy, now a restaurant known as Popjoy's (nobody seems to be able to explain the corruption of the name).

ELSEWHERE IN BATH

Apart from establishments already mentioned, day visitors are recommended (partly for reasons of time) to the **Moon and Sixpence Wine Bar** at 6A Broad Street, **Le Parisien** on Old Bond Street, and—for Malaysian dishes—**Bali**, on George Street.

Worth a detour (even on a day trip) is the **American Museum**, Claverton Manor, on the easern outskirts of the city. There are 18 rooms set out with American furniture dating from the mid-17th century to the mid-19th century, as well as galleries devoted to glass, pewter, and silver. Occasionally special weekends are devoted to such themes as the Civil War, the War of Independence, and Native American heritage. For details, Tel: (0225) 46-05-03. To get there by public transport take the number 18 bus from the abbey or the bus station as far as the university; from there it's a five-minute walk (ask the driver for directions).

During late May and early June you may want to extend your day well into the evening, as that is when the annual **Bath Festival of Music and the Arts** is held. Every year there is a special theme (1993 celebrated the 150th anniversary of the birth of Edvard Grieg, as well as featuring other 19th- and 20th-century composers). There's also a jazz program and a fringe festival, and not all events are evening ones. For details, Tel: (0225) 46-22-31 or 46-33-62 (box office).

STAYING IN BATH

Should you be tempted to spend the night in Bath, you may be able to find accommodations on short notice, although there is no guarantee. You are more likely to find a room at one of the larger hotels, such as the ▶ **Francis Hotel** on Queen Square, a Georgian building that was partly rebuilt after it was hit by one of the few Luftwaffe bombs to fall on Bath. It has a particularly spacious restaurant, although some rooms, while comfortable and well appointed, are small. Another possibility is the ▶ **Hilton National** on Walcot Street, a fairly functional hotel in which some of the more than 100 rooms have a river view. A new leisure center and 50 additional bedrooms have contributed to a smarter look here.

—Bryn Frank

GETTING AROUND

Windsor

By car, leave London via Hammersmith and follow the M 4 to junction 6. It's a 40-minute train ride from London's Paddington Station to Windsor and Eton Central; change at Slough. The trip takes 55 minutes from London's Waterloo to Windsor and Eton Riverside. You can also reach Windsor by Green Line bus from Victoria Coach Station.

Winchester

Winchester is about 65 miles (104 km) from London by rail, a trip of just over an hour; the day round-trip fare is about £13. Trains leave from Waterloo Station, which lies on London's Bakerloo and Northern Underground lines. From Winchester's train station it is only a ten-minute walk southward via Station Road and the Upper High Street to the heart of what remains of the ancient city. (The approach is as uninspiring as old Winchester is impressive.) You can also travel by long-distance bus from London's Victoria Coach Station, travel time about an hour and a quarter; the day round-trip fare is about £12.

It is possible to combine a day trip to Winchester and Salisbury, but if you are coming from London it will require an early-morning start and a late return. You'll need to change trains at Basingstoke, and you should be prepared to wait up to an hour for connections.

Salisbury

Salisbury is accessible by train from London's Waterloo Station, which lies on the Northern and Bakerloo Underground lines. The trip takes approximately an hour and a half. The round-trip fare is about £17.

You can also go by long-distance bus (National Express) from London's Victoria Coach Station. The journey takes about two and three-quarter hours, and the round-trip fare is £12–£16.

A busy full-day alternative is a guided bus tour from Evan Evans, which costs about £38 per adult. The tour includes all entrance fees (to the visitor center at Stonehenge, for example) and takes in Bath and its main attractions as well as Salisbury and Stonehenge. Details from Evan Evans, 26–28 Paradise Road, Richmond, Surrey TW9 1SE; Tel: (081) 332-2912.

For regular bus service from Salisbury to Stonehenge, see the end of the Salisbury section, above.

Bath

Bath is well known for its speedy rail connection to London's Paddington Station, which lies on the Circle, District, and Metropolitan lines of the London Underground system. Although it is 107 miles (170 km) from London by train, Bath can be reached in about an hour and a half. The train station (an elegant building in its own right) is convenient to the city center. The round-trip fare ranges between £24 and £44.

Bath is also accessible by long-distance bus (National Express) from London's Victoria Coach Station. The journey takes about three hours, and the round-trip fare is £13.25–£17.

ACCOMMODATIONS REFERENCE

Rates are projected 1994 prices for a double room with breakfast, unless otherwise indicated. As prices are subject to change, always double-check before booking.

Winchester

▶ **Forte Crest Hotel**. Paternoster Row, **Winchester** SO23 9LQ. Tel: (0962) 86-16-11; Fax: (0962) 84-15-03; in U.S. and Canada, (800) 225-5843; in Australia, (008) 22-24-46. £89 (breakfast not included).

▶ **Lainston House Hotel**. **Sparsholt**, Winchester SO21 2LT. Tel: (0962) 86-35-88; Fax: (0962) 776-72. £120–£240.

Salisbury

▶ **Rose & Crown Hotel**. Harnham Road, **Salisbury** SP2 8JQ. Tel: (0722) 32-79-08; Fax: (0722) 33-98-16. £100–£115.

▶ **White Hart Hotel**. 1 St. John Street, **Salisbury** SP1 2SD. Tel: (0722) 32-74-76; Fax: (0722) 41-27-61; in U.S. and Canada, (800) 225-5843; in Australia, (008) 22-24-46. £90–£105 (breakfast not included).

Bath

▶ **Francis Hotel**. Queen Square, **Bath** BA1 2HH. Tel: (0225) 42-42-57; Fax: (0225) 31-97-15; in U.S. and Canada, (800) 225-5843; in Australia, (008) 22-24-46. £108 (breakfast not included).

▶ **Hilton National**. Walcot Street, **Bath** BA1 5BJ. Tel: (0225) 46-34-11; Fax: (0225) 46-43-93; in U.S., (800) 445-8667; in Canada, (800) 268-9275; in Australia, (008) 22-22-55. £105 (breakfast not included).

NORTHWEST

Oxford

Visitors to Oxford, 59 miles (94 km) northwest of central London, tend to arrive with a ready-made image in mind: Matthew Arnold's description of "that sweet City with her dreaming spires." That is not always what they find, particularly if they arrive by public transportation. Emerging from the railway station, passengers are confronted by a brewery and an old jam factory. The latter, once the source of Oxford's famous marmalade, now does at least house an antiques market where the atmosphere is friendly and there are bargains to collect. Bus travellers are likewise dropped in one of the city's more nondescript quarters. The dreaming spires, however, are not far away. The city center is still dominated by the colleges that together make up the university, a few uncompromisingly modern but most still proudly displaying their medieval origins in their ancient stones. The University of Oxford is not some distant institution drawing its academic skirts away from the life of the city but is very much at the heart of it.

The best way to get a feel for Oxford is to find a vantage point with an overall view. One such spot is where the main streets, St. Aldate's, Queen Street, Cornmarket, and the High, converge, at Carfax. The 14th-century **Carfax Tower** (all that remains of St. Martin's Church, which was demolished in 1896) is open to visitors, who, when they have wound their way up the spiral stairs, will find all Oxford laid out before them. This is where you should begin your tour of Oxford.

MAJOR INTEREST

Carfax Tower
University colleges
Radcliffe Square
Bodleian Library
Bookstores on Broad Street
Sheldonian Theatre
Museum of the History of Science
Ashmolean Museum

To the east of the tower, the High Street—always known as "the High"—curves away to the distant hills. To the north is Cornmarket Street. Between these two streets is an enticing array of domes, pinnacles, and towers. St. Aldate's, to the south, is dominated by the ornate Tom Tower, marking the entrance to Christ Church College. Beyond it is the Thames, or (as it is more popularly known in its passage through Oxford) the Isis. To the west are sadder sights: Queen Street leads to a mishmash of modern shopping areas and parking lots. The old castle also lies this way, but the romantic battlements are now the site of the local jail, and all that remains of the Norman fortress is a grassy mound—the old "motte," still a very distinctive landmark.

From the Carfax Tower, the areas that reward exploration are apparent. The rich golden stones of the old, which on a sunny day seem to glow with their own inner light, offer a far greater lure than the neon and plastic of the new. Thus, visitors to Oxford are drawn to the city's main claim to fame, its ancient university.

Travellers here frequently ask to be directed to the university, only to be told that it is all around them—as you can clearly see from the top of Carfax Tower. The university is made up of 35 separate colleges, each with its individual history and traditions, yet all growing from a single root. To understand the system you must step back some 700 years. Medieval learning drew its strength from the church, which was the major center of study and which controlled virtually all forms of education. By the 13th century Oxford was home to a guild of teachers, the Universitas, whose students were housed in communal halls. From these grew the colleges, each with its chapel for prayers and its quadrangles, around which were grouped rooms for students and teachers. Common facilities, such as libraries, soon developed to serve all the colleges. But the heart of the teaching system remained the tutorial, the meeting of teacher and student in the comfortable, informal surroundings of a college room.

Great variety exists among the colleges, certainly in appearance. There are grand colleges, with architecture so classically formal it approaches pomposity, and others where you might feel you had strayed into the garden of some old country mansion. To understand the colleges, it may help to take a little time at the beginning of the tour to look at one in detail:

CHRIST CHURCH COLLEGE

As you descend Carfax Tower and walk south on St. Aldate's, the first college you come to is Christ Church. The site originally held an Anglo-Saxon nunnery, but the church was rebuilt several times before the Norman church of St. Frideswide was begun here in the 12th century. In 1525 Cardinal Wolsey arrived with typical bravado and plans to demolish all that was old and raise a new college with a new chapel. The cardinal's fall brought a change of plans and patrons. Henry VIII took over, and Cardinal College became Christ Church. In the process, St. Frideswide's was saved, first as the college chapel, later as **Oxford Cathedral**.

Given its powerful patronage, the college was inevitably built on a grand scale and improved and developed over the centuries, with much of its present formal beauty due to the influence of Sir Christopher Wren. The formal entrance, topped by the tall **Tom Tower**, is intended to impress the visitor, and it does. Each evening during term time the great bell in the tower tolls 101 times, once for each member of the original founders of the college.

Once inside the quad you find yourself in an enclosed space, the self-contained world of the college. All around are the buildings that house students and dons, but the sheer size of the open grounds prevents any sense of claustrophobia. Meanwhile, the eye is drawn to the tower and spire of the cathedral. Thus, the architecture expresses both the college's religious and scholarly heritage. Christ Church has an air of spaciousness, fronting a wide street with the open green of Christ Church Meadow alongside. Beyond the main quad are subsidiary quads and such important buildings as the college kitchens.

Famous alumni of Christ Church include the mathematics tutor C. L. Dodgson, better known as Lewis Carroll, who might have been amused by some of the antics of 20th-century undergraduates: A swan was once discovered languishing in Tom Quad, formally attired in black bow tie; on another occasion, when Dean Lowe of Christ Church landed in Christ Church Meadow in a helicopter, he was greeted by a choir of undergraduates singing "Lo, he comes in clouds descending."

Christ Church creates its own unmistakable atmosphere, just as every other college at Oxford does, and if it can boast of former members as illustrious as Lewis Carroll, William Penn, and W. H. Auden, so can they.

OTHER COLLEGES AND LANDMARKS

If you go back up St. Aldate's and then take a stroll east down Blue Boar Street, a quite different sense of space and time develops. The noise of traffic recedes, and the narrow lane briefly opens out into Oriel Square, bounded by the **Peckwater Quad** of Christ Church and Oriel and Corpus Christi colleges. What is at once so striking is that Oxford really is a mixture of quite disparate styles: **Oriel** is grandly Jacobean, while **Corpus Christi**, altered and enriched though it has been over the years, has a feel of almost domestic intimacy. It is typical of Oxford that there should be curiosities to look for, such as Corpus Christi's pelican sundial with its strange perpetual calendar.

Beyond the square, the way continues its ever more secretive path up cobbled Merton Street past **Merton College**, which received its first statutes (the laws for governing the college) in 1263 and is generally regarded as the oldest of the colleges—though the claim is strongly contested by two others, Balliol and University. Merton can at least claim to have some of Oxford's oldest buildings, and nowhere do you feel closer to the medieval heart of the university than in **Merton Chapel**, with its beautiful stained glass.

Merton Street bends through a right angle, and the mood changes again, dramatically, for there at the end is the High, dominated by colleges and two churches set among many old houses of character (virtually all now converted to shops). To the west are crowded city streets, to the east openness and light—no accident, rather a reflection of the fact that the former lay within the old city walls, the latter outside them. To the east the view is dominated by **Magdalen College** (pronounced MAUD-lin), its elaborate stonework gleaming from a recent cleaning. Magdalen is the focal point for one of Oxford's most popular traditions. Each May Day morning at 6:00 a hymn is sung from the tower, signaling the start of a prebreakfast round of roistering that fills the surrounding streets, not to mention the surrounding pubs, which are opened early for this one day of the year. From here you can hire punts to explore the River Cherwell. A favorite excursion is to punt down to the **Victoria Arms**—universally known as the Vicky Arms—for a well-earned pint of beer on the lawn. It takes approximately two hours from Magdalen Bridge. A shorter, one-hour trip is possible by hiring a punt upstream at Bardwell Road.

Heading west down the High toward the city center the scene is one of rather formal grandeur, with the Classicism of **Queen's College** striking the dominant note. But to reach the core of the university complex you must turn off the High onto Catte Street and follow the latter to **Radcliffe Square.** An urban space that captures the imagination, the square owes its impact to the genius of Nicholas Hawksmoor, who suggested that the library, the **Radcliffe Camera,** be built as a rotunda. His own design was not used, however, and the work was given to James Gibbs, though both men received fees. It sits there like the hub of a wheel, positively inviting you to look outward to the splendors on every side.

To the south is the **Church of St. Mary-the-Virgin** with its tall tower. The main body of All Souls College comes into view to the east, and Brasenose College is to the west, while to the north is the Bodleian Library. But it is not just the magnificence of the buildings that gives the square its special character: The Camera is the principal undergraduate library, so it is constantly surrounded by a clutter of bicycles and a whirl of students who are there to work, not merely to gaze.

Bodleian Library

The Bodleian Library, a research library used by scholars from all over the world, is rather more solemn. Statistics, for once, do give some notion of scale: five million volumes, spread along 81 miles of shelving, with seating for 2,078 readers. What statistics cannot do is convey the air of antiquity of a library whose heart is now four centuries old. Modernization has been slow. Heating was introduced only in 1821, which is why the oath all new readers must take includes a vow "not to bring into the Library or kindle therein any fire or flame." Visitors who want to see the oldest part of the library must make arrangements in advance, but it is well worth the effort. Visitors should call the Bodleian (Tel: 0865-27-71-65) and book a tour; there are four a day on weekdays, starting at 10:30 A.M., and two on Saturdays (except for degree days), from mid-March to the end of October, with limited visits in winter. No children under 14 permitted; admission by ticket.

BROAD STREET

Opposite the Bodleian is New College Lane, spanned by Oxford's version of the Bridge of Sighs, which unites the two parts of Hertford College.

Those tempted to explore will find ever more secluded alleyways, one of which, St. Helen's Passage, ends surprisingly at a country-pub-come-to-town in the shape of the thatched **Turf Tavern**. Just around the corner at the end of Broad Street is one of the undergraduates' favorite pubs, the **Kings Arms**, where you can choose between the big open bar at the front and the cozy paneled back bar, which until very recently was exclusively a male preserve. (Still reserved for men is the famous bathing spot on the Cherwell, Parson's Pleasure, where gentlemen may bathe in the nude.) Those who prefer wider vistas will certainly find them in **Broad Street**. Close at hand is the **covered market**. Stalls originally cluttered and blocked the surrounding streets before they were moved into this specially built market hall. Here the colleges buy their provisions; many of the vendors sell very traditional English food—from the specialists in game, whose stalls, in season, are festooned with pheasant and partridge, to the sellers of English cheeses.

But Broad Street also caters to a quite different need: For book lovers, it is as close to heaven as they are ever likely to get. Here virtually anything can be found, from the most esoteric textbook to the latest paperback. There are shops specializing in art books, children's books, and antiquarian books. **B. H. Blackwell**, the world-famous bookshop on Broad Street, is nearly as much an Oxford institution as the university itself. Trinity, Balliol, and Exeter colleges manage to squeeze in among the booksellers and still leave space for a small group of historic buildings, such as the Sheldonian.

The **Sheldonian Theatre** was designed not as a theater in the modern sense but as a site for ceremonials. The first work of Sir Christopher Wren ("the first" in the sense that it was the first to be begun; Pembroke Chapel at Cambridge, though completed earlier, was started later) soon found other uses. Home for a time to the university press, it later became a concert hall and remains one today. The Sheldonian and the delightful little **Holywell Music Room** up Holywell Street are part of Britain's musical history—Haydn performed here and so did Handel. In July there is the **Handel in Oxford Festival**; hearing the composer's works in the ornate setting of the Sheldonian is not unlike hearing Mozart's music performed in Salzburg.

Broad Street is a cheerful place, but it has had its

moments of horror. A stone cross inlaid in the middle of the road outside Balliol marks the spot where the Protestant martyr Thomas Cranmer, archbishop of Canterbury, was burned at the stake in 1556, and an old gate in Balliol quad is still said to show the scorching of the flames. Bishops Hugh Latimer and Nicholas Ridley were also burned nearby, and all three are commemorated in the Martyrs' Memorial in St. Giles.

The Ashmolean and Other Museums

Broad Street has one more building of note, not perhaps the grandest but one that has a fascinating history. The tiny **Museum of the History of Science** building, which now holds an array of beautiful old scientific instruments, began life in the 17th century as home to Elias Ashmole's Cabinet of Curiosities, the world's first public museum. The Ashmolean collection outgrew its old quarters and found a new, Classically styled home on Beaumont Street—it is not unlike a British Museum in miniature. The **Ashmolean Museum** today covers a wide range of exhibits, from Egyptian mummies to 19th-century paintings. The ceramics are particularly fine, and among the gems of the art collection are a number of beautiful, haunting paintings by Samuel Palmer. Opposite the museum is the **Playhouse Theatre**. For many years it was the University Theatre, and among those who returned to perform here, after achieving fame and fortune, was Richard Burton. It closed for a number of years but has reopened as an independent theater and a new lively center for the arts.

During the mid-19th century Oxford decided it needed a natural-history museum, and again a new style was pioneered, an almost riotously elaborate Gothic Revival design by Benjamin Woodward and John Ruskin that used the new building materials of iron and glass. This, the **University Museum**, is on Parks Road. As well as housing the natural-history collection, it is home to the Pitt-Rivers Collection of ethnography, an extraordinary assemblage of objects from around the world, including such bizarre items as shrunken human heads.

The 20th century all but abandoned architectural elaboration, and the **Museum of Modern Art** on Pembroke Street is housed in a converted warehouse—very bare, very austere, but a perfect setting for its constantly changing exhibitions. The restaurant in the basement is a popular place for a lunchtime snack, and the diners are often as colorful as the pictures on the walls.

A relatively new addition to the Oxford scene, opened in the spring of 1988, combines something of the museum world with a good deal of show business and high-tech wizardry. At **The Oxford Story** on Broad Street, visitors follow the evolution of the university and meet some of the great thinkers and personalities who have been "up at Oxford."

THE OTHER OXFORD

University Oxford is what most visitors rightly wish to see. There is another city, however—the one where William Morris began making motorcars. Car making has now moved out to new works at Cowley to the east of the city, but evidence of its old industrial life remains, nearer the center. A pleasant way to catch a glimpse of this other world is to stroll along the towpath of the Oxford Canal from Hythe Bridge. The canal that once carried coal from the collieries round Coventry and Birmingham now carries people on vacation, enjoying a gentle cruise through the countryside. The canal threads its way past little cottages and grander houses, many with gardens stretching down to the water's edge. Eventually it runs beside Port Meadow, an area of grassland that stretches across to the Thames. This is still common land, where local people turn ponies out to graze. The energetic can walk all the way to Wolvercote, a distance of 2 miles (3 km), and reward themselves with a drink at the **Trout**. The less energetic can turn off at one of the many bridges along the way to explore the area known as Jericho. This maze of narrow streets was once home to the working-class families of Oxford but has now become fashionable. The past is nevertheless preserved in simple pubs such as the **Bookbinders Arms** on Victor Street—a reminder that the Oxford University Press is not very far away. Oxford is still a city where town and gown both have important roles to play.

STAYING AND DINING IN OXFORD

Opposite the Martyrs' Memorial on Beaumont Street is Oxford's best-known hotel, the stately and very traditional ▶ **Randolph**. Those looking for something less overwhelmingly grand need only walk up St. Giles to the ivy-covered ▶ **Old Parsonage** at the end of Banbury Road. Good, cheaper accommodations can be found a little farther afield, at hotels such as the ▶ **Westgate** on Botley Road, eight minutes from the city center, near the railway station; and the ▶ **Courtfield Private Hotel**, on a tree-lined road close to the River Thames and picturesque Iffley village.

Along Banbury Road are two of Oxford's favorite, if contrasting, restaurants. **Brown's** has good food at reasonable prices and is invariably bustling, noisy, and crowded—but full of atmosphere. **Gee's Brasserie**, 61 Banbury Road, is very different: Housed in an elegant Victorian conservatory, it boasts one of the best and most sophisticated French menus in the country (Tel: 0865-535-40). Another popular restaurant in this area is **Munchy Munchy** at 6 Park End Street. Its plain appearance gives no hint of the exotic flavors of Ethel Ow's authentic Indonesian cooking; reservations needed for four people or more (Tel: 0865-24-57-10). Equally exotic is **Al-Shami** at 25 Walton Crescent, which specializes in Lebanese cooking, complemented by a Lebanese wine list (Tel: 0865-31-00-66).

—*Anthony Burton*

WARWICK

The historic town of Warwick and its magnificent castle hold a magnetic attraction for visitors the year round. Both have been the setting for major events in England's history, and Warwick has been the administrative capital of the county for centuries. Although the castle is rightly the focus of any trip to the town, the town of Warwick itself, 96 miles (134 km) northwest of London and beyond Oxford, has a particular charm and intimacy rarely found elsewhere. It is relatively small and contains many places of interest that can easily be visited in an afternoon after a visit to the castle. Visitors with more time may prefer to spend a day in Stratford and visit Warwick on Guide Friday's bus tour the next day.

MAJOR INTEREST

Warwick Castle—especially the tour of the private
    apartments
The Beauchamp Chapel in St. Mary's Church
Lord Leycester's Hospital
Regency town of Royal Leamington Spa

Warwick began as an Anglo-Saxon village standing on a sandstone outcrop above a natural ford across the River Avon, just west of its confluence with the River Leam. In A.D. 914 the town was fortified against the invading Danes by the Mercian queen Ethelfleda, daughter of Alfred the Great.

Later, in 1068, two years after the Norman Conquest, William I ordered castles to be built throughout his newly conquered kingdom, and a typical "motte and bailey" castle was erected here. A tall wooden tower within a stockade was built on the man-made sandstone mound that still stands to the west of the present-day castle, and the town's inhabitants would take shelter within the castle's bailey whenever danger threatened.

Throughout the centuries the town remained an important trading center because of its strategic position, but it also gained status as a result of the increasing importance of the castle and its inhabitants. An especially notable period in the castle's history was its occupation by the mighty Beauchamp family, who began a massive rebuilding program in the mid-13th century and continued to improve the castle until the end of their tenure in 1445.

For several hundred years after this the castle remained a vital link in the defense of the kingdom, a position ensured by its location at a strategic crossing place on the river. Successive kings awarded the castle to their allies and confiscated it from their enemies, which resulted in its buildings constantly being enlarged and improved upon. Today it presents to the visitor one of the finest arrays of fortified buildings in the country. Castellated battlements and awesome towers spread over the hillside between the town and the river, surrounded by superb gardens and enclosing an enormous mansion at their heart.

THE CASTLE

Warwick Castle became the subject of controversy in the 1970s when the present earl of Warwick sold a number of the family heirlooms and, finally, the castle itself, together with the remainder of its magnificent contents. The buyers were Madame Tussaud's—the owners of the famous waxworks museum—and, despite initial fears, they have proved extremely successful at making the castle a commercial success without compromising its historic integrity. They also have an ongoing policy of conservation and restoration as well as of buying items associated with the castle.

As one of Britain's major tourist attractions, the castle is filled to the brim with visitors in high summer (lines of visitors waiting to see the state rooms and private apartments have been known to stretch beyond the castle walls), so avoid visiting then if at all possible. However, if a visit in summer is unavoidable, take pleasure in knowing that you'll be experiencing the grounds at their best; you will often be able to see special events, such as Civil War reenactments or falconry displays, on the grounds. If you want to avoid the worst of the summer crush, visit in the early morning; Thursdays and Saturdays are said to be the least crowded.

Unlike for many other historic sights, a winter's afternoon can be one of the most rewarding times to visit Warwick castle. Visitors are few and the tour of the **private apartments** can be thrilling. The apartments have been arranged to replicate a royal weekend house party that occurred here in June 1898, complete with lifelike models of the guests and appropriate sound effects. Guests included the Prince of Wales (later King Edward VII), Lord Curzon, the young Winston Churchill, and a clutch of dukes and duchesses. It is one of the most well-presented exhibits of its kind, and visitors may feel like invisible party crashers who have travelled back in time as they walk around the house looking in on small groups of guests as they chat, listen to music, or dress for dinner in the guest bedrooms. All the rooms are furnished as they would have been in 1898 and dressed with the paraphernalia of late-19th-century aristocratic living.

The rest of the mansion consists of the 14th-century Great Hall and the various grand State Rooms (including the State Dining Room), which were used for formal entertaining. Nearby is the supposedly haunted Watergate Tower, and there is a splendid armory near the gatehouse. If you are not claustrophobic you can visit the gloomy dungeon with its instruments of torture.

Visitors coming by car can park on the grounds to the west of the castle, just off the Stratford road (A 46). If there is space in it, you might try a more convenient parking lot off Castle Lane, just above the castle and closer to the town center. Castle Lane is also the most convenient route for those arriving in town by train. All visitors enter the castle via the main entrance and gift shop in the stables on Castle Lane. Contact the castle directly for information about the special events that occur through-out the summer season (Tel: 0926-49-54-21). The tour of the castle and grounds will take at least three hours. On July and August afternoons Guide Friday often operates an open-top bus tour of Warwick from the stables coach park; for details, Tel: (0789) 29-44-66.

WARWICK TOWN

You can get a fine view of the castle if you walk to the "new" Banbury road bridge, which was built in the 1780s to replace the old bridge at the foot of the castle walls. This made possible the survival of the delightful collection of old buildings in Bridge End across the river. Fortunate visitors may be able to view the beautiful private gardens at 55 Mill Street, just east of the castle (occasionally open for charity), which also afford a magnificent view of the castle and the remains of the old bridge.

However, by far the finest view can be obtained from the river itself. Small rowboats and some charming, antiquated motorboats can be rented from the ever-helpful Mike Harrison and his family, who run the boathouse in St. Nicholas Park, across Banbury Road from the castle, from Easter to September, but check with the tourist office to make sure the boathouse is still open (Tel: 0926-49-22-12). The setting is magical. The park is full of delightful attractions for the whole family and makes a great spot for a picnic. The Jacobean mansion housing the **St. John's House Museum**, on the park's northern edge, is worth a visit for its interesting examples of social history, including a full-size Victorian schoolroom.

The most historic part of the town itself is contained within a triangle of roads north of the castle centered on St. Mary's Church: To the north is Priory Road, which runs along the southern edge of Priory Park (the priory buildings are no longer here; they were shipped to the U.S. in 1926); to the east is St. Nicholas Park and Coten End, which leads toward the town of Royal Leamington Spa (see below); to the west, Bowling Green Street runs from Theatre Street down to West Gate, one of the town's original gates; and to the south is the castle and its fine grounds, which stretch along the banks of the River Avon.

The base of this triangle is the High Street (leading into Jury Street), which separates the town from the castle and joins the East and West gates—the original entrances to the medieval walled town. Although the town's outline has survived, fire destroyed many of the original buildings in 1694. As a result, most of the houses date from the late 17th and early 18th centuries.

The fire also destroyed the main body of St. Mary's Church. Its nave and tower were rebuilt in the early 18th century. However, the jewel of the church—the 15th-century Beauchamp Chapel—survived, and should not be missed. This striking and richly decorated chapel was built between 1443 and 1464 in accordance with the will of Richard Beauchamp, the fifth and greatest of the earls of Warwick. In the center of the chapel lies a life-size gilded bronze effigy of the earl lying on an elaborately carved tomb of Purbeck marble. Among the "weepers" around the tomb is Richard Neville, who married Beauchamp's daughter Anne and was later known as "Warwick the Kingmaker." (Anne is seen grieving over his corpse at the beginning of Shakespeare's *Richard III*.) Later earls of Warwick and their families are also commemorated here, most notably Queen Elizabeth I's favorite, Robert Dudley, earl of Leicester, and his wife, Lettice. In the far corner of the chapel is the tomb of their only son—the "noble impe"—who died at age six. His tiny suit of armor is in the castle's Great Hall.

Among the most interesting of Warwick's ancient buildings are Oken's House, near the castle—now a world-famous doll museum—and Lord Leycester's Hospital, by the West Gate. Home to retired military veterans since 1571, the hospital was founded by Robert Dudley, earl of Leicester, in a group of buildings that also houses the former Guildhall (built by Richard Neville in 1450) and the candlelit Chapel of St. James, which is built over the town's West Gate. The half-timbered, overhanging façade of this group of buildings leans out over the footpath and has been much photographed. If you walk through the tiny passage between the houses you will discover a charming inner courtyard. The buildings date from the 12th through the 16th centuries. The Brethren's Kitchen here serves excellent light lunches and homemade teas from Easter to September (closed Sundays). Similar fare can be had at Charlotte's Tearoom on Jury Street or the charming little John Paul's tearoom at 5 New Street. For a more substantial meal, eat at the excellent Fanshawe's at 22 Market Place; Tel: (0926) 41-05-90.

The Warwickshire Museum (local and natural history of Warwickshire) is housed in the Market Hall on Market

Square. A weekly market and the annual Mop Fair, traditionally held on the first Saturday after October 12, still
take place here. (The Mop Fair was the event at which
servants and agricultural laborers gathered for the annual
hiring; nowadays it is mostly a fun fair.) Like many other
such halls, Warwick's Market Hall once stood on arcades
(now filled in) that sheltered the market stalls.

AROUND WARWICK

A mile north of town, at Guy's Cliffe on the Coventry
Road, the **Old Saxon Mill** steak house is in an unusual
building and has tables outside by the old mill wheel.
From here there is a spectacular view up to the gaunt
ruins of an 18th-century mansion where the great actress
Sarah Siddons worked as a young girl. Inside the Old
Saxon Mill you can eat an inexpensive meal while overlooking the river or have a drink while you watch the
water rushing underfoot. Go for the setting rather than
the food. Guy's Cliffe itself is named after the legendary
hero of the Dark Ages, Guy of Warwick, who ended his
days as a hermit in the caves above the river.

KENILWORTH

Dramatic ruins are now all that is left of the great castle at
Kenilworth, about 5 miles (8 km) north of Warwick. This
once-formidable royal stronghold was dismantled by
Cromwell's troops at the end of the Civil War. The 12th-
century keep of the castle and its outer curtain wall were
originally surrounded by a vast man-made lake, which
acted as a defensive system in the early Middle Ages.
Later, the lake became an important asset for entertainment and leisure, culminating in the three visits of Queen
Elizabeth and her 400-strong retinue to the castle when it
was the property of Robert Dudley, earl of Leicester. The
most well-documented of these was the July 1575 visit,
which formed the background for Sir Walter Scott's novel
Kenilworth.

Today the lake has been drained and the buildings are
decayed and roofless, but their sheer scale is very impressive indeed, and you can still see the walls of John of
Gaunt's Great Hall, the massive gatehouse, and the stables
erected by the earl of Leicester. You may find your visit
enhanced if you have already been to the World of Shakespeare exhibition in Stratford, which illustrates Elizabeth
I's triumphal procession to Kenilworth in 1575. Make

sure, too, that you have a close look at the postcard sold here that shows a drawing of Kenilworth as it was during Elizabeth's visit. There is, in addition, a small exhibition in the stables.

ROYAL LEAMINGTON SPA

A couple of miles east of Warwick on A 444 is the elegant Regency town of Royal Leamington Spa, as charming as Warwick but with a completely different atmosphere: Here the visitor is transported to the early 19th century, with its gracious, well-lit houses and spacious streets. Leamington, like Bath and Cheltenham, came to prominence on the late-18th-century wave of enthusiasm for "taking the waters." By 1814 several baths had been built, together with the large, handsome buildings housing the Pump Room, the Assembly Rooms, and the Public Baths. The town continued to prosper in the 19th century, a fact well illustrated by the broad avenues and crescents lined by handsome houses, which are embellished with porticos and ornate iron balconies.

Although two distinct towns, Warwick and Leamington Spa are divided only by their suburbs and the River Avon. Buses between the towns are frequent and are marked with the letter "C."

Staying in Royal Leamington Spa

Leamington's spacious elegance and excellent shopping make it a more attractive place than Warwick for an overnight stay—try the moderately priced ▶ **Lansdowne Hotel** on Clarendon Street for excellent accommodation and dinner. Those looking for an inexpensive meal should try **Alastair's Bistro and Wine Bar** on Warwick Street or **Rooster's** on Oxford Street. (See Getting Around at the end of this section for more on travelling between Warwick and Royal Leamington Spa.)

—*Angela Murphy*

Stratford-upon-Avon

If you only have time for one excursion out of London, Stratford-upon-Avon should be very high on your list of possibilities. This charming little town just 8 miles (13 km) or so southwest of Warwick was the birthplace of Shakespeare, and many buildings associated with his life here have been superbly restored. These houses and their contents today provide a fascinating picture of life in

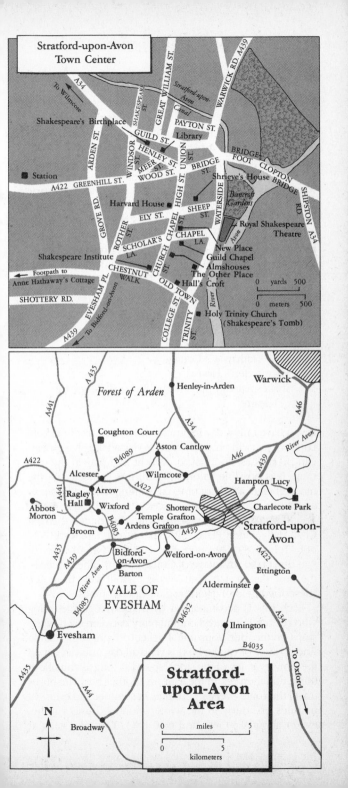

Elizabethan and Jacobean times. A day spent in Stratford can give visitors a very special insight into England's heritage—both rural and urban—as well as a more complete picture of the world's greatest poet-dramatist.

Ninety-six miles (134 km) northwest of central London, Stratford has been a place of pilgrimage since the early 18th century, when interest in Shakespeare's plays started to grow. Although a steady stream of visitors came to the town, it was not until the famous actor and impresario David Garrick organized the first Shakespearean Festival in 1769 that Stratford started to receive the widespread attention it still enjoys. There are many places of interest to visit here, ranging from the superbly preserved houses associated with Shakespeare to such oddities as the Teddy Bear Museum.

MAJOR INTEREST

Shakespeare's Birthplace
New Place and Hall's Croft
Anne Hathaway's Cottage
Mary Arden's House
Shakespearean plays at the Royal Shakespeare
　　Theatre

If you have only a day in Stratford and are travelling from London, you will probably want to visit all the Shakespearean properties, and maybe even fit in a play in the evening. It is possible to organize all this yourself, but the most efficient and least time-consuming method is to take advantage of the many services offered by the Guide Friday company in Stratford. You can contact them at Civic Hall, Market Place, 14 Rother Street, Stratford CV37 6EF; Tel: (0789) 29-44-66; Fax: (0789) 41-46-81. Even if you don't take advantage of Guide Friday's other services, the best way to start your visit is by following the route (described below) taken by their open-top buses.

Each bus is accompanied by a knowledgeable guide who recites a prepared commentary between each of the stops on the tour. Your initial ticket (bought at the Guide Friday office or on the bus) is valid all day. You can get off their buses at any of the stops, spend as long as you like at them, and then rejoin the tour on another bus. The buses travel the route every 15 minutes in summer and every 30 minutes or hourly in the winter months (buses run between about 9:30 A.M. and 6:30 P.M.). The tour starts at

Bridgefoot, outside the Pen and Parchment public house near the river (although you can join it at any point). It then meanders through town, stopping at or near the major attractions, before heading west to Anne Hathaway's Cottage in the adjoining village of Shottery, and Mary Arden's House in Wilmcote, just to the north of Stratford. You can also walk the tour, as laid out below, except perhaps for the journey to Wilmcote.

SHAKESPEAREAN STRATFORD

Before starting a tour of the Shakespearean properties, it is worth visiting the lavish sound-and-light presentation called **The World of Shakespeare,** on Waterside. This is designed to illustrate the everyday life of the Elizabethans and is a great help to the visitor. For further information, Tel: (0789) 26-91-90.

Shakespeare's Birthplace

The first stop on the bus tour is at the end of the pedestrianized section of Henley Street, where you will find the town's principal place of pilgrimage, Shakespeare's Birthplace. The house has been a popular attraction for 300 years, although nowadays visitors are no longer offered pieces of the bard's chair as expensive souvenirs. (Early commentators noted that the chair must have been unusually large, judging by the number of people who received pieces over the years.) The house is entered through a modern visitors' center, with its exhibition of costumes designed for television productions of Shakespeare's plays, and a garden that has been planted with the trees, herbs, and flowers mentioned in the plays. Inside, there are a number of exhibits that illustrate Shakespeare's life and work, and the house is furnished with Elizabethan and Jacobean furniture throughout.

Shakespeare's Birthplace, together with four other Shakespearean properties in the area, is owned and run by the Shakespeare Birthplace Trust, which also operates an extensive library, a records office, and a specialized bookshop at the visitors' center. Entry tickets can be bought at the individual sites, but it is cheaper to buy an inclusive ticket for all of the properties (available at any property). The other four sites are Nash's House, with the gardens of New Place; Hall's Croft; Anne Hathaway's Cottage in Shottery; and Mary Arden's House and Countryside Museum in Wilmcote.

New Place

Shakespeare's own house, New Place, where he lived during his retirement until his death in 1616, was demolished by its cantankerous owner in the 1760s. Its foundations are at the corner of Chapel Street and Chapel Lane, opposite the historic Guild Chapel, and now form part of a very pleasant garden, which includes a colorful Elizabethan knott garden. **Nash's House**, next door, was the property of Shakespeare's granddaughter, Elizabeth Hall, and her first husband, Thomas Nash. It is now the local history and archaeology museum. The **Guild Chapel** dates back to the 15th century, when the town was developed by the influential Guild of the Holy Cross. A religious foundation, the guild was dissolved in 1547, but by then it had already built the chapel, a series of almshouses, and the King Edward VI Grammar School, which Shakespeare attended less than 20 years later. The school, on Chapel Street, is still in use today and is open to visitors only occasionally—at which time it displays a plaque announcing the fact; ask at the Tourist Office for further details.

Hall's Croft

Shakespeare's daughter, Susanna, married a physician with an extensive medical practice; their house, Hall's Croft on Old Town street, is the last of the Shakespearean properties in town. This fine Tudor house has some exceptional Elizabethan and Jacobean furniture, but its main interest is its dispensary and other exhibits that illustrate the state of medicine in those times. In addition, the garden at Hall's Croft is a particularly pleasant place to have morning coffee, a light lunch, or afternoon tea.

If your time is limited you should go straight to Hall's Croft from New Place, leaving the Royal Shakespeare Theatre for later in the day. However, only a few minutes' stroll south from Hall's Croft is **Holy Trinity Church**, the beautiful medieval parish church where Shakespeare was both baptized and buried. This is worth visiting to see Shakespeare's grave and bust. The bust was made within seven years of his death, while his widow and many of his friends were still alive. Every year on the Saturday closest to Shakespeare's birthday (April 23) invited guests, including actors, local officials, and foreign ambassadors, celebrate the day by walking in procession to the church to lay flowers on the Bard's tomb. If you can plan your visit

to Stratford to coincide with the occasion, you will miss
the summer crush of tourists and, at the same time, see
some of the true life of the town. Another time to avoid
the crowds is the autumn Mop Fair (held on or near
October 12).

Anne Hathaway's Cottage

From Hall's Croft the bus tour heads west out to the
village of Shottery, where Shakespeare did much of his
courting. If you have time you can take a pleasant stroll
from the croft through fields out to Shottery and Anne
Hathaway's Cottage. From Hall's Croft walk north along
Chestnut Walk to Evesham Place—the footpath is signposted from here. Anne Hathaway's Cottage in Shottery is
a perfectly preserved thatched cottage that was the family
home of Shakespeare's wife, Anne. The house stayed in
the Hathaway family for several generations and contains
much of its original furniture. Like all the properties, it is
staffed by extremely knowledgeable guides and surrounded by a superbly kept, old-fashioned English garden. Just across the road from the cottage is the charming
Cottage Tea Garden, where visitors are served tea and
light snacks in a lovely little garden by a stream.

Mary Arden's House

Whereas Anne's parents were yeoman farmers, Shakespeare's parents were a comparatively wealthy couple.
His father was a glover and tanner and his mother, Mary
Arden, was the daughter of a prosperous farmer. The
Ardens' attractive farmhouse in the village of Wilmcote (4
miles/6½ km northwest of Stratford) is now a museum of
farming and rural life, and is the next stop on the bus
tour. This is the largest of all the properties associated
with Shakespeare, and, like the others, it has been im-
maculately preserved and, in places, reconstructed.

The farm outbuildings behind Mary Arden's House
now contain the **Shakespeare Countryside Museum**. This
extensive museum of farm and country life is linked with
the restored Glebe Farmhouse next door, which illustrates Victorian and Edwardian domestic and farming life.
The large complex is full of interesting objects and warrants an hour or so of your time. All year round you can
also see fine falconry displays from the resident falconer.
The museum operates a café in summer, or you can get
good bar food at the **Mason's Arms** nearby. A short stroll

to the east is the Stratford-upon-Avon Canal, and just south of here a series of 11 locks takes the canal down into town.

Charlecote Park

Legend has it that the young William Shakespeare poached deer on the grounds of nearby Charlecote Park, east of Stratford, and deer can still be seen grazing in the landscaped park. Whatever the truth of the legend, the magnificent Tudor mansion in its great park is well worth visiting for itself. Still the home of the Lucy family, the house is the property of the National Trust, which opens the ground-floor rooms to the public. A short video that gives a very attractive picture of some of the house's history can be viewed in the bakehouse. Watch it before going on an extended tour of the impressive Victorian living rooms, the vast kitchen and brewhouse, and the museum of local and family relics; open from April through October. Visitors without a car can either take a taxi from Stratford or catch the number 18 bus, which leaves hourly from Stratford's Wood Street.

ELSEWHERE IN STRATFORD

Back in Stratford, visitors may well find that they have had enough of Shakespearean connections for a while, however fascinating. If so, other places worth a visit are the **Brass Rubbing Centre** in the summer house in Avonbank Gardens, near the theater, the Teddy Bear Museum, and Harvard House. The late-16th-century **Harvard House**, on the High Street, is now owned by Harvard College. Erected by the grandfather of the college's founder, John Harvard, it contains a fascinating collection of books, pictures, curios, and period furniture.

If you have children in tow, the **Teddy Bear Museum** on Greenhill Street is a must. This rickety little four-story building is crammed to the rafters with teddy bears of every shape and size. Among the many bears on display are those donated by famous people—from royalty to rock stars. Stratford also abounds with antiques shops to browse in. As in all tourist-oriented haunts, however, you ought to shop around.

The Tourist Information Center is at the corner of the High and Bridge streets. Down by the River Avon are Bancroft Gardens and the basin of the Stratford-upon-Avon Canal, which branches off the river at this point.

From here, or just across the footbridge on Swan's Nest Lane, you can hire boats or take a short cruise on the river or the canal.

THE THEATERS

South of Bancroft Gardens and dominating the riverbank, is the large brick **Royal Shakespeare Theatre**, built in the late 1920s to replace the Victorian Memorial Theatre, which burned down in 1926. The shell of the older theater still stands, and the **Swan Theatre**, a replica of a Jacobean playhouse, has been built within it. The Swan generally puts on plays by Shakespeare's contemporaries or followers, such as Marlowe. It also houses the RSC (Royal Shakespeare Company) collection of paintings, costumes, and other mementoes, and is open daily. Tours of the collection and the backstage areas are offered in the afternoons. There is also a modern theater just along the road, **The Other Place**, which stages a variety of productions.

Shakespearean plays are performed from the end of March to the end of January, but advance booking is highly advisable at any time. The RSC also offers a variety of stopover packages that include theater tickets, meals, and accommodations. Information about these can be obtained from RST Restaurants, Royal Shakespeare Theatre, Stratford-upon-Avon, Warwickshire CV37 6BB. The box office is open from 9:30 A.M. to 8:00 P.M. on performance days; Tel: (0789) 29-56-23 to reserve seats, or (0789) 26-91-91 for 24-hour booking information.

DINING AND STAYING IN STRATFORD

Theatergoers and others can dine at the theater, either at the **Box Tree** restaurant overlooking the river or at the more informal **Terrace** restaurant. Just across the road is the popular actors' pub, the **Black Swan** (known locally as the "Dirty Duck"). For those who would rather eat in the center of town, the **Slug and Lettuce** pub-cum-bistro on Guild Street is a lively alternative, with an excellent range of dishes, in spite of its unappealing name. For reasonably priced accommodations, try the small but exclusive ▶ **Stratford House Hotel**, just 100 yards from the theater on Sheep Street, which has a good restaurant and will book theater tickets for you. Another pleasant hotel in a peaceful canal-side setting is ▶ **Duke's Hotel** on Payton Street.

—Angela Murphy

GETTING AROUND

Oxford

Oxford, 59 miles (94 km) northwest of London, can be reached by rail from Paddington Station, by bus from Victoria Coach Station, and by road via the A 40 and M 40. Rail service is frequent during the day, and the trip takes a little more than an hour.

Warwick and Stratford

If you want to travel to Stratford or Warwick by car from London, you can drive almost all the way along the newly completed M 40 motorway from west London. At junction 15 you can turn north to Warwick and Leamington Spa or south to Stratford-upon-Avon. The journey can take less than an hour and a half, weather permitting.

If you are not travelling by car, the fastest way to Stratford is via the "Shakespeare Connection" intercity rail service from London (Euston Station). The fast train to Coventry takes just over an hour, and Guide Friday has a special connecting bus that goes between Coventry and Stratford. The total travel time is usually under two hours, and there is a special late-night bus to pick up theatergoers from Stratford. You can, for example, leave London (Euston) at 8:30 A.M., arrive in Stratford at 10:35 A.M., do a day's sightseeing, attend a performance at the Royal Shakespeare Theatre in the evening, and arrive back in London in the early hours of the morning. For details contact British Rail (Tel: 071-387-7070) or Guide Friday (Tel: 0789-29-44-66). Visitors travelling on the weekend can upgrade to first class by paying a small supplement. If you want to visit both Warwick and Stratford, you will need at least two days. You might want to travel to Stratford, stay overnight there, and take Guide Friday's tour to Warwick the next day.

Three bus companies run trips to Warwick and Stratford from London: National Express (Tel: 071-730-0202); Evan Evans Tours Ltd. (Tel: 071-930-2377); and Frames Rickards (Tel: 071-837-3111). National Express provides frequent bus service between London, Leamington, Warwick, and Stratford that is cheaper than the road-rail services. The other companies operate day trips that include visits to Oxford University, Stratford, and Warwick Castle. However, if you just want to visit Stratford for the theater, you should take the round-trip bus organized by the Royal Shakespeare Company (Tel: 379-1564).

Although Leamington Spa, Warwick, and Stratford all have railway stations, they are on different branch lines, and Leamington Spa is the only one that can be reached directly by rail from London (out of Paddington Station). Although relatively scenic, these lines can provide both slow and infrequent service.

Once you have reached Stratford or Warwick, sightseeing on foot is both easy and rewarding. However, if you want to rent a car to go further afield, this can be arranged locally. Guide Friday in Stratford can arrange car rentals through the major international companies, such as Hertz or Avis. Alternatively, they may be able to arrange personal tours in a car driven by a qualified guide.

Regular Midland Red buses (X16) also run hourly (every two hours on Sundays) between Wood Street, Stratford-upon-Avon, and Coventry via Warwick, Leamington Spa, and Kenilworth Castle. The number 18 bus goes from Wood Street, Stratford, to Leamington Spa via Charlecote Park. For details, telephone the Midland Red bus information service (Tel: 0788-53-55-55).

ACCOMMODATIONS REFERENCE
Rates are projected 1994 prices for a double room with breakfast, unless otherwise indicated. As prices are subject to change, always double-check before booking.

Oxford
► **Courtfield Private Hotel.** 367 Iffley Road, **Oxford** OX4 4DP. Tel: (0865) 24-29-91. £38–£42.

► **Old Parsonage Hotel.** 1 Banbury Road, **Oxford** OX2 6NN. Tel: (0865) 31-02-10; Fax: (0865) 31-12-62. £125–£190 (includes Continental breakfast).

► **Randolph Hotel.** Beaumont Street, **Oxford** OX1 2LN. Tel: (0865) 24-74-81; Fax: (0865) 79-16-78; in U.S. and Canada, (800) 225-5843; in Australia, (008) 22-24-46. £150 (breakfast not included).

► **Westgate Hotel.** 1 Botley Road, **Oxford** OX2 0AA. Tel: (0865) 72-67-21; Fax: (0865) 72-20-78. £41–£52.

Warwick
► **Lansdowne Hotel.** 87 Clarendon Street, **Royal Leamington Spa**, Warwickshire CV32 4PE. Tel: (0926) 45-05-05; Fax: (0926) 42-06-04. £58.

Stratford-upon-Avon

▶ **Duke's Hotel.** Payton Street, **Stratford-upon-Avon,** Warwickshire CV37 6EF. Tel: (0789) 26-93-00; Fax: (0789) 41-47-00. £68–£89.

▶ **Stratford House Hotel.** 18 Sheep Street, **Stratford-upon-Avon,** Warwickshire CV37 6EF. Tel: (0789) 26-82-88; Fax: (0789) 29-55-80. £61–£76.

NORTH
Cambridge

In the perpetual pairing of Cambridge with Oxford, Cambridge always comes second. It is Oxford and Cambridge, or even Oxbridge, but never the other way around, except perhaps in the specialized world of the scientist. This may be a reflection of history, for the university at Cambridge began with an exodus of scholars from Oxford after a quarrel between town and gown at the beginning of the 13th century. Yet, paradoxically, Cambridge contrives to appear the older city, more closely tied to its medieval past. Here, the influence of the university is overwhelming; it is an inescapable presence in a way that is never quite the case at Oxford. But if it is the university that has made Cambridge the fascinating and beautiful place it is today, it is the River Cam that first brought the city into being. It was at the crossing of the river that the settlement of Cam-bridge grew, and it is the river that today threads together the different parts of the city's past to make a coherent whole.

MAJOR INTEREST

The Backs
University colleges
Kettle's Yard
Round Church
King's College Chapel
Fitzwilliam Museum

From the river, the visitor passes **the Backs,** which are exactly what the name suggests—the green space at the back of the colleges, along the river's edge. But the unimaginative name gives no notion of the enchantment here, where the stone towers and turrets of colleges and chapels are reflected in the quiet waters of the Cam. By far the best way to take in this view is from a punt, the traditional narrow, flat-bottomed boat propelled by pole. These can be hired either by the bridge at Magdalene Street or by Mill Lane.

It is also possible to take "chauffeured punts" and let someone else do the poling. Those who choose to be punted rather than punt may fancy themselves in some English Venice, a feeling reinforced as you pass under Cambridge's bridges, particularly the local version of the **Bridge of Sighs** at St. John's College. The oldest bridge, at Clare College, was built in the 1630s, and the oddest is the Mathematical Bridge at Queens' College. A shapely wooden arch, it was constructed entirely without nails from straight timbers that notch together like a Chinese puzzle. It was certainly a puzzle that proved too complex for generations of drunken undergraduates. They were capable of dismantling it, but putting it together again was quite beyond them. Eventually, the authorities had to step in, and the bridge sections are now bolted together.

The views of the colleges from the Cam include what is perhaps the city's most famous—**King's College** and its **chapel** (see below). The latter is on every tourist itinerary and deservedly so, for it is one of the great buildings not just of Cambridge but of the world. Its majesty is apparent from the outside, but its true glory is its interior. It was begun in the 15th century but not completed until the 16th, by which time Gothic architecture was at its most flamboyant. We should be grateful for the delays, for without them the building would never have been given its glorious, fan-vaulted ceiling.

Cambridge University is, like Oxford, the sum of its colleges, and while there are many similarities in organization, there are subtle differences as well. Colleges in both universities are usually built around squares, but what is a quad at Oxford is a court at Cambridge, and undergraduates here never have tutorials—they go for "supervisions" instead. For visitors, however, the most obvious difference lies in building materials: Whereas in Oxford stone rules, here warm red brick dominates. Most of the colleges are open to visitors except during the examination period, which runs from early May to mid-June. But even when they are closed, much of the colleges' magnificence is on display. Indeed, it is the cumulative effect of the college architecture that gives Cambridge its unique atmosphere and that visitors tend to remember far more clearly than any nice points or fine details.

CASTLE ST.

CHESTERTON LA.

MAGDALENE ST.

Pepys
Library

River Cam

To Stratford-upon-Avon

Kettle's Yard

Magdalene College

MADINGLEY RD.
A1303

NORTHAMPTON
ST.

BRIDGE ST.

PORTUGAL PL. PORTUGAL ST.

Round Ch
(Churc
the Holy Sepul

St. John's Chapel Tower

St. John's College

Sid
Sus
Co

Bridge of Sighs

ST. JOHN'S ST.

Trinity College

River Cam

SIDNEY ST.

TRINITY LA.

Caius College

TRINITY ST.

MARKET ST.

The Backs

SENATE
HOUSE
PASSAGE

Great St. Mary'

Clare College

Senate
House

Guildhall

Marl

Clare Bridge

KING'S PARADE

King's College Chapel

CORN
EXCHANGE ST.

QUEEN'S RD.

BENE'T ST.

Corn
Exchange

King's Bridge

King's College

St. Benet's

Queens' College

Corpus Christi

PEMBROKE ST.

Mathematical
Bridge

MILL LA.

GRANTA PL.

LITTLE
ST. MARY LA.

Pembroke
College

SILVER ST.

TRUMPINGTON ST.

Peterhouse

Fitzwilliam
Museum

NEWNHAM RD.

FEN CAUSEWAY

The geography of Cambridge is comparatively simple. Starting in the north, below the river crossing of Bridge Street, the main road divides. One branch becomes Sidney Street, changing to St. Andrew's Street and continuing as Regent Street. The second branch, starting as St. John's Street, continues on as Trinity Street, King's Parade, and Trumpington Street. Both these routes are lined with colleges, and the space between is given over to town affairs, to the Guildhall, the Corn Exchange, and the still-flourishing market—a proper market with stalls selling everything from fresh meat to fine books.

EXPLORING THE COLLEGES

Magdalene College

Beginning a tour of Cambridge on the far side of the Cam, at Magdalene Bridge (originally Great Bridge), the spot where the Roman road crossed the river, you come first to Magdalene College (pronounced MAUD-lin), founded in 1542. Although it is not one of the grander colleges, the splendor of its Renaissance gateway can be admired, while the extremely Gothicized church can be left to those with enthusiasm for heavy-handed Victorian restoration. The college has much of interest besides its architecture. The **Pepys Library** contains Samuel Pepys's bequest, which includes the famous diaries written in the author's unique shorthand and the more easily deciphered pocket book of Sir Francis Drake. In the 17th century there was a strong Puritan element in the college, and one member who left for the New World, Henry Dunster, went on to become the first president of Harvard College.

Magdalene and its immediate surroundings show how rich and diverse the charms of Cambridge can be. You could spend a contented day without straying more than a few hundred yards from here. Magdalene Street itself has a wealth of ancient buildings. Look, for example, at number 25, now a shoe shop but basically a timber-framed medieval building with an upper story jutting outward and embellished with lovely, ornate carving. Just north of the crossroads, on the corner between Northampton Street and Castle Street, is one of the city's most surprising finds, known somewhat prosaically as **Kettle's Yard**. Here is the house of the art collector Jim Ede, who died in 1990. Nothing on the outside prepares you for the interior. This really is a home, not a museum, so arranged that the visitor feels the owner might turn up at any moment to resume residence. Ede bought the then-unfashionable and unwanted work of his contemporaries—from Gaudier-Brzeska to Ben Nicholson—and he had special affection for the "primitive" paintings of Cornish artist Alfred Wallis.

Across the bridge, visitors who enjoy exploring back streets will find an area that once housed college servants but now comprises what the local real-estate agents would call "desirable residences." It also has its oddities and surprises. On the corner of Portugal Street, an aged police notice announces that hand carts and trolleys are not allowed in, while nearby Portugal Place has a genteel terrace that ends with the High Victorian Gothic of St. John's chapel tower. Back on Bridge Street is the popular student pub the **Baron of Beef**, and just a little closer to the city center is another of Cambridge's more pleasing oddities. The church of the Holy Sepulchre is usually known simply as the **Round Church**, for the very good reason that it is indeed round. Dating from about 1130, it contains a ring of stone heads—from fiercely mustachioed warriors to even fiercer demons—that stare down at the visitor.

St. John's College

The Round Church stands by the point where Bridge Street and St. John's Street diverge, at St. John's College, which boasts one of the most attractive and ornate gatehouses of all the colleges. Typical of many, it was built of both red brick and stone. In addition to a statue of the saint, the gatehouse bears a variety of heraldic emblems, from Lancastrian roses to mythical creatures with horns and tusks known as yales. They are the emblems of Lady Margaret Beaufort, under whose will the college was founded in the 16th century. These you might expect, but the builders had a sense of humor. A field of marguerites makes a visual pun on the founder's name, and among the daisies is a rabbit hole with a fox disappearing down one end and a rather smug rabbit popping out the other.

Trinity College

St. John's Street leads to Trinity Street and Trinity College, where you might notice that the heraldic ornaments on the great gate are the same as those at St. John's—not surprising, because Henry VIII was Lady Margaret's grandson. The statue of Henry clutches an orb in one hand and—thanks to generations of undergraduates—a chair leg in the other. (The king originally held a scepter, but as it was relentlessly removed and replaced by a chair leg, eventually the authorities abandoned the struggle and the chair leg remains.) Trinity's **Great Court** is the largest in Cambridge, and college athletes test their prowess by attempting to run a circuit while the clock is striking 12:00—as depicted in the film *Chariots of Fire*. The apple tree on the lawn is descended from one that stood in the garden of a former member of Trinity, Sir Isaac Newton. Opposite Trinity Great Gate is **Heffer's**, long established as the university's main bookshop.

Gonville and Caius College

Trinity Lane is one of those curved, narrow ways that promise fresh delights just around the corner. Here it leads on to Gonville and Caius College, begun by Mr. Gonville and enlarged by Dr. Caius and usually known simply as Caius (pronounced "keys"). It has three gates: The undergraduate enters in Humility to Tree Court, passes through Virtue to Caius Court, and leaves the college via Honour. The lane leads on past Senate House Passage and the 18th-century Classical formality of Senate House itself, where university degrees are conferred in a ceremony that, because of the numbers involved, takes two days. After that comes Clare College, closely followed by King's.

King's College and Queens' College

King's is a delight, but the **King's College Chapel** is the inevitable focus of attention. Seen from across the Backs it is majestic; up close the detail is revealed; and inside the full splendor appears. It might never have been so splendid but for the turbulence of medieval life. The chapel was begun in the 15th-century reign of its founder, Henry VI, but the long and bloody Wars of the Roses caused numerous interruptions, and it was completed by Henry VIII. His devices—the Royal Arms, portcullis, Tudor rose, dragon, and greyhound—can be seen everywhere in the building. More important, English architecture had reached a period of great elaboration; hence we have what is literally the chapel's crowning glory, the intricate tracery of the beautiful fan-vaulted roof. The chapel's proportions are noble, and the vast areas of stained glass send a warm light washing over the intricate details of carving and tracery. If you left Cambridge having seen nothing else, you would go away content.

King's has an appropriate companion in nearby Queens' College, named after its two founders, Margaret of Anjou and Elizabeth Woodville. Where the former college is all grandeur, the latter has a feeling of pleasant domesticity, with buildings of mellow brick that could be part of a country house.

King's Parade and Trumpington Street

Back on Trinity Street, now become King's Parade, the clock on **Great St. Mary's Church** rings the hours with a familiar chime, for it is the same as Big Ben's at Westminster—although first struck at St. Mary's. Church bells are also cause to visit St. Bene't's [i.e., Benedict's] Church, where modern bell-ringing, or change-ringing, was begun. There are two ways of ringing bells. The simplest is one in which the bells play a melody. In change-ringing, however, the bells ring peals, compositions, often quite lengthy, that may not appear to the uninitiated to have any melodic basis. Each peal is differentiated from the next by the order in which the bells are rung. It is a system of great, almost mathematical, complexity whose nearest musical equivalent might be a Bach fugue. Change-ringing, still widely practiced in English churches, was invented by a parish clerk at St. Benet's named Fabian Stedman. Another reason to visit the church: It boasts a Saxon tower, the city's oldest building.

Where King's Parade becomes Trumpington Street, water courses run down deep gulleys on either side. These once brought drinking water to the city's center, and the man largely responsible was Thomas Hobson, who owned extensive livery stables. His customers were forced to take whichever horse was nearest the door, a practice that gave rise to the expression "Hobson's choice."

Off Trumpington Street is Pembroke College, with a **chapel** by Sir Christopher Wren that was the first of his architectural works to be completed—giving Cambridge a Wren "first" to set beside Oxford's Sheldonian Theatre. Nearby **Peterhouse**, the oldest of the colleges, dating to 1281, has a famous curiosity. Looking up at the top of the building near the church, you can see an iron bar across a window. The poet Thomas Gray had it placed there to anchor a fire-escape rope. This proved too tempting for his fellow undergraduates, who put a tub of water at the bottom and yelled "Fire!" He was so upset by the experience that he packed his bags and moved to Pembroke College.

Trumpington Street leads on to the **Fitzwilliam Museum**, which has the solemn appearance associated with much Victorian architecture, having been built in 1848. Once past the somewhat dourly tiled entrance, rather reminiscent of a grandiose public lavatory, you will find a fine collection of art and antiquities, with the work of French and English Impressionists doing a great deal to lighten the overall sense of darkness that seems to pervade the museum. There are temporary exhibitions mounted throughout the year.

STAYING AND DINING IN CAMBRIDGE

If you are tempted by the thought of afternoon tea, then the thing to do is to leave the Fitzwilliam for **Fitzbillies**, Cambridge's most famous tea shop, at 52 Trumpington Street, or, if the riverside still exerts its appeal, the ▶ **Garden House Hotel** on Granta Place for cream tea on the lawn stretching down to the water. The Garden House is also recommended for an overnight stay. The ▶ **University Arms** on Regent Street is another excellent accommodation. The hotel is 150 years old and features a paneled restaurant with stained-glass windows of college crests. The recently enlarged but old, established ▶ **Lensfield Hotel** is a friendly, relaxed, family-run place; centrally located, it is within walking distance of colleges, shops, and the river. A mile from the city center and a few minutes from the railway station, the ▶ **Helen Hotel** has an Italian-style garden; owners Gino and Helen Agodino specialize in Italian cuisine.

Those on the lookout for something equally traditional but a little stronger than tea might care to sample the beer at the 17th-century coaching inn known as the **Eagle**, on Benet Street. And if a full-scale meal is in order, there is no shortage of restaurants. You might try the imaginative menu at **Twenty Two** on Chesterton Road, where offerings range from cold ginger-and-melon soup to lamb with rhubarb (Tel: 0223-35-18-80), or the hustle and bustle of popular **Brown's** on Trumpington Street, with generous portions of pastas, salads, pies, and grills, among other English, Continental, and American fare. **Midsummer House** on Midsummer Common has a distinctly metropolitan air, which extends from its elegant setting to its international cuisine (Tel: 0223-692-99). Fine though international restaurants are, visitors to Cambridge are more likely to want something as English as a punt on the Cam, and what could be more English than a cricket pavilion? **Hobbs Pavilion** restaurant on Parker's Piece is just that, though the proprietors cannot guarantee you will have a match to watch.

—*Anthony Burton*

GETTING AROUND

Cambridge, 55 miles (88 km) north of London, can be reached by rail from Liverpool Street Station, by bus from Victoria Coach Station, and by car via the M 11. There is frequent train service; the trip takes approximately one hour. The trip is slightly faster from King's Cross.

ACCOMMODATIONS REFERENCE

Rates are projected 1994 prices for a double room with breakfast, unless otherwise indicated. As prices are subject to change, always double-check before booking.

▶ **Garden House Hotel.** Granta Place, Mill Lane, **Cambridge** CB2 1RT. Tel: (0223) 634-21; Fax: (0223) 30-04-83. £125–£170 (includes Continental breakfast).

▶ **Helen Hotel.** 167–169 Hills Road, **Cambridge** CB2 2RJ. Tel: (0223) 24-64-65; Fax: (0223) 21-44-06. £45–£50.

▶ **Lensfield Hotel.** 53 Lensfield Road, **Cambridge** CB2 1EN. Tel: (0223) 35-50-17; Fax: (0223) 31-20-22. £60.

▶ **University Arms.** Regent Street, **Cambridge** CB2 1AD. Tel: (0223) 35-12-41; Fax: (0223) 31-52-56. £115–£120.

THE COAST OF FRANCE
AND BELGIUM

Less than 10,000 years ago, before the melting waters of the Ice Age raised the level of the sea and drowned the plains between France and Great Britain, you could have walked from the coast of one country to the other. When, in mid-1994, the Channel Tunnel is transformed from bore to reality, you may be able to do the same again. In the meantime you'll have to settle for a boat. But the ride is such a short one that hopping over to the Continent, just for the day, is a favorite excursion for the British, at least for those living in London and the southeast. With frequent sailings from several British ports, combined with regular train service from London to those ports, it is just as easy for visitors from abroad to add a taste of France or Belgium to a holiday in the London area.

MAJOR INTEREST

Boulogne
The Haute Ville
Rue de Lille specialty shopping
Cathedral
A walk around the ramparts
Place Dalton market

Calais
Town Hall
Parc Richelieu
War Museum
Restaurants
Shopping

Dunkirk
Museum of Fine Arts
Malo-les-Bains seaside resort

Dieppe
Seafood restaurants
St-Jacques historic area with cathedral
Saturday morning market
Castle

Bruges
Horse-drawn carriage tour
Belfry
Breidelstraat lace shops
Michelin-rated restaurants

The proximity of northern France to Britain does not imply the slightest compromise in its Gallic ambience. In fact you could drive for hours on end into the French hinterlands and not discover anywhere more French than the Channel ports and their immediate environs.

You get a whiff of France from the moment the ferry nudges past the end of the harbor walls with their complement of red-nosed fishermen wearing berets and smoking yellow-paper hand-rolled cigarettes. You'll swear you hear them muttering Gallic curses as your ferry's propellors churn up *their* patch of La Manche (the sleeve), as they call the Channel, disturbing all the *poisson* that were just about to take a bite of hook.

The simplest way to book is to choose your port, then the means of travel (where there are alternatives), and then walk into any British travel agent's office. A day round-trip excursion ticket from the British port costs about £16. Only a few agents, however, are able to sell the train ticket between London and the British port; for that you need to go to the railway station. At Victoria Station you can buy both rail *and* ferry, hovercraft, or Jetfoil tickets from the offices on platform 8 on the morning of departure—though leave yourself a few minutes to spare, as the lines can be long, especially during the peak summer months.

The choice of routes and sailings is enormous. For speed you can't beat the hovercraft services, the "flying cushions," or the new catamaran services, which cut the crossing time by more than half, between Dover and either Calais or Boulogne. But the disadvantage is discomfort. There is no room to roam on a hovercraft, the interiors being modeled on the lines of an aircraft. There are also no money-changing facilities, and no shops or restaurants (soft and hard drinks are brought to your seat, but not tea or coffee). When the sea is choppy the journey can be unpleasant, although when it's *too* rough they switch you onto a ferry.

Once you reach the French coast, an alternative to lingering in the ports is to rent a car and explore some of the surrounding area. As with Britain, the variety of scenery packed within small pockets of French territory is enormous, and each port will plug you into a distinctive brand of countryside as well as towns of enormous historic interest. Northern France has been, over the centuries, one of the most fought-over patches of land in the world, and it has plenty to offer its visitors.

Boulogne

Less than a two-hour sail from England, the port of Boulogne offers living proof that France really does begin just across the Channel. All things considered—ease of access, range of shops and restaurants, and overall ambience—it is arguably the best choice for the daytripper.

Boulogne is really a two-in-one town, an old and a new. Crowning a hilltop, and easily spotted from the approaching ferry long before it pulls into the docks, stands the largely intact old medieval city, the **Haute Ville**. From within its 13th-century ramparts, Boulogne feels more like a small provincial town buried in the rural heartland of France than a city that is just a swift ferry ride from British shores. The old town comes complete with narrow, winding, cobbled streets, with lots of interesting specialty stores lining the **rue de Lille**; a 13th-century belfry attached to the 17th-century town hall; a castle built in 1231 to defend the town walls against the threat of invaders; and a grand 19th-century **cathedral** built on a Norman crypt.

A leisurely stroll around the ramparts, with a pause to look down from any of the four bow-fronted gateways or 17 towers to admire the horizon of the town's high-pitched rooftops or the views of the docks and the distant surrounding forests, will take anywhere between 30 and 40 minutes. On the clearest of days you can just make out the coast of Britain.

Boulogne's Basse Ville, its new town, lies at the foot of the old town, and was largely rebuilt after hefty damage was done by Allied bombs during World War II (487 bombs landed here, destroying some 5,000 buildings). The waterfront is home base not only for the ferries but for the hundreds of trawlers that make Boulogne the largest fishing port in Europe; they unload some of the catch on the quai Gambetta, a scene that Edith Piaf used to enjoy from her apartment.

Travel on a Wednesday or a Saturday and you'll catch the tail end of the market on Place Dalton, a sightseeing trip in its own right. Pity the poor rabbits, calmly nibbling grass in their hutches, unaware they are up for sale at 25 francs per kilo.

High on the agenda of any day-tripper to France is a good lunch, and Boulogne's restaurants will not disappoint. Two worthy of special mention are owner/chef Tony Lestienne's thoroughly modern **La Matelote** on boulevard Ste-Beuve (Tel: 21-30-17-97) and **La Liégoise**, much favored by the upper echelons of the local business community, on rue Monsigny (Tel: 21-31-61-15).

There are sharks living in Boulogne. **Nausicaa**, arguably the best aquarium in Europe, has been opened on the site of the old casino. Incorporating many of the state-of-the-art display tanks so impressively used in American aquaria (Boston, Baltimore, New Orleans, Monterey, and other places), this new undersea exhibit is one of the most exciting ways to spend an hour while waiting for your ferry home. Those who consider that eating a good lunch is an even better way will be pleased to learn that **Le Matelote** has opened a branch in Nausicaa. The aquarium's explanatory signs are written in both French and English.

Calais

Calais is the nearest gateway to England, the quickest to reach, and is served by an armada of ferries that seem to shuttle in and out as frequently as commuter trains.

Although Allied bombers laid waste to much of Calais' medieval charms, many of the town's older buildings miraculously survived the assault. They include the most spectacularly flamboyant building, the town hall, fronted by Rodin's statue of the Burghers. The **town hall**, a red-brick, Flemish Renaissance Revival building in château style, appears far more ancient than its 20th-century construction. How on earth, you may wonder, did the architects manage to persuade the straitlaced city burghers to accept their plans for such a wild fantasy of a building?

The oldest building in town is the Tour du Guet, built in the 13th century on the Place d'Armes to keep an eye on shipping movements in the Channel. It is, unfortunately, closed to the public (the authorities don't want British visitors to look nostalgically back at the white cliffs). But you can walk around the delightful Parc Richelieu and watch the locals play *pétanque* (*boules,* as we know it) or visit the **War Museum**, housed in one of Hitler's bunkers that was used as the German navy's main telephone exchange in northern France.

British day-trippers in France fall into two distinct categories. There are those who grab a full breakfast on the morning ferry, make do with coffee and perhaps a bag of *frites* during the day, and hold out till early evening for real English fare on the ferry home. For others, the day starts as one long fast until the moment that the first crumbs of genuine baguette fly like shrapnel across the restaurant table.

At the **Côte d'Argent** (Tel: 21-34-68-07) you can dine on fish soup, coquilles Saint-Jacques, sole meunière, French cheese, chocolate mousse, coffee, an aperitif, and wine for around 150 francs, a fraction of its British equivalent (assuming you could ever find such a thing), and the meal will be served in great style. Sole, for example, comes on a huge, beautifully painted platter beneath a silver tureen that looks like a czar's helmet. The restaurant is located on the **Plage de Calais**, an apron of sandy shoreline sufficiently broad to be the venue for sand-yachting races. With hundreds of tiny old-fashioned wooden changing huts, it is one of the best beaches along the entire coast.

Although nowhere near as attractive a town as Boulogne, Calais' strength lies in its two shopping centers: between the Place d'Armes (where those without a car are deposited by the ferry bus) and the main street of rue Royale; and at the northern end of boulevard Jacquard just beyond the town hall, then along boulevard Lafayette. Among the best of the specialty shops are **La Maison du Fromage**, which sells more than 200 brands of cheese; **Au Royal Chocolat** for delicious cream-filled Leonidas chocolates from Belgium; **La Madrague** for a host of pretty household items; **Descamps** for luxurious bed and bathroom accessories; and **Cupillard** for its excellent range of kitchenware, including cast-iron Le Creuset pans and casserole dishes.

Dunkirk

Dunkirk (Dunkerque in French) is France with a Flemish accent. Flemish influences are everywhere evident, from the style of buildings to the unpronounceable names of some shops, not to mention items on the restaurant menus. The Belgian border, never a real cultural dividing line, is just up the road—nearer, in fact, to the town center than Dunkirk's own ferry port.

Dunkirk was badly damaged during World War I and virtually devastated in May 1940 during Operation Dynamo, the mass evacuation of Allied troops from the Continent. Its reconstruction afterward was with an eye more on commercial slickness than on aesthetics, though a few old buildings, including the town hall, the belfry, the medieval Leughenaer Tower, and St. Eloi church, survived. The **Museum of Fine Arts**, bang in the center of town on Place du Géneral de Gaulle, contains several important collections of Flemish and Italian paintings from the 17th century, while in the basement there is a display of souvenirs, documents, and a diorama detailing Dunkirk's role in both world wars (closed on Tuesdays).

Dunkirk's trump card is **Malo-les-Bains**, part seaside resort, part residential neighborhood, a 20-minute walk north of the center but a world away from its heavy maritime commerce (Dunkirk is France's largest port after Marseille and Le Havre). The broad Digue de Mer promenade, backed by cafés and crêperies, brasseries and restaurants, runs alongside three miles of beach that stretches all the way to the Belgian border. A good place to eat here is **La Mer du Nord** at 3 rue du Leughenaer, near the water.

Dieppe

The prettiest and most Gallic of the Channel ports, Dieppe is characterized by narrow streets and historic houses clustered around the harbor and behind its pebble beach. It is also France's oldest resort, popularized by the duchesse de Berry in the early 19th century when she made seabathing socially acceptable for ladies.

The town lies at the end of a route aptly known to many Parisians as the Road of the Sea. Dieppe has, in fact, long billed itself as the *plage de Paris*. Spreading out to the west as far as the castle and an intimidating line of cliffs is a deeply shelving pebble beach backed by a gusty promenade, the latter separated from the main hotels by La Pelouse, a broad ten-acre swathe of grass.

There are more good-value-for-money restaurants squeezed into Dieppe than in any other Channel port. Specialties include *sole dieppois* and *marmite dieppoise,* a fish soup (dieppoise style means cooked in cream and wine, or sometimes cider), as well as scallops. In fact, half the scallops eaten in France come from the waters off Dieppe. The **Marine**, a nondescript modern restaurant on the Arcades de la Poissonerie, serves very good fish. The owner has what the French call a British mustache; see if you can spot him.

The most interesting shops lie in the historic St-Jacques area around the cathedral. On Saturdays the area is the scene of one of the best markets in Normandy. Dieppe's **castle** houses a gallery of paintings by Pisarro, Monet, and other Impressionists who came to capture Dieppe's light, as well as prints by Braque—who spent his last years nearby—and a collection of locally made ivory carvings.

For those in search of character, a nice place to spend the night is the ▶ **Hotel Windsor** on the boulevard de Verdun. Its grand, old-fashioned staircase is hung with pictures of transatlantic liners; the rooms are large and many have sea views, although the furnishings tend to be frayed at the seams.

Bruges

The best reason for going to Belgium for the day is not Ostend, the Channel port, but Bruges, which is a swift train ride from the port. Bruges is the best-preserved medieval city in Europe, and the best way to plug into the ancient mood is from a horse-drawn carriage. A bowler-hatted driver will guide you along lime- and willow-shaded canals, over hump-back bridges, and down cobblestoned alleyways lined with fine gabled houses, merchants' mansions, ornate guildhalls, and other manifestations of the success of the city's ancient trade.

The more energetic can tackle the 366 steps to the top of the **belfry** in the Grote Markt, the town's main square. If you reach the summit just as the 47-bell carillon peals, your ears will tingle all the way to your boots. The place for lace, a local specialty, is Breidelstraat, while Steenstraat is lined with shops full of delicious Leonidas and other locally made chocolates (one shop is called **Sukerbuye**, "sugar-belly").

For lunch there's a choice of some 30 Michelin-rated restaurants to choose from, more per square mile than in any other provincial city in Europe. Try the **Huyze Die Maene** (House of the Morn) at Markt 17 for elaborate dishes and a magnificent view of the floodlit Markt. A longer visit, in fact, may seriously damage your health, but if you want to spend a night try the ▶ **Navarra** hotel on St. Jacobsstraat, a 17th-century former palace that was restored in 1983. Napoleon nearly slept here—a special swan staircase was built for the occasion, but he didn't show up.

—*David Wickers*

GETTING AROUND

Entry Documents

For France: Citizens of the United States and Canada require valid passports but not visas for tourist visits of 90 days or less. Citizens of Australia and New Zealand require passports *and* visas; to obtain a visa, check *well in advance* of a trip with the nearest French consulate. Residents of EC countries require only a passport or an identity card.

For Belgium: Citizens of the United States, Canada, Australia, and New Zealand may enter Belgium for tourist visits of less than 90 days with valid passports; citizens of EC countries may enter with a passport or an identity card.

Local Time
France and Belgium are one hour ahead of the U.K.

Telephoning
The international country code for France is 33. The country code for Belgium is 32.

Electric Current
Current in both France and Belgium is 220V, 50 cycles AC; North American appliances will need a converter and a plug adapter; British appliances will need a plug adapter.

Trains to Dover
Trains from London to Dover leave from both Victoria and Charing Cross stations. For the most part, trains from both go only as far as Dover's downtown station, Dover Priory, which is some distance from the embarkation areas; courtesy buses and taxis operate between the station and the harbor. There are, however, some trains from both Victoria and Charing Cross that go directly to Dover Harbour; check the timetable at the British Rail Travel Centre at either of those two London stations, at the International Rail Centre at Victoria Station, or call (071) 834-2345.

Boulogne
You can travel to Boulogne by ferry via either Folkestone (with Sealink; Tel: 0233-64-70-47, 1 hour and 50 minutes) or Dover (with P & O; Tel: 0304-20-33-88 in Dover or 081-575-8555 in London, 1 hour and 40 minutes), but the best service for day-trippers is the hovercraft from Dover (Hoverspeed; Tel: 0304-24-02-41 in Dover or 081-554-7601 in London), which takes 40 minutes and costs about £16 round trip. Aim to catch the 7:45 A.M. train from Victoria Station to Dover Harbour, which connects with the 11:35 "flight" to Boulogne, arriving in Boulogne just in time for lunch. There is a free bus from the hoverport at Le Portel into the town center. The return "flight" leaves Boulogne at 7:05 P.M., connecting with a train that will get you back to Victoria Station around 9:00 P.M. (These times and carriers are selected from among many options to give you an idea of the possibilities.)

Calais

Again, the Hoverspeed (Tel: 0304-24-02-41 in Dover or 081-554-7061 in London) crossing from Dover is the quickest, taking only 35 minutes. The Sealink (Tel: 0233-64-70-47) and P & O (Tel: 0304-20-33-88) ferries from Dover take around 1 hour and 40 minutes. None of the services dovetails into the train timetable, but London (Victoria or Charing Cross) to Dover (Priory Station) services are very frequent, as are buses, which shuttle arriving passengers to the port (some trains go all the way to Dover Harbour). You could, for example, catch the 7:30 A.M. train from Charing Cross to Dover Priory, arriving in good time for the 10:30 A.M. P & O ferry.

Dunkirk

The Sally Line (Tel: 0843-59-55-22) ferry sails from Ramsgate at 9:00 A.M. and takes 2 hours and 30 minutes to cross the Channel. The main drawback is that you have to get up in time to catch the 5:50 A.M. train from Victoria Station to make the most of the day. At Ramsgate you have to catch a taxi to the port, a 10-minute ride from the station. The ferry docks at the western end of the vast Dunkirk port, 13 kilometers (8 miles) from the town center— farther, in fact, than the distance between town and the Belgian border—but Sally operates a free shuttle bus into town. Although the sailing time is long, Sally Line ships are among the most comfortable on the Channel. Return on the 5:00 P.M. sailing, which will get you back to London at 10:32 P.M.

Dieppe

There is only one good reason for not going to Dieppe for the day: The trip from Newhaven on Sealink-Dieppe ferries (Tel: 0273-51-22-66) takes 4 hours. The most sensible approach is to stay overnight on the British coast in nearby Brighton (see above in Day Trips) and catch a morning train along the coast to Newhaven in time for the 7:00 A.M. sailing, returning on the 6:00 P.M. ferry.

Ostend/Bruges

Travel by ferry to Ostend takes nearly 4 hours, but there is an appealing alternative, the Jetfoil, a variation on the hydrofoil, operated by P & O (Tel: 0304-20-33-88) from Dover. This takes 1 hour and 40 minutes for the crossing, then another few minutes for the train to Bruges. To make the most of the day, catch the 7:45 A.M. train from

Victoria Station to Dover Western Docks, which connects with the 9:35 A.M. Jetfoil, arriving in Ostend at 12:15 P.M. local time. The Bruges train leaves Ostend at 12:34 P.M. and arrives in Bruges at 12:48. For the return jouney catch the 6:54 P.M. train from Bruges and you'll wind up back at Victoria at 10:04 P.M.

ACCOMMODATIONS REFERENCE
Rates are projected 1994 prices for a double room without breakfast. As prices are subject to change, always double-check before booking.

▶ **Navarra**. 41 St. Jacobsstraat, **Bruges**, Belgium. Tel: (50) 34-05-61; Fax: (50) 33-67-90; in U.S. and Canada, (800) 528-1234; in Australia, (02) 212-6444. £55–£72.

▶ **Hotel Windsor**. 18 boulevard de Verdun, 76000 **Dieppe**, France. Tel: (35) 84-74-52. £30–£35.

CHRONOLOGY OF THE HISTORY OF LONDON

The Ancient Past

London stands on a site where two spurs of gravel jutted out to face each other across the Thames, making the river fordable. This was the lowest crossing point on this section of river, and was used by people as long ago as the Stone Age, which began around 12,000 B.C. and lasted for 10,000 years. Hunters once pursued mammoth where commuters now chase after taxis, and these early wandering inhabitants left behind flint hand axes and arrowheads as evidence of their presence. There are few reminders of the Bronze Age, which lasted from roughly 2000 to 500 B.C., but by the time the Iron Age had arrived around 500 B.C. there was a permanent settlement in the area. This was a time of a strong Celtic presence in England; the Celts are the people we consider to be the first "British" race. Eventually, a fort was established, guarded by a rampart and ditch on what is now Wimbledon Common. Its inhabitants might well have been the first settled Londoners.

The Romans

The Romans (55 B.C. to A.D. 409) brought new standards of civilization to Britain, establishing cities joined together by a network of well-made roads. Their houses had surprisingly "modern" amenities, including baths and under-floor heating.

- **55–54 B.C.**: Caesar's expedition.
- **A.D.43–47**: Claudian invasion and conquest of

southern England. Foundation of London (Londinium).

- **60–61**: Revolt of Queen Boadicea of the Celtic
  Iceni people. Londinium burned to the ground.
  The revolt is soon crushed, rebuilding begins, and
  Londinium is established as the capital of the prov-
  ince.
- **c. 200**: The city walls are constructed.
- **c. 340–369**: Barbarians from continental Europe
  raid the British Isles.
- **410–446**: Roman withdrawal from Britain.

The Dark Ages and the Anglo-Saxons

The withdrawal of the Romans from London brought the
Dark Ages. The name should not be thought of as indicat-
ing a period of barbarism, but rather as reflecting our lack
of detailed knowledge of the period. The city was, it is true,
only a poor shadow of its former self as the great public
buildings fell into disuse and ruin. Invading armies—the
Angles, the Saxons, and the Jutes, now generally lumped
together as the Anglo-Saxons—from three parts of Germany played their part in adding to the destruction. Understandably, the more peaceful settlers generally preferred
the country to the town. Gradually, however, London began to regain its former importance, though it was to suffer
further raids by the Vikings from across the North Sea. The
arts were represented by rich ornamental work, such as
that found in the Sutton Hoo ship burial, now in the British
Museum, and by the superb illuminated manuscripts of
the Christian church.

- **c. 450**: First Saxon settlements in the British
  Isles.
- **457**: Celtic refugees from the southeast settle in
  London.
- **604**: First description of London as a Saxon town,
  subject to the king of Essex. Æthelbert of Kent
  establishes a bishopric, and Mellitus becomes first
  bishop of London.
- **616**: Mellitus driven out, and London reverts to
  paganism.
- **656**: King Sigebert of Essex converts to Christianity, and Finan becomes new bishop of London.
- **675**: Work begins on the first St. Paul's cathedral,
  under the direction of Bishop Erconwald.

- **839**: First Viking raid on London.
- **851**: Viking fleet attacks London and burns the city.
- **872**: Danes occupy London.
- **886**: Alfred the Great defeats the Danes and restores London to the kingdom of Mercia.
- **896**: New Danish invasion repelled.
- **994**: Olaf Tryggvason of Norway and King Swein of Denmark join forces to attack London, but the city stands firm.
- **1014**: Danes again in control of London.
- **1016**: London regained under Canute.
- **1042**: Saxon Edward the Confessor crowned, and begins work on Westminster Abbey.
- **1066**: King Harold marches through London after defeating the Danes at Stamford Bridge; English under Harold then defeated by William of Normandy at the Battle of Hastings.

Normans and Plantagenets

The first priority of the Norman conquerors was to consolidate their rule, and inevitably a particular emphasis was placed on the defense of the capital. Early fortresses here consisted of a motte and bailey; the motte, or mound, was topped by a wooden tower and surrounded by the bailey, or courtyard, with its protective moat. In time, the wooden tower was replaced by a stone keep, exemplified by the famous White Tower of London. The Roman walls of London were used as the basis for the fortification of the Norman city.

The Normans also brought with them elaborate religious rituals that required large churches, cathedrals, abbeys, and monasteries. Norman supremacy in church architecture had already been recognized under the Saxons by the use of Norman builders to work on Westminster Abbey. Now, however, churches were to reach even greater magnificence as the massive simplicity of the early churches gave way to the complexities of the full-blown Gothic. The nave of the rebuilt Westminster Abbey is an outstanding example.

London became the great trading and commercial center of the country. Outside the city, in what are now suburbs, the feudal society was based on the lord of the manor, who gathered his wealth from the labor of the villagers. The great lords fought against each other; secular power vied with ecclesiastical power; and even the monarchy was subject to a series of dynastic struggles within the ruling Plantagenet line. This was also an era of international wars and the long struggles of the Crusaders in the Holy Land, all combining to make it a period of seemingly endless turmoil.

- **1066**: William I crowned in Westminster Abbey.
- **1080**: Work begins on the White Tower of London.
- **1086**: The Domesday survey records many of the present London districts as settlements, for example "Stratford-atte-Bowe" and "Stevenhethe," or Stepney.
- **1087**: Coronation of William II (Rufus).
- **c. 1090**: Construction of the Great Hall of Westminster Palace.
- **1100**: Coronation of Henry I.
- **1135**: Coronation of Stephen.
- **1141**: During the civil war between Stephen and Matilda, Matilda (Henry I's daughter) takes possession of London, but the townspeople revolt and she flees to Oxford. Fulham Palace becomes the home of the bishop of London.
- **1154**: Coronation of Henry II, the first Plantagenet king.
- **1163**: Edward the Confessor canonized. Pilgrimages to his tomb in Westminster Abbey begin.
- **1189**: Coronation of Richard I (the Lionheart).
- **1191**: Henry FitzElywin appointed first mayor of London, an office he holds until 1212.
- **1199**: Coronation of John.
- **c. 1200**: Lambeth Palace built for archbishop of Canterbury.
- **1215**: King John lays down Charter, specifying mayors to be elected annually. Signing of Magna Carta.
- **1216**: Accession of Henry III. During his reign London is established as the capital and permanent seat of government.
- **1245**: Work begins on rebuilding Westminster Abbey.
- **1272**: Accession of Edward I during his crusade.
- **1274**: Edward I returns to London.
- **1290**: First Parliament meets at Westminster. Expulsion of the Jews from England.
- **1292**: Legal profession established. Student lawyers were based at the Inns of Court.

- **1307**: Accession of Edward II.
- **1327**: Deposition of Edward II in favor of his son, Edward III.

The Late Middle Ages

This was a period marked by wars at home and abroad: the dynastic struggles between the houses of York and Lancaster—the Wars of the Roses—following the Hundred Years War against France. As wars need to be paid for, there were numerous increases in taxation, which called forth violent responses, notably the Peasants' Revolt, during which London was stormed, the prisons thrown open, and the houses of the rich sacked. To add to the misery, the country was ravaged by the Black Death, which reduced the population as a whole by a third or more. In spite of this catalogue of horrors, the arts thrived. Architecture had one of its most exuberant periods of development, as exemplified by the styles known as Decorated and Perpendicular, both characterized by elaborate tracery. It was also during this period that English literature was born. In part it looked back to a world of mythical chivalry, the celebration of which reached its highest achievement in Sir Thomas Malory's *Morte d'Arthur;* but there was also a new interest in everyday life. Among Chaucer's pilgrims in *The Canterbury Tales,* who amused themselves on a pilgrimage to Canterbury by telling stories along the way, were many characters who could have been drawn from the common folk of London. Literature was given a further boost when William Caxton set up the country's first printing press in an alley near Westminster Abbey.

- **1337**: Start of the Hundred Years War.
- **1348**: Beginning of the Black Death.
- **1357**: The Black Prince brings the captured king of France back to London after the Battle of Poitiers.
- **1377**: Coronation of Richard II.
- **1381**: Wat Tyler leads the Peasants' Revolt and marches on London.
- **c.1386**: *The Canterbury Tales* completed.
- **1397**: Richard "Dick" Whittington becomes mayor of London for the first time.
- **1399**: Accession of Henry IV.
- **1411**: London guilds combine to build Guildhall.
- **1413**: Accession of Henry V.

- **1415**: Henry V escorted back into London by mayor and aldermen after his triumph at Agincourt.
- **1422**: Accession of Henry VI.
- **1435**: Jack Cade leads rebels against London.
- **1461**: Edward of York marches on London and is declared king. He becomes Edward IV. Lancastrian Henry VI exiled.
- **1470**: *Morte d'Arthur* completed.
- **1477**: Caxton prints his first book in London.
- **1483**: Death of Edward IV and alleged murder of the young princes in the Tower of London. Accession of Richard III.
- **1485**: The Wars of the Roses end with Richard III's defeat at the Battle of Bosworth. Henry Tudor crowned as Henry VII.

The Tudors

The accession of Henry Tudor brought an end to the strife and turmoil that characterized the Wars of the Roses. In the peace that followed, prosperity, based on a growing overseas trade, came to London. The arts flourished in this new atmosphere. Ecclesiastical architecture saw the last great flourishes of the Gothic style, epitomized by the brilliance of Henry VII's chapel at Westminster Abbey. Other religious houses were reduced to ruin by Henry VIII's break with Roman Catholicism. Secular architecture, too, saw dramatic changes, as the rich and powerful came out of their fortresses and built new palaces of a previously undreamed-of luxury. (Cardinal Wolsey's Hampton Court boasted a thousand rooms.) The miniaturist Nicholas Hilliard provided jewel-like portraits of the age, while the composer William Byrd gave British music a distinctive voice. But it was in the new London theaters that the arts achieved what now seems a Golden Age. Of the great dramatists of the age only one, Ben Jonson, was a native Londoner, but the capital drew in other men of genius, such as Christopher Marlowe and William Shakespeare.

- **1486**: First royal naval dockyard begun at Deptford.
- **1503**: Work begins on Henry VII's chapel, Westminster Abbey.
- **1509**: Accession of Henry VIII.
- **1515**: Cardinal Wolsey appointed lord chancellor.

- **1519**: Hampton Court completed.
- **1531**: Construction of St. James's Palace.
- **1533**: Henry VIII marries Anne Boleyn, who was later to be executed on Tower Green.
- **1536**: Dissolution of the monasteries. Many London monasteries pulled down. Others are put to new uses: The monks' refectory hall at Westminster Abbey becomes the dining hall of Westminster School.
- **1547**: Accession of Edward VI.
- **1553**: Accession of Roman Catholic Mary Tudor. Sir Thomas Wyatt leads rebellion in favor of Lady Jane Grey. After fighting in the streets of London, Wyatt is defeated.
- **1558**: Accession of Protestant Elizabeth I.
- **1573**: Birth of Ben Jonson.
- **1576**: Burbage builds London's first theater.
- **1577**: A second theater is built on Curtain Road, Shoreditch: first performance here of *Romeo and Juliet* and *Everyman in His Humour*.
- **1587**: Execution of claimant to the throne Mary Stuart, Queen of Scots.
- **1588**: Elizabeth I addresses fleet at Tilbury before it engages the Spanish Armada.
- **1599**: Overseas traders found East India Company in London.
- **1603**: Death of Elizabeth I.

The Seventeenth Century

This was a period of dramatic change in England, and particularly in the capital. The Stuarts lost the throne in the Civil War and regained it at the Restoration, and the century ended with the throne secured for the Protestant House of Orange. It was a time of contrasts and conflicts—austerity and flamboyance, Protestantism and Catholicism. Many left the country to seek freedom in the New World. For London it was a time of devastation and renewal. The plague years were followed by the Great Fire, from which a new London rose. The Gothic past was left behind and new architectural idioms, both Classical and Baroque, came to the fore. The new London was developed by such masters as Inigo Jones, who designed the Queen's House at Greenwich, and Sir Christopher Wren, whose St. Paul's Cathedral was to dominate the city skyline until the age of the skyscraper. In music, Henry Purcell reigned supreme.

- **1603**: James VI of Scotland, a Stuart and son of Mary Stuart, crowned James I of England.
- **1605**: The Gunpowder Plot conspirators attempt to blow up Parliament.
- **1608**: Thames freezes over; great "frost fair" held on river.
- **1613**: Work begins on New River to provide first water supply for London.
- **1619**: Inigo Jones's Banqueting House begun.
- **1625**: Accession of Charles I. Ceremonial return to London in state barge ruined by torrential storm.
- **1642**: Charles I attempts to arrest five members of Parliament in the House of Commons. Civil War. Charles loses control of London.
- **1649**: Execution of Charles I outside the Banqueting House.
- **1653**: Oliver Cromwell becomes Lord Protector.
- **1660**: Restoration of Charles II.
- **1662**: St. James's Park redesigned in the French style and opened to the public.
- **1665**: The Great Plague.
- **1666**: The Great Fire of London.
- **1675**: Work begun on St. Paul's Cathedral.
- **1685**: Accession of James II. Edict of Nantes revoked: French Protestant refugees (Huguenots) settle in London.
- **1688**: Accession of William and Mary.
- **1689**: Purcell's *Dido and Aeneas* performed in Chelsea.
- **1691**: Lloyd's insurance company formed in Edward Lloyd's coffeehouse on Lombard Street.
- **1694**: Formation of Bank of England

The Eighteenth Century

The period tends to be associated with the name "Georgian," for George I came to the throne in 1714 and George III was still there when the century ended. Inevitably the name suggests an urbane Classicism in architecture and decoration, as seen informally, for example, in Church Row, Hampstead, and formally in the Paragon, Blackheath. It was the age of Adam, Sheraton, Chippendale, and Wedgwood. Musical life was dominated by Handel. In literature, the novel was born in the works of Richardson, Fielding, and Sterne, and toward the end of the century Romanticism flourished in the hands of Blake and Wordsworth. A different view of London appeared in the works of William Hogarth, whose Gin Lane showed a London steeped in debauchery. It was also an age of great change: Britain lost a colony in the American Revolution but began building a new empire in India. More dramatic still were the profound changes brought about by the Industrial Revolution, which began to gather momentum in the second half of the century.

- **1702:** Accession of Queen Anne.
- **1714:** Accession of James I's great-grandson George I from Hanover in Germany.
- **1715:** Handel's *Water Music* composed for Thames pageant.
- **1719:** First general hospital built at Westminster.
- **1727:** Accession of George II.
- **1733:** Westbourne River dammed to create the Serpentine in Hyde Park.
- **1739:** London gets a second Thames bridge at Westminster.
- **1749:** Henry Fielding takes his seat as a Bow Street magistrate.
- **1751:** Act raising the price of gin limits the ruinous effect of cheap drink.
- **1753:** Thomas Chippendale establishes his furniture works on St. Martin's Lane.
- **1759:** Opening of the British Museum.
- **1760:** Accession of George III.
- **1761:** Robert Adam appointed as architect to the royal works.
- **1785:** First issue of *The Times* appears.
- **1794:** Work starts on Grand Junction Canal, linking London to the Midlands.

The Nineteenth Century

In many ways, the new century saw a continuation of trends begun in the previous period. Industrial development continued, particularly in the field of transport. London's docklands began a long period of expansion, and by the end of the century the city was at the hub of a complex rail network. The great railway stations, such as Paddington and St. Pancras, are among the capital's finest Victorian buildings. As the Georgian age passed and the Victorian age began, a new style in architecture found favor—the Gothic Revival, epitomized by the Houses of

Parliament. Literature, from the gently ironic novels of Jane Austen to the teeming world created by Charles Dickens, continued to be the leading artistic medium. It is perhaps a commentary on the times that 1851 saw both a celebration of Britain's leading role in world affairs in the Great Exhibition and the start of Mayhew's chronicles of the desperate poverty of many of the capital's citizens.

- **1802**: West India Docks opened, first of a series of new docks.
- **1808**: Trevithick demonstrates his steam locomotive in London.
- **1811**: Work begins on Waterloo Bridge.
- **1812**: John Nash begins new design for Regent's Park and Regent Street.
- **1820**: Accession of George IV.
- **1835**: Opening of new Houses of Parliament.
- **1836**: First steam railway in London. Dickens publishes *The Pickwick Papers*.
- **1837**: Accession of Queen Victoria.
- **1843**: Opening of the first tunnel under the Thames.
- **1851**: The Great Exhibition in Hyde Park. Henry Mayhew begins work on *London Life and the London Poor*.
- **1863**: The first underground railway opens.
- **1864**: Work begins on the Embankment, covering London's new main sewer.
- **1888**: London given a new governing body: the London County Council.
- **1890**: First electric trains run underground.
- **1895**: Trial of Oscar Wilde at Bow Street.

The Twentieth Century

The role of London in the life of the country has changed in the present century. Trade and manufacturing have declined as the emphasis has shifted toward the financial institutions. Two world wars have taken their toll, and the bombs of the Blitz brought greater changes to the face of the city than any event since the Great Fire. Equally important has been the role of transport, with the airplane and especially the automobile changing the whole pace and pattern of life. The confidence shown by the builders of the past has only rarely been matched in more recent times, most notably in buildings such as the 1930s Underground stations and the 1986 Lloyd's building of Richard Rogers. In the arts, literature has continued to play a dominant role, but music, which had declined, has experienced a revival. The visual arts, too, have fared well, and now have an appropriate setting in the recently refurbished Tate Gallery. The new arts of cinema, radio, and television have become increasingly dominant.

- **1901**: Death of Queen Victoria and accession of Edward VII.
- **1906**: Suffragists establish headquarters at Clement's Inn.
- **1910**: Accession of George V.
- **1914**: Outbreak of World War I.
- **1918**: Armistice ends World War I.
- **1922**: First radio broadcast from London.
- **1924**: The first Empire Exhibition at Wembley.
- **1929**: First public television broadcast from London.
- **1936**: Death of George V, abdication of Edward VIII, and accession of George VI.
- **1939**: Outbreak of World War II.
- **1940**: Battle of Britain, and start of the Blitz.
- **1945**: End of World War II.
- **1951**: Festival of Britain. Beginnings of South Bank arts complex.
- **1952**: Accession of Elizabeth II.
- **1963**: Establishment of National Theatre in London.
- **1986**: New Lloyd's building opened.
- **1991**: Opening of the Sainsbury Wing of the National Gallery.

—Anthony Burton

INDEX

Ck $ exchange rate
220/240, 50 HZ   Need Adapter or Converter
                     plus adapter plug

Write to^{20} for info, etc

Tickets for a Play (Shakespeare)

Visitor Travelcard
5-hrs ahead U.S.

Underground (Tube) Map!
Bus Map!

Tourist Pass? P. 141 .

Riverbus (primarily commuters) 142